MW00837957

Forensic Materials Engineering

Case Studies

Forensic Materials Engineering
Case Studies

Peter Rhys Lewis
Ken Reynolds
Colin Gagg

CRC PRESS

Boca Raton   London   New York   Washington, D.C.

Library of Congress Cataloging-in-Publication Data

Lewis, P. R. (Peter Rhys), 1945–
    Forensic materials engineering: case studies / by Peter Rhys Lewis, Ken Reynolds, and Colin Gagg.
        p. cm.
    Includes bibliographical references and index.
    ISBN 0-8493-1182-9 (alk. paper)
    1. Forensic engineering. I. Reynolds, Ken. II. Gagg, Colin. III. Title.

TA219.L49 2003
620—dc21   2003048886

Visit the CRC Press Web site at www.crcpress.com

© 2004 by CRC Press LLC

No claim to original U.S. Government works
International Standard Book Number 0-8493-1182-9
Library of Congress Card Number 2003048886
Printed in the United States of America 1 2 3 4 5 6 7 8 9 0
Printed on acid-free paper

Dedication

To all those who seek the truth in human affairs

Preface

Case studies of product failure are the most valuable source of information for manufacturers to improve their products. There is no better way in which product designs can be changed so as to minimize if not eliminate premature failure. Case studies are the mainspring of forensic engineering, which is why we are opening our own case books to a wider audience than the insurers, lawyers and private clients who originally commissioned them. Some of them have already been presented to our post-graduate students at The Open University (T839 Forensic Engineering), and elsewhere such as the annual ANTEC conferences of SPE (Society of Plastics Engineers). We make acknowledgment at the appropriate point in the text.

There are now several compilations of case studies, in the U.S.,[1,2] Japan[3] and in Europe.[4] A start has also been made on the World Wide Web, where ease of access makes this medium an ideal source for users.[5] All such modern compilations include cases from around the world, simply because of product globalization. Indeed, many of the cases published by the journal *Engineering Failure Analysis*, for example, emanate from rapidly developing economies such as those of mainland and offshore China, Malaysia and other parts of South East Asia as well as Eastern Europe.[6] One serious problem with many such compilations, however, is that they tend to ignore many vital aspects, such as the litigation involved in a case, or the turning points in investigations. We believe that these aspects are neglected at peril because if they focus on just the technical details, they do not tell the story of what actually happened. Product failures are more realistic when related as stories in chronological sequence, rather than a logical way that makes one wonder why the products failed in the first place. We have adopted the chronological approach because it makes the technical matter more interesting, and so encourages the reader to learn why products failed and what design changes are needed in the future to prevent similar accidents. Traditional compilations are also limited by the nature of the materials studied, nonmetallic materials being severely neglected, despite their increasing importance in safety-critical and structural roles. However, some case studies of plastic products have been published independently in the last decade.[7,8]

Chapter 1 reviews some of the conceptual tools that that have become widespread in industry. Although these tools can help improve product design to ameliorate if not eliminate failures, they stand or fall on the abilities of product engineers to recognize failure modes in a very wide variety of different situations. This is where the specific skills of forensic investigation become paramount. One analogy that is appropriate to the work of a forensic investigator is that of the forensic pathologist, and the parallels between the two activities are explored in Chapter 2, a chapter that also includes an introduction to the properties of different materials. A very high proportion of failures are caused by unexpected loading, or repeated loading, or by loading in the presence of aggressive chemicals, or by unexpected levels of stress at specific points in a product. Such mechanical failures demand some background information about the nature of loads, their magnitude and how they relate to the properties of the material of which a product is made. The nature of loading patterns is discussed in Chapter 3, which deals with the difference between load and stress for an elementary situation that involves only tensile forces. The concept of loading path is developed. The approach is vital to understanding more complex loading patterns, such as the type that occurs in automobile accidents. A variety of different techniques (the so-called "toolbox" of Chapter 4) is available to study the physical remains after an accident. Some tools are very simple: a hand magnifier is often the only tool that is needed. Even so, the high magnifications from a microscope are often needed to reveal the failure mode of a specific product. What is seen is not always perceived, however, which is the justification for the small amount of background theory supplied in the earlier chapters. All these parts of the book are provided with illustrative examples taken from our case notes, many of which have some intrinsic interest for their relevance to the changing pattern of failure. Thus Chapter 4 includes mention of the failure of a soldered joint in a circuit board. Thermo-mechanical fatigue is an important generic failure mode for all electronic equipment, use of which has grown exponentially in the last decade. It is therefore a failure mode that will grow in importance as equipment ages. Hopefully, designers will recognize the significance of the failure mode and rectify their products accordingly.

The following chapters are grouped according to the kind of defects that lead to failure. Chapter 5 deals with manufacturing faults in products. It ends with another area of interest: the application of new technology to improve manufacturing performance. Thus gas molding seems to be a process that offers everything without any drawbacks, apart from a license fee for the use of patented technology. The reality is somewhat different, as the case study about heavy-duty chair arms shows. Chapters 6 and 7 discuss the frequent failures encountered with materials used for fluid containment (Chapter 6) and storage vessels (Chapter 7). While pipe and cylindrical storage vessels could not be simpler in shape, they can suffer from poor design or materials selection. Failure of such systems is very unforgiving because escape of fluid can cause very serious property damage, especially if undetected in the early stages of failure. The expansion in use of plastics in this area has been remarkable, and they find widespread application for transportation of many utilities such as gas, liquid fuels and water (quite apart from speciality chemicals).

The workplace is often the scene of severe accidents that may put employees at risk of serious injury. This area of investigation, which has grown from legislative pressure to protect employees, especially in hazardous occupation sites such as mines, steel mills and foundries, is the subject of Chapter 8. One of the cases concerns failure of a scaffolding barrier, a case that illustrates the importance of appreciating the wider picture. The immediate cause of failure appeared to be at one end of a safety rail, although the actual cause of the problem lay at the other end. One of the most common workplace accidents involves slips and falls, often from a ladder. While a deceptively simple tool, a ladder can be very dangerous if simple rules are not rigorously obeyed, as the final case studies of the chapter show, making a link to earlier problems with stepladders (Chapter 3).

One of the most rapidly growing markets is for medical devices, such as implants or tools for surgeons and doctors. Legislation imposes onerous duties on designers to protect the patient from unwanted side effects of implants. Product quality and integrity must be of the highest standard possible, and there are relatively few materials that meet these needs. The human body is also a very unpredictable environment, which is why product failures must be investigated thoroughly. Implants and prostheses have often failed in the past, and it is only by learning from past mistakes that progress can be made (Chapter 9).

Of all accidents that are familiar to the public, those on our roads and highways can be the most serious both to drivers and other users. Vehicular accident is the most common cause of accidental death, yet until Ralph Nader[9] began his quest to improve auto safety, that area had been largely neglected by designers. Not so any longer. And it is one of the most challenging areas of investigation, often because of the destruction of vital evidence of causation. This is why analysis of trace evidence (such as headlamp filaments) becomes a key task in reconstruction of the events leading to car accidents (Chapter 10). Fraudulent insurance claims is the topic discussed in Chapter 11, where forensic information allows insurers to check the validity of claims made upon them. And although the large majority of cases discussed in this book are civil law cases, those of a criminal nature are equally accessible to engineering analysis (Chapter 12).

The final chapter examines patent cases where a patentee sues an alleged infringer. Unlike most of the failed product cases, a high proportion of such cases proceed to trial, so they are of particular interest for the detailed level of forensic scrutiny. Failure to honor the intellectual property rights of others can be just as serious a design disaster because of the financial consequences to the loser. If a patent is found valid and infringed, backdated royalties must be paid to the successful litigant, and the right to manufacture the product suspended. The largest settlements (e.g., *Polaroid v. Kodak*) have involved hundreds of millions of dollars in compensation, and such actions can seriously weaken companies. The cases describe common consumer products like lawnmowers, wheeled garbage containers and residual current devices (RCDs). This is a specialized area of forensic engineering that rarely receives attention from engineers, but which may affect working practice more severely than often supposed.

The terminology used throughout is American English (e.g., "plaintiff" for "claimant," "coal mine" for "colliery," etc.).

REFERENCES

1. Shipley, R.J. and Becker, W.T. (Eds.), *ASM Metals Handbook,* 10th ed., Vol. 11, *Failure Analysis and Prevention,* ASM, Materials Park, OH, 2002. An introduction to the subject is provided by Wulpi, D., Understanding How Components Fail, ASM International (2002).

2. Esaklul, K.A. (Ed.), *ASM Handbook of Case Histories in Failure Analysis,* ASM, Materials Park, OH, Vol. 1, 1992; Vol. 2, 1993.

3. Jones, D.R.H. (Ed.), *Failure Analysis Case Studies,* Elsevier, New York, Vol. 1 (1998); Vol. 2 (2001).

4. Seiko, R., *Failure Case Studies in Engineering,* Butterworth-Heinemann, Oxford (1993).

5. For example, The Open University Department of Materials Engineering maintains a website of case studies at http://materials.open.ac.uk.

6. The journal *Engineering Failure Analysis* is published bi-monthly by Elsevier and edited by D.R.H. Jones.

7. Ezrin, M., *Plastics Failure Guide: Causes and Prevention,* Hanser-SPE, Munich, 1996.

8. Wright, D.C., *Failure of Plastics and Rubber Products,* RAPRA, Shropshire, U.K. (2001).

9. Nader, R., *Unsafe at Any Speed,* Grossman, New York, 1965.

Acknowledgments

We thank The Open University for use of case study material first presented in two post-graduate courses (T838 Design and Manufacture with Polymers, 1998 and T839 Forensic Engineering, 2000). The two courses, run jointly with London Metropolitan University, were developed with financial assistance from EPSRC (one of the U.K. Government Research Funding Councils). One of the case studies (container failure of Chapter 5) has also appeared in T353 Failure of Stressed Materials. The external examiners for T838 and T839 (Professors Bob Young of UMITS. Roy Crawford FRAEng of Queeens University, Belfast, and Dr. Colin Goodchild of Glasgow University) gave helpful advice in preparation of case study material. Drs. Bob Dyson, Mark Alger and Mike Fitzpatrick of London Met University also assisted in course development. Dr. Dai (D.R.H.) Jones of Cambridge Universtiy was consulted during preparation of T839, and encouraged publication of many of the cases in the journal *Engineering Failure Analysis*.

We also express our appreciation to the experts and investigators with whom we have worked on many of the case studies presented in this book, and the many solicitors, loss adjusters and insurers for their instructions on most of the cases.

P.R.L. thanks The Royal Academy of Engineering and The Open University for their financial support of several visits to the Failure Analysis and Prevention Special Interest Group (FAPSIG) of the Society of Plastics Engineers ANTEC conferences in the U.S. Several of the cases mentioned in Chapters 6, 7 and 9 were first presented there, and they have been updated as necessary for this book. Drs. Meyer Ezrin (University of Connecticut), Donald Duvall, and Professors Jan Spoormaker (Delft University), Alan Lessor (University of Massachusetts) and Alex Chudnovsky (University of Illinois at Chicago) provided helpful feedbadk for cases presented at several FAPSIG sessions at recent ANTEC conferences.

P.R.L. would also like to acknowledge the inspiration of Sir Geoffrey ALlen FRS in sponsoring the course PT614 (Polymer Engineering) and others through SERC and Open University funding. He also thanks those of his students who helped investigate some of the cases in this book, including

Drs. Geoff Attenborough, Bob Ward, Paul Hawkins and Kamal Weerappe-ruma (Haycarb, Sri Lanka).

We acknowledge the assistance of our able colleagues in the Department of Materials Engineering at The Open University, especially Dr. George Weidmann (co-investigator of the plastic tank failures of Chapter 7); Gordon Imlach (micrography, DSC, FTIR); Dr. Jim Moffatt (mechanical testing); Mike Levers (photography); Stan Hiller and Richard Black (micrography); Naomi Williams (SEM) and Dr. Sarah Hainsworth (ESEM); Ian Norman (computing and scanning); Jennifer Seabrook (secretarial); Peter Ledgard and Charles Snelling (sample preparation); Clive Fetter and Robert Wood (editors on T838 and T839); and Roger Dobson (course manager for T838 and T839).

P.R.L. also thanks Dr. John Bellerby and Dr. Mike Edwards of the Royal Military College of Science (Cranfield University) for interesting discussions on various case studies while he was an external examiner for their Forensic Engineering and Science Master's Course. He acknowledges helpful discussion of cases with his fellow examiner on the course, Dr. Maurice Marshall, lately Head of the Forensic Explosives Labs of the U.K. Government at Fort Halstead. He also had fruitful discussions with Dr. Sarah Hainsworth of Leicester University and Dr. Mike Fitzpatrick of The Open University.

Last, but by no means least, we thank our families for their patience and understanding, which helped us bring this work to fruition.

Peter R. Lewis
Ken Reynolds
Colin R. Gagg

The Authors

Peter R. Lewis, Ph.D., was educated as a physical chemist at Manchester University (B.Sc. Hons Chem, class I). He worked on the synthesis and properties of thermoplastic elastomers and was awarded a Ph.D. in 1970. He spent a year as an ICI postdoctoral fellow under Professor S.F. Edwards in the Department of Theoretical Physics, before being appointed a lecturer in metallurgy at Manchester. During his 5 years in the department, he became involved in consulting with local companies about manufacturing problems. One intractable problem involved failure of miner's lamps in mines caused by a series of material, design and manufacturing mistakes. His work helped hignlight the problem of introducing new materials without sufficient development.

Dr. Lewis joined The Open University in 1975, where he helped pioneer new distance learning courses in materials processing and basic science for technologists and engineers. He also pioneered the development of specialist postgraduate courses for practicing engineers leading to a master's degree. The work was funded by the British government through the Science Research Council. Dr. Lewis chaired the first distance learning course in polymer engineering (1984), the first course in the new structure, collaborating with others in the sector. This led directly to a teaching company with the Acco-Rexel Group, with several students helping the industry invest in new technology. At the same time, he continued working with a range of companies experiencing manufacturing problems and helped resolve legal disputes ranging from contractual failures to personal injuries. He has appeared as an expert witness in numerous trials in U.K. courts in the Patents Court, High Court, Technology Court and County Courts.

Dr. Lewis became involved in the Integrated Graduate Development Programme with London Metropolitan University in the 1990s, obtaining grant funding for two new courses, Design and Manufacture with Polymers (1999) and Forensic Engineering (2000). The latter is the first distance learning course in the subject, and attracts about 100 students annually. Dr. Lewis has published failure cases in journals such as *Engineering Failure Analysis* and *Interdisciplinary Science Reviews* and presented numerous papers to ANTEC conferences of the SPE (Orlando, Dallas, San Francisco and

Nashville). He has produced more than 300 technical reports and several books dealing mainly with failure of polymeric and composite products.

Ken Reynolds, M.Sc., the son of a village blacksmith, has had a lifelong interest in the working and heat treatment of metals. He left school at 16 and took a job in the quality control laboratory of a nonferrous foundry and tube works where he soon became the works troubleshooter and dealt with customer complaints. Later he was transferred to the research department of the same industrial group where he worked for 5 years on the development of titanium alloys for aerospace. During this time he studied for external degrees from London University and gained an honours degree in engineering metallurgy and later a master's degree with a thesis on the hot workability of titanium tin aluminium alloys.

Mr. Reynolds entered the academic world as a lecturer in physical and industrial metallurgy at Birmingham College of Advanced Technology, later to become The University of Aston, which pioneered 4-year "thin" sandwich degree courses with integrated industrial training. During this time he was called upon to give evidence at several coroner's inquests as to the cause of failure of machinery and components involved in fatal industrial and road traffic accidents. The forensic science service at that time was staffed mainly by scientists, so Mr. Reynolds organized a series of short professional development courses in failure investigation at Aston specifically oriented toward forensic engineering. These courses were well supported by industry as well as independent engineers working for insurance companies.

As a UNESCO consultant in 1970–1971 Mr. Reynolds helped establish the National Institute of Foundry and Forge Technology in India and immediately afterward undertook a project in Iraq advising on the setting up of colleges for engineering technicians. Upon his return to the U.K. The Open University had just been established. Mr. Reynolds was appointed a senior lecturer in the technology faculty and contributed to all their courses in materials over the next 25 years.

Mr. Reynolds retired from the academic world in 1996 but continues to practice as a forensic metallurgist. To date, he has dealt with over 1300 cases. While at The Open University, he met Peter Rhys Lewis. They have collaborated on several legal cases and compiled a master's course in forensic engineering, which led to *Forensic Materials Engineering: Case Studies*.

Colin R. Gagg, M.Sc., holds an honours degree in engineering technology and a master's degree in management and technology of manufacturing. He is a chartered engineer and professional member of the Institute of Mechanical Engineering. His practical experience includes 2 years at the Structures

Laboratories of Imperial College of Science, Technology and Medicine and 4 years at the Engineering Department of the University of Toronto. He currently holds the post of research projects officer at The Open University and, for the past 10 years, he has been a member of the Forensic Engineering and Materials Group.

Mr. Gagg's prior research interest focused on advanced processing techniques such as Ospray processing, thixo-casting and melt spinning, from which a long-standing avenue of interest developed, engineering in medicine. His current research interests lie in two distinct areas: solder studies and forensic engineering. Solder assessment focuses on creep, creep rupture and monotonic characteristics of lead and lead-free solder systems. A principal aim of the work is to ensure that stress analysis and modeling for life prediction employ appropriate and reliable data. In addition to research publications, results generated have been fed directly into mainstream course production and into a specifically tailored course for the Taiwanese market. The second channel of research pursuit is forensic engineering, an area of research that is fed directly into the teaching stream as case study input.

Mr. Gagg's academic interests center on forensic engineering, where he is a contributing author for a postgraduate forensic engineering course. He maintains his enthusiasm for teaching the subject by tutoring 20 to 30 postgraduate students per year and serving as a member of the examination board for the course. He is also an examiner for M.Sc. dissertations in the manufacturing program at The Open University.

Mr. Gagg has written 24 papers for journals and international conferences and has produced more than 100 technical reports dealing with failure of metallic products. His consulting activities include resolving production difficulties and component failure issues. He acts as a single joint expert in product failure, personal injury disputes and failure during surgical procedures. He has appeared as an expert witness in court proceedings related to personal and fatal injury.

Contents

7 Failure of Storage Vessels 215

Introduction

1

The subject of this book is forensic engineering, an area of engineering that has grown substantially in recent years as product users have demanded ever-increasing levels of quality. Premature product failure cannot only deprive the user of that product, but it can also lead to personal injury and other detrimental effects. If a ladder suddenly collapses due to the fracture of a key part, the user may be thrown off and sustain injury. If the radiator of a new car suddenly runs dry and the engine seizes up, the owner will want redress.

These are all examples of problems to which the forensic engineer can make a neutral and objective contribution in helping to investigate and determine the cause of the accident. It is also a subject that has grown with the application of new investigative tools such as Fourier transform infrared spectroscopy (FTIR) and scanning electron microscopy (SEM), techniques also used widely by forensic scientists. Consideration of the documentary evidence that inevitably accompanies any dispute that leads to court action is also a task that forensic engineers can perform. Thus engineering drawings of a product are or become available during disputes, and they may need to be interpreted for dimensional tolerances or any other feature that may have caused a problem.

1.1 Forensic Engineering

What is forensic engineering? To answer the question, we need to look at the meaning of the words (an activity that we will encounter later when discussing intellectual property matters). Consultation of *Chambers English Dictionary* gives the following definitions:

Forensic = 1. belonging to courts of law
2. appropriate to, or adapted to, argument
3. loosely, of or pertaining to sciences or scientists connected with legal investigations

Engineering = the art or profession of an engineer
Engineer   = one who designs, or makes, or puts to practical use,
                engines or machinery of any type

Thus forensic engineering could mean, under the loose meaning of (3) above, "of or pertaining to engineers connected with legal investigations." But with which legal investigations is a forensic engineer concerned? Such investigations could include:

- Product failure (e.g., breakage of a critical part of a product as in the ladder case just mentioned)
- Process failure (e.g., a manufacturing process fails to achieve the intended effect)
- Design failure (e.g., many products fail prematurely)

But not all such failures lead to litigation. Product failure occurs frequently with consumer products, for example, but it is rare to resort to the law to alleviate the problem. A new car may develop an unexpected defect, such as a leaking radiator. If covered by a warranty (as most new cars are today), then the seller will repair the damage at no cost to the user. One typical condition of warranties is that the car is maintained according to the manufacturer's instructions; if not, the warranty may be void. Product or component failure is relatively common with a wide range of products, and there are well-established routes to replacing failed products without resorting to litigation. Components with a limited life are thus routinely replaced as a precautionary measure, and others are replaced when wear becomes visible and dangerous (such as car tires). However, some failures are more critical than others, for example, because they may involve safety-critical parts. Such parts are essential to the correct functioning of a product, and their failure can lead to safety risk to the user.

A primary thesis of this book is that all unexpected failures, however trivial they might at first glance appear, should be investigated to determine the cause or causes. The more serious the failure, such as with safety-critical components, the greater the need to investigate. Thus, in the case of the faulty car radiator, if the failure led to seizure of the engine, then the consequence of the original failure is much greater expense, both to the user and the manufacturer. If seizure of the engine in turn led to a car accident, then the safety issue becomes paramount.

So what are the consequences for the manufacturers? They will be concerned about their own quality methods used to make the part that failed, whether or not there was a design defect, or the problem could have been caused by the user (e.g., by not maintaining the water level in the radiator).

In most failures, it is the methods and techniques of forensic engineering that, when applied objectively, can isolate the cause or causes of failure. Action can then be taken to alleviate the problem.[1-3]

1.2 Causal Analysis

So what are the basic methods for determining failure modes? Some common examples illustrate methods we all use and take for granted everyday. Thus when a car fails to start on a cold, damp morning, there is a range of possible explanations that come to mind (perhaps aided by the need to meet an appointment). The battery may not be fully charged, so the engine cannot turn, or charge may be leaking away and the spark plugs not igniting the gasoline vapor in the engine. Short circuiting of charge is a common problem if the plugs are damp. Alternatively, gasoline may not be reaching the engine because the tank is empty. There is a range of possible causes that can be tackled systematically in turn to arrive at the correct failure mode. Now consider a much more serious example. A car suffers an engine compartment fire; inspection reveals a leak from a plastic fuel pipe. How could such a leak occur? Examination of the pipe shows that it could have simply slipped off while the engine was on, or alternatively, it may have fractured. The cause could have been a variety of possibilities, including use of the wrong material, aging, or chemical attack. Such a failure is clearly safety-critical, and deserves detailed investigation to determine the cause.

Both examples illustrate a central point about failure analysis: there is an implicit assumption that there are rational causes for failure and reasonably objective ways of determining those causes. Of course, it is assumed that you, the reader, have some inkling of the way such common machines operate. This may not be true of all machines, even in a domestic environment. Microwave ovens, personal computers and CD players come to mind. One way out of the impasse usually involves reading the operating manual, which provides basic guidance on common failure modes (but does not normally provide an understanding of the basic principles underlying their operation) and how to recognize their symptoms (often in the form of a "fault-finding" guide). Computers are usually supplied with their own "help" guide in the software, of no use if the computer itself crashes! Even the written guides that accompany the machine are of no use if there is a mechanical or electrical effect within the machine.

Typical fault-finding guides from car maintenance manuals (Figure 1.1) are usually tabulated and suggest several possible causes for one specific symptom. For the cooling system part of the fault-finding guide shown in the figure, five general symptoms are listed, and possible causes are provided under each

Figure 1.1   Fault-Finding Checklist for Overheating or Overcooling of Automobile Engine

Cooling System Faults	
Overheating	**External Coolant Leakage**
☐ Insufficient coolant in system or thermostat faulty	☐ Deteriorated or damaged hoses or hose clips
☐ Radiator core blocked or grill restricted	☐ Radiator core or heater matrix leaking
☐ Electric cooling fan or thermoswitch faulty	☐ Pressure cap faulty
☐ Valve clearances incorrect	☐ Water pump seal leaking
☐ Pressure cap faulty	☐ Boiling due to overheating
☐ Ignition timing incorrect/ignition system fault — gasoline models	☐ Core plug leaking
☐ Inaccurate temperature gauge sender unit	**Internal Coolant Leakage**
☐ Airlock in cooling system	☐ Leaking cylinder-head gasket, cracked cylinder head or cylinder bore
Overcooling	**Corrosion**
☐ Thermostat faulty	☐ Infrequent draining and flushing
☐ Inaccurate temperature gauge sender unit	☐ Incorrect coolant mixture or inappropriate coolant type

heading. It is up to the user to investigate each possible fault mode systematically in turn to find the faulty component. By eliminating parts that are functioning correctly, the faulty part should be located quickly and remedial action taken. Since internal combustion engines work on the same general principles, the tabulated data are generic to many different makes of car. Such checklists are certainly a useful starting point for troubleshooting, but they must be used with common sense so that unsuspected failure modes are not discounted. Checklists often fail to mention a rather common failure mode: using the device incorrectly or in a way likely to cause failure. An example that springs to mind is spilling coffee on a computer keyboard; because water is conducting and likely to penetrate onto the printed circuit below, failure is almost inevitable. Even with simple mechanical tools such as ladders, unintended abuse by the user sometimes leads to very serious accidents.

1.2.1   Fault Tree Analysis

One simple way of showing the interrelationship of many different possible causes producing a single symptom is called fault-tree analysis,[4] also known as cause-and-effect analysis (Figure 1.2). Thus an overheating car engine can be caused by too low a coolant level (Figure 1.1, line 1). This in turn could be caused either by internal or external leaking of the coolant. An internal leak could be caused by a broken cylinder head gasket or a cracked cylinder head. Such internal leaks usually lead to water entering the main oil sump, which turns milky by emulsification, and is instantly recognizable when seen. Alternatively, the water is leaking to the exterior environment, and possible causes include a broken hose, damaged seals (to the pump for example) or

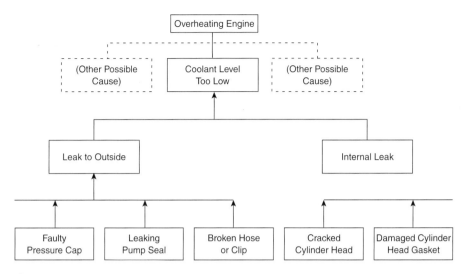

Figure 1.2   Fault tree diagram showing causal connections for an overheating automobile engine.

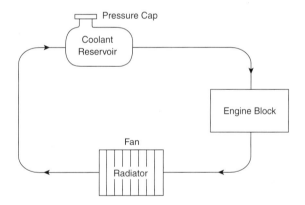

Figure 1.3   Simple diagram of the cooling system of an engine.

a faulty pressure cap (Figure 1.3). There are several dotted lines on the fault tree that indicate other possible causes (which might be peculiar to a particular model of a certain make of car). Fault tree diagrams are useful because they place analysis on a systematic footing, and give a mechanic or fitter a logical path to follow during examination. Each failure mode will exhibit well-defined features, so if inspection of the engine near the cooling hoses shows one point where there are dried traces of impurities from the cooling system, then the adjacent hose will need further, much closer examination.

With machines in which the working principle is totally known or if the principle of operation is known in outline form only, it is often possible to

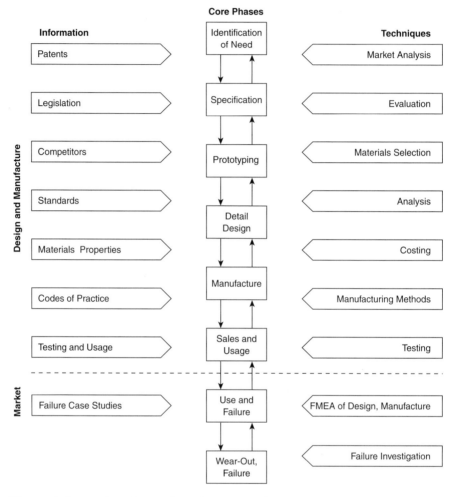

Figure 1.4 Product design flow diagram with core activities in center, information sources at left and methods at right.

evaluate failure using common sense ideas. The basis of analysis proceeds by a logical analysis of the way failure has occurred. If the original failure is buried under consequential damage, then the task is more difficult than for simple failures. Alternatively, or in addition, the failed component may lie deep within the machine, and the failure only inferred from the lack of a particular function. However, clues to the failure may be exhibited by contact traces of wear or abrasion, for example, where none would normally be expected. Analysis of such traces is known as trace or contact analysis and can be extremely useful in locating the source of a particular problem. Forensic investigation often starts after simple inspection by a mechanic or fitter reveals a component that should not have failed, or shows defective design or manufacture, especially if the failure has led to an accident in which injuries have occurred.

1.3 Product Design and Manufacture

Manufacturing is about making products to a recognizable specification (often a Public Standard), so it is useful to consider the sequence of steps that results in a finished product (Figure 1.4). Failure to achieve a product that can survive its environment, for example, must be tackled at a very early stage in product design. This is the stage of product conception (identification of a need), followed by planning and modeling, leading to a product specification. Provided the models achieve the desired technical effect, then detailed consideration of materials of construction follows. Testing and evaluation lead to a prototype or prototypes capable of production. At all stages, study of the failure of models and prototypes is an essential part of the development process, leading to improved prototypes. The process is an iterative one, where failure at any stage causes reconsideration of the specification or materials. Such failures are, of course, a normal part of new product development.

When a successful prototype emerges, production can be planned. This is usually a costly operation due to the cost of tools and machines to run them, and demands careful planning and testing. Following product launch, when the product is sold into the open market, product failure looms large in the design equation. Product quality will be a touchstone for public perception of the product itself, so any failures require immediate attention of the design team. Failure investigation using forensic methods is the key to identifying any design flaws or production defects, and correcting them as early as possible.

One tool for attempting to find and eliminate product defects of any kind (manufacture, design or material) before or after launch is known as Pareto analysis;[4] an example of a Pareto diagram is shown in Figure 1.5. The basis of the analysis is simply the collection of failure data from the production line (usually via the quality team), and sorting of that data into generic groups. It essentially classifies product defects in terms of their importance, so that the team can gain an overview of product problems. One limitation of restricting attention to the "vital few" is that a safety-critical defect among the "trivial many" may cause greater problems in the long term. Similar statistical methods form part of reliability engineering, now just another tool in total quality management, or TQM.[4] The team can then concentrate on those most serious defects, using fault tree analysis. A related method when applied in mass manufacturing industry is CEDAC (cause-and-effect-with-

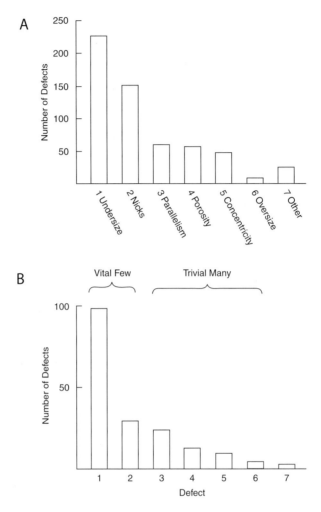

Figure 1.5 (A) Pareto diagram for several types of defects. (B) Interpretation of Pareto diagram.

added-cards), using diagrams such as that shown in Figure 1.6, and flow charts similar to that shown in Figure 1.7 to find "root causes."[4]

Another technique of some value in tackling product defects is known as failure modes and effects analysis, or FMEA.* This technique is in widespread use in many industries, and required by many standards and codes of practice. It is based on assessment of the real or suspected defect in terms of three criteria — occurrence, severity and detection — and is discussed further below. All such techniques are, however, simply management tools

* In addition to Chapter 17 in Dale's book, many large companies (such as Ford) have produced their own FMEA manuals, and there is at least one standard, *Analysis Techniques for System Reliability: Procedure for FMEA*, 1st ed., 1985, International Electrotechnical Commission IEC Standard No. 812.[5]

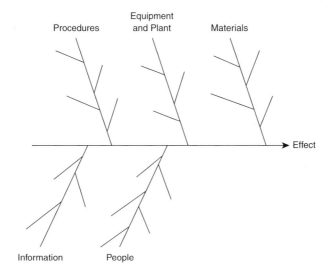

Figure 1.6   CEDAC or cause-and-effect diagram, also known as an Ishekawa diagram.

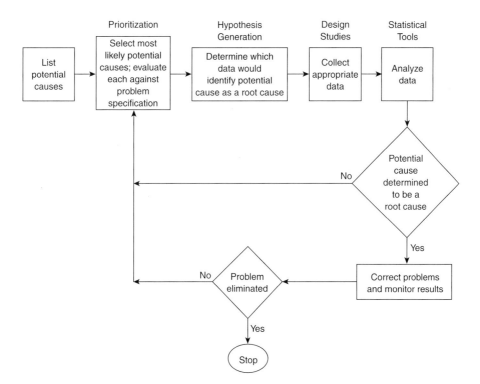

Figure 1.7   Flowchart for finding the root cause(s) of a problem.

to allow design and production engineers a way of interacting and talking to one another in a systematic fashion about product failures and the effects that led to failure. If there is no deep appreciation of product defects and their criticality, no management or statistical method will solve the problems of product failure.

1.4   Product Defects

What are some of the common defects found in products? The first task is to define more closely the meaning of the word "defect." One working definition might state that

> a defect is a feature or characteristic of a product or component which inhibits or prevents the correct functioning or processing of that product or component

The term "feature" is used in a neutral way to denote any characteristic of a product or component that does not normally appear in a specification (such as an engineering drawing). Thus variations in surface texture often appear on plastic moldings or cast metals as a result of the manufacturing process. The definition of features, which are also defects, is useful because it immediately allows us to examine those features that can affect product function in more detail. There are at least two types of defects:

1. Those already present in the product before sale or use which lead quickly to rejection or functional failure (in which case they are clearly defects), and
2. Defects that develop over time in a product, and so can increase the failure rate after normal use of the product

Such an approach exceeds the narrow legalistic view of defects. For example, the U.K. Consumer Protection Act (1987) defines a defect as follows:

> There is a defect in a product … if the safety of the product is not such as persons are reasonably entitled to expect….

The set of defects thus defined are of course safety-critical defects and, while of overriding interest for much litigation, do not cover aesthetic defects or defects that render a product inoperable.

Table 1.1   Typical Product Defects

	Primary Defects	Secondary Defects
Design: geometry	Dimensions (overfit, underfit) Stress raisers	Cracks from stress raisers
Design: materials	Poor materials Voids Inclusions Contamination	Degradation
Manufacture	Poor molding, casting, etc. Weld lines Contamination Cracks	Distortion over time
Assembly	Poor fit Poor welding, etc.	
Finishing	Surface blemishes Packing flaws	Degradation on surface

1.4.1   Primary Defects

Primary features that are often defects in components would typically include the following:

1. Sharp corners in stressed areas
2. Internal voids or inclusions that raise the stress to unacceptable levels when the product is loaded
3. Deviations from acceptable dimensions so that the component does not fit with others during assembly (underfit or oversized, such as sinking of the surfaces of castings or moldings)
4. Poor quality material of construction (e.g., contaminated material)
5. Cracks in components

Any such features can occur in combination with one another, and may also interact, such as a void near a sharp corner, a serious defect in a product where the stress is imposed at the corner. A more complete list of defects is given in Table 1.1. Note, however, that not all such features may be defects by themselves. Whether or not a feature can be regarded as a defect depends on the product specification, and the role of that feature in product failure. It may, for example, be acceptable to tolerate a certain level of cracks in a product if they are well below criticality. Indeed, the subject of fracture mechanics is devoted to the study of such subcritical cracks and how to recognize under what conditions they may become critical, so as to avoid those conditions and prevent catastrophic failure.

1.4.2   Secondary Defects

Features of the second kind that occur generally over a period of time typically include:

1. Wear of parts that move against one another
2. Cracks that develop over time or cycles of use
3. Corrosion or degradation by contact with the environment
4. Change in dimensions with time
5. Material changes with time

among many other potential features either within the body or at surfaces in products (Table 1.1). As with primary features, they will become defects if they could potentially lead to fracture or failure or rejection for aesthetic reasons. The distinction between product features and defects is closely related to the product function, its environment and usage (the specification).

Some of the most severe features that are often primary defects in product parts are those caused by stress concentration, such as by sharp corners or by cracks or from impurities or voids within samples.[6,7] When products are loaded as part of their normal function, the stress at such defects is raised above acceptable limits. Such stress raisers cause the local stress to rise above the intrinsic strength of the material concerned. The net result is that cracks are initiated at such defects (to become secondary effects) and can either grow very rapidly, producing a sudden fracture, or can grow stepwise over time a number of load cycles in a process known as fatigue.

1.5   Product Testing

Due to the high cost, 100% testing is rarely used for most mass-manufactured products. Samples are usually chosen to be representative of the batch, as in SPC, or statistical process control.[4] Tests are normally carried out under standard conditions, defined either by a national or international standard, or often by an internal company standard. While they may provide a degree of quality control, it must be remembered that the major goal of standard tests is to attempt to simulate conditions of use of the real product. The standard tests may be more or less successful in this regard. If the tests are successful, then a high quality product is made. However, if the test or test method itself fails to detect product defects, then faulty products can enter the market and cause problems. Failures of the test method itself can occur in several ways:

1. Inability to reproduce conditions of use.
2. The test technique is not monitored correctly.
3. The test may not adequately detect product defects.

There is of course failure to test under realistic conditions at all, the results of previous experience being preferred. An example of such a failure occurred where hot water seals achieved their intended purpose during intermittent conditions of use, but failed completely during near continuous exposure. Testing was not performed under the changed conditions, so the failure mode was missed entirely (see Section 6.7).

1.5.1 FMEA

An important tool for considering potential and actual failure modes in products is FMEA (failure modes and effects analysis). It is not in itself a product test method but rather a way of assessing product defects and, if necessary, specifying changes to product testing or suggesting new test methods.[4,5]

Pareto analysis, FTA and SPC (statistical process control) are all techniques used by design teams both for new and existing or long-standing products. Most factories gather statistics on their product lines through quality departments. Many inspectors are not engineers, however, and may not recognize a particular problem as rating high in importance compared with others. Thus surface blemishes are easy to spot on the line and are clearly defects of a kind, but not usually serious enough to affect product safety. Such obvious (patent) defects may be contrasted with latent defects, which lie hidden within products or components. The study of latent defects is the particular responsibility of the design team, who will use FMEA (failure modes and effects analysis) to identify, classify and act upon. They may be defects in products returned from customers, defects found internally or by other methods such as routine testing and inspection.

A common design defect in many products, for example, is sharp corners in products which, when stressed, raise the local stress above the failure stress of the material concerned. Thus fracture will start at such corners, and propagate into the interior of the sample. If the product shape is made by a mass manufacturing route such as injection moulding or casting of a metal alloy, it will occur in every product so that its likelihood of occurrence (L) is 10 on a scale of 1 to 10. If the severity of the consequences of fracture is high (say 8), and it is easy to detect (with a value of say 8), then the product of all three factors is 640. This number is known as the risk priority number (RPN), in effect a criticality threshold, so

$$RPN = (\text{likelihood of occurrence, L}) \times (\text{severity, S}) \times (\text{detectability, D}) \quad (1.1)$$

The design team assigned to an FMEA analysis will by experience set a threshold value above which action must be taken. Suppose in this case, the RPN is 250. The team must now discuss ways of eliminating the defect, which in this case is easily done simply by modifying the tool plans by increasing the radius of curvature at the corner in question.

FMEA is not the only answer to improving quality, but what it can do is focus the minds of designers onto product quality in a systematic and rational way. Potential problems can be tackled at an early stage in design development rather than in a panic when failures come back from customers. FMEA is also crucially dependent on the skills of the members of the team. The method stands a much greater chance of success in solving problems if the engineers know how to recognize defects, and how to correct them once identified.[8] The method has to be taken seriously by management if it is to achieve the goal of reducing product failure. Too often the method is given lip service, so that serious product failures may continue to plague specific industries.*

1.6 Litigation

Although the majority of product or process failures are resolved by on-the-spot inspection, by compensation from the seller or from insurance cover, there nevertheless remains a core of failures that cannot be easily resolved without litigation. It may come from allegedly faulty components supplied by an outside contractor, or as a result of an accident in which a component is identified as defective. One party either does not believe, or does not accept the claims of the other side or sides (for multiparty disputes). This may occur for several reasons.

- The evidence of failure is unclear or ambiguous.
- The evidence was destroyed by the accident, or was not preserved, or was modified by later events.
- The evidence may offer conflicting interpretations of what happened.
- Faults responsible for the failure may have been introduced by third parties.
- Faults may be present but have no connection with the cause of failure.
- The failures may be widespread and thus more serious than isolated incidents (design failure).
- Process failures may be endemic (often contractual problems).

---

* A case study of the implementation of FMEA at Allied Signal in the U.K. is described in Dale's book on page 360 (Chapter 17). He discusses the tendency of many automotive company suppliers to regard FMEA as a mere paper exercise.

Commercial disputes often result in litigation, where a court is asked to examine the facts, and interpret the relevant law concerning the dispute. There are other ways of resolving commercial disputes, and such so-called "alternative dispute resolution" or ADR methods have developed as quickly as court costs have escalated.[9] That is, of course, the reason for their success, because the role of lawyers is minimal, with experts performing a more important task than is the case in a formal court of law. Such ADR methods include arbitration before a single assessor (often an expert engineer) and mediation, where a lawyer consults the parties separately to test their evidence. It is arranged on a fixed date, with each party sitting in separate rooms together with their respective expert witnesses. The mediator moves from room to room, putting points to each party raised by the other side. The quality of the evidence raised by each expert is tested by the mediator in turn until one side or the other starts to yield ground. This is the turning point, because now offers of settlement can be made and modified until a deal is possible without the need for court action. The whole process concentrates minds, due to the sharp deadlines imposed by the mediator. Since decisions are reached in private, there is no public record, an advantage for some, but a disadvantage if a major design problem does not reach the public record.

There are several formal tribunals available for commercial litigants in the U.K., with state courts acting as the first port-of-call in the U.S. Some of these disputes involve the interpretation of the law itself, and the ultimate decision then becomes part of the case law in that area. Such cases might, for example, involve the first to be brought under a new statute (as specified in an Act of Parliament or Congress), and the judgment could be important for what the wording of the Act means when applied to real situations and problems. Such "test cases" are especially important in intellectual property disputes, where the current statute law is in some areas of technology being outstripped by events. Thus computer technology, software and biotechnology developments are so fast nowadays that it is a struggle for the statute law to keep pace.

1.6.1 Trials of Disputes

Disputes are finally resolved by trials, when all other avenues have been exhausted. So what is so important about a trial? A trial is a public forum where the opposing parties in a dispute confront one another, and attempt to convince a court of the rectitude of their own case. It is often the first time for confrontation, or at least the first time when others are present to order and marshal all the evidence in a systematic and fair way. Much research will have been prepared well before the trial, with the collection of evidence to be presented to the court, and the preparation of arguments to be used for one case or the other. The arguments are prepared in the form of "pleadings," documents presented by each side in support of their case, and prepared by the lawyers with the aid of experts if technical issues are at stake. Frequently, so-called "skeleton arguments" can also be presented as more evidence comes to light as trial approaches, and the original pleadings must be revised.

Expert engineers play a key role in marshalling the evidence, both real and often voluminous documentary evidence. Thus if a product fails, there will always be in-house documents from the manufacturer relating to quality control, for example. Such documents are usually "discovered" (a legal term for obtaining information from the other side in a dispute) well before trial to all parties in an action, and may include, in technical cases, the following:

- Maps, plans and engineering drawings
- Quality control records
- Testing records
- Models and prototypes
- Specifications and standards
- Internal memos and correspondence between the parties (privileged documents being excluded)

Such documents assume great importance as a trial approaches, because they help to flesh out the background as well as provide key details about the product in question. A plaintiff who has suffered individual loss or injury from a product failure does not have the information about the way in which the product was made and its quality checks after manufacture. The plaintiff will often have an expert report on the failure, however, that will point to areas that should show how the defect could have arisen or was not detected by the quality managers of the manufacturing company. The expert performs a valuable role here, by specifying what discovery should be made in order to clarify the failure, following production of his or her report or reports concerning the failure.

However, it is the material evidence that usually forms the starting point for a forensic investigation, and it is often that very evidence that provides a much more detailed picture of what actually happened in an accident, for example. The evidence often gives vital clues as to how an accident was initiated, perhaps from traces of contact with other bodies, or from features that reveal the way in which the product was made originally. Analysis can also show whether or not the material of construction was appropriate to the function it performed in service, or whether it was affected by processing during manufacture, or by its working environment. It is the role of the expert engineer to initiate such investigations.

1.6.2 Evidence and Trial Procedure

The raw evidence available for a court to consider comes in several different forms. It usually includes the following for a typical technical case:

1. Real evidence (the failed product or products, tool parts under question, models and prototypes, etc.)
2. Testimony from witnesses of fact relating to the incident(s)
3. Testimony from expert witnesses
4. Pleadings in the case (drawn up by the lawyers for both sides)
5. Documents discovered from both sides related to the facts at issue

The detailed sequence of events at trial varies from country to country, but so-called "common law" countries (mainly English-speaking jurisdictions, such as the U.S., Canada, Australia and the U.K. plus its many former colonies) have broadly similar processes. The essential goal is to present the evidence in a logical and coherent way to the judge or jury who, at the end of the process, will need to decide which party wins the argument and the damages to be awarded. Jury trial is more common in the U.S. for all kinds of civil disputes, while single judges are the norm in Britain. Juries are always used in criminal actions in both countries. The claimant or plaintiff usually opens the trial with a speech from his or her lawyer, which outlines the case against the defendants. It is usually short, and is followed immediately by examination of the first witnesses of fact for the plaintiff (possibly including the plaintiff). This is always started by the plaintiff's lawyer, so the questioning is friendly, being designed to put the witness at ease, and elicit favorable information about the plaintiff's case.

Cross-examination by the defendant's lawyer is often aggressive in tone and searching in nature. It is when the work of the court really begins, because the testimony is scrutinized for inconsistency, ambiguity and deliberate falsehood. The latter is rare in civil actions, but unfortunately much more common in criminal trials. Sometimes cases collapse at this point if the plaintiff (for example) contradicts his or her own previous evidence (from a witness statement), and cannot explain the discrepancy or discrepancies. In a recent case where the writer was to appear as an expert for the defense, this is exactly what happened when the plaintiff contradicted himself on the witness stand, even when the questions from the cross-examiner were put fairly and calmly. The cross-examiner had intended only a few questions, because the case actually hinged on expert evidence, but the questions came thick and fast as the plaintiff's evidence began to unwind. The case ended the next day, because the plaintiff faced yet more searching cross-examination, and his credibility before the court was, by this time, rather low. In addition, the cross-examiner had been using the plaintiff's numerous documents to frame his questions. The judge had scrutinized many of the documents and found them lacking key details (some pages appeared, on the face of it, to have been deliberately obscured during photocopying). The judge asked for the originals, but they were not produced by the time the case collapsed, with the defendant dropping his counter-claim, and winning all his (substantial) costs.

The end result could not have been predicted before the trial started but this example demonstrates very effectively the power of cross-examination to reach the truth of a matter in dispute. The experts were thus never called, and the technical merits of the case never tested. Halted trials are not uncommon, and it is even more common for civil trials to stop at the doors of the court when final offers are made between the opposing lawyers. It is a crunch point for both parties, because they know that all the evidence will be tested in minute detail. Any weaknesses will be exposed in the light of open court (normally held in public), so both sides face stark reality before the trial commences and often reach an acceptable compromise without needing the added expense of a trial. In trials involving several defendants, the lawyers must decide whether or not to proceed to trial irrespective of the merits of a case. A settlement may be reached before trial because the costs of going to trial are out of all proportion to the costs of the dispute itself. For example, no fewer than ten different subcontractors were sued by a university due to corrosion failures that necessitated extensive repairs. Because each party agreed to a modest settlement, their costs were much lower than if the case had been heard in a trial that was estimated to last 10 weeks. The defendants had strong technical evidence that supported their case that the college was actually at fault for not treating the water supply correctly with anticorrosion chemicals. The costs of all ten companies would have included appearances of their senior managers and operatives in the trial together with ten experts instructed by each company, as well as the much greater costs of the ten teams of lawyers. So they agreed to a commercial settlement without testing the merits of the case, a sensible end to what could have been a long trial (with no necessary clear conclusion), adverse publicity and substantial loss of goodwill.

Often the evidence is tested by "without prejudice" (i.e., nothing can be used later in a court) meetings between the experts. It may end up in a total disagreement (in the worst examples) with an "agreement to disagree," or with partial agreement on the technical issues. This is very valuable to the court, which usually asks for a statement of the areas of agreement and disagreement, because it saves time by focusing on the critical points in a case.

1.6.3 The Role of Forensic Engineers

Expert witnesses such as forensic engineers and scientists have a special place in any trial because they can give opinions about events, a role denied to witnesses of fact.[10,11] But most of their work is done well before trial, in the form of site visits, laboratory tests and experiments, literature searches and presentation of detailed reports. The expert will be given the failed product, as well as background information on the accident (such as witness statements), and be instructed to prepare a report that should include

1. The nature of the failure and its consequences
2. Analysis of the failed product itself
3. Interpretation of the evidence of the failed product
4. Possible causes of the failure
5. The likely cause of the accident, and, where possible
6. A reconstruction of the sequence of events

Criminal cases of course focus on the crime rather than a product failure, *mutatis mutandis*. The expert may feel some responsibility to the solicitor or company paying for the service or, if an expert within a company, some loyalty to that company. Even if the case or failure never reaches court action, the report should always be completely objective, and all attempts to bias the conclusions one way or another from outside pressure (whether real or imaginary) must be resisted. A report must be, and be seen to be, a fair attempt to explain a failure in a perfectly neutral way. There are several ways of achieving this central objective, but one of the most important is to let the real evidence speak for itself. In a way, a piece of real evidence is a "silent witness" that will reveal all kinds of detail about the failure that may not be immediately obvious to the untutored eye but which an expert will locate and show the court.

Photographic evidence (still images given directly, and reference to videos or film footage) of such details is normally presented in the report, together with analysis of the material of construction, an account of any mechanical tests on the material, evidence from new, intact products and so on. A picture of the sequence of events in the accident will emerge as the evidence from the failed product builds up in the report. Finally, a reconstruction of events allows the investigator to revisit the facts which have been established, and in turn draw conclusions about the cause of the accident. Computer simulations or graphic animations are also useful in explaining mechanisms to a judge with no technical training. The expert should be able to say how the product has been made, and whether the material and process route has been well chosen. Much information will necessarily be missing at this stage of an investigation, so the expert can point out what extra information is needed from the manufacturer in order to test the conclusions reached in the report. If, for example, the product failed because of faulty manufacture, the expert should be able to list the internal documents needed for the process of discovery, the legal process initiated by the instructing attorney.

1.6.4 Expert Reports

As a result of some abuse of the system of giving expert evidence to courts in the U.K., a new system of presenting reports has been introduced in the last decade (known as the Woolf reforms, after the name of the judge who recommended reform). Similar problems have occurred in the U.S. Courts, according to one American commentator.[12] Experts employed by the courts are licensed state by state, but such safeguards may still not prevent "hired guns" from appearing for disputants. Essentially, experts must address issues in an action totally impartially, and show no bias to their instructing client. Experts should be cautious in extending their opinion to subjects about which they may have no expertise, give details of their qualifications, provide references to literature used in their report and state who carried out tests or experiments (along with their qualifications). Where there is a range of opinion on causation, it should be stated, and the reasons why a particular opinion is supported. A summary of conclusions should be provided, together with a statement that the expert understands his duty to the court. Just as important is a statement of instructions given to the expert (written or oral), including all facts that may be material to his or her opinions. Finally, the expert must verify the report by adding a formal statement of truth:

> I confirm that insofar as the facts stated in my report are within my own knowledge I have made it clear which they are and I believe them to be true, and that the opinions I have expressed represent my true and complete professional opinion.

These requirements provide some reassurance to the court that the expert evidence is really unbiased, and that the expert is not a hired gun. The intention of such changes is to reduce wasted costs of trials, and lower the time needed to bring actions to trial (many years in some important cases). ADR is encouraged by the new philosophy for the same reasons. For example, if a product failed through abuse by the injured party, then the report to the lawyer acting for the same party will be of no further use for litigation. It is up to the lawyer to assess the quality of the report, whether or not it is fairly based on the evidence and whether or not it is worthwhile to instruct another expert, or get a second opinion. Experts may differ as to the cause of the accident, especially where critical information is missing. Experts can also be wrong! It is a sad fact that many investigators fail to probe deeply when presented with instructions either from within their own company (for internal reporting) or from lawyers. The authors have numerous examples of expert reports where the investigators have made a superficial inspection of the failed product and drawn the wrong conclusions. Such reports are brief, and often include no plans or photographs of the product to support the conclusions. The danger from the superficial approach to problems is that the whole legal machine is put into motion on an unsupported base. The machine often continues on unabated (sometimes for years) until another expert produces a more firmly based report, which contradicts or qualifies the original opinion. This situation creates an unwelcome build-up of costs, money that will have been wasted. The moral is that failure reports must from the outset examine the evidence in sufficient depth to draw reasonable conclusions. It perhaps goes without saying that all reports should be written in clear and concise language, without ambiguity or contradiction. After all, it is a nontechnical judge or jury who will have to reach their own conclusions about the facts of a case. It is easy for scientists and some engineers to make a report too complex, and so lose the lay reader. If complex arguments or higher level mathematics are needed, they should always be put in an appendix, so as not to break up the logic of a presentation.

1.7   Engineering Materials

The case studies in this book deal with the problems of a wide range of materials, and include many metal, alloy and polymer products. Mechanical failure still forms one of the most important types of product demise, and the cases in this book are predominantly of this nature, especially when thermal and chemical effects are included. This is not to say that other failure modes cannot occur, but rather that they are dealt with elsewhere. Software failures, for example, are a relatively recent problem, but cannot be discussed within the scope of this work. Civil engineering failures, too, are beyond its scope, although many such failures do involve classical failure modes of mechanics and materials; the subject is well studied in other works.[13] The case histories presented here show how different forensic tools can be used to determine the cause or causes of product or process failure. Metallic materials are central to engineered products and deserve major examination. Because they have been used in major structural applications for so long, much knowledge has been gained by study of their main failure modes. Even so, it took many years before low-cycle fatigue was recognized as an important fracture mechanism. It is now thought, for example, that many early failures of bridges were caused in this way, although it was not recognized at the time. Cast iron structures, in particular, fell with some regularity, culminating in the Tay bridge disaster of 1879. Recent reanalysis of the witness evidence and the photographic archive of the remains indicate that low-cycle fatigue of the tie bar lugs contributed to its final demise.[14] A similar problem occurred in the early 1950s with the British Comet aircraft, one of the first to be designed to fly at high altitude with a pressurized fuselage. Several disappeared over the Mediterranean, but careful and painstaking detective work on the remains recovered at the scene established without doubt low-cycle fatigue cracks from window cut-outs in the fuselage. When fatigue cracks reached a critical size, they grew catastrophically and the planes disintegrated. Many more recent disasters have also been caused by fatigue of structural components in an airframe.

As a relatively new class of materials, polymers have found widespread application in many consumer and industrial products, often in a safety-critical role. New polymeric or composite materials offer many advantages in a variety of ways, be it in greater design freedom or lighter weight and so on. But there are some disadvantages, especially as experience of long-term usage is often absent. Many new polymers have been invented and used only within the last 50 years or so (polysulfones, for example, are of even more recent application), so longer-term experience of their behavior is either absent or difficult to access. Knowledge of the failure modes of such materials is a vital part of their safe application, and case studies are an important way of gaining more precise knowledge of their properties. Textbooks tend to ignore many of the realities of product failure, which is rather unfortunate given the importance of the subject to designers. Textbooks also tend to emphasize theoretical aspects of particular materials, without mention of the practical problems of using those materials in often demanding and safety-critical roles. Reference works are available that provide basic definitions and background information.[15]

References

1. Noon, R., *Introduction to Forensic Engineering*, CRC Press, Boca Raton, FL, 1998.

2. Brown, S., Ed., *Forensic Engineering*, Part I, ISI Publications, Bermuda, 1995.

3. Carper, K.L., Ed., *Forensic Engineering*, 2nd ed., CRC Press, Boca Raton, FL, 2001.

4. Dale, B., *Managing Quality*, 3rd ed., Blackwell Business, Oxford, 1999.

5. *Analysis Techniques for System Reliability: Procedure for FMEA*, 1st ed., 1985, International Electrotechnical Commission IEC Standard No. 812.

6. Young, W.C., *Roark's Formulae for Stress and Strain*, 6th ed., McGraw-Hill, New York, 1989.

7. Pilkey, W.D., *Peterson's Stress Concentration Factors*, 2nd ed., John Wiley & Sons, New York, 1997.

8. Finlay, A. and Lewis, P.R., Total Quality Manufacture of Stationery Products with FMEA Methods, Teaching Company Quality Seminar, Institute of Marine Engineers, April 22, 1992.

9. Acland, A.F., *Resolving Disputes Without Going to Court*, Century Business Books, Evergreen, CO, 1995.

10. Reynolds, M.P. and King, P.S.D., *The Expert Witness and His Evidence*, 2nd ed., Blackwell Scientific, Oxford, 1992; Smith, D., *Being an Effective Expert Witness*, Thames Publishing, Norwich, U.K., 1993.

11. Bronstein, D.A., *Law for the Expert Witness*, CRC Press, Boca Raton, FL, 1999.

12. Huber, P.W., *Galileo's Revenge: Junk Science in the Courtroom*, Basic Books, New York, 1991.

13. Ratay, R.T., Ed., *Forensic Structural Engineering Handbook*, McGraw-Hill, New York, 2000.

14. Lewis, P.R. and Reynolds, K., Forensic engineering: a reappraisal of the Tay bridge disaster, *Interdisciplinary Sci. Rev.*, 27(4), 287–298, 2002.

15. Walker, P., Lewis, P.R., Reynolds, K., Weidmann, G., and Braithwaite, N., Eds., *Dictionary of Materials Science and Technology*, Chambers-Harrap, Edinburgh, 1993.

Materials in Distress

2

2.1 Introduction

All materials have limits as to what they are able to withstand in terms of forces that can be applied and environmental conditions under which they can safely operate. Designers and manufacturers strive to ensure their products meet the appropriate materials and engineering specifications and should survive an acceptably long, trouble-free service lifetime in a particular application. However, no material is universally suited for every type of engineered product and no product is unbreakable or will not fail in some way if the service conditions are hostile. When a product does not achieve the expected level of performance it is said to have "failed." That does not necessarily mean that it has broken but simply that it may have worn at an unusually high rate, suffered debilitating environmental attack or degradation or anything that would prejudice its future performance if it had been allowed to remain in service. The statistical incidence of failures for a particular product, whether it be a single item or a complex assembly such as a motor vehicle, exhibits a characteristic "bathtub" shape as illustrated in Figure 2.1.

Initially the high incidence is associated with not getting the product quite right in terms of satisfying every aspect demanded of the application, or minor difficulties with quality of materials or manufacturing. When these initial difficulties are resolved the incidence of failures flattens off to a very low level and remains so for the intended lifetime of the product and beyond. However, the incidence later rises steeply due to products literally "wearing out." A characteristic "wear and tear" failure mode of individual components soon becomes recognized and, for this reason, preventive maintenance to replace such parts before they fail catastrophically both greatly extends the

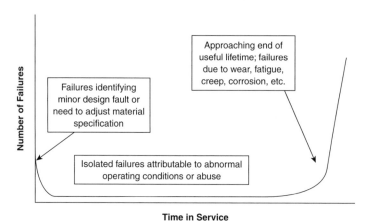

Figure 2.1 Incidence of failures during the lifetime of a manufactured product.

useful lifetime of the machine and promotes safety. For an aircraft there are no layovers at 40,000 ft.

The metallurgist and the materials engineer may aptly be regarded as the pathologists of the engineering failure. The medical pathologist is called upon to ascertain the cause of death by applying knowledge of the way the human body works and how disease and trauma affect cells, tissues and organs. Hence, if the driver of a crashed vehicle is found to be dead after an accident it is vitally important to establish whether death was due to some natural cause such as a stroke or heart attack that led to loss of control or whether it was the result of violent impact in the collision. A number of parties will be keen to know the findings, not only those investigating the cause of the accident but also insurers of the driver and owners of property damaged in the accident. A whole chain of litigation may be initiated on the basis of the pathologist's findings.

But what if the driver was not killed but claims the vehicle suddenly went out of control as it was entering a curve and, when the wreckage is examined, it is discovered that some vital part of the steering or braking system is broken? It is just as important to establish whether this was broken in the collision or was the cause of the driver's loss of control. This calls for investigation by someone able to relate the way the part failed to the circumstances of the accident. The necessary skills include the ability to interpret fractures and identify failure modes in terms of the mechanical properties and manufacturing methods of metals, plastics and other materials used in engineered products. Armed with such knowledge and experience, it becomes a fairly straightforward matter to determine whether a particular component recovered after an accident was damaged or broken by sudden, massive overstress in an impact or whether it failed spontaneously as the result of gradual wear and tear or some progressive weakening ("disease") such as corrosion or fatigue.

It is useful to illustrate the similarity between the forensic engineer's and the medical pathologist's categorizations of the cause of demise of a subject, as discussed below.

2.1.1   Cause of Demise — Engineering Example

Congenital (*early demise*) — A serious design fault or manufacturing defect, rendering a component so weak that it fails on the first occasion it is subjected to forces near the top of the anticipated spectrum of service loadings. For example, an aluminum alloy wheel for a racing car made from a rather poor quality casting, which had been wrongly machined so that part of the hub was cut away. It failed at the first curve in its first race when the vehicle braked from 165 mph.

Congenital (*slow demise*) — A minor material or manufacturing fault that leads to progressive weakening over a period of service; for example, a surface defect in a forging initiates a fatigue crack that runs to completion after many thousands or millions of stress cycles.

Disease — Corrosion, degradation, wear or similar damage that reduces the effective cross section of critical load-bearing components, or introduces stress raisers that serve as initiation sites for fatigue, for example, wear of a crankshaft journal introduces a step in a previously radiused surface.

Consequence of previous operation — Failure stemming from an earlier repair or adjustment, for example, welding that alters the microstructure, introduces residual stress or causes cracks in heat-affected zones that lead to eventual failure by fatigue. Carrying out some minor maintenance or repair with a dissimilar material that sets up corrosion or suffers environmental degradation, gradually reducing the effective cross-sectional area or strength until the component is no longer capable of supporting the normal service loads.

Trauma — Sudden failure caused by gross mechanical overstress incurred in, for example, a collision, i.e., applying forces well beyond the magnitude and/or acting in different directions from those the design was intended to withstand. Traumatic failure is always associated with damage and deformation of adjacent parts in the load transfer path. For a traumatic failure the applied force must be sufficiently high to cause fracture at a single application.

In general terms "failure" is the inability of a product to meet or continue to maintain the performance or strength criteria in the application for which it was designed. It does not necessarily imply that it has broken or wasted away so that it no longer possessed the strength or properties it had when first put into service. A product may fail because it is part of a system that breaks down under some abnormal condition and unexpectedly places greater demands on one component than the design anticipated. Investigation of the mode of failure may then become the means of ascertaining where the fault lies in the system as a whole.

The engineer specialist in failure investigation and forensic work is usually presented with some product or component that is, or is likely to become, the subject of litigation between various parties. These may be damaged parts, photographs, etc. of the scene of an accident and/or circumstances of failure, or some consumer product that is alleged to be faulty and has caused injury or financial loss. The expert is instructed to address three basic questions:

1. How did it fail?
2. Why did it fail?
3. Who or which party was responsible?

To illustrate what is meant by "failure" let us consider the failure modes of the simple bookshelf placed on two supports, as illustrated in Figure 2.2. The design brief was for a straight shelf on two wall brackets capable of holding a single row of books. The unloaded shelf is shown in Figure 2.2A where the supports have been positioned at the extreme ends. When books are placed on the shelf it begins to sag, as shown in Figure 2.2B, and the curvature reduces the bearing on the supports. Eventually, but before the shelf is filled with books, the bowing is so great that one of the ends slips off its bracket and all the books fall to the floor. However, as soon as the load is taken off the shelf the shelf springs back to its original straightness. The shelf has failed in the elastic regime and nothing has broken. The shelf could be used again if an additional support were introduced near the middle to prevent the bowing or the shelf should be made thicker or redesigned to increase its structural stiffness (not "strength") so that it does not deflect so much under load. The fault is the responsibility of whoever disregarded the weight of the books when designing the shelf and chose to support it on two end brackets.

Next, consider a similar design, Figure 2.2C, but making the shelf in a thermoplastic material. The books are stacked along the shelf but initially the bowing is not sufficient to slip through the supports, although the bow probably will be noticeable because plastic has a considerably lower modulus of elasticity than wood or metals. However, thermoplastic material creeps (deforms permanently) over a period of time so the bowing gradually becomes worse until, eventually, this shelf again falls through the supports. But this time when it is picked up the bow will remain, so the shelf cannot

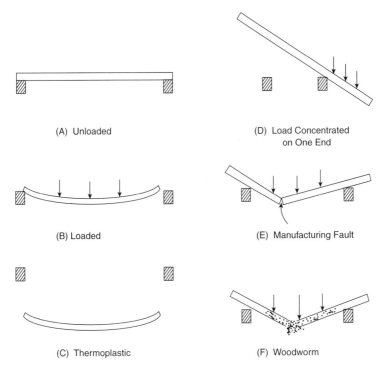

(A) Unloaded

(B) Loaded

(C) Thermoplastic

(D) Load Concentrated
on One End

(E) Manufacturing Fault

(F) Woodworm

Figure 2.2   Failure modes of a simple bookshelf.

be replaced. The failure is permanent and is due to a materials selection fault, again the responsibility of the designer. The remedy, if the thickness and aesthetic appearance of the shelf must remain the same, would be to use a plastic material that does not creep at ambient temperature, for example, a molded thermoset, or, alternatively, to build in reinforcement so that the overall stiffness is increased.

Now consider Figure 2.2D. Let us suppose this is the designer's attempt to overcome the problem with the wooden shelf of Figure 2.2A by bringing the supports closer together. This time if books are loaded from the right-hand side their weight sets up a lever moment that exceeds that of the empty shelf to the left of the fulcrum. Thus as soon as the leverage reaches the critical value the shelf suddenly tips and spills the books. Again a design failure, but this time one easily overcome by spacing the supports further apart or firmly fixing the shelf to both supports so that the unloaded end cannot be lifted when weight is being added to the other.

Finally, consider Figure 2.2E and Figure 2.2F, in which the design appears to be satisfactory but the shelf fails at the site of a local weakness. In Figure 2.2E it is assumed that a crack-like defect stemming from the manufacturing process had provided a localized stress concentration site for the tensile stresses acting along the bottom surface of the shelf. It would also reduce the effective cross-sectional area at that point, which would further increase the stress level. As books were placed on the shelf the bending action would generate increasing tensile stress in the bottom fibers. If the defect were severe the shelf might break at this position before it was fully loaded. However, if the shelf could be fully loaded without causing instantaneous fracture, then it is possible the defect might propagate slowly over a period during cycles of stress associated with adding and removing books a few at a time. Eventually the defect could reach a size where the shelf was no longer capable of withstanding one final stress cycle, so it would suddenly give way under a load that had been satisfactorily withstood on many previous occasions before the crack had grown so far into the section. This is what happens in a fatigue failure.

It is a fairly straightforward matter to ascertain from the appearance of the fracture surfaces whether the failure was of an instantaneous form or whether it was a progressive fatigue failure. Such an examination would also reveal the size and nature of the original defect, from which it should be possible to establish at what stage in the manufacturing process it was introduced. In the above circumstances responsibility would rest with the manufacturer, not only on the grounds of introducing the defect in the first place but also for failing to detect it in the finished product by appropriate quality control procedures.

The failure in Figure 2.2F illustrates the kind of progressive weakening in service that may be caused by environmental conditions. The illustration represents a gradual eating away (literally) of cross-sectional area by wood-boring insects, but a similar weakening could result from fungal attack under moist conditions, as well as other forms of environmental degradation for other materials. In either case, visual and microscopic study of the fracture would reveal the cause. Tests might be conducted on samples cut from near the break in order to demonstrate the reduction in strength that had resulted from the attack. Clearly neither the designer nor the manufacturer could be held responsible for the consequences of such failures.

2.2 Manufacturing Defects

These are the "congenital" faults in a product that may sometimes result in failure the first time it comes under load although, more usually, the faults lead to progressive weakening and eventual failure by fatigue. Manufacturing techniques may be divided into the following broad categories, each of which is prone to the introduction of defects characteristic of the material and the particular shaping process used to form the product.

1. Flowing to shape in the liquid, powder or semiviscous state — sand casting, continuous casting, injection molding, extrusion, rotomolding, etc.
2. Deforming to shape in the hot solid state — forging, rolling, extrusion, drawing, thermoforming, etc.
3. Cutting to shape in the solid state — machining processes such as turning, milling, sawing, drilling, etc.
4. Joining together using a liquid phase — fusion welding, soldering, brazing, adhesives, sintering, etc.
5. Joining together in the solid state — riveting, bolting, mechanical fasteners, etc.

In addition, one or more of several post-shaping processes may be applied to a formed product to control its mechanical properties, resist environmental degradation or improve service performance, including:

1. Bulk heat treatment throughout the component section — hardening and tempering of steels, controlled transformations, precipitation hardening treatments, annealing
2. Surface heat treatments — case hardening, induction hardening, thermal toughening (e.g., glass)
3. Coatings — diffusion, plasma coatings, spraying, dipping, electroplating, anodizing
4. Mechanical treatment of the surface — peening, polishing

Details of and variations within these themes are beyond the scope of this book. Suffice it to remark that each of these shaping processes and secondary treatments presents the opportunity to incorporate characteristic defects, and it may be essential when investigating the cause of a particular failure to have knowledge of the potential defects that may have been introduced during manufacture.

2.2.1 Defects by Omission

One of the simplest errors is the omission of a key stage of the manufacturing process, not so much in shaping the product where a mistake would be obvious as in treatments used to achieve specific microstructural conditions or surface properties. Using the "wrong" material is another error; most steels and aluminum alloys look the same regardless of their chemical composition, but fractional or small percentages of alloying elements are absolutely vital in determining the level of mechanical properties. Such faults are often difficult to spot because the physical appearance of the defective product may

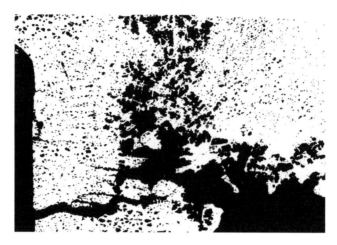

Figure 2.3   Casting shrinkage in a section cut from a wheel hub.

give no clue as to its mechanical strength or structural condition yet have disastrous consequences on performance in service. Perhaps the best example is the selection and heat treatment of steels to develop the desired combination of hardness, strength and toughness to meet the service requirements of a vast number of diverse engineering products, ranging from cutting tools, hammers and dies for working other materials, to all manner of structural fabrications and commodities used in the modern world. Few tests can be carried out on a finished product without damaging it or destroying parts beyond use, so if it meets the dimensional specification, is certified as having been made from the correct material and exhibits the appropriate surface finish, all that can be done in the way of quality control is nondestructive testing. However, such tests did not prevent a serious accident caused by the failure of a vital steel pin shortly after being put into service; the pin should have been heat treated to give a tough core and a hard, brittle outer skin, but instead it had received the wrong heat treatment, rendering it hard and brittle throughout. Consequently, the pin failed the first time it was subjected to a shock load that would easily have been withstood if the part had received the correct treatment.

The pouring of molten metal into molds is widely used for the manufacture of complex shapes, as well as being the first stage in the manufacture of wrought products. However, casting can lead to a variety of defects and some are extremely difficult if not impossible to eliminate entirely in a large product, shrinkage in particular. Figure 2.3 is the cross section of a wheel hub for a trailer made by casting liquid steel into a sand mold. The mold should have incorporated a reservoir of liquid of sufficient size and should have been so placed as to feed further liquid as the casting solidified in order to compensate for the liquid-to-solid volume contraction in the body of the casting. When everything is solid the casting is broken out of the mold and the feeder cut off along with other extraneous channels required to admit the flow of liquid metal into the mold. The dark areas apparent in Figure 2.3 are shrinkage voids in the center section of the casting, which should have been wholly sound metal. When this particular casting was made the feeding was inadequate, so shrinkage cavities formed in the last portion to solidify which, unfortunately, happened to be the most highly stressed area when the wheel was mounted on the axle of a trailer. The hub of the casting had been machined but this had not cut into the shrinkage zone where the cavities could have been detected but, instead, had cut away metal that had been perfectly sound. The inevitable result was that the finished wheel was so weakened by the defect that the first time the loaded trailer turned a corner the wheel collapsed, resulting in serious damage to a very costly piece of equipment that was carried on the trailer.

In machined products the major problems emanate from sharp re-entrant sections, such as keyways, grooves and slots. Time after time early fatigue failure of machined components can be attributed to crack initiation at such sites, due to their localized stress concentrating effect. Often the remedy need be nothing more than incorporating a radius that reduces stress concentration to a tolerable minimum so that the local stresses never reach a level high enough to initiate fatigue cracking. Another similar cause of early demise by fatigue is thread forms that have been poorly machined or subjected to bending rather than the purely axial forces that they are intended to withstand. Polymeric materials are especially prone to premature failure from stress raisers, tough plastics often becoming quite brittle when a sharp corner is designed into a product. Such design defects are obvious on visible features on an injection molded product, but become latent defects if on hidden, interior parts of the product. The solution is the same: incorporate a generous radius on the molding tool.

2.2.2 Welding Defects

Defects stemming from welds and repairs are numerous in both metals and plastics and all may result in premature failure. The major problems are:

1. The joint is a "casting" and may contain all the defects associated with the casting process, as well as possibly not having adequately fused with the materials joined.
2. The neighboring material goes through heating and cooling cycles that can reduce its strength or cause embrittlement. (This part is known as the heat-affected zone.)

3. Localized heating may soften the parent material or cause changes in composition, such as contamination by oxides.
4. If a protective gas or flux shield is required it has to be maintained throughout the process.
5. Shrinkage and thermal contraction effects must be accommodated.
6. Alloying ingredients, especially those controlling grain structure and properties, must be maintained within the fusion zone and not lost.
7. The assembly should cool at an acceptable rate after welding to prevent undesirable transformations in the heat-affected zones.

In nonfusion welding processes such as friction welding, explosive welding, stud welding, roll bonding and many other related techniques the main advantage is that defects arising from solidification of liquid are avoided. The plastic deformation associated with solid-state welds usually imparts greater strength and physical integrity to the weld zone, which is also of much smaller volume than a fusion weld. Even with techniques like spot welding, seam-welding and flash-butt welding, where the deformation is assisted by electrically generated thermal energy to produce some very local melting, the deformation part of the process consolidates the joint by minimizing the defect level. Hence, in routine and proven designs of such joining processes the occurrence of defects is low. When defects do occur they are usually attributable to lack of control of the process parameters.

A widely adopted technique to extend the life of expensive capital plant such as earth-moving equipment is renewing or building up worn parts without the expense of replacing the whole component. Done correctly this is a sensible practice, but done incorrectly it can be disastrous. Potential pitfalls include lack of penetration, undercutting of adjoining sections, porosity, slag entrapment, contraction cracks and hydrogen build up from moisture in the air or condensation on cold metal, which may cause delayed embrittlement. All of these pitfalls can lead to premature failure and it is not unusual to find such faults responsible for serious accidents.

Fusion welding is a microcosm of all the defects associated with castings but, in addition, there are problems with distortion and residual stresses caused by thermal contraction after the weld has solidified. Regions under high residual tensile stress are a common source of fatigue failures especially if there are minute surface imperfections or geometrical irregularities to serve as initiation sites. Small differences in composition or microstructure between the deposited weld metal and the parent material can also set up corrosion cells that may lead to wastage of section in critical regions or sometimes result in failure by stress corrosion.

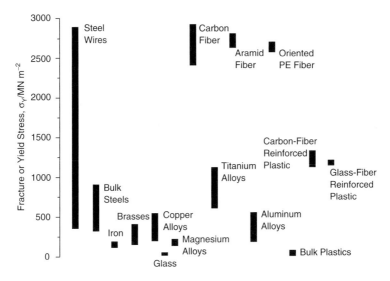

Figure 2.4 Strength range of various structural materials.

2.3 Failures under Mechanical Overload

The strength of a material is usually measured in some kind of laboratory test on a standard test piece. By far the most commonly quoted measurement is the *tensile strength* and such values are widely used to make comparisons of different materials, such as illustrated in Figure 2.4. However, the way the force is applied and the geometry of the test piece itself affect the result and there are other mechanical properties that are equally important as absolute tensile strength in determining the ability of a component to withstand externally applied loads, for example, toughness (which is a measure of the ability to absorb energy as a fracture develops) and ductility or malleability (the capacity to be deformed before fracture occurs). In many materials events begin to happen that would destroy the integrity of an engineered component long before the tensile breaking force is reached. Among the most difficult types of material to use successfully and safely in highly stressed situations are those that behave in a brittle manner despite having very high tensile strength.

Other strength data commonly quoted are determined by means of compression tests and shear tests where the units are the same as for tensile tests, i.e., force per unit area, but others are expressed in different units and must always be related to the geometry of the test piece and the way the test was conducted. Highly sophisticated tests that measure properties such as fracture toughness are of vital significance in material specifications and design parameters for structural products used in aerospace, pressure vessels, etc.

Different types of materials exhibit different behaviors depending on the way their constituent atoms and molecules are bonded and how these stack together to form crystal structures. The art of materials science is to control these arrangements by mechanical processing and heat treatment in order to make a product with the required properties for a particular application. The engineering dimension comes in when the product has to be designed to resist all the foreseeable loadings likely to be encountered under service conditions and to ensure that a given component will safely withstand the stresses and strains (and abuse) likely to be experienced during its entire service lifetime, regardless of whether these are static loadings or loadings of a cyclic nature likely to be applied many millions of times.

Again, it is not the purpose of this book to survey all the different types of mechanical test and property data that may be called for in a forensic investigation in order to establish whether a particular failure resulted from mechanical overload. However, it is useful to understand why different materials react in different ways under overstress conditions and how the nature and level of forces that had acted may be deduced and order of magnitude estimates made.

Figure 2.5 illustrates three characteristic forms of force-extension curves obtained from a tensile test in which a test piece containing a gauge length of uniform cross-sectional area is subjected to an increasing axial force until it fractures. The ends of the test piece are usually of larger cross-sectional area than the gauge length in order that the test piece does not break in the grips of the testing machine, although it is quite common to measure the strength of items like wires, fibers or textiles directly. During the test, extension is measured as the force is increased and, after converting the force to stress (= force divided by cross-sectional area of the gauge) and the extension to strain (= extension per unit length of the gauge), a stress strain curve is produced similar to those shown in Figure 2.5A, B and C.

The constituent atoms in metals are arranged in regular crystal structures but no individual atom has to be permanently bonded to any particular neighbor. Initially they act as if they are on springs so when an external tensile force is applied they are pulled further apart and if the force is relaxed they go back again. Thus the early part of the force-extension plot is linear and the extension is elastic and reversible when the force is reduced to zero, as denoted in Figure 2.5A and the early part of Figure 2.5B. The energy absorbed is represented by the area under the line up to the value of the force acting and is recovered when the force is removed. All engineering products have to be designed so that they will never be exposed to forces exceeding this limit of elasticity, since if they were ever exposed to greater forces they would

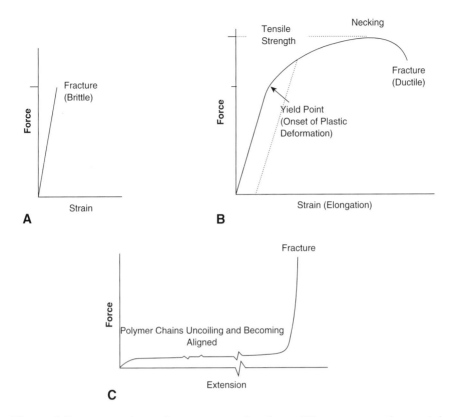

Figure 2.5 Forms of tensile test curves for three different types of material. (A) Brittle (e.g., ceramic). (B) Ductile (most metals). (C) Thermoplastic polymers.

become deformed permanently. The force at this limit of the elastic deformation is called the "yield stress" (or sometimes quoted as an offset yield or proof stress) because the plastic deformation beyond this limit cannot be reversed. Should this stress be exceeded in service the component will be permanently altered in shape and will no longer be suitable for its intended purpose. This is represented by the dotted line in Figure 2.5B, showing how the elastic contraction from the higher force intercepts the strain axis, showing that the test piece is now longer than when it started. If the force is then reapplied and the test continued the yield point is now higher than it was originally.

Great use of this is made in manufacturing since plastically deforming is the only means of increasing yield strength in metals that cannot be hardened by heat treatment (for example, sheet, strip, sections and tubes in brasses and many aluminum alloys). In forensic examination any evidence of plastic deformation on a failed product thereby confirms that the component must have been subjected to stresses above its yield point and, further-

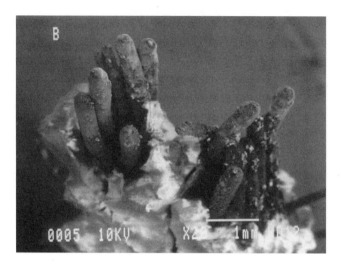

Figure 2.6 Cup-and-cone tensile fractures of high tensile steel wires in bead of burst tire (scanning electron micrograph).

more, that the direction of the external force that caused it must be consistent with the nature of the deformation.

If the tensile test is continued until the test piece fractures, the curve passes through a maximum, which is the value quoted as the tensile strength, but then drops down until the test piece breaks at a lower value of applied force. This is because the cross section of the test piece begins to neck down in one position and all deformation thereafter is confined to the region where the necking is taking place. If the applied force is divided by the actual area sustaining it, then the "true stress" continues to increase, albeit at a much lower rate than the earlier part of the deformation curve. The "extension" axis is also no longer an accurate figure for the amount of deformation, because this is now confined to the necking region, not over the whole gauge length of the test piece. When this, too, is corrected and substituted on the strain axis, the true stress-true strain curve continues to rise and the fracture appears in a very different position from the engineering stress strain curve.

Usually this difference between the tensile strength and fracture stress may be ignored but it does become significant when examining a component that has broken in tension across a screw thread or a locally narrowed section like a keyway or circlip groove. In estimating the applied force that caused this damage account must be taken of the actual cross-sectional area over which it acted, not the nominal cross sectional area.

Because of the way necking takes place in a tensile test the fracture of a circular cross section exhibits a waisted appearance over the neck terminating as a cup and cone fracture at the narrowest part, as illustrated in Figure 2.6.

Such fractures are commonly found in the high tensile bead wires from burst tires and in wire ropes that have been subjected to gross overload.

All common engineering metals are ductile, although some alloys (i.e., mixtures of metal atoms on an atomic scale) may become brittle under certain circumstances, for example, steel fully hardened to form the cutting edge of a tool. Ceramic materials (e.g., glass, sintered oxides, etc.) are intrinsically brittle because their constituent atoms are chemically bonded and unable to be displaced like metals. Nevertheless, they still behave initially as if the atoms are held together by springs, so their force-extension curve is a straight line, as in Figure 2.5B, terminating in sudden fracture. They do not display any significant plastic deformation prior to fracture; if the broken pieces are offered up to each other the specimen looks just as it did before the test. When the applied force reaches a critical level, microcracks suddenly run together, join up, and the product fractures. On account of this behavior brittle materials tend to be restricted to applications where the loads are predominantly compressive.

Elastic energy is stored as the applied force is increased and when fracture occurs this is suddenly released, causing the product to break up into several pieces as cracks propagate unrestricted from one free surface to another. By careful replacement of the broken pieces it is possible to identify the nature of the external force and the position where it acted. The ability of ceramic products to withstand high levels of applied tensile force may be substantially increased by building in compressive stress at the surfaces when the product is manufactured as, for example, in toughened glass. External force must first overcome this compressive force before it can place any tensile strain on the glass. However, when such products do fail the stored elastic energy is greater so the product breaks up explosively into myriad small pieces as this energy is released.

2.3.1 Polymeric Materials

Thermoset plastics materials are also brittle because their long polymer chains are linked by chemical bridges (*cross-links*) that anchor them together to retain their as-molded shape. By introducing high tensile strength fiber reinforcement (e.g., very fine glass, carbon or aramid fibers) numerous interfaces are formed within the brittle polymer matrix that prevent the microcracks running all through the material when the critical tensile stress is reached. The microcracks do in fact begin to run through the plastic matrix but they soon meet a fiber that blunts the tip and stops them from going any further by reorienting the crack parallel with the tension axis at the interface. This effect is readily recognizable when a semitransparent fiber-reinforced product has been subjected to gross overstress by the milky white translucent area that develops around the point where the damaging force was applied due to the scattering of light by the myriad interfaces.

In amorphous (noncrystalline) elastomeric materials the long molecular chains are not cross linked by strong chemical cross-link bridges but are simply tangled together, held by very weak bonds. Such materials include natural rubber and the large range of synthetic elastomers such as NBR (used in fuel pipes) and fluoroelastomers such as Viton (which became more widely known after the Challenger space disaster). Their inherent flexibility and reversible elasticity make them key engineering materials because they can absorb vibration, and so reduce the debilitating effects of fatigue, for example. The same property makes them ideal seals against fluid movement in engines and motors.

Thermoplastic materials such as polyethylene or polypropylene are usually partly crystalline, which makes them much more rigid and thus suitable for use in engineered products. However, they are still much less stiff than the same geometry in a typical metal, so their design to withstand imposed loads must be changed quite drastically. They can also be transformed into very strong flexible products by straightening out the molecular chains. This shows up well in their tensile force-extension curves, as in Figure 2.5C.

When the force is first applied there is only slight resistance so the extension increases rapidly while the applied force is doing nothing more than straightening out the chain. Extensions of several hundred percent may occur without any sign of fracture, though the cross-sectional area of course becomes correspondingly smaller as the strain increases. Eventually, all the chains become straightened out so the tensile force is now acting along the line of the molecular chains. Because these are strong chemical bonds the force rises steeply as very little strain is possible. Eventually the test piece breaks where the chains have the least overlap. Narrow strips may be split away easily to give very strong fibers (e.g., polypropylene), which can subsequently be woven into products like string, binding tape and rope, which have high tensile strength and are flexible. Even stronger materials such as carbon fiber can be made by simultaneously heating and stretching, while other high performance polymers can be made by control of chain orientation during manufacture (e.g., UHMPE fibers such as Spectra and Dyneema) or synthesis (e.g., aramid fibers like Nomex, Twaron and Kevlar).

One disadvantage of some common thermoplastic materials for load-bearing applications is that they soften and deform slowly under quite modest loads at high temperatures. There are two thermal measures that are important: T_g (the glass transition temperature) and T_m (the melting temperature) if the polymer is partly crystalline. T_m is always above T_g and many engineering thermoplastics have a T_m above 200°C. The ultimate use temperature lies somewhat below T_m due to material softening as T_m is approached. A good example is nylon 6,6 with a T_m of about 266°C, which makes the material ideal for under-the-hood applications, especially when reinforced with short glass fibers, with exposure temperatures of about 150°C. The same basic polymer also makes tough textiles when spun into a fiber, such as that widely used in stockings and hose. By contrast, aramid materials such as Nomex are stable up to temperatures of about 500°C, so they can be used in fire-resistant garments for firefighters and race car drivers, for example. The same fibers are also extremely tough both as free fiber and in composites, and their much lower densities make them attractive materials for ballistic protection when compared with metals.

2.3.2 Fracture Surfaces

The paths of overstress fractures are distinctly different in ductile and brittle materials and enable the nature and line of action of the forces that caused them to be readily identified. If the material is brittle fracture follows a line at 90° to the maximum principal stress acting; if it is ductile it follows the line of maximum shear stress, which is at 45° to the principal tensile stress. These characteristic directions for cylindrical sections broken under conditions of uniaxial tension, shear and bending are represented in Figure 2.7.

Fractures in the bending mode are also included in Figure 2.7. Bending differs from uniaxial tension and compression inasmuch as the stress distribution across the section under load is not uniform. In bending, the stress in the outermost fiber starts at a maximum value in tension and then falls to zero at the neutral axis before rising to a maximum compressive value at the outermost fiber on the opposite side. If the material is ductile the outermost fibers stretch by deforming plastically and those on the inside of the bend deform under compression. It is only when the outermost fibers reach the limit of their plasticity that cracking starts and then continues to propagate across the section as bending continues. A small shear lip at 45° is usually formed as the two halves of the fracture finally break apart, though very ductile materials may fold completely flat before any cracking has occurred. By contrast, in a brittle material, as soon as a crack initiates in the tension surface it immediately runs across the section toward what had been compressed fibers but the remaining ones now have to carry the entire tensile force. As the fracture runs across to the opposite side from where it started at least one step, but sometimes two or three steps parallel with the axis appear.

Interpreting fractures is a highly skilled art and cannot be dealt with exhaustively in a book such as this one. However, one note of caution must be expressed with regard to steel components that have been surface hardened to very high strength levels to impart wear resistance, in which state the outer

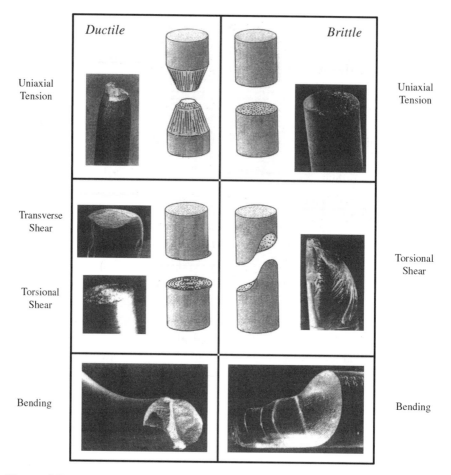

Figure 2.7   Characteristic fracture paths in ductile (left) and brittle (right) materials subjected to different overstress modes.

skin becomes brittle. While the bulk of such a component will be heat treated to achieve the desired high strength and toughness and satisfy all the design parameters, it may fail in a brittle manner, if subjected to bending impact or some condition where the tensile stresses at the surface are not uniform. A crack initiated in the brittle case or surface layer may run right across the section in a brittle manner. More often though, the case cracks and the underlying material deforms before it eventually fractures, as happened to the ball stem shown in Figure 2.8.

Steels are also anomalous inasmuch as under impact bending a section that is ductile when tested at room temperature may fracture in a brittle manner at subzero temperatures. This *ductile-brittle transition temperature* as it is called is sensitive to a number of metallurgical factors, including carbon and impurity levels, grain structure, the presence of any nonmetallic

Figure 2.8 Cracks in the brittle surface hardened layer on the stem of the steering ball joint damaged in the accident.

inclusions and, in particular, any notches or stress concentrations. A small number of World War II Liberty ships suffered brittle fractures in arctic waters that caused them to break in two in rough seas, the fractures starting at the corners of welded hatches on the deck and suddenly running down the sides. The principal cause was the manner in which four deck plates had been welded around the hatch openings coupled with the susceptibility of the weld metal to brittle fracture. Whereas the old methods of riveting the plates would have stopped the crack when it reached the edge of the plate, the all welded construction allowed the cracks to run right around the ship like a girdle. Recognizing brittle fractures in failed components is easy, but establishing the cause is much more challenging on account of the number of possible contributing factors.

2.4   Fatigue Failure

Fatigue is a phenomenon that results in the sudden fracture of a component after a period of cyclic loading in the elastic regime. Failure is the end result of a process involving the initiation and growth of a crack, almost invariably at the site of a stress concentration on the surface, though occasionally at a slightly subsurface defect such as a sharp unfavorably oriented inclusion. This initial crack grows progressively at 90° to the direction of principal tensile stress during the action of further load cycles which, for steels, exceed

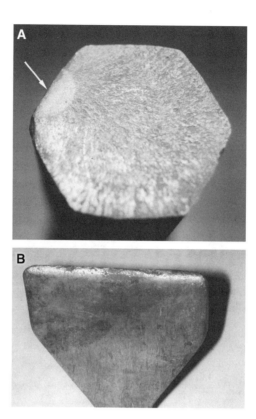

Figure 2.9 Single bending fatigue fracture in a pneumatic tool. (A) Fracture surface on the shank. (B) Blunted cutting edge that set up abnormally high cyclic bending stresses in the shank.

approximately 40% of their tensile strength but for most materials there is no safe limit below which it ceases to propagate. Eventually the effective cross-sectional area becomes so reduced that the component ruptures under one final cycle of a load near the top of its normal service spectrum, but one at a level that had been satisfactorily withstood on many previous occasions before the crack propagated. The final fracture occurs suddenly in a ductile or a brittle mode, depending on the characteristics of the material.

Fatigue fractures exhibit a characteristic appearance, which reflects the initiation site and the progressive development of the crack front, culminating in an area of final overload fracture. Figure 2.9A shows a typical single initiation fatigue fracture, in this instance a percussion tool used for road breaking. This particular tool was a tarmac cutter having a wide, chisel-shaped blade that had been allowed to become blunt (Figure 2.9B). As quite usual for such a tool, the shank was subjected to a levering action that applied bending cycles just above where the blade flared out, predominantly in the

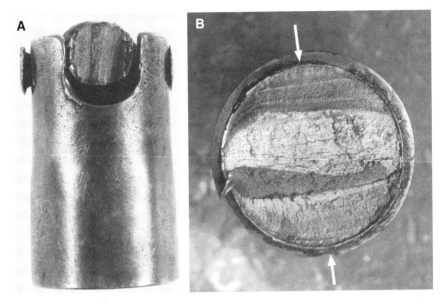

Figure 2.10 (A) Double bending fatigue failure of a scaffold spanner handle. (B) Double bending fatigue failure of a rotating shaft.

same direction. A tiny indentation near the shoulder had served as the initiation site for the fatigue crack. The tool had been hardened and tempered to give a high hardness but in this condition the steel had fairly low ductility and fracture toughness. Consequently, the crack did not have to penetrate very far into the section before it suddenly ran to completion during one particularly severe bending cycle.

A characteristic of all fatigue fractures is that the initiation site is almost invariably at the surface where there exists some change in the section (like a slot for a keyway or circlip, or the root of a screw thread) that acts as a localized stress concentrator, although very exceptionally it may start just below the surface at the site of some internal flaw or inclusion. Usually the initiation site is easily recognized with the naked eye or with the aid of an eyeglass. From this site the crack front spreads into the underlying section, forming a series of concentric wave fronts resembling the ripples on a still pool disturbed by a pebble. These are actually positions where the developing crack arrested while it awaited another load cycle sufficiently high to drive it further. In fact, the surface marks are commonly referred to as "beach" markings because they resemble the striation patterns left in the sand when an incoming wave pauses before retreating. With an incoming tide the next beach mark is a little further up the beach, although broadly of the same shape.

Figure 2.10 shows a double bending fatigue fracture that initiated at two sites diametrically opposite at the root of a slot. This was a reversible box

Figure 2.11   Multisite initiation fatigue fractures. (A) Crop sprayer bearing arm that failed in reverse bending. (B) Rotavating machine drive shaft that failed under cyclic torsional forces.

spanner used for tightening and releasing clamp bolts on scaffolding, where the box end could be fitted over the nut and the hand bar swung side to side through 180° when tightening or releasing, to avoid lifting the box off the bolt head and repositioning it for the next half turn. Fatigue cracking initiated on opposite sides of the groove cut-away in the handle. Cracking had reached the stage where only the narrow band of metal at right angles to the pivot was still holding the handle to the box section. This suddenly broke in a ductile overload manner as a workman was striving to loosen a tight nut while dismantling the scaffold, causing him to fall to his death. (This accident happened in the days before the present safety at work legislation was introduced.)

A fatigue fracture may exhibit several initiation sites, all of which begin to grow into the cross section under the externally applied loadings until eventually there is insufficient cross section remaining to withstand one final cycle. Thus a rotating shaft failed suddenly by propagation of the top crack in Figure 2.10B, which was initiated at a small defect near the arrow. There are two initiation sites, however, showing that the shaft was subject to bending along the axis defined by the arrows. Figure 2.11A is an example of a multi-initiation site fatigue failure of the pivot bearing arm for a crop sprayer. This predominantly follows the path of a double bending stress system, but the

Figure 2.12   Fatigue crack surface in an NBR lip seal of an automotive brake hydraulic system.

sprayer was tilted at different angles, all subjected to up and down forces as the tractor bounced over uneven ground. Hence one crack might initiate at one side but before it had grown very far another initiated further along on the same side, followed by another at a different place, and the same thing was happening on the opposite face. The net result is a fracture such as illustrated here, with several distinct initiation sites, all eventually linking up before running together in the final ductile overload fracture along the centerline of the cross section. In the drive shaft (Figure 2.11B), separate fractures initiated at the roots of individual splines and began to propagate in helical paths, but then linked up as they entered the main shaft. The final failure was ductile overstress of the last remaining area at the central axis.

Fatigue is a "disease" that affects all materials, but without a doubt the majority of such failures, certainly those that are publicized, are metals, often steels, simply because these are the most widely used structural materials. Recent rail disasters in the U.K. (Hatfield) and Germany (Eschede) were caused directly by fatigue of steel rail and a wheel, respectively. The single worst aircraft disaster ever (JA8119 on a Boeing 747) in Japan in 1985 was caused by fatigue of a rear pressure bulkhead from a faulty repair. One of the worst crashes in the U.S. was the Chicago crash of 1979, when an engine fell off a plane in flight due to a fatigue crack in the support pylon. Composite materials have a much better record in safety-critical components, and have displaced many metal parts such as helicopter rotor blades and propellors. Elastomer seals can fail by fatigue just as any other material, such as the lip seal from an automotive hydraulic brake system shown in Figure 2.12. The sudden failure of the brakes caused a road accident, which is one very good

Figure 2.13   Classical fatigue failure of an automobile engine crankshaft, initiating at the shoulder of the journal and propagating through the web.

reason why small leaks on brake systems should always be investigated and the safety-critical parts replaced.

If single incident mechanical overstress failures are discounted then something on the order of 75% of all service failures of engineered products are attributable to fatigue, a figure certainly borne out by engineers involved in accident investigation. The insidious nature of fatigue is that the crack does not appear in the initial stages although damage is occurring on an atomic scale at the site where it does eventually appear. Only cycles of stress above a particular threshold value will actually cause this damage and propagate the crack. But all these stress cycles are in the elastic regime, so there is no external sign of the distress in the form of deformation. Plastic deformation only appears during the final fracture and even then only if the material is ductile. In high strength/low ductility materials such as the heat-treated steel in Figure 2.9 there is often no external sign of deformation, although examination of the last area to fracture may well exhibit a ductile mode; just as often, it may be brittle. After the fatigue crack has initiated and while it is still propagating into the cross section, it may be detected using one or more of several different nondestructive inspection techniques, like dye penetrant, magnetic particle inspection and ultrasonics (which are described in Chapter 4), but the difficulty is that many initiate in positions where they are inaccessible to routine inspection, for example, the crankshaft deep inside an internal combustion engine as illustrated in Figure 2.13. This particular failure initiated where the original radius of the bearing journal had been partially removed when the crankshaft was reground, leaving a step that served as the local stress raiser.

Extensive use of fatigue data is made when load bearing components are designed, particularly if they are subject to cyclic loadings. The reader is advised to refer to the many specialist books on this subject, as a detailed discussion is beyond the scope of this text. After all, the forensic engineer's

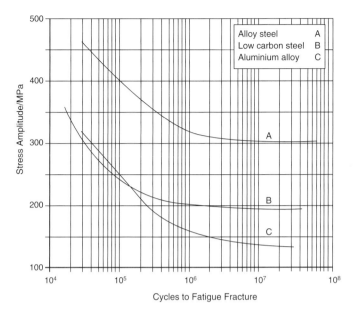

Figure 2.14   S-N for two steels and heat-treated aluminum alloy. Notice the leveling off at 40% of tensile strength for the steels.

task is usually to identify the mode and cause of a particular failure and this, more often than not, is because a product has been exposed to unusual conditions or was abused in some way that the designer never intended or foresaw. However, it is useful to refer to the form of S-N curve, as depicted in Figure 2.14. These diagrams summarize data from a series of tests in which standard specimens are subjected to cyclic loads of a particular stress amplitude, S, until fracture occurs. The number of cycles to failure, N, is represented on a logarithmic scale. Tests are carried out over a range of stress levels, all below the elastic limit of the material. S-N curves supply useful data for design, provided that the frequency and maximum amplitude of cyclic stresses likely to be encountered in service can be estimated. There are various ways of taking into account the variations in stress amplitude and frequency likely to be experienced by a specific component in a particular application.

For steels the S-N curves level off at approximately 40% of their tensile strength, and this is defined as the "fatigue limit." In principle steels should survive indefinitely if a component is used in situations where the maximum level of cyclic stress is unlikely to exceed this fatigue limit, but there are complications in relying on this, not the least of which is because the level of stress at all positions within a shaped component under different applied loads is difficult to predict, even using finite element analysis methods. However, for nonferrous metals and most other solids used in engineering there

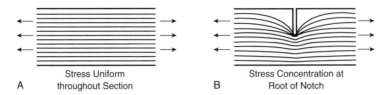

A   Stress Uniform throughout Section   B   Stress Concentration at Root of Notch

Figure 2.15 Schematic representation of localized stress concentration arising from notches and surface defects. Ductile materials deform and reduce stress intensity by increasing the radius at the root. Brittle materials fracture as soon as the critical stress intensity level is reached.

is no well-defined limit, the S-N curve would continue to fall, although at a diminishing rate at the lower stresses. Accordingly, for design purposes the stress level at which specimens survive for 10^8 cycles is used, and this is called the "endurance limit."

No amount of care in designing against fatigue can ever ensure that fatigue failures will never be experienced. In recognition of this many critical parts are replaced well before their fatigue lives are due to expire, by applying what is called "preventive maintenance." A safe life is set for a component based on the worst situation where cyclic loadings may be approaching, say, 50% of the fatigue life. When this life is reached the part is taken out of service and replaced with a new one. While this is successful in safety-critical situations many engineering parts still continue to fail by fatigue and will continue to do so — and cause accidents because it is practically impossible to guard completely against minor faults in design, manufacture, maintenance or repair, let alone surface damage and wear that may occur in service. The problem is localized stress concentrators somewhere on or slightly below a free surface.

Figure 2.15A is a schematic diagram depicting a uniform stress distribution across a section carrying a tensile load. The lines represent the stress intensity, which is completely uniform across the whole section. However, consider what happens to this stress distribution if a notch is cut into the side. The load is the same but the stress must rise as it is being carried by a smaller cross-sectional area. It becomes highly concentrated at the root of the notch, as depicted by the stress distribution lines in Figure 2.15B. This stress at the root of the notch is determined by its depth, L, and radius at the tip, r, according to the relationship:

$$S = 1 + 2\sqrt{L/r}$$

A circular hole (L = r) would thus concentrate the stress by a factor of 3. The stress concentration factor is often known as Kt. If the stresses were cyclic

Figure 2.16 Fatigue initiating at the corners of a keyway slot in an 80-mm-diameter drive shaft and following the root of the screw thread.

and the nominal level was below the fatigue limit, then clearly the introduction of a stress raiser could raise them locally to well over the limit and a fatigue failure is to be expected sooner or later. Figure 2.16 is a typical example of a fatigue fracture initiating at the corner of a keyway in a circular shaft and subsequently following the stress concentration around the root of a screw thread. The minimal area of cross section at the moment of the final break is a clear indication that in the absence of the keyway the uniform stress level would have been well below the fatigue limit of the metal. The local stress concentrating effect could have been reduced considerably if the bottom of the keyway had been radiused instead of being machined to a sharp 90° corner.

The above example should make it abundantly clear that in conducting an examination to ascertain the cause of a failure it is vitally important to identify the initiation site(s) of a fatigue fracture and hence ascertain the nature, magnitude and direction of the forces that caused it. From there onward it is a fairly straightforward matter to establish what or who was responsible.

The fatigue path follows a route that is at 90° to the maximum principal tensile stress within the component, whereas ductile failures are at 45° to this, following the direction of maximum shearing stress. For example, a torsional fatigue fracture of a shaft follows a helical path (Figure 2.17B). In this instance the torsional forces were caused by the shaft being driven in both directions so fatigue initiated in two places and both cracks grew independently toward each other following the characteristic helical paths until they met.

Figure 2.17 (A) Overstress torsional failure of a 30-mm steel shaft. (B) Reverse bending torsional fatigue failure of a 20-mm-diameter steel drive shaft.

2.5 Corrosion

Metals and alloys corrode because the electrons associated with each atom are not tied up in chemical bonding to other atoms but, instead, exist like a cloud or gas surrounding the regular array of atoms in the crystal. If placed in a chemical solution, the outermost metal atoms can lose electrons and become positively charged ions, in which form they are able to enter solutions. In this state they are able to take part in chemical reactions as positively charged ions (written Fe^{2+} or Fe^{3+} for iron, depending on whether two or three electrons have been given up) and the freed electrons are able to form an electric circuit. This process is called "corrosion," and results in a wasting away of the surface of the metal and the formation of a chemical "corrosion product." The consequential loss of cross-sectional area thus reduces the capacity of the component to support load. The propensity to corrode depends on the potential of the atoms at the surface to enter solution is called the "electrode potential" of the particular metal. The rate of corrosion is determined by the current that flows through whatever electrical circuit is established. Table 2.1 lists the electrode potentials of the common metals.

Table 2.1 Standard Electrode Potentials of Common Metals in Conducting Solutions of Their Ions in Relation to a Hydrogen Electrode

Metal	Electrode Potential (V)
Gold	1.42
Silver	0.80
Mercury	0.79
Copper	0.34
Lead	−0.13
Tin	−0.14
Nickel	−0.25
Cobalt	−0.27
Cadmium	−0.40
Iron	−0.44
Chromium	−0.70
Zinc	−0.76
Titanium	−1.63
Aluminum	−1.66
Magnesium	−2.37

If any two of these metals are in contact in a solution that can accept ions (a solution that need be nothing more than slightly acidic moisture), they may set up an electrical circuit in which the driving voltage is the difference between their respective electrode potentials. The metal having the more negative potential will give up electrons and corrode, while the less negative or positive metal does not. The corroding metal becomes the anode and the receiving metal becomes the cathode in the corrosion cell. Thus if aluminum is connected to iron in a corrosive medium their potential difference is ($-0.44 - (-1.66) = 1.22$ V) and the aluminum, being the more electronegative, becomes the anode and corrodes at a rate proportional to the electrical resistance of the circuit. If copper were in contact with the iron then their potential difference would be $0.34 - (-0.44) = 0.78$ V and the iron, being the more electronegative, would be anodic to the copper and would corrode.

This explanation is oversimplified in order to illustrate the general principles. A number of scientific factors have not been taken into account and in practice real corrosion cells are more complex. For example, the relative areas of the two metals forming the anode and the cathode are important. A small aluminum rivet in a large sheet of steel (iron) would corrode very rapidly because it constitutes a small anode in a large cathode, whereas the rate of the corrosion of aluminum sheet if the rivet were steel would be less because the anode current would be spread over a much greater area. The insulating effect of films and corrosion product set up in a corrosion cell also exerts a pronounced effect on the rate of attack.

The cause of failure resulting from such general wastage type of corrosion is usually obvious, for example, where a steel member of a vehicle has rusted through or an aluminum alloy structural member flaked away over a period of several years due to exposure to road salt in winter weather. Occasionally, however, the corrosion may not be visible from the outside and could remain undetected up to the moment when sudden catastrophic failure takes place in an area inaccessible to painting or protection such as between two closely fitting plates or inside a boxed structure (Figure 2.18).

Two distinct types of corrosion are recognized, namely, wet corrosion and dry corrosion. Both result in the wasting away of a component, reducing the thickness of section and thereby the load carrying capacity of the affected structure until failure takes place by mechanical overstress or fatigue. Dry corrosion is essentially high temperature oxidation and is controlled by the rate at which oxygen can diffuse through the existing oxide skin and react with the metal beneath to form additional oxide. This may be an adhering tenacious film that largely prevents further oxygen from reaching the metal or it may be porous and nonadherent, allowing a continuing reaction progressively eating away the cross section. Dry corrosion is seldom a problem

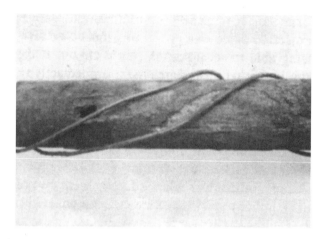

Figure 2.18 Galvanic corrosion and perforation of steel pipe caused by contact with copper heating spiral inside wet lagging.

for structures and components operating in normal environmental conditions, although it clearly has serious consequences for parts operating at elevated temperatures.

It is not generally realized that stainless steels rely on a thin surface film of chromium oxide which forms virtually instantaneously in an oxidizing atmosphere. If the film is broken by scratching or abrasion it reforms and effectively becomes self healing. However, under chemically reducing conditions stainless steel is no better than plain unalloyed varieties. A family went away on vacation and inadvertently left a pork chop on the draining board of their new stainless steel sink unit. When they returned 6 weeks later and scraped off the offending mess they discovered the shape of the chop outlined in pinholes through a disintegrating draining board. Several other metals, for example, aluminum and titanium, derive their corrosion resistance from a tightly adherent surface oxide film that is very stable despite the underlying metal itself being chemically reactive, particularly in the case of titanium. In contrast, if the surface oxide film is porous or cracks up because it has a larger specific volume than the metal from which it formed, like hydrated iron oxide ("rust"), then it will have practically no protective effect whatsoever.

2.5.1 Stress Corrosion Cracking of Metals

For certain metallic alloys the effects of brittle fracture, stress and corrosion combine to produce the troublesome phenomenon of stress corrosion cracking. This requires all of the following acting together:

1. A susceptible composition and microstructure.

Figure 2.19   Stress corrosion cracking in a deep drawn brass cup (left) beside a cup from same material (right) but stress-relief annealed before exposure to the same environment.

2. External or residual internal tensile stress from a manufacturing operation. Residual stresses exist as "balanced" regions of tension and compression and cancel each other out across the body of the component, but the susceptible state is when the tensile component exists at an outside surface.

3. A mildly aggressive chemical environment that on its own would cause no significant corrosive attack.

If these are all present then crack-like defects that start as corrosion crevices can grow rapidly and proliferate throughout the microstructure. In brasses the phenomenon is known as "season cracking" because it was first observed when cartridge cases showed spontaneous cracking in the monsoon season as the British Empire spread across India. Deformed grains of single-phase brass provided the susceptible microstructure, residual stress from crimping the deep drawn cartridge cases gave the residual stress pattern and, because they were usually stored near stables, traces of ammonia from horse urine in the humid atmosphere provided the mildly aggressive chemical agent. Figure 2.19 shows stress corrosion cracking in a deep drawn brass cup exposed to ammonium (NH_4^-) ions, such as often present in proprietary metal polishes. As the cracks appeared the residual hoop stress was relaxed, so the strips of broken metal bent outward under the stimulus of the residual component of longitudinal stress. The cup placed beside this was made in exactly the same way and from the same sheet of metal, but before exposing to the corrosive atmosphere was given a stress relief anneal. This did not soften the metal or alter its grain structure in any way, but it did eliminate the residual stresses; hence, no cracks. Figure 2.20 shows a silver-plated goblet, one of an expensive set purchased overseas, which failed for the same reason.

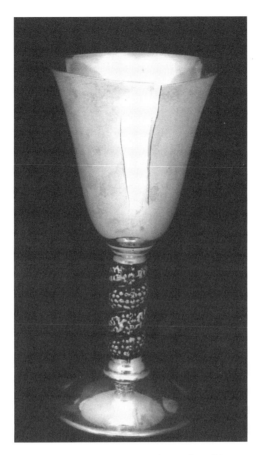

Figure 2.20 Stress corrosion cracking in silver-plated brass goblet.

Most of the higher strength engineering metals may suffer stress corrosion failure if the conditions are right. Stainless steels and aluminum alloys are susceptible in chloride (Cl^-) environments. One obvious remedy for all is to eliminate or significantly reduce the level of residual stress resulting from forming or welding processes. Hydrogen is also a troublesome element in this respect as it is believed it may form molecular hydrogen within the crack region and extend the crack by causing an internal gas pressure, or the formation of solid hydrides within the microstructure that can also subject the crack to additional mechanical stress. These stresses may extend the cracks themselves or enhance the corrosion mechanism as before. Examples of both these types of failure are discussed in later chapters.

2.5.2 Environmental Cracking of Plastics

Metals are not the only materials susceptible to the corrosive effects of their environment and stress corrosion cracking. Many plastics are also affected in a similar manner, for example, acetal plastic moldings used widely in plumbing fittings. In this instance it is the chlorine in the water that is usually responsible. The stress corrosion cracking tends to be limited essentially to crack tips, but can be just as devastating in its effects on the structural integrity of products. Failures have been widespread in the U.S. with acetal fittings in domestic hot water systems. Chlorine in the water supply is an extremely aggressive and reactive oxidizing chemical, but even its more benign form as the chloride ion can create severe problems in all types of products. Other reactive chemicals can also degrade polymers, some of the best known being oxygen and ozone cracking of elastomers. Both failure modes can be seen on old automobile tires, oxygen attack taking the form of "crazy-paving" cracking, where the cracks form a random pattern of cracks in the tread and sidewall. By contrast, ozone cracks are oriented at 90° to the principal stress, and are usually much more severe.

While chlorine attack on many plastics involves chemical attack and degradation of the chains, another type of attack, known as environmental stress cracking (ESC), involves only physical interaction. Many polymers are susceptible to certain organic fluids to which they become exposed while in service. Cracks develop only when the product is strained, but may occur in unloaded samples due to the presence of "frozen-in" strain from the manufacturing process. Injection molded products are more susceptible because of the high levels of such strain usually present.

2.6   Creep

Creep is a time-dependent phenomenon in which a component gradually deforms under a steady tensile load that is well below the elastic limit of the material. It is due to the atoms or molecules within the microstructure continually adjusting to accommodate the externally applied forces. In this process damage to the crystal structure may occur, internal voids appear and cracks may spread which eventually culminates in a creep rupture failure. This may not take place until the component has been in service for several hundreds or thousands of hours. In metals and alloys the temperature at which creep becomes significant is approximately 30% of their melting temperature in Kelvin and strain occurs at an increasingly faster rate up to 60%, at which temperature the metal softens and begins to recrystallize. Above 60% of the Kelvin melting temperature the component will rupture in a very short time due to mechanical overstress as a result of the material continually softening.

Because the engineering metals generally have high melting temperatures, creep failures are only experienced in components operating at high temperatures. Nickel alloy blades that are used beyond the combustion zone in aircraft engines consistently operate under high centripetal stresses at temperatures above 1000°C, whereas aluminum or magnesium alloys are restricted to the cooler blades at the front. In contrast lead, hardly a structural material, melts at only 327°C and creeps under its own weight in hot sunshine, as may be observed by the appearance of splits and tears in roof coverings and gutters.

However, some thermoplastic materials do creep appreciably and failures are to be expected when containers made of such materials (e.g., polyethylene buckets) are used for transporting or storage of warm liquids. Most people who have carried loaded plastic bags from a supermarket on a hot day have experienced failure of the handles before they reached their cars. Examination of the bags will reveal that they stretched appreciably and narrowed down before breaking, which explains why they had begun to cut into the fingers. The creep is due to the time-dependent unfolding of polymer chains under constant stress, but the problem can also affect large permanent structures like storage tanks if the design has not allowed for the maximum load to which the structure will be subjected (the load imposed on the walls by a full tank). Provided the walls are correctly designed with maximum thickness to lower the stress (usually by simply increasing the wall thickness), then such tanks have a long and useful life ahead of them.

Establishing the Load Transfer Path

3

3.1   Loads, Forces and Design

The design of any functional article or component is not simply a matter of what it looks like, what materials it is to be made from and how it integrates with other components in the assembly, but must also take into account that it must be strong enough to resist safely all foreseeable loading conditions likely to be encountered in service. However, nothing is unbreakable. Hence if a broken or damaged component is produced that might have been responsible for, say, a road traffic accident or one resulting in serious personal injury, it is vitally important to establish whether its failure could have been the *cause* of the accident or was a *consequence* of the accident.

To resolve this requires consideration of the nature, magnitude and direction of forces that caused the damage in relation to those that the component was intended to withstand. If the design or fitness for purpose of a mass produced component were at fault, then there would be a spate of practically identical failures as soon as it was put into service which would quickly lead to identification of the problem followed by remedy of the design, material or manufacturing process and, most probably, a recall of all the product. Where an isolated failure is encountered an abnormal event or condition must be sought, such as a gross mechanical overload greater than the component was intended to withstand or had experienced up to the failure incident, or some material or manufacturing fault that led to progressive weakening over a period of time, such as fatigue, wear or corrosion. These processes gradually erode the component's capacity to carry the normal service loads and, if the weakening continues undetected, ultimately lead to a sudden, often catastrophic failure.

The forensic engineer may thus be presented with a broken component and the circumstances (and photographs of scene and wreckage) of an accident for which it may have been responsible. The first step in the investigation is to ascertain from the state of the damaged parts the direction and order of magnitude of the force(s) involved, so that these can be traced from the critical (broken) component through all the linkages to the source of the external loading. An external force applied to a system of linked components can only set up stresses in individual members if they remain linked so that each is able to react to the force acting on its neighbor. If one member is stressed to a level where it suddenly fractures (regardless of whether this is due to overstress or pre-existing weakness at that point) this interrupts the load transfer so that members beyond the break are no longer required to react to the external force. By estimating the stress levels in the various members of the linkages and comparing these with the fracture of the critical component it is then a straightforward matter to establish whether or not the critical component was causative of or a consequence of the accident.

The principle is that if there is evidence of mechanical distress or damage on *both* sides of a fracture then abnormally high forces had been transferred before the component broke and the component broke simply because it was the weakest part in that particular load transfer path. If, however, there is no sign of prior mechanical distress on either side of a break, then the fracture must have occurred before adjacent links in the system had reached stress levels capable of causing deformation, i.e., none was grossly overstressed. Evidence should therefore be sought as to whether an inherent material or manufacturing fault had existed or some progressive deterioration could have been responsible for a spontaneous fracture under a foreseeable loading condition. If such a fault is identified in a linkage which played a vital role, for example, in the steering or braking system of a vehicle, then there is a high probability that it could have been the cause of loss of control and causative of an accident.

3.2 Abnormal Externally Applied Force — Stepladder

The direction and order of magnitude of a damaging force is sometimes all that is necessary to establish the cause of an accident. For example, people suffering serious injuries while using lightweight stepstool ladders frequently seek to establish that manufacturing fault was responsible. It is human nature to blame someone else for one's misfortune. Steps and ladders are required to carry labels stating their maximum working load and pictorial "Do's and Don'ts" for safe use. In their statements of circumstances of the accident claimants usually assert they had erected the steps properly on a firm, level floor. Yet the very nature of the damage may be such that it could not possibly

Figure 3.1 Stepstool ladder placed in the doorway where an accident occurred.

have been caused by the forces generated if these safety instructions were being properly observed.

Figure 3.1 shows a stepstool ladder alleged to have failed within an hour or so of purchase while being used to paint the gutters of a house. The user was a tall, heavy man but within the weight specified on the labeling of the steps for "light domestic use." The foot of the left stile is bent inward and the steps can no longer be placed on the floor without the front frame tilting so far that anyone attempting to climb them would topple sideways. The stile is a rectangular box section aluminum alloy that has buckled inward opposite the bottom tread, and the rivet holes at that side are torn, as shown in Figure 3.2. The plaintiff alleges the steps were of defective construction and/or that the box section was not strong enough or that there was a fault in the metal.

As in all designs of step stool ladders the front and back legs splay outward so that, whether viewed from the front, back or the sides, when they are opened out and placed on a firm, level floor the four feet are farther apart than any of the steps or side braces. Thus any load acting downward from someone mounting or standing on the upper treads generates compressive forces in the stiles that are reacted to by the floor and hence set up force components acting to spread the feet *outward*. How then could the bottom

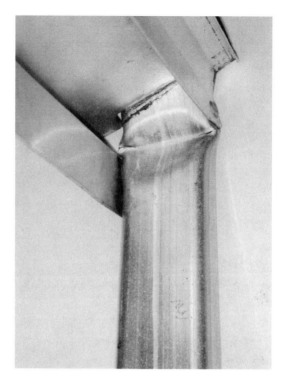

Figure 3.2 Closer view from the underside of the collapsed stile showing buckle.

of the left stile have been bent *inward*? Yet the deformation opposite the bottom tread is on one side only and has been caused by an inward acting horizontal force acting with the tread serving as a fulcrum. Loosening of the rivets and slight tearing of the rivet holes were consistent with this action and no sign of any similar distress could be found anywhere else in the structure. Moreover, the rivets had left witness marks showing that they had been properly set when the front frame was assembled. There is no evidence of faulty construction or material weakness and, even if there were, the force that caused this failure was directed from the outside of the left foot and was reacted to by the bottom tread but not producing any damage whatsoever to the tread itself or the right-hand stile.

The most likely way a force system of sufficient magnitude could have been set up is if the steps had been lying sideways with the right stile flat on a firm surface while a downward force was directed against the bottom of the left, as depicted in Figure 3.3. This would bend the left foot downward about the fulcrum of the bottom tread and in doing so would stretch the rivets and produce the buckle. How could such a situation arise? Simply — by the user overreaching sideways while near the top of the steps, causing them to topple sideways onto their right side. On the way down some part

Figure 3.3 Position of the steps when the leg was bent, after they had become unstable.

of their anatomy struck the projecting foot of the left stile as the right stile lay nearly flat on the ground. The full weight of their falling body was applied to the foot of the left stile, producing exactly the form of damage shown in Figure 3.1.

Sometimes the falling body may land on the back frame and bend the leg in a similar manner and the back cross brace may be buckled. In one particular accident where the user's body landed directly above the cross brace the back leg was pushed down over the brace and penetrated the user's buttock, causing severe injury. He was a large man weighing some 130 kg (280 lb), and stated he had stood tiptoe on the very top of a set of steps to remove a suitcase from his attic and, as he pulled it out, the steps "suddenly collapsed."

Such damage as described following an accident is invariably the result of some kind of instability while the person injured was climbing or working from the steps near the top. Sometimes the instability is caused by overreaching, possibly to lift something heavy off a shelf, and other times by the steps not being opened fully and locked in position to prevent them folding forward, or if the feet were not set on a firm, level surface. With tall ladders it is essential to have a second person standing on the bottom rung ("footing" the ladder) so that no rocking movement is possible while the user is working near the top. In fact, the stiles of ladders are usually so strong that the maximum recommended static weight of a user acting at any angle will not bend a stile. Dynamic forces are necessary that are generated only when the user's body is falling and these forces must be reacted to by something external to the structure.

3.3   Establishing the Load Transfer Path

When faced with a damaged or broken component from, say, a road traffic accident, it is always useful to consider the load transfer path and estimate the order of magnitude of forces that would have had to be transferred through the various linkages up to the particular component. This is often essential to establish whether spontaneous failure of the component could have been responsible for loss of control or whether it was broken by collision forces in an accident attributable to some other cause. The force required to break or deform it in the manner observed must have been transmitted through all the linked components in the system and should therefore be consistent with the deformation and damage, or absence of such, displayed by each of them. If the failed component had contained some major weakness and had broken spontaneously prior to the external (collision) forces being applied, none of the intervening components linked to the point where the external force was applied would display any significant mechanical distress, because there was nothing to react to them. The fractured component would not have been unable to react to the external force as it should have done and so the load transfer path terminated.

Here is an example of the application of the method to establish the cause of a motorcycle accident. Lawyers were completely misled by an expert who failed to consider the load transfer path when examining parts from the steering of a high performance motor cycle. The expert concentrated on the part that had broken and carried out an exhaustive laboratory study of its metallurgical condition and mode of fracture in seeking to establish that here was a pre-existing manufacturing fault.

A young man was seriously injured in an accident only 3 days after he had purchased a powerful motorcycle. No other vehicle was involved. The rider was riding along a country road with a rather poor surface and recalled that as he was entering a slight right-hand curve he suddenly felt the steering "go loose" and noticed sparks from the road beneath his front wheel. The steering was pulling him uncontrollably toward the left and he crashed into a tree. The police accident report stated the road was dry but the tarmac surface was ridged and slightly pot-holed and there was a scattering of loose gravel along both sides. There was no sign of abrasion or tire skid marks on the approach to the curve, but there was a deep gouge across the grass verge leading directly to where the machine had run into a tree. Pieces of the front wheel were scattered around the tree and a few smaller ones were found on the road. A vehicle inspector found the forks were twisted and the steering

Figure 3.4   Fracture at the top of the steering tube of a motorcycle. Sections have been cut away for metallurgical examination.

tube had sheared off near the top, just below the upper taper roller bearing. He commented that if this tube had failed as the vehicle was entering the bend the rider would have been unable to steer the machine, although all cable controls (in particular to the front disc brake) would be unaffected.

The engineering expert instructed by the young man's lawyer concentrated his attention on this fracture. The engineer observed that the top of the steering tube had both an internal thread and an external thread and that the fracture had initiated where their roots coincided, i.e., across the thinnest cross section of the steering tube (Figure 3.4). He sent the broken pieces to a metallurgical laboratory, which cut sections and reported it was a virtually instantaneous ductile tearing fracture displaying no evidence of metal fatigue. In addition, the laboratory carried out hardness tests and a microstructural examination (hence the pieces cut away in Figure 3.4) and found these to be typical of the quality of steel used for such steering tubes. The laboratory concluded that the tearing fracture had started at the front of the tube where the roots of the internal and external thread coincided, i.e., where the wall cross section was least.

The engineer then sent the remains of the front wheel (Figure 3.5) that had shattered into several pieces to another laboratory that reported it was a magnesium alloy casting to a standard specification. This second laboratory found a small casting defect in one of the fractures but concluded this defect would have exerted no significant effect on the strength of the wheel and had been exposed as the wheel fractured.

In the light of these findings the engineer concluded that the cause of the accident was loss of steering control due to sudden failure of the steering tube as the front wheel went over a pot hole in the ridged road surface. He advised the injured man's lawyer that they had grounds to pursue a claim against the motorcycle manufacturers on the basis of

Figure 3.5   Pieces of front wheel recovered after the accident.

manufacturing weakness in the steering tube, namely, the reduction in wall thickness where the internal and external thread roots coincided.

The lawyers were not too confident that they could succeed in such an action, recognizing that the defendant manufacturers would argue that this particular steering tube was no different from thousands of others fitted to their machines and such tubes had no history of spontaneous failures such as alleged. Unfortunately the engineer died before they had gone beyond the initial stage of litigation, so they decided to seek a second opinion. All the earlier reports were made available to a second expert, who immediately recognized that the two specialist laboratories had each been sent only one damaged item from the machine. Each laboratory had reported on the one part as instructed, without having an opportunity to see any of the other components from the motorcycle. The engineer had done nothing with the rest of the machine except take two or three general photographs. Neither he nor the laboratories had considered the load transfer path.

The second expert was provided with the laboratory reports but immediately recognized that the chain of damage started at the front wheel and finished at the broken steering tube. He first considered the rider's statements and then followed the load transfer path, starting from the tree instead of the fracture in the steering tube.

Although the rider claimed he remembered seeing sparks coming from the road below the front wheel immediately before he lost control, no signs of abrasion could be found anywhere on the pieces of rim from the front wheel. A magnesium alloy casting exhibits little ductility, so it had shattered into pieces rather than deforming as a steel wheel would have done. All but a few tiny pieces had been recovered and none of them showed any evidence

Figure 3.6 Bead of a front tire showing the kink where the steel bead has been deformed by the tire being impacted against the wheel rim.

of abrasion or wear. Assembling the pieces revealed that the fractures spread out from a single point on the left rim, consistent with a forceful impact concentrated at one spot. The impact had been cushioned by the tire, as there was no deep indentation in the metal of the rim itself. Figure 3.5 shows the major pieces juxtaposed, and Figure 3.6 shows the inside of the tire with a pronounced kink in the bead consistent with being flattened against the outer flange of the rim.

It was a tubeless tire and no evidence of puncture could be found, so the air must have either escaped through cracks in the metal wheel or by displacement of the tire bead from the wheel rim by an external force. The bundle of high tensile steel wires inside the rubber forming the bead (which holds the tire onto the wheel rim) had been deformed to the profile of the outer rim, as evident in Figure 3.6. This forceful impact had clearly occurred when the wheel hit the tree, as there were several small splinters of bark embedded in the fracture of the major part of the wheel still attached to the hub, which could only have occurred after the tire had been displaced from the disintegrating wheel.

This big force against the front tire had been reacted to by the magnesium alloy wheel and must, in turn, have been reacted to by the axle in order for

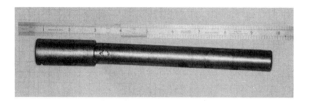

Figure 3.7   Bent axle from the front wheel.

Figure 3.8   Brake disc, bent and bolts missing where trapped in the calliper.

the wheel to break up in this manner. Figure 3.7 shows the axle placed on 1-mm² paper, clearly revealing that it is bent toward one end. A steel axle does not deform in this way unless one side is restrained while the other is acted upon by a force sufficient to deform it. This necessary displacement is revealed by the way the fork stanchions have been twisted out of line, as illustrated in Figure 3.8. The same force had twisted the brake disc, breaking two bolts at one side, while it had been restrained by the calliper (Figure 3.9). Thus the big force against the tire must have been transmitted through the wheel into the axle and then to the forks, twisting them sideways, as illustrated in Figure 3.10. This force must have then been reacted to by the head frame tube of the chassis. All external forces on the forks are transmitted to the headframe of the machine via the bearings at the top and bottom of the steering tube.

The steering tube exhibited a ductile shear failure just below the top bearing, as already shown in Figure 3.4, and had bent immediately above the bottom bearing as a result of the bottom of the fork being pushed backward, as illustrated in Figure 3.9. (Surprisingly, the first engineer had made no mention of this in his report and had not taken any photographs of this region. From the dimensions of the tube in the vicinity of the bend and

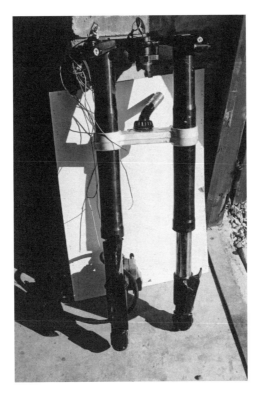

Figure 3.9 Front forks, twisted out of line. Notice the position of the brake calliper and the bottom of the steering tube bent as the forks were pushed rearward.

estimating the tensile strength of the steel from its hardness value, it is possible to make a reasonable estimate of the bending force, but this was unnecessary in this instance.)

No sign of damage or deformation could be found beyond the bearings in the frame of the machine. Hence the steering tube is where the energy of external impact had been finally expended and is where the chain of damage terminates. Although the force that broke the steering tube had been reacted to by the headframe of the machine and transferred into the chassis, it must clearly have been below the level necessary to cause any plastic deformation of the metal structure. Sometimes a bearing may show small indentations on the race where rollers or balls have been forced in during collision impact, but in this instance there was no sign of this effect (often referred to as "brinelling" after the hardness testing method that forces a hardened steel ball into the test specimen to produce a spherical indentation).

The above analysis demonstrates that the steering tube had been fractured by collision forces generated when the front wheel hit the tree. A shearing fracture had occurred across the threads where the roots of the inner

Figure 3.10   Closer view of the lower section of a steering tube, sawn to remove the mating fracture of the threaded portion still remaining in the upper bearing. Notice the absence of bending deformation on the upper portion of the steering tube still remaining in the top bearing.

and outer threads coincided, which was the minimum cross-sectional area of the entire length of tube. As this section fractured in shear the bottom of the forks continued to be pushed backward, which consequently bent the bottom of the steering tube forward just above the lower bearing, as evident in Figure 3.10. Hence the steering tube had *not* failed spontaneously and caused the rider to lose steering control while the machine was traveling along the road. A steering tube is never subjected to such forces as would cause it to fail in this manner during normal riding, even on the most bumpy of road surfaces. If the steering tube had contained any significant manufacturing fault at this position, the fracture would have exhibited a progressive fatigue mode, not ductile tearing. The defect would have been exposed by the fracture. Furthermore, if this section had failed before the machine hit the tree the steering tube could not have reacted to forces of sufficient magnitude to disintegrate the front wheel, bend the axle and cause so much damage to the forks and brake disc.

Not surprisingly, on the strength of this second opinion, the litigation was abandoned.

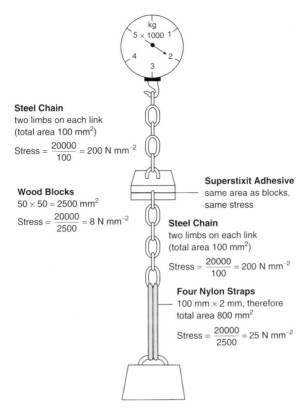

Steel Chain
two limbs on each link
(total area 100 mm²)

Stress = $\dfrac{20000}{100}$ = 200 N mm⁻²

Wood Blocks
50 × 50 = 2500 mm²

Stress = $\dfrac{20000}{2500}$ = 8 N mm⁻²

Superstixit Adhesive
same area as blocks,
same stress

Steel Chain
two limbs on each link
(total area 100 mm²)

Stress = $\dfrac{20000}{100}$ = 200 N mm⁻²

Four Nylon Straps
100 mm × 2 mm, therefore
total area 800 mm²

Stress = $\dfrac{20000}{2500}$ = 25 N mm⁻²

Figure 3.11 Forces acting on linked components subjected to same load.

3.4 Effect of Faults and Weaknesses

Consideration of the load transfer path such as above does not require precise calculations of stresses and strains or finite analysis modeling, though sometimes these methods may be necessary in the investigation of major disasters such as airplane crashes. For the more mundane investigations it is usually quite sufficient to make a qualitative assessment of the nature, magnitude and direction of the load transfers. However, a semiquantitative approach may be extremely useful when a component in the load transfer path is suspected of containing some weakness or defect that may have been responsible for a failure.

Consider the system illustrated in Figure 3.11, which, let us suppose, is to extol the virtues of a new, instant "super-glue" for a TV advertisement. Two blocks of wood 50-mm square are coated with the adhesive and stuck together. Nylon straps suspend a 2-t mass from the crane hook. Steel chain is used to fasten the straps to the wooden blocks and attach the load to a crane weigher. The weigher registers 2 t. The intention is to show how good the glue is. But let us estimate the stresses in the various links comprising this load transfer path, first to discover which is likely to fail first if the load were increased up to the point where something *would* break and then to investigate differences if a defect were present in one or another of the component members of the linked assembly. For the purpose of this exercise we shall ignore the weight of the straps, the wooden blocks and the chains, as these would be relatively insignificant compared with the 2 t being lifted. We take the order of mechanical strength of each of the three components to be:

Component	Stress (N mm^{-2}) under 2000-kg Load	Mechanical Strength of Material (N mm^{-2})
Nylon straps Four, each 100 mm × 2 mm Total cross section = 800 mm^2	25	Tensile failure 75
Steel chain Two limbs each 50-mm^2 area Total = 100 mm^2	200	Yields at 400 Tensile fracture 650
Adhesive spread over blocks 50 mm^2 = 2500 mm^2	8	Fails at 15

While the 2000-kg mass is off the ground it applies a force of 20 kN (near enough) acting on all components in the load transfer path (including those inside the weigher) which is reacted to by the crane or whatever is supporting the weighing machine. On the 2500-mm^2 area of adhesive this generates a stress of 8 N mm^{-2}. The total cross-sectional area of the four 100-mm × 2-mm nylon straps is 800 mm^2, so the mean stress when supporting the load of 20 kN is 25 N mm^{-2}. Every chain link comprises two limbs totaling 100 mm^2 cross-sectional area, so the mean stress in each limb is 200 N mm^{-2}. Joints made with this adhesive are known to fail at stresses in the region of 15 N mm^{-2}, so the joint is, in fact, by far the weakest link in this load transfer system. It does not fail (in the short time, at least) because the stress acting is only just over one half this level. Its weakness relative to the other members in the system is not immediately apparent due to the much greater cross-sectional area of the wooden blocks. However, if the applied load were increased this is where the failure should occur because the chain links and the nylon straps are working well within their limiting stresses and neither would be expected to show any kind of mechanical distress, although they would stretch elastically under the stress. Elastic deformation is recovered when the force is removed.

Which member would fail first if the load were increased to, say, 4 t? This would double the stresses given in the table, from which it is quite obvious that the adhesive would have failed before the stress reached 16 N mm^{-2}. However, at a 4-t load the stress in the chain links would be 400 N mm^{-2}, which is just at its yield point, so some of the links might have begun to elongate. The nylon straps would have reached only two thirds of their breaking load.

Now let us remove the wooden blocks and, using only the chain and the nylon straps, gradually increase the load until something broke. Which would it be? When the load reached 6 t the nylon straps would fail as the stress in them would be 75 N mm^{-2}. However, the chain would also have stretched considerably because the stress of 600 N mm^{-2} is well above the yield point of the metal but still below its tensile strength. So we would expect to see an appreciably elongated chain attached to the broken straps.

Now let us suppose that the weld in one of the chain links was defective. By how much would its load-bearing cross section have to be reduced for the link to fail *before* the adhesive joint? Clearly this must be a load below that to break the adhesive joint, i.e., 15 N mm$^{-2} \times 2,500$ mm^2 cross-sectional area = 37,500 N. (In reality this would be a far more complex problem than it seems, because the fracture toughness of the steel and the form of the defect would need to be taken into account to make an accurate calculation.) Nevertheless, if we take the simplistic view that the cross-sectional area of the chain link must be so reduced that its remaining area (A) multiplied by the nominal tensile strength of the steel (650 N mm^{-2}) has to be equal to or less than the breaking load of the adhesive joint (37,500 N), then A works out at 57.7 mm^2. As each limb of the chain should have been a 50-mm^2 cross section, then the one with the defective weld must have been effectively reduced to only 7.5 mm^2. Hence, on inspection we should expect to find a sizeable defect occupying something like 85% of the original cross-sectional area of that limb. Even though this is not a precise figure it shows we should be looking for a sizeable pre-existing defect in the fracture surface of the broken limb.

There would also be another feature to look for. Because steel is a ductile material and yields before it fractures, the defective limb would break under the applied load but the opposite limb would deform plastically, open up and allow the connecting link on the loaded side to escape. None of the other links in the chain would display any sign of distress because under a load of 37,500 N the mean stress in the limbs of nondefective links would be only 375 N mm^{-2}, which is below the steel's yield stress of 400 N mm^{-2}.

Finally, to bring this semiquantitative consideration of load transfer to a conclusion, if such a chain were used on its own, for towing a broken down vehicle, for example, and if the entire length of chain were overloaded beyond the yield stress of the steel, then every link would deform before the weakest one broke. The entire length of chain between the attachment points would be found to have stretched when the pitches of the individual links were measured. However, if there was no general stretching of the chain, this would indicate a failure caused by some localized condition leading to overstress, such as a defect in that particular link or some unusual mechanical condition that led to overstress, for example, a kink, while the rest of the chain was not loaded to its yield stress.

Practicing engineers may question the validity of assumptions and approximations made in estimating forces as outlined in this section. Of course it would be better to carry out laboratory tests and make simulations to obtain accurate values, but the problem is that damaged components produced are one-offs from a particular accident and the evidence must be preserved with minimum disturbance for examination by other experts representing various parties who may be joined in litigation. Quite often there is insufficient material to remove sections for standard test pieces without destroying what some expert may later assert was vital evidence. The usual material and mechanical specification for a part may be available but the reason for a particular one failing may be that it did not meet that specification at the time of manufacture or that its properties may have been altered by something that was done to it in service, like inadvertent heat treatment from a nearby welding operation softening or cracking a quenched and tempered steel. Hence the forensic investigator must rely on nondestructive (or nondamaging) tests and observations to ascertain whether the material was ductile or brittle or had deteriorated in some way in service. With metals a Vickers diamond pyramid hardness test, which leaves only a tiny indentation on the surface, is very useful for estimating the yield and tensile strength of a broken component in the vicinity of a fracture and, with a small item like a rivet or fastener, is the only means of doing so.

3.5 Cause of Failure of Axle Bracket in Racing Motorcycle Sidecar

We conclude this chapter with a case that ran for 8 years with the plaintiff's expert striving to prove that poor design compounded by a manufacturing fault was responsible for a very serious accident in a motorcycle race that resulted in the 24-year-old rider being confined to a wheelchair for the rest of his life. The young man had purchased his machine at the start of the racing season and, after doing well at preliminary meetings, had reached the final of a national grasstrack championship. His sidecar frame was hand built by a specialist firm whose chassis were regarded throughout Europe as among

Figure 3.12 View from the rear of the racing motorcycle sidecar as recovered. The sidecar wheel bracket is broken and completely separated from the chassis.

the best available, and used exclusively by a three-times-in-succession national champion. Six machines roared off in the final race and the young man was in fifth place as he entered the first curve. Suddenly, just as he started the slide at the bend, his machine went "tail light" and somersaulted through the air, twisting around and turning over as it did so. The sidecar passenger was flung clear of the track, but the rider was thrown to the ground and his machine appeared to land on his back before coming to rest several yards further along the race track.

When the machine was recovered it was discovered that a triangular bracket that held the sidecar wheel was broken and partially separated from the sidecar chassis. This bracket was a unique design that allowed the sidecar wheel to be adjusted forward and backward along the sidecar chassis with the axle mounted in an eccentric hub that enabled the wheel to be set at various angles of "toe-in" and inboard inclination. It was the ease of making these fine adjustments, absolutely critical in a championship race, that made it so popular with the racing motorcycle fraternity. The chassis and the bracket were made from high strength steel tubing joined by bronze welding, a conventional method at that time (early 1990s) for cycle and motorcycle frames. The steel tube and joining method were those recommended for cycle frames by Reynolds TI in its technical brochures. The sidecar axle was a hardened and tempered alloy steel as used for stub axles of small motor cars.

Figure 3.12 is a rear view of the machine, as recovered, with the sidecar wheel offered up approximately in the position it was in when the bracket fractured. The engineer for the defendant company was the first to examine the damaged machine. A tie rod from the bracket to underneath the saddle was broken, though it was said this was badly cracked but still hanging together when the machine was lifted off the track. The tire bead had separated all around the outer rim and the inner tube had a 3-in.-long split near the valve. The sidecar chassis frame was unaffected apart from slight bruises where the clamps holding the bracket had been attached, but both front and rear clamps had opened out as a result of the bracket being pushed down onto the chassis, and two of the four bolts on each had been sheared off at their brazes. After considering the load transfer path, this expert's conclusion was that all the damage had been caused by the sidecar wheel violently impacting the ground as the machine rolled over toward the end of the somersault, after it had passed over the prostrate body of the rider but before it came to rest further along the racetrack. A video recording had been made of the incident by an amateur cameraman who had positioned himself with a good view of the machines at the first curve. This expert's conclusion was entirely based on visual examination and nothing was disturbed or dismantled pending expert examination commissioned for the claimant, who had instituted proceedings against the designers and the manufacturer of the sidecar chassis and the eccentric hub.

The plaintiff's engineer agreed all damage occurred as described above, but he reached an entirely different conclusion. He observed that all the braze fractures had occurred at the interface between the steel and the braze alloy and that nearly 30% of the fracture area of the brazed joint to the eccentric hub was more heavily stained than the rest. He regarded this as evidence that this part of the braze had been cracked for some time before the accident. He also found different degrees of staining on the fractured interfaces of the smaller brazes on the clamp bodies (Figure 3.13) and interpreted these stains as signs of stress corrosion. There were several other features that we need not discuss here, but which he regarded as further evidence that the brazed joints had been progressively weakening for some time before the accident. His conclusion therefore was that failure of these weakened joints had occurred as the machine was rounding the curve and, as the eccentric hub cracked, its movement caused the tire to rub against the chassis and exert a strong braking effect. It was this, coupled with misalignment of the sidecar wheel, that caused the machine to go tail light and begin to somersault.

This engineer's detailed allegations may be broadly summarized as follows:

1. The design of the eccentric hub and the clamps was defective in relying on butt joints in high tensile steel tubes to be hand made by bronze welding.
2. The brazing had been carried out defectively. The large braze to the eccentric hub had not wetted properly (based on the area of discoloration on the exposed fracture surfaces) and this had caused fatigue

Figure 3.13   Close view of the clamp to the sidecar chassis showing the sheared lug. Notice the left end of the clamp has lifted off the chassis tube under the same force system that sheared the lug weld.

    cracking to propagate through the rest of the joint until it was no longer capable of withstanding the service loadings.

3. Entrapment of residual zinc plating solution in crevices behind the clamp lug brazed joints had caused stress corrosion cracking of the bronze alloy over a period of time and had reached the stage where four of the eight lugs were so weakened that they cracked open on the last occasion the bolts were tightened. This loosened the attachment of the bracket and allowed the sidecar wheel to move backward and become misaligned.

    In a nutshell, this expert had advised the rider's legal representatives that the accident was caused by sudden, final fracture of the hub weld as the machine rounded the curve, allowing the sidecar wheel to become misaligned and finishing off the loose clamp lugs. The tire rubbed against the chassis frame, causing the machine to become tail light and somersault.

    The defendant's engineer was not impressed by these assertions, and was confident he could rebut all three on technical grounds. However, he first wished to examine the axle, which appeared to be bent slightly downward, as suggested by the small gap that had opened up at the top of the hub, indicated by the arrow in Figure 3.14. Figure 3.15 is a view with the sidecar wheel laid flat below the chassis. It seemed from the damage to the clamp still remaining on the chassis that a considerable downward force had acted to cause much deformation damage to the bracket and fracture of the hub. Accordingly, a joint investigation, attended by the manufacturer and the claimant's legal representative, was carried out during which the position of

Figure 3.14 Sidecar wheel offered up to the broken bracket. Notice the gap (arrowed) suggesting the axle is bent downward.

Figure 3.15 Sidecar wheel turned around and placed under the chassis. Notice the broken tie rod and how the rear leg of the bracket has broken at the hub joint. Notice also that the bottom of the rear clamp has been broken away, allowing the bracket to separate from the chassis tube.

the axle was carefully marked and then removed from the hub. It was found to be bent downward by some 15°. The hardness of the steel was measured in order to estimate its tensile strength and confirm that it was in the specified hardened and tempered condition. The defendant's expert later applied engineering standard bending formulae to calculate the external force that would have been required to produce this degree of bend. The figure obtained was 8.5 t force applied in the plane of the wheel at the midpoint of the wheel bearings. The axle had bent downward so this force must have acted from the top of the wheel or possibly, but much less likely, by the bottom of the

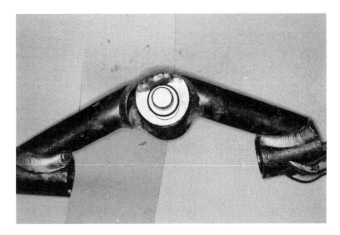

Figure 3.16 Unused bracket tested to destruction in the compression test. The fracture is virtually identical to the accident bracket.

wheel being pushed inward. The defendant's expert then obtained an unused bracket from the manufacturer, fitted with an axle, and tested this in a compression test machine. The clamps began to deform at 7.4 t, and the brazed joint could be heard to crack at 8.2-t force and finally split open as shown in Figure 3.16 at 9.1-t force, with the break virtually identical to that of the accident bracket. There was no sign of any defect in the fracture surfaces of the bronze weld. The cracking followed the interface between the bronze and the steel.

Suspecting that the discoloration of the fracture surfaces of the plaintiff's bracket was postaccident and most probably resulted from exposure to moist atmospheres during the 8-month storage period between the accident and the expert's examinations, part of this laboratory-produced fracture was masked off and the hub was left in an outdoor store. The exposed area of fracture quickly started to become discolored. This was because the fracture followed a brittle intermetallic layer formed at the interface of the bronze and the steel, which corrodes rapidly in moist air. The masked region was hardly affected after 2 weeks but 3 months after the masking was removed it was indistinguishable from the rest of the fracture interface. Hence, as neither expert had seen the hub fracture until several months after the accident and the machine had been stored in a farm barn for this period, there was no way of deducing what the fracture would have looked like immediately after the accident. The topography of the fracture displayed none of the characteristics of metal fatigue, so the defendant's expert continued to believe it was an instantaneous fracture caused when the wheel hit the ground.

The plaintiff's expert had obtained a replacement clamp and put it through tensile tests to determine the force required to break the allegedly unsuitable bronze welded joints on the lug. Instead of the interface failing as he had predicted, the steel lug stretched, opened out and eventually fractured, and the bolt used to hold it in the grips of the testing machine was badly deformed. The bronze weld was unaffected, mainly because it was of much greater cross-sectional area than the steel tubes that it joined. The plaintiff's expert also carried out stress corrosion tests but was only able to produce cracks by exposing the replacement clamp to concentrated ammonia fumes with the joint under so much tension it had deformed. In all normal moist atmospheres, including that developed in contact with animal dung, the defendant's expert determined that no cracking could be produced in the braze.

Still refusing to accept the simple interpretation of the load transfer path from the wheel through to the sidecar chassis, the plaintiff's expert commissioned a thorough FE (computer modeling of finite elements within a structure) strain analysis of the bracket, but, for some unaccountable reason, not including the axle or the wheel. The analysts were unable to offer any figure for the forces necessary to cause the kind of fracture observed because the data necessary for bronze welded joints were unavailable.

After spending 7 years and a great deal of money conducting technical investigations, the plaintiff's engineer had nevertheless not considered the load transfer path associated with the deformation damage to all the components from the sidecar wheel to the chassis. For example, he devoted considerable attention to the fractured lugs of the clamp but made no attempt to explain why the clamps themselves were heavily deformed, as illustrated in Figure 3.17 and Figure 3.18. Eventually, the two experts were ordered to produce a joint report summarizing and commenting upon each other's evidence and their opinions as to the cause of the accident. As a consequence of this, the plaintiff was advised by his legal representatives that he had no chance of succeeding at trial, so the claim was abandoned.

The lawyers accepted the defendant engineer's explanation for the cause of the accident, based on simple consideration of the load transfer path from the wheel to the sidecar chassis. The crucial evidence was the bending of the axle. Stub axles do not deform until they are subjected to loads that exceed the yield stress of the steel from which they are made. Thus a force on the order of 8.6 t must have been directed at the rim of the wheel but, more importantly, this must have been reacted to by whatever was holding the opposite end of the axle and, in turn, by all the components transferring this force to the sidecar chassis. If any of these linkages had not been capable of transferring forces of this magnitude they would have failed in some way before the axle bent. If we start with the wheel, we see that the axle was stressed above its yield point and bent downward. This force was reacted to by the hub at the top of the bracket. The bracket was subjected to compression, which cracked the bronze weld at the hub exactly as reproduced in the

Figure 3.17 Underside view of rear clamp.

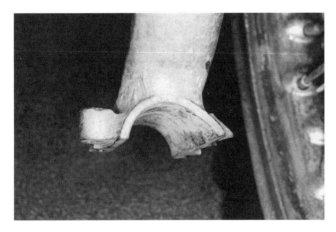

Figure 3.18 End view of rear clamp, illustrated in Figure 3.17, showing how compression force has deformed semicircular shape.

laboratory test (Figure 3.16). This compression force was transferred to the clamps holding the bracket to the chassis, which opened out as illustrated in Figure 3.19 and confirmed in the photographs in Figure 3.13, Figure 3.17 and Figure 3.18. The damage terminated at the chassis frame, which had suffered only slight bruising by the clamps. All the energy of the impact against the wheel was dissipated in fracturing and deforming the other components.

If the plaintiff's expert had considered this possibility at the outset before starting his detailed scientific tests, he would have realized that if the weld at the hub had broken first, there would have been no path by which the load to deform the clamps and bend the axle could have been

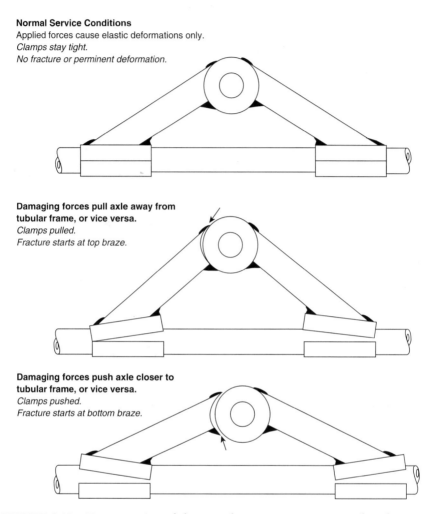

Normal Service Conditions
Applied forces cause elastic deformations only.
Clamps stay tight.
No fracture or perminent deformation.

**Damaging forces pull axle away from
tubular frame, or vice versa.**
Clamps pulled.
Fracture starts at top braze.

**Damaging forces push axle closer to
tubular frame, or vice versa.**
Clamps pushed.
Fracture starts at bottom braze.

FIGURE 3.19 Upper portion of the rear clamp, as in Figure 3.18, but drawn to show extensive deformation caused by compressive loads acting through brackets.

transmitted. Whenever and however the axle became bent the hub mounting must have been strong enough to react to and transmit the applied force to the chassis.

The final capitulation by the plaintiff's expert was when analysis of the video, frame by frame, revealed the wheel to be in its normal position and alignment on the sidecar chassis during most of the somersault, after the machine had struck the rider's prostrate body. One of the last frames showed the sidecar wheel violently striking the ground at the end of the somersaulting, after which the wheel appeared to be thrown outward almost horizontally, clearly establishing that this was when the damage was done.

A "Toolbox" for Forensic Engineers

4

4.1 Introduction

A range of scientific instruments and techniques is necessary to "solve" the variety of cases presented in the remaining chapters. Such procedures are needed to obtain evidence about the products involved and the materials of which they are made. In other words, "tools" must be selected that are appropriate to report on the issues put to the investigator. The interpretation of these data requires some expert knowledge. Furthermore, expert findings must be presented in a form that lawyers can understand and incorporate into their legal proceedings, as well as one that allows the courts to reach a judgment.

The objective of any forensic engineering investigation is to determine the cause or causes of accidents or failures. Forensic engineering is, therefore, primarily a problem-solving exercise. With any analytical assignment, there is a need to be aware of available tools, the information they provide, their limitations and any "trade-offs" that may be inherent in a particular technique. However, there is no pressing need to understand any deep underlying theory, just as when driving a car it is not necessary to know the way a car engine works.

Many failure problems will lead to litigation, perhaps because the damage is capable of several different interpretations. Thus the approach taken to any material evidence, such as a fractured component, is fundamentally constrained by the need to preserve and conserve it for possible examination by others. Items submitted for examination may be vital legal evidence that cannot be chopped up or machined into test specimens. The exception is where the item is very large, so selecting samples for test specimens will not destroy anything critical. Forensic investigations are, therefore, fundamentally different from routine quality control, where thousands of components will be available for examination. The different approach of forensics is biased to nondestructive methods of inspection, simply so that the evidence is preserved. That is not to say that destructive or partly destructive methods cannot be used at all, but rather that they should be used only as the last resort. Indeed, all the parties in a dispute will need to agree on a testing program, at which all can be present when any element of destruction is proposed.

The purpose of this chapter is to outline a "typical" range of techniques and associated instruments that can be called upon by the forensic engineer. These range from photography, crack detection, metallography, and high- and low-power microscopy through to chemical and mechanical analysis.

4.2   An Initial Approach to a Failure

At the outset of any investigation there is one abstract tool that can often be taken for granted: *There is a tendency to neglect the vital importance of our eyes — the simple power of visual observation, so that others may see what we have seen and the importance attached to it.* As the great detective Sherlock Holmes said to his medical doctor sidekick, "Watson, you see but you do not perceive." When the forensic engineer examines debris from an accident he or she must look at much more than its general features. The aim must be to seek evidence elucidating what might have caused the debris to reach its current state. Photographing the whole item is of little use when the clue to its failure lies in one small area or a surface feature that would pass unnoticed by a nonspecialist observer.

Acute observation will allow more than scrutiny of artifacts under examination; it may also provide an insight into the situation that led to failure in the first instance. Observations of this nature allow assessment of the *circumstances* from which the physical evidence was gathered. This might take the form of

- A visit to the scene of the accident
- An invitation to select evidence for laboratory examination
- Examination of "scene of incident" photographs taken by the police or factory inspectors

It is essential to ensure that the right objects are selected for examination, and the correct circumstances surrounding an event become familiar.

Such visual evidence will need to be recorded in photographs. "A simple picture is worth more than a thousand words" is literally true, as well as more convincing. Visual observations of an incident or a failed product must be recorded by camera or video film at the scene of an incident or at the time the product has failed, or during the dismantling of a device. The value of recording evidence is shown by a case that involved contamination of an industrial site.

Scene of Incident Inspection.   A sheet metal fabricator wanted to pinpoint the source of contamination of material and finished goods held in the company stockyard. The nature of work being undertaken at the site demanded the use of galvanized, clad or prepainted stock material to generate a specific surface finish on the end product. Contamination from the work yard of an adjacent company had caused areas of staining and corrosion over the stock material, rendering it worthless for the manufacturing process.

A visit to the site was made in order to take photographs and select samples of the contaminating material, for analysis and identification of the contaminant source. The samples were taken from selected areas around the work yard of the adjacent company, and a photographic record was made of each site of contamination. However, the following day it was decided to return to the adjacent site to take additional photographs because the lighting levels were better (the sun had come out). On entering the yard, all evidence of contamination had been removed by a bulldozer, only hours after the initial visit.

Sample evidence and related photography, gathered from the first visit, were sufficient to prove the source of the contamination. It is impossible to know when circumstance may intervene.

4.2.1   Significance of Initial Observations

An example that relied on understanding the circumstances that surrounded an event concerned the failure of a hoist carrier. This example will also highlight the use of the human ear as a prime investigative tool. In a factory making upholstery, slices were taken off a large block of polyurethane, rolled up and then carried over the slicing machine to a dispatch area. The carrier was a bar with chains and hooks at both ends, and a shackle attached to a wire rope hoist at the center. The carrier bar broke at its center and one half of the transported material fell onto a man's head, causing serious injury. A graphic representation of the relevant components is shown in Figure 4.1. The bar appeared to be far stronger than it needed to be to carry the few kilograms weight of the roll. Photographs taken by a factory inspector were available and calculation showed that the bar was only lightly loaded during the lift and traverse to the dispatch area.

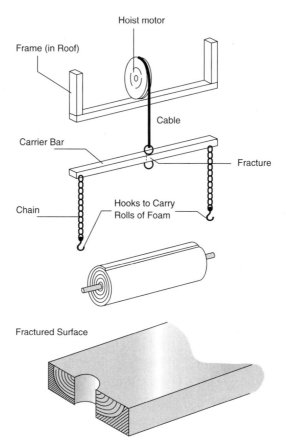

Figure 4.1   Graphic sketches of hoist, lifting bar, foam roll and fracture surface.

A visit to observe the replacement bar in operation revealed the cause. On the return from the dispatch area the bar had to be lifted up until it came up against the stop for the hoist pulley. It swung wildly from side to side. The operator raised it at full speed, traversed back to the slicing machine and then lowered it so that the chains could be attached to the next roll. Every time it reached the top of the return lift, the swinging end of the bar slammed against the frame on which the hoist was mounted. Eventually the bar broke at the center as a result of metal fatigue. The clue to the cause of the fatigue was the loud clank as the swinging bar came up against the hoist limit switch. Without *hearing* this in action, it would have been difficult to discover where the fatigue stresses originated. They had nothing to do with loads carried by the hoist. It was the repeated violent slams on the return journey, and when the hoist was not carrying any load, that caused the failure.

What can be found by simple observations may turn out to be highly significant and pre-empt the need for further or detailed laboratory examination. In the case described, it was *prior* events that revealed how failure occurred. Laboratory examination of the fractured carrier bar would not have identified the cause of failure, and would be quite irrelevant as the solution to the problem lay in circumstances *prior* to failure.

Visual observation can be used as a comparator. The following case illustrates how simple comparative observations can be used in a manner similar to fingerprint identification. A stolen Jaguar was recovered. In the course of the theft, the car had sustained damage to the windows, roof and bodywork. In addition, the hubcaps for all four steel road wheels were missing. However, the owner stated that the steel road wheels had been substituted for his original alloy wheels, an expensive "extra" for that make of vehicle. He submitted a substantial claim to his insurers for bodywork repairs, and for purchase of new alloy road wheels to replace those stolen from his vehicle.

Similar to fingerprints, the observation of "hub-prints" (the impressed markings from the wheel hub into the wheel rim, and vice versa) can identify mating surfaces that have been in intimate contact for extended periods of time. Examination was restricted to one side of the Jaguar. Road wheels on the opposite side were left untouched to facilitate a similar investigation by other interested parties.

Initial observation of the wheel rims revealed no finger markings in the wheel grime (Figure 4.2A). As the inner surface of the rim contains a deep well, it is natural to hold or grasp the wheel with your fingers in this well to take the weight of the wheel, and provide a balanced lift. Lack of any markings in the road grime was indicative of wheels that had not been removed for some considerable period of time and travel.

Arc lengths generated from bolting the wheel rim to the hub (Figure 4.2B) were measured and a match was observed between the flange and rim. In addition, machining marks from the flange had been impressed onto the wheel rim, and were clearly seen within the arc markings. The pitch of these machining marks was identical on both flange and wheel rim.

Seven additional matching features were found on each wheel, verifying the initial observation that the steel road wheels had been on the vehicle and not removed for a substantial amount of time and mileage. The claim was undoubtedly fraudulent. When advised of the criminal nature of fraud, the Jaguar owner rapidly withdrew his claim. Furthermore, the insurers advised him that they would not cover repair costs for damage sustained during the theft, nor would they insure him at any future time.

4.3   Assessing the Situation

When undertaking any failure analysis the initial evidence from the scene of an accident has to be evaluated by visual observation, based on a common

Figure 4.2 Undisturbed road dirt layer on a wheel rim (A), compared with impressed markings transferred from the wheel hub to the wheel (B).

sense approach along with a refusal to jump to conclusions. This can mean a long and often tedious examination of the evidence left by an accident. Other debris may hide critical trace evidence, for example. Observations made at the scene must be chronicled, usually with the aid of sketches, note taking and photography of the debris. The more complex the debris field, the greater the need for multiple images of the remains, so that the final resting position of key components is recorded. Such activity is essential before laboratory analysis.

4.4   Inside the Toolbox

After site inspection, gathering relevant information and collecting failed samples, what range of methods are available for analysis of samples? The forensic engineer has a variety of apparatus and inspection techniques that can help glean information from a failed artifact. These range from a simple eyeglass and macro-photography on the one hand, to hardness testing, mechanical testing and microanalysis on the other.

4.4.1 Photography and Sample Handling

The importance of photography has already been mentioned. However, forensic photography demands more than a "point-and-shoot" approach to recording information. Photograph the general area in or around the vicinity of the incident. Many pictures should be taken as is thought necessary to define and isolate key features on samples. At a later date such pictures, as an *aide-memoir*, may well become invaluable. Photograph the artifact as a whole, especially in the vicinity of any broken pieces, and use a macro lens to record fine detail if necessary. The photographic record should provide information on size and condition of all pieces, and should show the relationship of any fracture to its component parts. Sometimes this can be difficult, as it is essential that the fracture surfaces are not actually brought into contact with one another (to prevent damage to the fracture surfaces themselves). In addition, samples are usually three dimensional, so it can prove difficult to reassemble several broken parts on a planar surface for ease of imaging. Plasticene or Blu-Tack is useful here. Also, if dimensions are critical, small parts can be photographed on graph paper.

Careful examination and photography of the fractured artifact should follow, concentrating on any relevant details on external surfaces that are visible to the eye without any magnification. Lighting conditions are important in bringing out hidden detail in the picture. Shadows can often obscure such detail, and shadow-free photographs can be achieved only with very even illumination. The illumination source can be shielded either by an opaque screen (such as grease-proof paper) or a ring-illumination source used directly with the camera. Positive use of shadows is also very important, however, in highlighting relief on surfaces and is normally achieved with oblique or slanting illumination from a point source, such as the sun or a fiber-optic light. Figure 4.3 is a photograph of a truck clutch plate that failed in service. Due to a combination of an incorrectly adjusted clutch plate, and an inexperienced driver, the surface of the clutch pressure plate became subjected to a series of sudden frictional heating cycles followed by quenching. Quenching, at the surface of the clutch plate, arose from a combination of a large thermal mass of the clutch, and the cooling effect of its rapid movement through surrounding air. The net result of such thermal cycling was the development of a large number of radial cracks that are shown in the macrograph. When the clutch eventually disintegrated, pieces of the plate flew into the cab, seriously injuring the driver. In this instance, oblique photographic lighting was used to record both cracking and thermal discoloration.

Figure 4.3 Photo-macrograph of a thermally fatigued clutch plate of a truck. Dimensions: outside diameter, 42 cm × 2.5 cm thick. Oblique lighting, from top right.

Among the first on the scene of an accident would be the police photographer, or safety officer (or factory inspector) if the accident is an industrial accident. When recovering evidence for further observation, preservation of any dirt or grease marks on samples can be vital if critical evidence of its past history is not to be lost. Such trace evidence (witness marks) can help in reconstructing past movements of the sample, such as contact with other, perhaps mating parts. The need to maintain fracture surfaces in their state as found immediately after an accident cannot be emphasized enough. With certain materials, touching such surfaces can initiate corrosion, so it is important to minimize handling. When being removed from the accident scene, failed samples should be protected by wrapping carefully in bubble-wrap film, and then sealed into labeled plastic bags. Blu-Tack or Plasticine can also prove useful in protecting surfaces, as well as for mounting samples for photography. It finds an additional application in removing grease and dirt at a later stage in an inspection, after original pictures have been taken. By using a dabbing action, Blu-Tack will lift and clean most dirt and loose corrosion product from fracture surfaces.

4.4.2 Product and Material Standards

Compliance with product standards and regulations is now a major issue for many manufacturers. Unless products comply with specific standards, the ability to sell can be compromised in many markets. The American Society for Testing and Materials (ASTM) and British Standards Institution (BSI) have produced standards covering safety, performance and reliability of most products, including the influence of mechanical and environmental factors. In addition, each standard is reviewed and updated periodically, thus ensuring continued relevance.

When considering any failure, an appropriate standard written to encompass the component or its application (e.g., wire ropes, chains, seatings, etc.) may be applicable. Standards are an invaluable comparator against which failed components can be matched. Furthermore, it is not just ASTM and BSI that can be searched; equivalent standards exist in Europe (ISO), Germany (DIN), Japan (JIS), and elsewhere. All are excellent sources of reference. Because the majority of accidents occur within the home, domestic appliances are particularly well covered by appropriate standards. In the U.K., there more than 50 deaths and some 12,000 accidents requiring hospital treatment each year, involving consumers using ladders around the home (Source: DTI, U.K., July 2001). A person falls and suffers injury, and damage is found on the stiles or rung hooks, feet, etc. The user seeks to sue the supplier, alleging manufacturing defect or flaw, poor construction, insufficient strength of alloy sections, etc. Such allegations are usually unfounded as there are stringent standards (i.e., BSI, 2037:1994) covering the design, materials, construction and performance for such ladders and steps. Analyses of stepladder failures are presented in Chapter 3, and associated workplace accidents are presented in Chapter 8.

Within any standard, much of the required "background work" will be included and will be of particular value in product liability disputes. All that may be required of the expert is a comparative analysis between the relevant standard, and the product/component in dispute. It should become apparent if a product did not conform to the required standard.

4.4.3   Macroscopic Examination

Macroscopic examination involves observation of a failed component, fracture surface or section under low magnification (10 to 50×), preferably using a stereomicroscope. For field observations, a simple eyeglass is all that will be required. The macroscopic study will reveal information representative of the entire piece.[4] In addition, the amount of information that can be obtained from examination of a fracture surface under low magnification is surprisingly extensive. Fracture characteristics such as direction of crack growth and origin of failure can be determined, as in the fatigue failure shown in Figure 4.4. Furthermore, size and distribution of inclusions, uniformity of structure and grain size, segregation and presence of fabricating defects will be readily discernible. Macroscopic examination of fracture surfaces can also reveal information relevant to failure mode (fatigue, shear, brittle or ductile), indentations and surface damage suffered in service (some of which may have induced a fatigue failure) and environmentally enhanced failure (corrosion, stress corrosion cracking, hydrogen embrittlement, etc.).

Figure 4.4   Single bending fatigue failure of the drive shaft from an agricultural baling machine. Shaft diameter: 25.4 mm (1 in.).

4.4.4   Examination under Magnification: Optical Microscopic Inspection

The primary purpose of a microscopic examination is to reveal detail that is too small to be seen by the naked eye or by macroscopic examination. Magnifications would usually range from 20 to 500× for a standard optical microscope. Microscopic examination of etched sections can be used to reveal grain structure such as grain size, inclusions, phase distribution, cracks, porosity, internal defects, surface coatings, etc., as well as thermal and mechanical history and external features such as corrosion. In short, microscopic examination can reveal a great deal about the past history of a specimen and how it will (or did) react in service. However, it should be remembered that the technique will reveal detail about a particular (and often small) portion of the specimen that may or may not be representative of the entire article.

4.4.5   Metallographic Sectioning

When metallic composition or bulk structure needs to be checked or inspected, a polished section can be prepared by cutting a small sample from the object under observation. This form of observation is by necessity a destructive technique, so care is needed in the choice of sectioning site. Further, it has to be remembered that the specimen itself may become evidence, so must be carefully conserved for possible viewing by others. The cut and polished samples may be lightly etched by chemical swabbing to outline the crystal structure. This is the technique termed *metallography*. Metallographic examination provides a good indication of the class of material involved and whether it has the desired/required structure and how it had been manufactured and heat treated. It is particularly useful for seeking internal defects in welded or brazed assemblies.[2,3]

In other words, the microstructure of a material can be equated to a fingerprint taken during the course of a criminal investigation. To illustrate the unique nature of material microstructures, the following section will present a review of the chemical makeup, properties and associated microstructures of cast irons. Chapter 5, Section 5.4 demonstrates the importance of distinguishing between different forms of cast iron that is wholly dependent on observing the microstructure of a failed casting.

4.4.5.1 *Cast Irons*

Carbon not only reduces the melting point of iron from 1530°C for pure iron to 1143°C when 4.3% carbon is present, but this element also significantly increases the fluidity which enables very good castings to be made. Moreover, when the liquid metal solidifies in the mold and the carbon separates as graphite, there is practically no volume contraction as occurs with other metals. The castings are free of shrinkage effects that are sometimes very troublesome when castings are made in other metals such as steel, bronze or aluminum. The family of iron-based alloys that contain between 2.5 and 4.5% carbon are therefore extremely useful engineering materials and are called *cast irons*. As their name implies they are used solely to make castings, as they cannot be hot or cold worked like steels that contain less than 1% carbon.

There are several varieties of cast iron, their properties depending very much on the form (the "morphology") in which the carbon separates during the solidification process. This is determined by their composition and, equally important, the rate at which they cool in the mold, and sometimes, with certain types, by any heat treatments applied to the solidified castings. Traditionally cast irons were regarded as always brittle, but over the last half century methods have been introduced for modifying the form of the graphite during solidification or by subsequent heat treatment of castings in which the carbon is in the form of iron carbide (Fe_3C). The result is many varieties of cast irons that exhibit respectable degrees of ductility and toughness.

The traditional "gray" cast irons, so called because they expose a dull gray fracture when broken, are brittle and display no ductility whatsoever. They are nevertheless quite strong and easy to cast, and are widely used for general engineering castings that do not need to possess ductility, for example, the bed for a lathe or a press. The reason for their inherent brittleness is that the graphite present in their microstructures is in the form of flakes. These flakes take a three-dimensional form similar to the leaves of lettuces packed in a box, where the lettuce leaves are the graphite and the surrounding "air" ranging from the equivalent of pure iron to a high-strength steel. In a

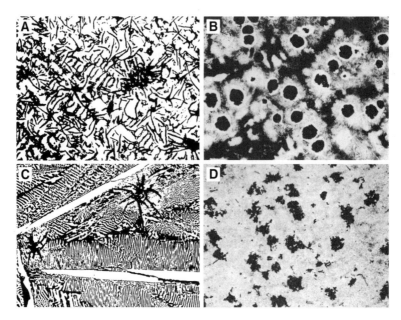

Figure 4.5   Microstructures of four different types of cast iron. Linear magnification: 75×. (A) Flake graphite ("gray") cast iron. (B) Nodular (spheroidal graphite) cast iron. (C) Chill ("white") cast iron where carbon is present as Fe_3C. (D) Malleable (blackheart) iron.

plane section, the "lettuces" look like separate flakes, but in three dimensions, each group of flakes has grown from the same nucleus.

By making additions to the ladle of fractional percentages of either magnesium or cerium (a rare-earth metal), the graphite separates in the form of spheroids, quite separate from each other, in matrices that again can be anything from the equivalent of pure, soft iron to a high strength steel. These are called "nodular" or "spheroidal graphite" (S.G.) cast irons.[4]

Figure 4.5A shows a typical microsection of a gray iron casting and Figure 4.5B shows a typical microsection of a ferritic SG iron, both as polished and photographed at a linear magnification of 75×. By making a casting solidify in the mold very quickly, the carbon does not appear as graphite but instead separates as iron carbide (Fe_3C), rendering the casting extremely hard and brittle. Figure 4.5C shows such a structure, the section polished and etched but again as a linear magnification of 75×. If a casting with such a microstructure is broken it exposes a silvery white, sparkling fracture, which is why these types of casting are called "white" cast irons. For certain applications where high hardness and maximum abrasion resistance are required, for example, the nose of a plowshare or the surface of a roll for cold working metals, castings are often made with chills inserted in the molds so that the metal that solidifies in contact with them develops the iron carbide microstructure.

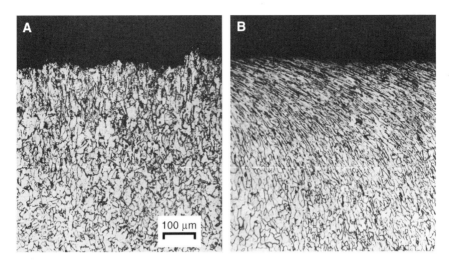

Figure 4.6 Microstructure of a sheared rivet (A) transverse section of a fracture surface, and (B) parallel to the line of action of force showing deformation of the grain structure.

Finally, there is a fourth group, the *malleable* cast irons, which have to be cast as wholly white iron and subsequently heated for several hours at temperatures where the iron carbide breaks down to form clusters of graphite. Strength is determined by whether they are produced with a ferritic or a pearlitic matrix after the heat treatment. Figure 4.5D shows such a structure, where the graphite appears as the ragged black areas and the matrix is equivalent to a medium carbon steel. A casting with this type of microstructure will be strong, tough and reasonably ductile, hence the name "malleable" cast irons. However, the application of such malleable castings has been largely ousted by the SG irons which are cast directly into the molds and require virtually no subsequent treatment.

As an analytical technique, metallography is relatively simple to undertake; it consists of four steps:

- Selection of section
- Surface preparation
- Etching
- Examination under magnification

However, since metallography is a necessarily destructive operation, care is needed in the choice of section (and the section itself becomes part of the evidence and so must be conserved, for possible viewing by others). Care is also needed to ensure that the chosen section will reveal material that will be representative of the metal under examination. The actual position of

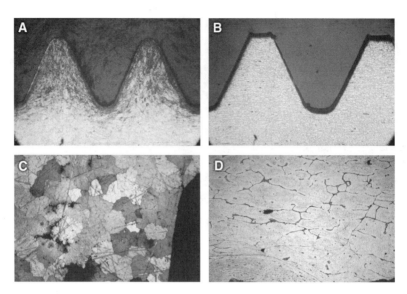

Figure 4.7 Manufacturing route revealed by metallography. A rolled screw thread on alpha brass (A), and a machined brass screw thread on alpha + beta brass (B). Cast structure of aluminum alloy (C), and hot extruded aluminum alloy (D).

sectioning should always be recorded. The orientation of the section may also be of importance if the section is selected to show, or is suspected to possess, directionality. Figure 4.6 is an illustration of a rivet that was sheared off in a collision which demonstrates how easy it can be to misinterpret microscopic evidence through selecting an inappropriate section. Figure 4.6A and B are sections taken at 90° through the sheared end, where Figure 4.6A is the structure transverse to the direction of the shearing force and Figure 4.6B the longitudinal view of the same section. Without knowing the direction of sectioning, Figure 4.6A gives no indication that the fracture was the result of transverse shear forces whereas Figure 4.6B shows the direction of shear and the grain distortion quite clearly.

Examination of metallographic sections can be invaluable to the forensic engineer. As a tool, this technique can reveal important information such as case depth of a case- or induction-hardened product, thickness and adhesion of plated coatings and heat-affected zones (HAZ) of welds — all of which may have a direct bearing on the cause of failure. By observation under magnification, the metallographic section may also reveal information regarding the method of manufacture (casting, hot forging, cold drawing, etc.; see Figure 4.7), and thermal history (either intentionally during manufacture or accidentally during service) of a component.

Other service effects such as work hardening, oxidation or corrosion and crack characteristics can be revealed. A case that required identification of a

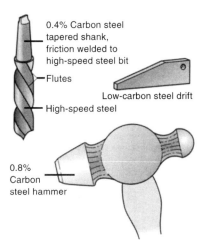

0.4% Carbon steel
tapered shank,
friction welded to
high-speed steel bit

Flutes

Low-carbon steel drift

High-speed steel

0.8%
Carbon
steel hammer

Figure 4.8   Sketches of the components and their respective compositions.

metal eye splinter will illustrate just how valuable metallography can be as a
tool. A workman in a machine shop was removing a large drill, with a Morse
taper shank, from a radial arm drilling machine. He said that he had used a
soft (steel) drift to remove the drill from the machine, striking the drift with
an ordinary engineer's hammer. This method was a normal everyday (and
correct) procedure for drill removal. However, while undertaking the routine,
the workman was hit in the eye by a flying metal splinter. The eye splinter
was submitted to ascertain which of the tools being used was the likely source.
The components and their respective compositions are shown in Figure 4.8.
Because all four components in this case were made from different materials,
it was decided to examine their respective microstructures and compare them
with those of the splinter, in order to establish the source of the splinter. The
microstructures are shown in Figure 4.9.

Direct microstructural comparison clearly reveals the eye splinter is a small
piece of HSS, broken from one of the outer flutes of the drill, not the hardened
steel hammer head, the medium carbon steel drift or the soft iron Morse taper
shank. It was therefore a straightforward task to arrive at a sequence of events
that caused the metal splinter to pierce the workman's eye. The simple answer
was that the workman must have struck the drill flutes with the hammer when
extracting the drill from the machine, and NOT used the drift as claimed. A
trained workshop engineer would know full well that drill flutes are exceptionally hard, with little or no temper — therefore prone to splinter or shatter
under impact loading — and the hardened steel face of a hammer is perhaps
the worst tool he could use to knock it free. The resultant eye injury was
therefore a direct consequence of the workman's irresponsible mistake or poor
working practice, as well as lack of eye protection.

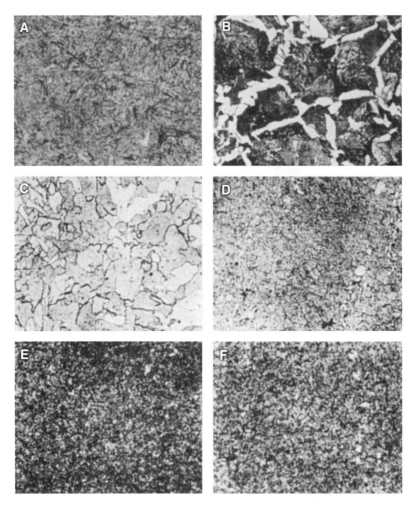

Figure 4.9 Micrographic montage showing the structures of each component and the eye splinter. (A) Martensitic structure of the hammer head. (B) Annealed 0.4% carbon steel drift. (C) 0.2% carbon steel tapered shank of the drill. (D) Splinter fragment removed from eye. (E) HSS steel drill tip fragment transverse section (longitudinal flutes). (F) HSS steel drill tip fragment longitudinal section (transverse flutes).

4.4.6 Scanning Electron Microscopy (SEM)

Advances in electronics and instrumentation have brought microanalytical techniques out of the realms of research and into the hands of everyday failure analysis. One of the best-known instruments is the scanning electron microscope (SEM). Fractography (observing the fracture surface of materials) is one of the most popular uses of the SEM. To illustrate the potential of SEM for forensic examination, Figure 4.10 typifies a fatigue failure of a fracture toughness sample. The fracture *surface* is shown at two different locations

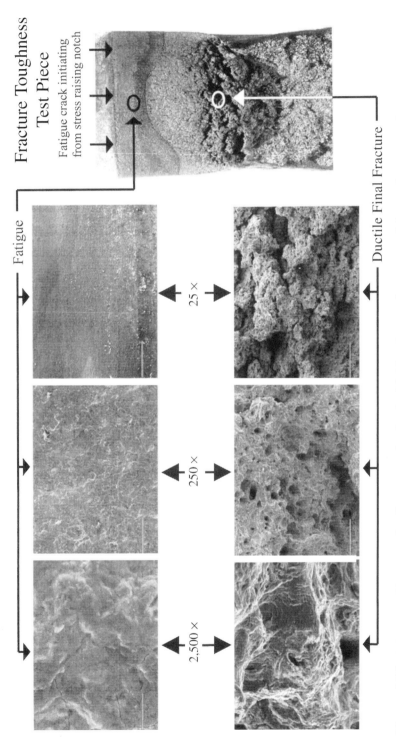

Figure 4.10 Montage of fractographs illustrating the depth of field and magnification capabilities of scanning electron microscopy (SEM). The fracture surface shown is that of a steel fracture toughness specimen. The power of the SEM to differentiate between different fracture mechanisms is clearly demonstrated.

under a range of magnifications, thus allowing direct comparison of the mode of failure experienced at each location. Having the ability to expose or compare surface features that are impossible to discern with the naked eye or the optical microscope has revolutionized forensic investigations.

A scanning microscope is much more complex to operate than optical instruments, due to the need to observe specimens in a vacuum because electrons are scattered by air. However, the benefits are numerous, and include

- Large depth of field, so that features of a rough surface are all in focus
- Very high degree of resolution (down to 0.5×10^{-6} m)
- Nondestructive for conducting materials
- Elemental analysis using EDAX (energy dispersive x-ray analyzer)

4.4.6.1 The Environmental Scanning Electron Microscope (ESEM)

One drawback of conventional SEM is the need to coat the sample surface of nonconductors with carbon or gold so as to bleed away the incoming electrons. If this is not done, the electrons build up on the sample, and prevent or inhibit image formation. A very high vacuum is needed in conventional SEM because air molecules scatter and absorb the electron beam. However, the environmental scanning electron microscope (ESEM) allows a small bleed of gas to pass over the sample being examined without entering the main column of the instrument. As the primary electron beam hits the surface, any electrons that stay on the surface are neutralized rapidly by reaction with positive ions formed by interaction of the primary beam with the gas molecules bled into the microscope. This enables the electrons to be carried away from the surface of the sample, preventing the harmful build-up. A low vacuum ESEM was used for investigating a failed catheter (Chapter 9, Section 9.4), in which the pressure is kept rather low at about 30 Pa (note 10^5 Pa ~ 1 atm). However, higher pressures are available in some instruments, rising up to about 15 torr and above (where 760 torr ~ 1 atm). The prime interest in these instruments is for observing living things, or materials that would deteriorate rapidly at low pressures. Thus water-absorbent fibers and wood lose water very rapidly at low vacuum, suffering severe damage. Care is still needed for all polymers, however, as the highly energetic electron beam (accelerated through 20,000 V, typically) can itself cause direct damage to samples by chemical reaction with the polymer chains. Application of the SEM during the course of an investigation into a hit-and-run road traffic accident shows the use of conventional SEM with nonmetallic materials.

A car struck a wooden post after knocking a cyclist off his bicycle. However, the driver of the vehicle did not stop, he just drove on — a typical "hit-

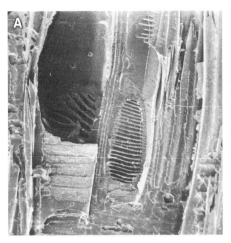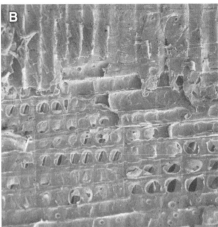

Figure 4.11 Micrographs of birch (A), and pine (B) (magnification: 45×).

and-run" accident. A witness saw the car drive off but was unable to get the vehicle license plate number. Nevertheless, the witness *was* able to provide a detailed description of make, color, etc. of the suspect vehicle. A vehicle matching the description was located sometime later, and a sliver of wood was found *behind* one of its headlights. The vehicle owner "recalled" that he had run into his own wooden fence, which had damaged the front wing. The wooden sliver must have become trapped behind the headlight as a direct result of his "bump."

Comparative observation on a SEM revealed a different story. A sample taken from the suspect's fence proved the wood to be birch (Figure 4.11A micrograph), whereas the sliver recovered from behind the headlight was pine (Figure 4.11B micrograph). Samples from the post that had been struck at the accident scene showed that it was also pine. Thus a simple comparison of respective microstructures revealed that the car in question *was* the vehicle involved in the hit-and-run incident.

Both the SEM and ESEM may be coupled to an energy dispersive x-ray analyzer (EDAX) for quantitative, or semiquantitative analysis. EDAX analysis can be performed in a SEM for understanding the chemistry of materials. When the electron beam in the SEM strikes the sample, it excites the atoms of an element, producing x-rays characteristic of the element. The scan is typically displayed in graphical format, with the X-axis showing photon energy and the Y-axis indicating the number of times energy of that photon keV has been generated. Chapter 5, Section 5.2 shows an elemental scan for an aluminum alloy rivet that had been recovered from a failed container. The EDAX scan showed that the rivet was of the correct composition. No sample was destroyed, or altered microstructurally to make this analysis. It is not as precise as a chemical analysis but quite adequate for checking material specifications.

The SEM will provide fractographic and microstructural information, where the EDAX will provide accurate quantitative information on local variations in material composition. In addition to resolving chemical composition, EDAX can be utilized to ascertain unusual microconstituents or contaminants within the material, even down to a single inclusion particle. The advantages of EDAX are that it is fast and easy, but sometimes requires followup work; for example, it will reveal Fe and O, i.e., the elements, but will not readily distinguish Fe_2O_3 or FeO phases. In addition, EDAX can be utilized for quantitative analysis of thick and thin films, semiconductors and some polymers. In difficult cases involving chemical attack, the data provided by microanalysis can be crucial to successfully completing the failure investigation.

An investigation that readily demonstrates the use of the SEM coupled with the power of EDAX involved the theft of a large quantity of copper alloy. A factory, manufacturing extruded copper alloy tubing for steam condensers, suffered a break-in and a large quantity of metal was stolen. The metal in question was a rather unusual brass of 76Cu-22Zn-2Al, and the factory was the only one in that area using aluminum bearing brasses in its manufacturing process. At that time, commercial brasses used for steam condensers and general manufacture of tubing were 70Cu-30Zn and 70Cu-29Zn-1Sn.

A suspect who worked in a nearby iron foundry was apprehended in connection with the robbery. He claimed that he had spent the evening in question drinking with his four buddies, and had never been near the brass tube factory. However, swarf was dug out of the suspect's boot, and compared with a piece of swarf from the floor around a large lathe used to skim billets prior to extrusion. The SEM comparison is shown as a montage in Figure 4.12, where the top half was swarf dug out of the suspect's boot and the bottom half was swarf recovered from the crime scene. As a lathe tool wears, it develops a serrated cutting edge that will produce characteristic score marks rather like the marks on a bullet fired down the barrel of a particular rifle. It can be seen that there is a perfect wear pattern match between the two pieces of swarf that can be considered comparable to a "fingerprint" in conventional detective work. Elemental x-ray analysis on the SEM confirmed that the sample removed from the suspect's boot was an aluminum bearing brass. Therefore the combination of wear fingerprint and alloy composition was more than sufficient evidence to place the suspect at the scene of the crime. It later transpired that the suspect *and* his drinking buddies were perpetrators of the robbery.

Examples of ESEM are given in Sections 6.6 and 9.5.

Figure 4.12 SEM montage of two separate pieces of swarf. The top half was recovered from the boot of a suspect and the bottom half was recovered from the crime scene. Note the perfect tool wear pattern match between the two pieces.

4.5 Mechanical Testing

When considering a metal in relation to an engineered product, the emphasis tends to be on its mechanical response to service loading. Most materials have an elastic limit beyond which other events occur. A totally brittle material will fracture suddenly (like glass) or progressively (like concrete or cement). Most engineering materials do something different; they deform plastically (change their shape in a permanent way).[3,4] It is important to know when and how they do this, and to be able to correlate the data to normal service loads.

4.5.1 Tensile Testing

Component failures can occur by overloading (car accidents, hoist chains, cables and almost anything that is broken in collisions) or the result of poor design, incorrect material selection, manufacturing defects or environmental factors. Mechanical properties of a failed component are, therefore, of prime interest in any failure investigation, as they will provide an insight as to how the component would perform under "service" loading conditions. Some of the most widely quoted mechanical properties are those determined by a tensile test. The tensile test may be used in the selection of material for a particular purpose, or for deciding that the size or shape of a component, manufactured from a specific material, is sufficiently strong to fulfill its design purpose.

60 mm Parallel Length

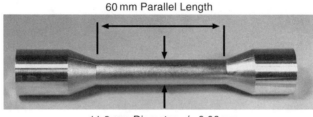

11.2 mm Diameter +/– 0.06 mm
(100 mm² CSA)

Figure 4.13   Specimen geometry for tensile test bars, taken from BS18: 1987.

Specimens for tensile tests are usually machined to a circular cross section or are wires. However, specimens from plates or sheets may be of rectangular section. Each must have a portion of uniform cross-section on which extension measurements are made. To give an indication of size, a typical tensile test bar is shown in Figure 4.13.

In addition to verifying the mechanical response of materials, tensile testing is used as a quality control tool, at the point of product manufacture. Testing at this point will ensure that quality and design specifications are met and maintained before the component or product enters service.

A few of the limitations to the use of tensile testing as a forensic tool are listed below:

- Specimen size and geometry generally require access to volumes of material. This is very rarely the case during a failure investigation.
- Specimen machining costs and preparation time are high.
- There is difficulty in machining a test sample from some materials (i.e., tool steel).
- Specimen dimensions influence load/extension data.
- Care must be taken in identifying the position and direction from which the samples have been taken.
- The associated capital equipment and operational costs are high.

Although generating a wide range of mechanical data (tensile strength, modulus of elasticity, elastic limit, yield point, ductility and breaking strength), the tensile test does not tell the whole story and further mechanical information may be required to permit a satisfactory conclusion to any failure inquiry. When considering that it is often tensile strength of a material that is of importance, hardness testing is a simple nondestructive procedure that will give a reasonable estimate of tensile strength, is nondestructive and can be undertaken on small samples.

4.5.2 Hardness Testing

A hardness test involves measuring the size or depth of an indentation created under pressure from an indenter, usually a diamond or a hardened steel ball. The size or depth of damage gives a measure of the tensile stress of the softer material. Hardness testing can also be used to estimate the resistance to wear (or abrasion) of a material, its tensile strength and the type of heat treatment that it has been subjected to. In addition, because it leaves only a tiny indentation on the surface of the specimen, hardness testing has the advantage of not markedly altering any evidence the surface may contain.[5]

Although a large number of cases presented in this work utilize the Vickers hardness test, it is important to remember that there are a *variety* of hardness test methods, some of which are outlined below. These vary from a scale of what scratches what (Moh's) through measuring the size of an impression left by an indenter under a known load (Vickers and Brinell), to measuring the depth to which an indenter penetrates under specified conditions (Rockwell B & C scale). The Vickers test using a diamond pyramid can be used with very small loads (down to a few grams), and will give results comparable with standard tests that produce indentations measuring up to 1 mm across. In addition, there are also ultrasonic methods of hardness testing.

4.5.3 Moh's Hardness Test

The Moh's hardness scale — commonly referred to as scratch hardness — is widely used by mineralogists. It is used when examining metals, where a hardened steel scriber or file may be used to see whether it scratches the surface. It is a quick and easy test to determine whether a component, such as a transmission shaft, has been case hardened. If a metal file slides over the surface without scratching it, the material is said to be file hard, which usually means the surface has a hardness above 800 on the Vickers scale.

4.5.4 Vickers Hardness Test

The Vickers hardness test involves measuring the size of an impression left by a 136° diamond pyramid indenter (see Figure 4.14), under a specified load. A hardness machine is used to hold the sample being examined and for applying the diamond indent. The indent diagonals are measured with a calibrated, low power optical microscope and the measured value is known as the Vickers hardness number Hv (see Table 4.1).

Microhardness measurement is possible using the Vickers test, but does require a polished surface. With indentation loads of less than 500 g the results are not quite the same as those obtained with the standard Vickers hardness test.

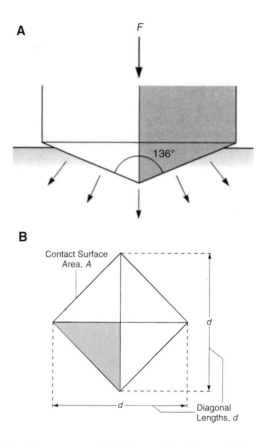

Figure 4.14 (A) Vickers pyramidal diamond indenter. (B) Impression on the surface of a test specimen.

4.5.5 Brinell Hardness Test

Similar in principle and operation to the Vickers test, the Brinell hardness test involves a hardened steel ball indenter. Hardness is expressed as the Brinell hardness number, BHN or HB. The Brinell test utilizes either a 1- or 10-mm-diameter steel ball in place of a diamond pyramid. Because the ball is steel, it can itself deform under load and will result in misleading readings on hard surfaces (hardness > 600 Hv). Use of the 10-mm ball allows one indentation to sample over a larger area of the component than can be accomplished with a Vickers diamond indenter. For the failure investigator it is, therefore, a useful method for testing items such as castings, where coarse grains can give different readings in different places if a small indenter (such as a 1-mm ball or Vickers diamond) is used.

4.5.6 Rockwell Hardness Test

The Rockwell C scale (R_c) is the most widely used hardness scale for workshop measurements of steel tools and hardened artifacts since they are relatively unaffected by shallow surface effects such as decarburization. The objects to be tested are indented with a diamond cone and the depth of penetration measured. The significant difference in principle is a prior application of an initial light load, followed by a further load being applied, at which point the *additional* depth of penetration is measured. Application of a preload means no surface preparation is required. Readings are taken directly from a dial and therefore minimal skill is required to perform the test. For testing the hardness of nonferrous materials, the Rockwell B hardness test is used, where a steel ball is used as an indenter.

4.5.7 Tensile Strength and Hv

It can be shown that the Vickers hardness test (Hv) bears a direct relationship to the tensile strength (σ_{TS}) of a material. However, the way in which a material responds will depend on the ratio of its yield stress (σ_y) to Young's modulus (E). For softer metals with a low σ_{TS}/E, it is found that

$$Hv = 3\sigma_{TS} \qquad (4.1)$$

where Hv is the Vickers hardness number. (*Note:* Hv is cited in units of N mm^{-2}, so σ_{TS} must have the same units in the above equation.)

For materials with higher σ_Y/E (including a wide range of metals, glasses and plastics), the relationship between Hv and σ_{TS} becomes more complex. However, for steels there is a useful empirical relationship between tensile strength (in MN m^{-2}) and Hv (in N mm^{-2}), namely,

$$\sigma_{TS} = 3.2 \ Hv \qquad (4.2)$$

Typical values of Hv for a range of material are shown in Table 4.1. When specimens are small or when standard test bars for tensile or shear testing cannot be taken from material evidence, a hardness test may be the only means of obtaining a useful estimate of the tensile strength of the material. A relationship between the different hardness testing methods can be shown in an approximate equivalent hardness table, shown in Table 4.2.

Any investigative tool can be used in isolation, or in combination with others to reinforce findings. A particular case relating to production difficulties of surgical eye probes concisely illustrates the versatile use of both hardness testing and electron microscopy during the course of an investigation.

Table 4.1 Typical Values of Vickers Hardness Number, Hv, for a Range of Different Materials

Material	H_v N mm^{-2}	Material	H_v N mm^{-2}	Material	H_v N mm^{-2}
Tin	5	Limestone	250	Tungsten carbide	2500
Aluminium	25	MgO	500	Polycarbonate	14
Gold	35	Window glass	550	PVC	16
Copper	40	Fused silica	720	Polyacetal	18
Iron	80	Granite	850	PMMA	20
Mild steel	140	Quartz	1200	Polystyrene	21
Fully hardened steel	900	Al_2O_3	2500	Epoxy	45

Table 4.2 Relationship between Brinell and Rockwell Methods of Hardness Testing

$H_{v\ 30}$	Brinell	Brinell	Rockwell (R_c)	Equivalent tensile strength of steel (MPa)
700	615	665	60.1	2100
600	550	564	55.2	1850
400	379	379	40.8	1250
200	190	190	(11.0)	620
100	95	95	Unsuitable	300

Over many years, a manufacturer had been producing titanium (Ti-6Al-4V) surgical eye probes. Unexpectedly, he began to experience problems during a final thermal hardening process. The treatment, successfully used in the past, was failing to produce desired strength and "springiness" within the finished units. The Ti-6Al-4V had been drawn directly from the manufacturer's own stock. Briefly, two samples of eye probes were examined: one from a successful batch that exhibited the required mechanical characteristics of hardness and degree of stiffness and the other from an unsuccessful batch. Additional instructions from the manufacturer were to recommend a suitable thermal treatment that would allow the hardness level of the unsuccessful batch of probes to be increased to a value approaching 500 Hv.

Microhardness testing found that the unsuccessful batch had a hardness range of 201 to 210 Hv, compared to 511 to 537 Hv obtained for the successful batch. Microstructural observation revealed fine equiaxed alpha grains and intergranular beta — typically a Ti-6Al-4V structure (Figure 4.15A), whereas Figure 4.15B shows equiaxed recrystallized grains of alpha — typically a commercially pure (CP) titanium structure. To verify the findings, elemental

Longitudinal Section   Transverse Section

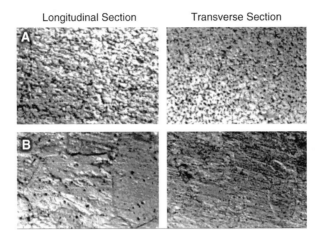

Figure 4.15 Optical micrographs obtained from a "good" eye probe (A) and from a partially fabricated probe from the suspect batch (B). Magnification: 400×.

x-ray analysis was undertaken and confirmed that two different titanium systems had been used, i.e.,

- The successful batch of eye probes had been manufactured from Ti-6Al-4V alloy.
- The unsuccessful batch had been manufactured from CP titanium.

Further thermal treatment on the CP titanium was undertaken in an attempt to improve the hardness by grain size modification. The type of thermal cycle, hardness and resultant microstructures are presented in Figure 4.16. The microstructure that displayed the highest hardness and minimal scatter was obtained by thermally treating the CP titanium for 0.5 h at 950°C, water quenching plus 8 h at 500°C, followed by air cooling. It was evident that thermal treatment could be utilized to enhance the hardness of CP titanium. However, this was a simple grain modification phenomenon.

Advice given to the manufacturer was twofold: with company product liability in mind, opinion was that the CP titanium eye probes be scrapped. Furthermore, it was recommended that the manufacturer urgently focus attention on stock control procedures especially for such expensive materials. It was failure of such procedures that had allowed incorrect material to enter the production line initially.

4.5.8 Bend Tests

Tension is also encountered in bending, and there are several kinds of test for bending simple shapes like beams of uniform section. Thus a beam can be loaded at three points and strained to failure. As the beam is deformed,

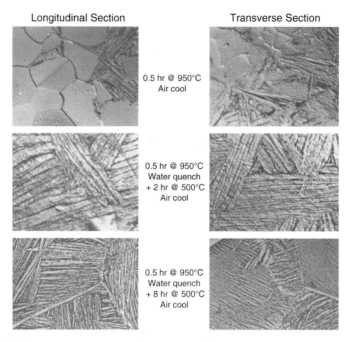

Figure 4.16 Microstructures of commercially pure (CP) titanium obtained by thermal treatment (magnification: 400×).

one surface is deformed into a convex shape and the material here is in tension, while the opposite surface is deformed into a concave shape where it is under compression. It is often thought that forensic work, being scientific by nature, must always be accompanied by long mathematical arguments. However, this is not the case as simple logic matched against the evidence is the only way in which causation is determined. Nevertheless, there are occasions where quantitative evaluation becomes valuable. A simple equation used for evaluating stresses and strains on beams in bending is the "engineer's bending equation":

$$M/I = \sigma /y = E/R$$

where M is the moment on the beam, I the second moment of area of the beam section, σ the stress at a distance y across the beam section, E the tensile modulus of the beam material and R the radius of curvature of the bent beam (Figure 4.17). Some of these variables become constant when a single type of beam is considered under two different loading conditions. Thus E is constant (same material) and I is constant (same section shape).

A particular case that required calculation of strain on the outside of a bend occurred when a manufacturer encountered a problem when forming

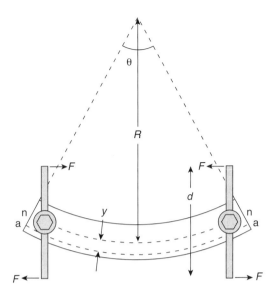

Figure 4.17 A state of bending caused by applying equal and opposite forces at the ends of a beam.

5-mm-thick sheet aluminum in a vehicle body pressing plant. The manufacturer supplied samples of both intact and cracked press formed bends and verified that all parameters (tooling, processing, etc.) were identical.

Visual observation of the two panels showed that forming processes had *not* been identical (Figure 4.18). Measurement of the uncracked sample revealed an inside radius of 7 mm, whereas the cracked sample had been formed to an inside radius of 3 mm. A simple bending strain calculation (Figure 4.19) indicated that the strain of the outer skin was of the order of 26% in the satisfactory batch, compared with 45% in the unsatisfactory.

It was therefore considered that the bend radius was the major cause of the cracking, as the smaller radius was introducing 45% strain at the outer surface of the bend — well above the ductility of the aluminum sheet.

4.5.9 Torsion Testing

Torsion testing provides a method for determining the modulus of elasticity in shear, shearing yield strength and the ultimate shear strength. It is useful for examining and testing parts such as axles, shafts, couplings and twist drills, and can be used to good advantage in the testing of brittle materials. Torsion testing has the advantage of no necking (as in a tensile test) or friction. Furthermore, the test data are generally valid to larger values of strain than are tension test data. However, torsion testing as a tool for the failure investigator will be subject to the same limitations as tensile testing above. Many engineering components have safety devices based on shear

Figure 4.18   Sections across 90° bends from cracked and uncracked aluminum vehicle body panels. Note the two different radii. For scale, leg length = 50 mm (2 in.).

Bending strain calculation:

$\varepsilon_x = \dfrac{y}{R}$ where y = distance from neutral axes and R = radius of curvature of neutral axes. In this case, $y = y_{max}$ = distance to outer fiber

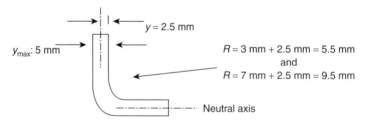

Situation (1) where inside radius of bend ≈3 mm:

$$\varepsilon_x = \frac{y}{R} = \frac{2.5 \times 10^{-6}}{5.5 \times 10^{-6}}$$

$$= 0.45 \text{ or } 45\% \text{ strain}$$

Situation (2) where inside radius of bend ≈7mm:

$$\varepsilon_x = \frac{y_{max}}{R} = \frac{2.5 \times 10^{-6}}{9.5 \times 10^{-6}}$$

$$= 0.26 \text{ or } 26\% \text{ strain}$$

Figure 4.19   Strain calculations at the outside of a bend.

pins that limit the amount or torque or bending moment that may be transmitted. In this way these cheap devices protect the rest of the more expensive mechanism from expensive overload. They function in a similar way to a fuse in an electrical circuit. Indeed in some circumstances shear pins are called "fuse-pins" or "fuse links." Flywheels, storing energy in rotating machines, may cause severe damage if the machine is suddenly stopped for any reason. By incorporating a shear pin the damage is greatly reduced. Their designers need to know the applied force that will cause them to fail by shear overload. Many airliner engines are attached to their mounting pylons in this way, and are designed to shear away if engine vibrations risk damage to the airframe.

4.6 Indirect Strain Measurement

Hardness measurements are one way in which the material response to a given load can be measured directly in a standard way. The strain produced by application of the load changes the dimensions of a small part of the surface of the material. However, are there any other ways in which the strain to which a sample has been exposed can be determined? The question is important for forensic work as large deformations and strains are frequently found in failed specimens, such as car parts recovered from accidents. Strain *monitoring* techniques are well known for structural analysis of components at the design stage of product development. A standard load will be applied to such products, and the strain in different parts of the structure monitored by strain gauges.

4.6.1 Brittle Lacquer

Brittle lacquers can be used to provide a simple and direct way of estimating the degree of strain in deformed bodies. The product is coated with a thin layer of brittle polymer, using a solution of the polymer in an organic solvent. After drying it forms a thin uniform film that is well bonded to the underlying metal. When strained to a high degree, the metal deforms plastically, and the thin film also deforms. Because it is brittle, however, the film cracks at only very small strains, so that it is covered with a pattern of cracks that reflect the underlying plastic deformation of the metal product. The cracks are oriented at right angles to the tensile strains in the metal, so the method allows easy identification of the plastic deformation. In other words, the crack pattern bears witness to the loading history of the product, as shown in Figure 4.20, for example.

This basic idea can be used for identifying loading patterns in failed products, and the case where a cyclist was injured after riding into the back

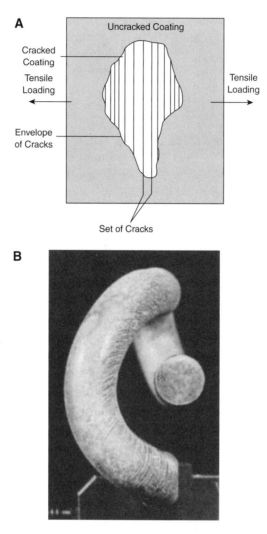

Figure 4.20 A schematic diagram of parallel cracks in a lacquer under tensile loading (A) and cracks in the brittle lacquer on a pandrol clip used for holding down railway lines, caused by elastic strain (reversible) (B).

of a parked vehicle describes the technique of brittle lacquer coating in action. In this case the brittle lacquer coating was applied as a protective (and decorative) finish. A young man suffered injury when riding home on a bicycle, after working a night shift. It was raining and just starting to get light. He claimed a poor weld on the frame head tube broke, causing him to ride into the back of a van that was parked without lights. The bicycle frame had been sent to a laboratory, where the head tube was cut out for closer examination. Subsequently, the section was sent for independent opinion as to the cause of failure.

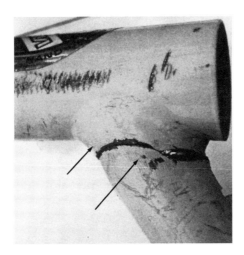

Figure 4.21 Head tube of a cycle frame showing cracking, resulting from plastic strain prior to fracture, in its "brittle lacquer" paint coating.

On receipt of the head tube section, the first observation was the clear presence of cracks in the yellow paint (Figure 4.21). It was determined that other markings on the head tube were severe scratches, emanating from vice jaws — the frame had been held in a vice while hack-sawing the section and had nothing to do with the actual failure. However, the weld at the bottom of the head tube of the cycle frame revealed an interesting pattern of strain cracks. The paint had acted as a brittle lacquer, and bore witness to the fact that the steel tube had undergone extensive deformation under frontal impact *before* the weld failed.

The scenario can be reconstructed: the rider, head down, half asleep after a night shift, gritting his teeth as he rode into the rain, ran straight into the back of the unlit parked van; the weld failed under the impact. There was no evidence whatever of fatigue cracking in the fracture surface. If there *had* been a preexisting crack, the paint film on either side of it would *not* have exhibited strain cracks.

4.6.2   Crack Detection Methods

Cracks on the surface of a component can often be seen by eye. These cracks are convincing pieces of evidence for structural failure. A crack is an opening of the material that must have been formed by strain, no matter how small. Several methods are available for detecting hairline cracks and are used to discover whether there are any cracks in a worn component, such as a crank-shaft, before regrinding or refurbishing. Such methods are routinely used for inspection of safety-critical parts, such as bodies and wings of aircraft, pressure vessels and so on. For example, in July 2000 hairline cracks in parts of the wing structure of a British Airways Concorde were detected by routine inspection using ultrasonic and dye-penetrant methods. However, it has to be emphasized that they were not relevant to the subsequent Paris disaster. Welds in oil and gas pipelines are usually inspected using portable x-ray apparatus, where the simple product structure allows easy use.

4.6.3 Other Crack Detection Techniques

Ultrasonic crack detection is a technique in which a pulse of ultrasound is injected into a component from a transmitter probe and the echo detected using a receiver probe. Both surface and internal defects can be detected by this technique.

Dye-penetrant examination is a versatile and simple technique but is only suitable for defects that break into a free surface. The component is sprayed with a penetrating dye, which is allowed to soak into the cracks by capillary action. The surface is then cleaned off with a removing solvent. However, the dye remains in any crack-like defect. The component is then sprayed with a chalky powder that acts as a "developer." This draws out the dye from the defect and highlights its presence in the white developer layer. This technique however cannot be used to measure the penetration depth of the crack. In addition, the sample has to be cleaned before and after testing, as the liquid penetrant may corrode the metal. It proved useful in an investigation on a broken ice skate blade (Figure 4.22A). The stainless steel blade under suspicion was from one particular batch, and had been returned broken after only a few hours of use. Dye-penetrant examination revealed many sites where surface cracking had initiated and propagated in service (Figure 4.22B). Simple metallography revealed a brittle microstructure, being a direct result of incorrect (too high) tempering temperature of the batch in question. The blade fabricator was obliged to review his quality control and monitoring methods.

Magnetic particle inspection is a technique only applicable to ferromagnetic materials. The component is painted with a white paint and then placed in a strong magnetic field. The attachment of strong horseshoe permanent magnets is often sufficient. Any cracks in the component produce local magnetic poles and when "ink" consisting of iron, or iron oxide, particles in paraffin is sprayed on to the component the particles settle at these poles and highlight the crack. Once again it is only applicable to surface cracks in ferromagnetic materials, but is very quick and cost effective. A similar technique is that of ultraviolet (UV) examination of fluorescent inks.

Radiography can be used to detect cracks. However, it is not always successful in detecting cracks unless the line of the crack is parallel or nearly

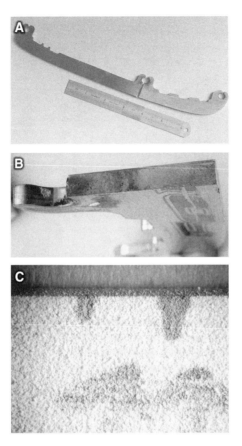

Figure 4.22 Broken ice-skate blade (A), optical photograph of fracture surface (B) and surface cracking revealed by dye-penetrant examination (C).

parallel with the x-ray beam, Figure 4.23. Radiographs will reveal whether defects or discontinuities are present in castings, forgings and weldments, in addition to polymeric and other nonmetallic parts. Information that can be gathered from radiographs would include surface cracking, internal voids, reinforcing flow patterns, density of reinforcing and fiber orientation (particularly at critically stressed points).

Soft x-rays are useful for showing the internal structure (including internal cracks) of composite material products, and even thermoplastic components. The technique was used in a dispute concerning the quality of gas injection–molded office chair arms (Chapter 5, Section 5.10). The defendants would not allow the samples to be sectioned physically, so the expert for the claimants suggested a trip to the local hospital to radiograph the arms nondestructively. On inspection of the radiograph, it was seen that the gas pocket

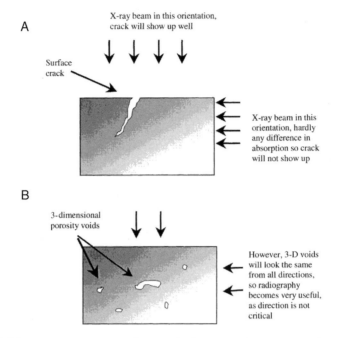

Figure 4.23 X-ray orientation for crack detection (A), compared with three-dimensional voids (B).

had penetrated the lower zone of attachment to the shell. The point being made is that the defect was detected *without* physically altering the component.

The technique has further advantages for failure investigation in that information obtained from a radiograph is often of value when choosing a location for sectioning. For example, radiographs can be utilized to determine a site that will provide optimum information for metallographic sectioning and examination. More to the point, it will allow choice of sectioning site that will not *destroy* useful information. However, one major limitation of the technique is that, for all samples, cracks that are inclined or perpendicular to the beam are very difficult to detect as they have little effect on beam absorbance (Figure 4.23).

This method is vital to personal injury cases, such as when a young man suffered injury when using a circular saw. A tooth came off an almost new blade and went right through his eye, lodging close to his brain. The final position was so delicate that surgeons could not risk removing it. However, x-rays taken at different angles allowed identification as a tungsten carbide tooth of the same dimensions as those on the failed blade, two of which were found to have broken off due to faulty brazing.

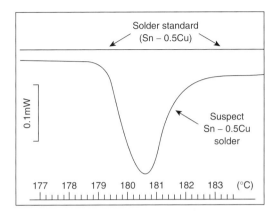

Figure 4.24 Comparative differential scanning calorimetry (DSC) scan of suspect eutectic Sn-0.5Cu solder against that of a known standard sample. Melting temperature for the solder is 227°C. The suspect solder displayed a low temperature (~186°C) melting phase.

4.7   Chemical and Thermal Analysis

4.7.1   Differential Scanning Calorimetry (DSC)

Differential scanning calorimetry is a technique used to examine the thermal properties of materials under carefully controlled conditions. Only milligram amounts of material are needed, so although the method is destructive, sampling is minimal. The sample is heated at a constant rate (typically 10°C/min), and the heat flow into or from the sample automatically recorded by the instrument. Heat is absorbed when a sample melts (an endothermic change), and the melting point T_m is often characteristic of the chemical composition of the material under study, as the following examples indicate.

An electronic circuit board fabricator began to experience component registration difficulties on a batch of surface mount (SMT) boards that had been fabricated by wave soldering. The board profile was one that had up to that time never given rise to any production problem. However, for the batch in question, the incidence of chip misregistration (along with associated board rework) climbed to an intolerable level. The board fabricator suspected the solder itself as the potential source of his problem.

It was a eutectic tin–copper alloy, from which a sample of the parent stock was submitted for examination. Analyses were undertaken and compared to that of a known pure sample. DSC revealed (Figure 4.24) a liquid phase, existing at approximately 179 to 182°C. It was immediately apparent that such a liquid phase would allow time for surface mount components to "float" out of registration, rather than freezing instantly at the eutectic temperature. The source of this unexpected phase was subsequently traced to cross contamination from a previous melt, requiring the solder producer/supplier to review his quality control procedures — with some urgency!

As electronic components and devices become smaller, the incidence of early failure is also on the increase. For domestic products, failure may be acceptable but for avionics applications a zero failure rate is pursued.

A further case concerned a printed circuit board (PCB) subcontractor who undertook the manufacture of a prototype board, utilizing a production line that had been recently shut down because of a lack of firm orders. However, it very quickly became apparent that the prototype was prone to unacceptably high failure during its "burn-in" stage. Electrical testing and observation under low power optical magnification located the problem to a series of ceramic chip capacitors (Figure 4.25A). Subsequent examination of a metallographic section, taken through one of the problem components (Figure 4.25B), suggested that there was no obvious fault with the discrete component. However, closer examination of the interface between the joint solder and copper board tracking on an SEM revealed internal cracking just above the solder intermetallic line (Figure 4.25C and Figure 4.25D). EDAX analysis of the solder showed that it was within specification (Figure 4.25E) and was not the direct culprit.

Thermal profiling of the board showed a localized hot-spot in the region of failure, generated by local power components. However, cracking of the type observed was a direct result of thermal fatigue. This failure mode had been induced by the cyclic nature of board burn-in combined with a mismatch of thermal expansion coefficients of the ceramic capacitor and FP4 resin circuit board. The fatigue mode had been exacerbated by having a localized hot-spot.

Differential scanning calorimetry is even more useful for polymers, where additional information includes the glass transition temperature (T_g, the temperature at which the plastic becomes elastomeric) and the decomposition temperature, when the material decomposes. While pure metals melt at sharply defined temperatures and alloys melt over a range, polymers melt over a wider range that is less sharply defined. That range is also sensitive to the heating rate and the molecular weight of the polymer as well as changes in chemical composition.

The variable degree of crystallinity in polymers is yet another difference between the two classes of material. Many polymers are totally noncrystalline and only exhibit a glass transition temperature. Thus PMMA (Plexiglas or Perspex) is quite transparent and has excellent optical properties, precisely because it is noncrystalline. Other polymers show some crystallinity, but only rarely does it approach 100%. Ultra-high-performance materials such as

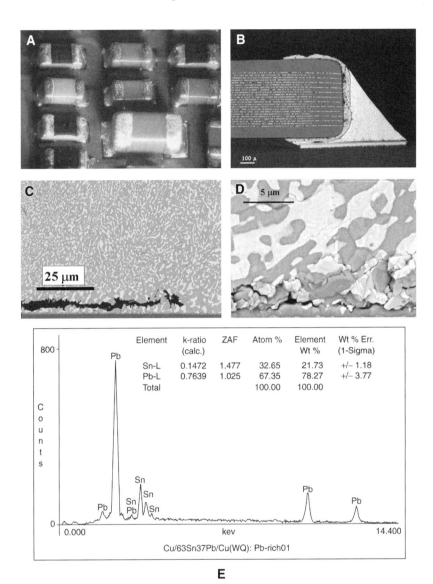

Figure 4.25 (A) Ceramic capacitors on printed circuit board (PCB). (B) Section through a failed ceramic capacitor. (C and D) Cracking within solder joint. (E) EDAX analysis of solder.

aramid (Kevlar, Twaron) or UHMPE fiber (Dyneema, Spectra) are exceptional in that the polymer chains are fully aligned along the fiber axis. The degree of crystallinity in common partly crystalline polymers such as polypropylene is thus variable, depends on how the polymer has been processed, and can be measured using DSC. Values of T_g and T_m are tabulated.[6] A case example where DSC proved of great value in unraveling the truth

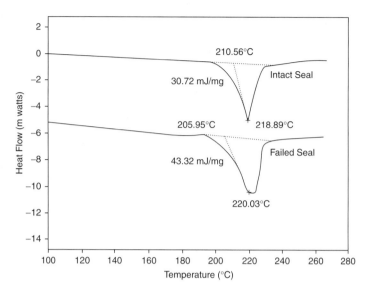

Figure 4.26 Melting behavior of new intact and failed seals made from Hytrel thermoplastic elastomer as shown by DSC spectra.

concerned the widespread failure of simple round washers for sealing radiator bleed valves. A new polymer, a thermoplastic elastomer (Hytrel, a block copolymer of a polyester and a polyether) was introduced in the U.K. to overcome the problem of leaking taps from fiber washers. It worked well in both hot and cold water taps, but failed in radiator valves. Comparison of an intact new seal and a failed seal showed a significant increase in crystallinity (Figure 4.26). Exposure to continuous high temperatures of a central heating system could increase the crystallinity with adverse effects on the strength of the seal, ultimately leading to cracking. The DSC curves show the increase in heat of fusion from about 30 mJ/mg to well over 40 mJ/mg as a result of exposure.

4.7.2 Infrared Spectroscopy

Spectroscopy involves exposure of a thin sample to a beam of infrared radiation and recording the absorption spectrum of the material. The nature of the polymer chains produces absorption at particular wavelengths which are characteristic of the polymer, and so is a primary aid to identification of the material. When fillers and other additives are used in the material, more complex spectra are obtained simply because extra absorption occurs. There are at least two ways of preparing the sample thin enough for analysis. Films must generally be 20- to 60-μm thick, so that the infrared beam can pass through the sample. A thin film can be cast from a suitable solution of the polymer (not always easy since many polymers are insoluble in common

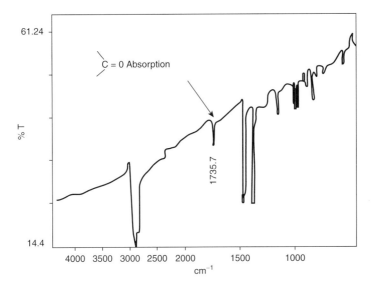

Figure 4.27 Infrared spectrum of polypropylene component inside metal crutch, showing carbonyl absorption indicative of oxidative degradation.

solvents) or a thin slice cut using a microtome. Even a slice cut using a sharp scalpel can yield useful information if a microtome is unavailable. Solvent casting is useful where the matrix polymer must be determined because most inorganic fillers are insoluble and not carried over into the thin film. However, cut sections are vital if the material is to be examined in its original state. FTIR (Fourier transform IR) is a sophisticated form of spectroscopy where the thin sample can be scanned repeatedly so as to improve resolution.

The method is so important for polymers that it is routinely used for failed materials, although care is needed since the method is partly destructive. For example, when a disabled woman was badly injured by fracture of her crutch, the plastic part that cracked was analyzed as shown in Figure 4.27. The spectrum from a solvent-cast film showed that the material was a polypropylene copolymer. However, it exhibited anomalous absorption at 1736 cm^{-1}, as found by comparison with reference spectra.[7] Oxidation of the material is usually found at this position, and can be caused by poor processing at too high a temperature. When material degrades, the chains are broken and the strength falls, which explains why the crutch broke when the woman put her weight onto the device. The plastic connector fractured and she was injured as a direct result.

A second, quite different example reinforces the point. A rotational molder of large products like mancabs and road cones suffered a number of premature failures due to brittle cracking. The process route involves placing preweighed polyethylene powder into a tool that is then closed and rotated

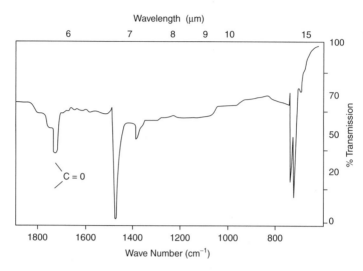

Figure 4.28   Infrared spectrum of a roto-molded polyethylene road cone showing intense absorption due to oxidation and UV attack leading to brittle cracking.

in a large oven. The plastic melts and sticks to the walls, where it solidifies
when the oven is cooled. High process temperatures are needed due to the
high viscosity of molten polymer. Oxidation tends to occur at the outer
surfaces of the product, and when exposed to sunlight, the chains degrade
preferentially at these points. Figure 4.28 shows the enlarged oxidation peak
in a thin solvent-cast film from a road cone that had been attacked by the
UV radiation present in sunlight (the same radiation produces sunburn).
The problem was solved by adding a UV absorber (which acts like sunburn
cream) and antioxidant to the raw power polymer.

Derived infrared techniques offer completely nondestructive analysis of
small samples. Thus FTIR microscopy involves using an infrared microbeam
to be shone through film, fibers or even dust samples in an optical microscope. The technique was used almost incidentally in a failed catheter case,
and showed the presence of degraded products that should not have been
present if the material had showed any integrity (Chapter 9). The surfaces
of samples can be analyzed using attenuated total reflection (ATR) spectroscopy, where the IR beam is channeled onto the surface and reflected back
for analysis in the usual way.

4.7.3   Chromatography

Another technique unique to polymers is GPC, or gel permeation chromatography. It yields information on the molecular mass (molecular weight) of
a polymer (or the chain length). As mechanical strength is directly related to
molecular mass, it is a powerful method when investigating failed polymers.

The technique uses a polymer solution in suitable organic solvent that is introduced into a column containing a cross-linked gel. As the solution passes down the column, the smaller chains are absorbed by the gel, leaving the longer chains to be eluted first. The smaller chains are then released, so giving a distribution curve for the sample. The molecular mass distribution will typically show a single peak and a tail at either side. Degradation of chain length that occurs in oxidation will show as a lateral shift of the whole curve to lower molecular mass. The method was used in a battery case problem, where GPC showed the chain degradation on exposed surfaces when compared with hidden surfaces (Chapter 7).

4.7.4 Other Methods

There is a multiplicity of other techniques that are used to probe polymer structure and the pathology of chain materials.[8] Spectroscopy is not limited to infrared radiation, but can include UV and Raman (far infrared). One very important type of analysis is NMR (nuclear magnetic resonance) which detects hydrogen nuclei in different environments. The method has become well known for magnetic resonance imaging (MRI) of the brain, but is well used by organic chemists for structure determination. It is a very powerful method for probing the structure of polymers. As such, it was used in an intellectual property case to check on the presence of a particular ingredient in wall plaster mixes.

The problem arose when a new type of plaster was developed to replace asbestos-modified plaster. Asbestos was added to extend the viscosity range of the solidifying plaster, a key property for plasterers in achieving that perfectly flat finish. Because of the toxicity of asbestos, the company decided to replace the ingredient with a polyelectrolyte. Then a senior manager left and set up his own company making the same product. This was a breach of confidentiality, so we were asked to compare the two plasters for the secret ingredient. It proved intractable: FTIR could not disentangle the several ingredients from one another, as the spectrum from bone glue dominated the absorption. In desperation, a selective solvent (deuterated DMF) was used to extract selectively the polyelectrolyte. It succeeded in confirming that the two plasters did indeed contain the same secret ingredient when their NMR spectra were compared. The dispute was resolved without going to court, and the original company won its case for its monopoly rights.

4.7.5 Integrity of Analysis

When such special methods are use for analysis, care is needed to ensure that they retain their integrity. One test for integrity is reproducibility: can another expert perform the same test and achieve the same result? It means that all experimental conditions must be recorded and published, or passed on to other experts. It is also a test worth performing on one's own results, to check that the spectrum really is showing what it is meant to show and not an artifact. Using automatic recording instruments demands that calibration tests are performed at regular intervals to check machine integrity. For DSC, indium, a low melting metal, with known melting point of 156.6°C, is analyzed during routine calibration. A standard spectrum of polystyrene is used for the same purpose in FTIR spectroscopy, as it possesses numerous absorption peaks at known wavelengths. Internal standards such as tetramethyl silane (TMS) are routinely used in NMR to measure chemical shifts of an unknown compound. Several different techniques that measure the same quantity are also used to corroborate results independently. Many of the more recent methods can also be checked by an interlaboratory test, where a compound of known composition is sent to each lab and analyzed blind. This has been done for GPC, and revealed frighteningly large discrepancies.

The importance of the reproducibility test was highlighted recently during the investigation of failed electric plugs. The Noryl casings were cracking and exposing live wires to the fingers of the user, making the manufacturer directly liable for any injuries. The plugs in question had been moulded at a factory in China, and it was our opinion that the process itself had caused widespread cracking of the transformer plugs. However, a forensic group in Japan disputed our conclusion. They claimed that too much fire retardant had been added to one batch of the material in Europe, so weakening the moulded plug casing. They based their conclusions on alcoholic extracts of the plugs analyzed using FTIR. When we analyzed the same plugs using SEM-EDAX (a method quite independent of FTIR), we could not corroborate their findings, and requested checks on their method. We never received their experimental details, and the original conclusions of faulty molding were finally accepted. Quality checks in the factory have been improved to prevent a recurrence of the problem.[9]

The same general principles apply to all the techniques of analysis and inspection described in this chapter and, if not applied rigorously, can lead to the kind of ambiguity and contradiction that led to the dispute in the first place. Although lawyers will often want the bare minimum of testing to be undertaken in a dispute, they do not normally have to appear in a witness box to defend the results.

4.8 Closing Comments

There are several points to make concerning failures of engineered products. First, it is surprising how much can be gleaned from the material evidence of failure, especially when linked to witness or other documentary evidence. It is this approach to evidence that is the clue to unraveling product failures and accidents. Above all else, a common sense approach is required. In effect, the investigator tries to explain the failure by sifting the evidence carefully so as to reveal key or critical parts that show how the incident occurred. On occasion, this may be limited to a bundle of documentary evidence, where the expert will be required to "weed-out" relevant information on the matter at hand. At times it might be review of a fracture surface that shows fatigue striations; at other times it might be the trace of a metal part on a roadway. Every so often, the microstructure of a small particle will reveal its origin, and hence allow a sequence of events to be constructed. Often the sifting process will be long and painstaking (especially when a large and complex device, such as an aircraft, fails) but at other times, it may be the speed of reaction to unfolding events that solves the problem at hand. Thus, a photograph taken "just in time" can short-circuit an investigation, particularly when the evidence is deliberately removed or tampered with at a later time.

Second, there is no doubt that experience and a working knowledge of typical failure modes of products can help elucidate the problem. Then, when abnormal features are revealed, another cause of failure must be sought. Thus abuse in service will often be shown by an abnormal pattern of wear or traces on the failed product that indicate lubricant starvation, for example. On the other hand, if no such traces are found, then an unusual or unexpected cause may be suspected. Stress corrosion cracking is sometimes difficult to recognize, especially if the chemical or corrosion products that initiated failure have long since disappeared. However, modern methods of analysis will usually pick up traces of the chemical on the fracture surface, so that positive conclusions can be drawn. SEM-EDAX is a good example of one such technique that yields not only excellent deep images of the fracture, but can also show up the chemical cause of fracture using elemental analysis of the x-rays emitted by the specimen.

Third, individual experience of failure can be vastly extended and enhanced by learning from others. An awareness of the growing publicly available literature, which examines product failure in depth, should be developed and continually honed. Such articles usually focus on specific failures investigated by others, and highlight the way investigations are tackled, the methods chosen for analysis and the chain of reasoning that reveals the cause or causes of that particular failure (or small group of failures). These reports show graphically what tools have been chosen from the toolbox of methods, why they have been chosen and what evidence they can reveal by careful application. It is also true to say that, for metals, methods such as hardness testing and microscopy (both optical and electron optical) allied to metallography are the first options in any laboratory investigation. In the same way, FTIR, DSC and microscopy are common starting points for studying failed polymer products.

References

1. Davies, J.R., Ed., *Metals Handbook Desk Edition,* 2nd ed., ASM, Materials Park, OH, 1998.

2. Newby, J., *ASM Handbook, Vol. 1: Properties and Selection: Irons, Steels, and High Performance Alloys*, 10th ed., ASM International, Materials Park, OH, 1990.

3. Newby, J., Ed., *ASM Handbook, Vol. 8: Mechanical Testing*, 9th ed., ASM International, Materials Park, OH, 1989.

4. Newby, J., Ed., *ASM Handbook, Vol. 9: Metallography and Microstructures*, 9th ed., ASM International, Materials Park, OH, 1989.

5. Weidmann, G., Lewis, P., and Reid, N., Eds., *Structural Materials,* Materials in Action Series, Butterworths, London, 1990.

6. Brandrup, J. and Immergut, E.H., Eds., *Polymer Handbook,* 3rd ed., John Wiley, New York, 1989.

7. Hummel, D.O., Ed., *Polymer and Plastics Analysis*, 2nd ed., Carl Hanser Verlag, Munich, 1978.

8. Crompton, T.R., Ed., *Analysis of Polymers: An Introduction*, Pergamon Press, Oxford, 1989.

9. Lewis, P.R., Premature fracture of Noryl transformer plugs, oral presentation, FAPSIG session, ANTEC 2003, Nashville, TN, 2003.

Failure Due to Manufacturing Faults

5

5.1 Traumatic Failure

Nowadays it is unusual for components with serious faults to find their way into service, principally because of the rigorous quality control procedures used in manufacture. However, from time to time failures are encountered and, when the fault has a serious weakening effect, failure often occurs on the first occasion the component comes under heavy load. Chapter 2 quoted the example of a set of racing wheels for a sports car, one of which had spokes drastically thinned down to where they blended into the hub due to poor machining practice. The outer part of the wheel broke away from the hub as the car entered the first curve in a race, traveling at about 160 mph. The tire and outer rim bounced over the safety barrier into the crowd and the car struck the barrier and was almost completely wrecked. There was nothing seriously wrong with the metal or the casting — the responsibility rested entirely with the firm that undertook the machining.

Almost every casting is a one-off, in the sense that faults stemming from the way a particular volume of metal solidifies — shrinkage, porosity, gas entrapment, blowholes, misruns, cold shuts and so on — may not be repeated in other castings made in the same foundry. Figure 2.3 (see Chapter 2) shows severe shrinkage in a malleable cast iron wheel hub from a trailer that failed immediately after being loaded for the first time and turned into the road. Figure 5.1 is a section across an aluminum alloy brake lug from an almost new motorcycle, which broke away and rendered the brake inoperative on the first occasion the rider had to make an emergency stop. A young child was killed. The lug was an integral part of a cast brake plate that was grossly

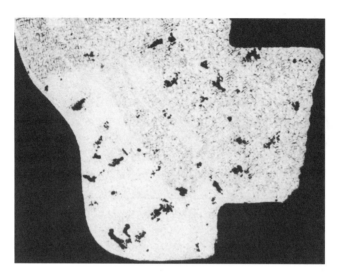

Figure 5.1 Section across the fractured brake lug from the motorcycle (fracture at right-hand side).

weakened by gas porosity and shrinkage. A similar fault accounted for the failure of a robot arm casting in aluminum alloy. The robot was designed for use in a nuclear installation but the arm broke off the body while it was undergoing proving tests. The seriously defective condition of the flange that carried the arm was obvious from the state of this machined surface, so the casting should have been rejected out of hand and certainly not built into a robot destined to be used for handling radioactive materials. Unfortunately the project was behind schedule, so the casting went straight into the machine shop as soon as it was delivered and the machinist did not consider it part of his duty to report such faults. This was a difficult casting to make and a number of replacements were x-rayed and found to be similarly defective. The problem was traced to gases released from the resin binder used to form the sand molds in the foundry coupled with inadequate feeding of the heavier sections of the body casting.

Another example, not involving a casting, concerned pivot eyes welded to the ends of hydraulic cylinders forming part of a lifeboat davit on a ship. Superficially, the welds appeared to be sound, but the first time they were deployed in a proving test the eyes broke off and revealed there had been practically no fusion between the eye and the base of the ram. Figure 5.2 shows the ends of three of these rams; the two with the large diameter eyes facing the camera had failed and caused extensive damage to the installation.

Figure 5.2   Defective welds on hydraulic lifeboat davits.

5.2   Failure of Freight Containers

The next case relates to a simple manufacturing mistake that cost an insurance company a great deal of money. It concerns freight containers made of aluminum alloy, the kind of containers universally used for transporting goods by ship, rail or road and seen all over the world in port installations and wherever freight is carried. Contents of these containers vary enormously, from being packed throughout with light items of clothing to carrying a single item of heavy machinery. The advantage of such containers is that they may be sealed at the point of loading and remain secure until arrival at their destination. This case began when a dock worker noticed a split in the end panel of a fully loaded 10-m-long container being lifted from the vessel. There was no obvious sign of external damage and the piece of machinery was still firmly anchored inside. Shortly afterward, a spate of similar failures were experienced at other ports and preliminary inquiries confirmed that all these containers were made at the same factory during the same 2-month period.

   The riveted seam between the two end panels in the side of the container had split open bottom to top as shown in Figure 5.3. It was subsequently determined that all the other containers had split in the same position and all had been carrying heavy items of machinery as distinct from bulky loads distributed throughout the container length. The costs escalated alarmingly,

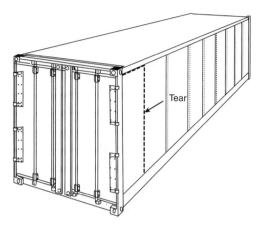

Figure 5.3 Position of seam that failed in container wall.

involving not only the transfer of the load to another container, but also finding an empty container and shipping it to the port, loss of earnings of the damaged container and cost of repair. There were at least four good reasons for requiring an urgent investigation:

1. Whether or not the owners had a case for claiming damages from any other party such as the harbor boards or the container manufacturers
2. Identification of the fault and a satisfactory method of repair; it would be wrong simply to repair the joints according to the original design before vindicating the design
3. Whether further failures of similar containers were to be expected and, if so, whether these might be avoided by reducing the recommended load carrying capacity
4. Whether partial failures of this kind might lead to complete unzipping and failure of the containers during a voyage or when offloading, with risk of serious accident and consequent damage to the cargo

As a preliminary to this investigation, a mechanical engineer with extensive experience in riveted stressed skin structures in aircraft had concluded there was nothing wrong with the original design or method of construction of these containers. This was borne out by the continuing satisfactory performance of the vast majority of these containers, some of which had been in use for several years. This led to the view that something had gone wrong with the manufacturing processes or material quality control, which accounted for structural weakness in these particular failed containers.

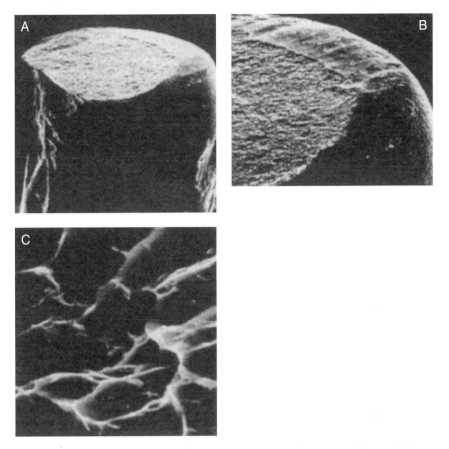

Figure 5.4   Scanning electron micrographs of rivet fracture: (A) ×20; (B) ×55; (C) ×6000.

The side panels were sheets of aluminum alloy that were attached to one another and the frame by riveting along vertical lap joints incorporating top-hat channel sections to act as stiffeners. All the failures involved the "unzipping" of the vertical lap joint between the first and second sheets in from the end of the container. The rivets had sheared across at the interface without causing any tearing or ovality of the rivet holes. Figure 5.4 shows three SEM views of a typical fracture surface at various magnifications. These are clearly single shear overstress fractures. A rivet was also sectioned, polished and etched for microstructural examination. This confirmed the shearing mode, as evident in Figure 5.5, by the way the grain structure has flowed adjacent to the fractured edge. The above interpretation explains the lack of any stretching of the holes in the sheet on either side of the rivets, so the investigation concentrated on what might be wrong with the rivets.

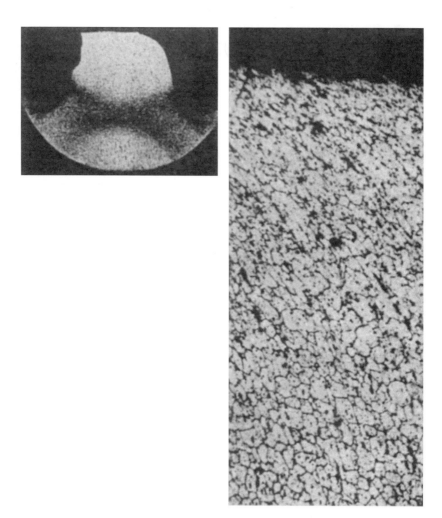

Figure 5.5 Microstructure across section of fracture (magnification: left, 20×; right, 100 μ = 2cm).

The first question is whether the rivets were the right composition. An element scan utilizing pulse counts of x-rays of characteristic wavelength for the elements likely to be present was carried out in the SEM and compared with that of an unused rivet of the correct composition (HR15 alloy to BS1473). The traces were as shown in Figure 5.6. While element scans are not precisely quantitative, the fact that the two are practically identical established that the correct alloy had been used for rivets in the failed containers.

Examination of the failed rivets under a low-power microscope revealed no physical sign of any internal fault or of a progressive failure mode such as fatigue, wear or corrosion. However, if one rivet near the end of a seam had failed it would have thrown an extra load onto its neighbors and these

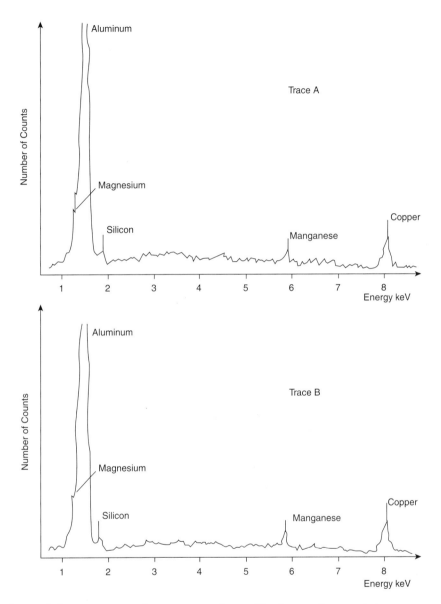

Figure 5.6 X-ray scans from SEM analysis of broken and unused rivets.

might then in turn become overstressed, causing the entire set to progressively unzip. Hence the next task was to examine the specification for the rivets on the engineering drawing. The relevant notes and diagram are reproduced in Figure 5.7 and Figure 5.8. It will be noticed that the rivet stock should be supplied in the H2 condition (as manufactured by the shaping and heading operations), but before use must be solution treated and then used within 48 h.

PART	BS. 641:1951 ³/₁₆ ᵢₙ x ½ ᵢₙ RIVET FOR CONTAINER SIDEWALL
MATERIAL	ALUMINIUM ALLOY HR 15 (B.S. 1473)
CONDITION	TB – Stock to be supplied in H2 condition Solution Treat and use within 48 hr

Figure 5.7 Extract from workshop drawing of rivet for container seams: drawing notes rivet with dimensions.

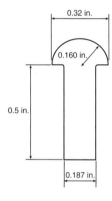

Figure 5.8 Detail drawing of rivet.

High strength in certain aluminum alloys, particularly those used in airframes, is achieved by a precipitation hardening mechanism. This involves a rearrangement of atoms within the crystals by soaking the alloy at a temperature not far below its melting point, so that alloying elements dissolve in solid solution, followed by quenching immediately into water. This retains the elements in the solid solution, but over a few days at room temperature they begin to precipitate and cause a dramatic increase in yield and tensile strength accompanied by a reduction in ductility. When this process takes place at room temperature it is called natural aging or *age hardening*; when it is accelerated by heating for an hour or so in the region of 200°C it is called artificial aging or *precipitation hardening*.

There is a problem with precipitation-hardening alloys: although they retain a high degree of ductility in the solution-treated condition, as they harden they gradually lose this and the ductility in the fully aged condition measured in the tensile test may be as low as 8% elongation, even lower in the really high strength alloys. This means that if parts are to be deformed to any extent such as setting the head of a rivet, this operation must be carried

Table 5.1   Chemical Composition for HR15 Alloy Rivet Stock (% by weight)

Element	Balance
Copper	0.2–0.8
Magnesium	0.2–0.8
Silicon	0.5–0.9
Iron	0.7
Manganese	0.4–1.2
Zinc	0.2
Chromium	0.1
Titanium*	0.2

*And /or grain refining elements

Table 5.2   Mechanical Properties of HR15 Alloy

Condition of Supply	Heat-Treated Condition	Diameter (mm)	Tensile Strength (MN/m²)
H2 – Annealed and cold drawn 20–40% reduction of area	TB – Solution heat treated and naturally aged	Up to 2	385

out before the aging gets under way, usually within an hour or so of quenching from the solution treatment. Table 5.1 and Table 5.2 are taken from BS1473 for HR15 alloy. The tensile strength given is for the TB (naturally aged) condition. In the H2 as-wrought condition in which these rivets were supplied, the tensile strength would be approximately 240 MN m^{-2}, but the metal would have high ductility and could be worked without any risk of cracking. In contrast, in the aged TB condition a rivet would not possess enough ductility for it to be set without the head splitting. Thus immediately before setting them in the container seam, the stock rivets would have to be solution treated, quenched and then set within a time window of about 1 h before the age hardening process began.

It is quite clear from the hardness tests on the failed rivets that they had not responded to the age hardening process as they should have and were consequently well below the strength levels that ought to have been achieved. The cause was obvious — they were of the correct composition but had not been solution heat treated before setting. This was borne out by their microstructures and, in fact, had already been suspected by the investigating metallurgist from the microstructure of the failed rivet shown in Figure 5.6. If the rivet had been solution treated the grains would have been much larger

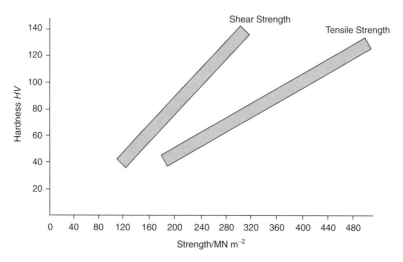

Figure 5.9   Correlation of hardness with the tensile and shear strengths for the aluminum alloy HR155.

and if it were in the naturally aged or precipitation hardened condition the amount of deformation along the sheared surface associated with the fracture would have been far less.

It was quite straightforward to establish whether the essential solution treatment had been omitted, thereby prevented the rivets from hardening to the required level. There is no way to tell from the microstructure whether a component is in the precipitation-hardened condition, but the condition may be readily established by measuring hardness. A hardness test can be carried out on a microsection, as it only requires a flat surface of sufficient area for a diamond point to make an indentation less than 1 mm across. Although the rivets were too small to be tensile tested and the broken ones could not be held in grips for a shear test, there is a close relationship between hardness and tensile strength. Hence, because measured shear strength of metals is usually about 60% of their tensile strength, hardness can be used to estimate the shear strength, even of a broken rivet, using the relationship shown in Figure 5.9. Measuring the hardness of ten rivets from the failed seam, as well as samples from the other seams in this container and from another container that had failed similarly, revealed none of them to be in the TB condition specified. The rivets used to make the seams were the correct alloy and in the as-manufactured condition specified on the order, but as they were not solution treated before setting they could not age and consequently reach the specified level of tensile strength.

Apparently, for about a month someone at the factory making the containers had omitted the solution heat treatment. While the metallurgical investigation was in progress, a mechanical engineer was addressing the complementary questions of what level of stress the rivets were subjected to when they failed and why only containers used to transport machinery had "unzipped." At first sight this may appear to be a rather academic question; the behavior of the rivets themselves may be thought to provide a sufficient answer. Because they fractured in shear they must have experienced a set of shear stresses with little or no normal stress. Furthermore, the magnitude of this stress must have exceeded the shear strength of the rivet — the material failed by overstressing. On the other hand, fully loaded containers without the defective rivets did not fail, so the shear stress on their rivets must have been less than the shear strength of the rivets in the specified condition.

The shear stress is therefore known to lie between these limits, but it is not known accurately, so the magnitude of the safety margin is not known. To allow for the unknown, it is usual in design to use a static *factor of safety* (or load factor) of a component, which is defined as

$$\text{factor of safety} = \frac{\text{nominal static strength of the component}}{\text{nominal static loading of the component}}$$

"Strength" means the maximum value of load the component can bear in a given situation — for example, in tension, compression or shear — without failing in a given way (for example, by fracture). "Static" implies that the loads are assumed to be constant and do not vary with time. The word "nominal" is used here to mean "according to the specification and the design calculations." These calculations are usually based on a simplified model of the component, and may ignore some of the complications of service conditions. If these complications could be taken into account quantitatively, on the one hand they would erode the nominal static strength and, on the other hand, they would inflate the nominal static loading. The factor of safety must be large enough to cover the uncertainties in strength and loading, which is why it is sometimes referred to as a "factor of ignorance."

It is essential that the static factor of safety be large enough that *at all times* within the lifetime of the component, the true strength will exceed the true loading. Whenever there is a service failure, the static safety factor should be reexamined. The investigating engineer has two options. He could choose a theoretical model of the loaded container and then analyze it to find the loads acting on the rivets, which would provide an estimate of the nominal static loading on a given rivet. Alternatively, the distortions in the sidewall of a loaded container could be measured and, using this information, infer the loads that are transmitted to the rivets. This should provide a more accurate estimate of the static loading on a rivet.

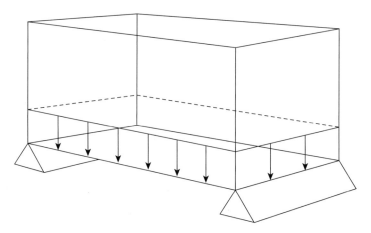

Figure 5.10   Modeling container as a box beam.

It is a problem to decide how the container should be loaded and difficult to anticipate every service load that might be encountered, for example, when a container is set down heavily in transit. It should not fail under such *foreseeable* conditions, but no design can be expected to allow for *gross* misuse as, for example, being driven into the arch of a low bridge. "Reasonable" overloads are not easy to quantify, but in general they are taken as loads that take into account foreseeable handling.

The engineer began by considering a theoretical model of a fully loaded container standing on its four bottom corner fittings, likened to a hollow box beam 2.4 m deep supported at its ends and subjected to the maximum load of 30,840 kg for this type of container, distributed uniformly along its length as indicated in Figure 5.10. The top and bottom of the box act as chords or flanges carrying the compression and tension forces due to bending, while the sides of the box act as webs, primarily carrying shear forces. The key point is that the side panels are important structural parts of the complete box. The shear force gives rise to shear stresses acting vertically on each cross section. However, these must vary in magnitude from place to place; for example, they must be zero at the top and bottom of each cross section because these surfaces are free and have no vertical forces acting on them from the outside. If the rivets were in the "TB" condition with a shear strength of 234 MN m^{-2}, then the safety factor would be in the region of 3.3 whereas for the defective rivets having a shear strength of only 165 MN m^{-2}, the safety factor would be reduced to 2.3.

The simple model used for this analysis neglects two factors that could be significant. First, some shear would be carried by the frame at the floor and the roof of the container, which implies the average shear stress calculated would be high. Second, it assumed that the shear load was shared equally by all 48 rivets, whereas the distribution would in fact be parabolic, with the maximum loading being near the middle of the seam. This distribution could result in the rivets near the middle, which is where the splits appeared to have started, being exposed to a shear stress well above the average, in which case the factor of safety may have been almost eliminated. To take into account these two factors would be a daunting theoretical task. Furthermore, when the panels of a stressed skin container are loaded in shear a secondary force field develops due to buckling, the so-called diagonal cross tension field, which imposes additional shearing force on the rivets. An alternative approach to the problem would have been to measure strains in a real container loaded to its full capacity and then infer from these strains what the stresses must be. It is a technique often used to study stress distributions in complex systems. However, the investigation did not justify this costly and time-consuming analysis. Furthermore, it would only have supplied data for a static container, whereas these containers split while they were being handled, so a dynamic analysis under transient loading conditions is really required.

Whatever theoretical modeling is undertaken, what is definitely known is that the original design of these containers had been approved and tests on prototypes had met the requirements of all relevant standards without reservation. Moreover, the vast majority of these containers, presumably not constructed with defective rivets, were still giving satisfactory service several years after the design was introduced.

Another factor that came to light during the stressing examination was the effect of load distribution inside the container. A single heavy item, such as a machine tool, places a different loading on the sidewalls than the same total load distributed evenly. If the container being handled bumps into something, then the inertia loads also add significantly to the shear stress on the rivets and is an obvious explanation as to why the splits occurred while containers were being off-loaded and why all those that failed had held heavy items of machinery. It is easy to appreciate that a container packed full of clothing, for example, would be much less vulnerable than one with a single, heavy item fastened to the floor near the middle. Additionally, the heaviest part of a machine tool might be at one end, which would increase the shear forces in the riveted seams at that end of the container.

The formal report concluded that a batch of containers had been produced with a side-wall strength below that which was intended, because the rivets had been set in the wrong condition, that is, without having been solution treated as specified on the drawing. The factor of safety in the basic design was adequate, but in the containers that split open it was reduced to an unacceptable level because the rivets were too weak. The failures were caused by transient overstress during handling. The manufacturer of the containers was thus held liable on the ground that they failed to solution treat the rivets before setting. There was no suggestion anything was wrong with the stock of rivets, which were in the condition specified and contained no fault that would have contributed to the failures. The packers, port handling authorities and shipping companies cannot be blamed. Containers inevitably get bumped from time to time and there is no evidence that these particular containers were treated any differently from all the others.

5.3   Failures of Gears in Oil Pump

This is another case about faulty heat treatment, but this time the material was steel and involved three separate firms in a chain supplying a major manufacturer with oil pumps for agricultural tractors. The oil pumps were mounted inside the engine crankcase and were fairly simple devices, consisting of two meshing spur gears driven by a shaft inside a housing. Oil was drawn in and forced around by the outside teeth of the contrarotating gears into a delivery pipe to the crankshaft bearings and camshaft of the engine. A number of failures were experienced after a few tens of hours work, resulting in complete engines being written off at busy times in the farming season, all of which claims had to be met under the tractor manufacturer's warranty.

The failures were all found to result from fatigue initiating at the keyway of the drive gear, so the tractor manufacturer sought to recover its costs from the oil pump suppliers. The oil pump suppliers merely assembled parts they bought as finished products and their records established that all the faulty gears had come from one large batch supplied by the same subcontractor. This subcontractor, a specialist gear manufacturer, carried out a failure investigation on several of the gears and found every one of the fatigue fractures had initiated at a small preexisting crack at the edge of a keyway for the drive shaft. These cracks, though small, were identified as quench cracks arising from the case-hardening heat treatment process. They had not been detected during final inspection at the time the oil pumps were assembled. This was clearly evident from the black scale on both faces of the initial crack, which contrasted with the bright surfaces of the fatigued area propagating from it. Although the dimensions and surface hardness of the gears were satisfactory, the analysis of the steel was slightly different from what the subcontractor had ordered from its suppliers and as stated on the delivery note. The subcontractor had forged the stock, machined the gears, put them through their case-hardening heat treatment process and finish ground the teeth before dispatch to the oil pump manufacturer. Consequently, this firm accepted liability for the defective gears but sued its steel supplier, a small stockholding firm that bought steels of various compositions and rolled them into sections and specific sizes ordered by a large number of small engineering customers. Fortunately, this firm carried product liability insurance because the root cause of the fatigue failures was that the wrong grade of steel had been supplied, which was totally unsuitable for the type of heat treatment process used to case harden the gears.

Steels for general engineering purposes are alloys of iron containing up to 0.8% by weight carbon together with small percentages of other elements such as manganese, chromium, nickel and vanadium. Without a doubt they comprise man's most versatile engineering materials, mainly because their carbon content allows a single product, say a chisel, to be heat treated so as to achieve extremely high hardness at the cutting edge, a middle section strong and tough and a softer head that is malleable. Unfortunately, when medium and high carbon steels are heat treated to maximum hardness they are also brittle and may sometimes crack under thermal contraction stresses during heat treatment processes. The other alloying elements modify the heat treatment response and impart specific properties in their own right, though not on such a dramatic scale as carbon.

Additional carbon may be introduced into the surface of a shaped product to a controlled depth, enabling the maximum hardness and wear resistance possible to be attained in the outside skin. This is the purpose of case hardening used to develop maximum wear resistance in parts which are in sliding contact, such as gear teeth, while retaining less hard but much tougher properties in the main body of the product. Typically, hardened cases are between 0.4 and 1 mm deep and, of course, the carburization process can only be applied to products made from steel when they have already been manufactured to the required shape and dimensions.

The oil pump gears had been forged to shape, machined to size and case hardened. Final grinding was used to correct any slight distortions resulting from the case-hardening process. The preexisting cracks discovered in the failed gears were typical of quench cracking. So on what grounds did the gear manufacturer seek to sue its steel suppliers?

Comparison of the analyses of the steels specified to make the failed gears and the one that was delivered by the material supplier were as follows:

	Carbon (%)	Manganese (%)	Nickel (%)	Chromium (%)
Ordered	0.2 max	0.6–1.0	0.6–1.0	0.4–0.8
Failed gear	0.38	1.62	0.16	0.04

The significant figure is the carbon content. The specified steel has a low carbon content and does not undergo an appreciable volume change when it transforms during quenching; it hardens to a limited extent but does not become brittle. The small percentages of manganese, nickel and chromium increase strength but not at the expense of toughness. It is a low alloy steel intended for case hardening.

The steel supplied was a medium carbon heat-treatable manganese steel, widely used in engineering applications requiring strength and toughness, for which it is used in a quenched and tempered condition. If quenched too rapidly products may develop quenching cracks due to the volume increase as the metal undergoes rapid transformation from its high temperature state to the temperature of the quenching bath. If and when such cracks form, they usually appear where there is a change in section — in this respect, the corner of a keyway is an ideal position. Hence, if a high content carbon case is built up on a product made from the specified steel and is finally quenched to harden the case, the volume expansion of the underlying steel will not crack it. If the same thickness of case is built up on a product made from the medium content carbon steel, the case is very likely to crack during a severe quench.

Thus the cause of the gear failures was clearly established. Responsibility was shared by the steel supplier and the gear manufacturer. The supplier had mixed the same sized bars of two different steels and had color coded the medium carbon–manganese steel as for the low carbon. Notwithstanding this, the gear manufacturer could have and should have discovered the quench cracks if adequate inspection and quality control procedures had been in force. Not all the gears would have been quench cracked (the tendency for this particular composition of steel depending very much on the quenching medium and the actual procedures for each batch) so they could have identified the faulty ones before they were dispatched and assembled into the oil pumps. Although the "wrong" steel was used, gears that had not quench cracked would have performed equally well and lasted just as long as if they had been made of the specified material.

5.4 Manhole Step

This case concerns the failure of a step built into brickwork near the top of a manhole that broke the day after installation, causing a workman to fall to the bottom of the manhole and suffer serious injury. The step was a U-shaped iron casting. It had the specification for manhole steps, BS1247 Part 1:1990, integrally cast into the top tread of the footrest. Two long limbs at the top of the U were set horizontally into the brickwork, leaving the loop of the U to form the footrest. Several such castings were set into the brickwork to form a staggered column of steps, which also became handles for the person

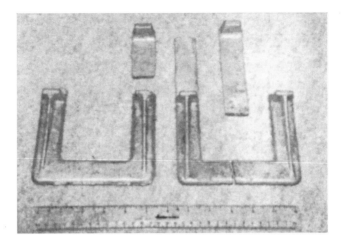

Figure 5.11   Failed manhole step (left) beside deliberately broken one (right).

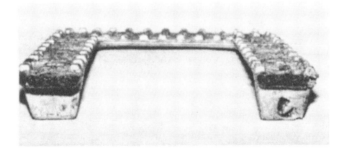

Figure 5.12   Fractures of the accident step.

climbing in or out. The castings were hot-dip galvanized before being dispatched to a builders merchant, who had sold several hundred to a subcontractor constructing manholes in a sewer system.

The broken footrest end of the accident step, along with the remains of two other steps from the subcontractor's unused stock that had been broken deliberately as a test after the accident, were submitted for examination. Figure 5.11 shows the accident footrest on the left and one of the tested steps on the right, viewed from the underside. The short piece of limb above the accident step is from another of the tested footrests, to illustrate the length of the limbs that had been left set in the brickwork. Figure 5.12 is the accident step, viewed slightly from above, showing the fractures. There is a large casting blowhole in the flange at the right-hand side and a smaller one at the outside edge that is part of the fracture, as can be seen in the closer view depicted in Figure 5.13. It occupies approximately 5% of the total cross-sectional area of both fractured limbs. These blowholes had been formed by

Figure 5.13   Closer view of fractures. Notice the large blowhole is not in the fractured area. The smaller one (arrowed) represents approximately 10% of the total fracture area of both limbs.

Figure 5.14   Etched microstructure of flake graphite cast iron (magnification 75×).

gases evolved at the interface between the metal and the sand mold when the liquid iron was poured. Holes formed by gases being released within the body of liquid metal during solidification would be much smaller and distributed uniformly throughout the cross section.

The foundry can therefore be blamed for releasing a casting containing visible blowholes, but the total cross-sectional area of only the one limb is reduced by 5% or so; hence they would have minimal effect on the bending strength. As there is not the slightest suggestion this could be a fatigue failure, these faults cannot be responsible for the sudden fracture that occurred the first time the footrest came under load.

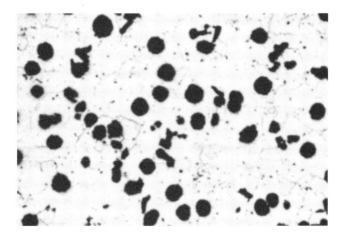

Figure 5.15 Etched microstructure of spheroidal graphite cast iron (magnification 75×).

There was no sign that either limb had deformed during the course of fracture. This is not consistent with a spheroidal graphite cast iron conforming to BS1247. Castings made to this specification should have a minimum of 7% elongation in a tensile test, so both limbs should have deformed before and during the course of fracturing. A section was therefore cut from the left side of the fracture illustrated in Figure 5.13, so that a cross section of the fractured end could be polished and etched for microstructural examination. This revealed the structure to consist of graphite *flakes* set in a mainly ferritic matrix. Hence this casting exhibited the microstructure of a common gray cast iron and would be brittle, not ductile and shock resistant. Figures 5.14 and 5.15 are typical microstructures of these two types. Due to the graphite appearing in the microstructure as flakes instead of spheroids this casting would display no ductility whatsoever in a bend test and its tensile strength would be only two thirds of what it should have been.

In order to cause the graphite to separate as spheroids a small amount of magnesium (0.5% by weight) has to be added to the ladle before the metal is cast and, additionally, there are certain limits to impurity levels that must be observed. If the magnesium is not added, or the ladle of liquid metal is held too long before casting, then the magnesium burns off, and the metal will solidify with a flake graphite microstructure. There would have been no outwardly visible sign that the microstructure of this step casting was defective. The form of the graphite would only have been detectable in the foundry by a destructive test, though a test bar could have cast at the same time if any fault had been suspected. The subsequent galvanizing process had no effect on the microstructure or mechanical properties.

It might be argued that the blowholes could have been a reason for rejecting this step at every stage in its handling, that is, before it left the foundry, when it was galvanized, when it was sold or even when set in the brickwork of the manhole. However, while it was obvious that this casting was not of high quality, no one handling it could have had any idea it was brittle and likely to fail as it did, particularly as lettering was integrally cast-in to the effect that it conformed to the required specification.

Neither of the two blowholes in the one limb of the U can be held responsible for the failure that actually occurred. The larger blowhole in the flange was not associated with the fracture and was not subject to any significant level of stress in service. The smaller one was in the most highly stressed part of the limb and undoubtedly would have weakened it, although the limb would still have possessed about 84% of its intended strength; taking into account the second limb, the step as a whole would have possessed over 90% of its intended strength.

The ladle of metal had obviously not been treated with magnesium or, if it had been, the magnesium must have burned off before casting; in fact the distribution and form of the flake graphite in the microstructure indicated that this is most likely what had happened. The implication is that all castings made from the last metal in this particular ladle would have solidified with flake graphite structures and would be susceptible to sudden fracture when loaded. Presumably all of these must still be in service or have already broken. The fact that this is the only step reported to have broken may be because it had not been set in mortar so that the flange was right against the face of the brickwork. The short, exposed parts of the limbs behind the flange would therefore have been subjected to bending. The brittle flake graphite iron was unable to withstand these tensile forces on the upper surface of the limbs and broke. If the same step had been well bedded in mortar, with its flanges flush with the brickwork, the greater part of the bending force in the rear limb might have been eliminated. The flange would have countered the levering action from the step and transferred the bending moment as a compressive force in the ribs on the underside of the step. Flake graphite irons are easily fractured by the tensile forces generated when a thin section is subjected to bending. Hence it could be argued that whoever set this particular step in the brickwork contributed to the cause of it failing as it did. Notwithstanding this, if the casting had possessed a spheroidal graphite structure, the limbs would have bent until the flange came against the brickwork and so transferred the load on the footrest to the rib beneath. It would not have failed catastrophically.

Responsibility for the footrest having the wrong microstructure and not conforming to the specification number integrally cast into the tread rests solely with the foundry. Its insurers accepted liability and settled the claim in full.

5.5 Failure of Threaded Iron Pipe Coupling

Another case concerns a different type of cast iron where something went wrong in the foundry.

The casting in question was a small straight coupling, joining two lengths of 1-in. (25-mm) iron pipe in an oil line to a central heating installation in an office block. A persistent odor of oil in the boilerhouse had been reported, so a service engineer was sent to investigate. He determined that the source of the smell was a slight seep of oil from the threaded pipe coupling close to the burner, so he tightened the union until the ooze appeared to have stopped. He packed up his tools and departed. That night there was a serious fire that caused a great deal of damage. The source was found to be an escape of oil through a split at one end of the pipe coupling.

There were deep indentations on one flange cut by the grips of a large stilson type wrench, the indentations being consistent with the direction of tightening. The wall was split right through from the end with this flange to halfway along the body of the fitting. A metallographic section cut transversely across the split revealed a structure characteristic of a malleable cast iron — of the variety called blackheart, which consists of graphite rosettes in a ferritic matrix — except for a narrow band on either side of the split, which exhibited a flake graphite structure. The casting should have solidified with all the carbon present as iron carbide (cementite, Fe_3C) which is the essential starting condition for the malleabilizing process. When the castings are put through the malleabilizing heat treatment the purpose is to cause a controlled breakdown of the cementite constituent into iron and graphite, but the graphite formed in an entirely different way from the flakes in a common gray cast iron. Figure 4.5D shows this form of microstructure. It appeared as ragged clumps or rosettes surrounded by virtually pure iron. For some reason this particular casting had solidified with a band of flake graphite structure through the wall, which could not change its physical form during the heat treatment that broke down the iron carbide. Thus after the coupling had undergone the malleabilizing heat treatment, this remained as a narrow band of brittle material extending right through the pipe wall.

The cause of the failure was obvious. The service engineer had tightened the coupling to stop the ooze, by screwing the coupling further onto the tapered thread. He had applied far too much torque by using unnecessarily large stilson grips, which cracked the band of flake graphite. Shortly after he left the premises the residual hoop stress must have caused the flange to split open, possibly due to vibration when the burner started up. The consequence was a major conflagration as the escaping oil ignited and was continually replenished from the storage tank.

Although some blame was attached to the service engineer's employers for the engineer's use of excessive force to tighten the coupling, the major responsibility rested with the foundry. The cause of the band of flake graphite is a complex metallurgical effect arising from the use of iron chaplets within a sand mold to support the cores required to form hollow sections. We need not go into the detailed explanation as to how this results in a band of flake graphite structure, except to say that it would have been a one-off effect in a large number of coupling castings made at the same time and the foundry would have had no means of detecting its presence. This one would possibly never have failed if the service engineer had not used such excessive force.

5.6 Replacement Gears for Gearbox of Heavy Trucks

No injury or accident was involved in this case, but it was the basis for a substantial claim against a small company that specialized in the manufacture of replacement gears for machinery and vehicles for which spares were no longer available.

The manufacturers of one particular make of heavy commercial vehicle were taken over by a larger company and, although the vehicles had long enjoyed a reputation for sturdiness and reliability for haulage work, the new owners of the business announced they would no longer supply spare parts when existing stocks were exhausted. The two largest gears in the gearbox tended to wear faster than the others and it became impossible to replace them, even when the other parts still had a great deal of useful life remaining. The specialist firm set out to manufacture replacements and soon had orders for several dozens of sets of these two particular gears. The firm had taken measurements and characterized the hardness of the worn gears and manufactured new ones of identical dimensions using one of the strongest steels available. The specialist firm machined the gears and sent them out for heat treatment because, in addition to hardening and tempering the whole gear, the teeth had to be surface hardened to match the hardness of the originals.

All seemed to be well until the first pair of gears was returned, having failed by teeth breaking off in just over 3 weeks' service (Figure 5.16). Their failure was attributed to poor gear changing practice, as the gearbox had no synchromesh and double declutching was necessary when changing gear. Another two gears were fitted, but a similar failure occurred after only 2 weeks. As it was a major job of replacement the truck owners were displeased

Figure 5.16   Broken teeth on gear wheel.

to say the least because, in addition to the costs, the vehicle was not earning its keep while it was off the road. Also, the truck owners had purchased nine pairs of the replacement gears intending to use them for other vehicles in their fleet.

The manufacturer suspected there might be something wrong with the surface hardening heat treatment, and discovered the hardness of the teeth that had broken were higher than they had specified. The customer returned all the unused gears and the manufacturer sent them off to have the teeth tempered to reduce their hardness. They did so in the belief that the fractures were due to the teeth being brittle. A modified set was put in the gearbox but this set failed after 4 weeks, every tooth breaking off the inner ring gear. Hardness checks revealed that they had been softened to the modified hardness. The vehicle operators initiated proceedings against the manufacturer to recover their losses.

Metallurgical investigation of the failed and unused gears found nothing wrong with the composition or heat treatment of the steel. However, two of the original gears that had gradually worn out over a long period of use — distinct from teeth breaking off —were also produced. These provided the answer to the premature failures. The diameter across the outer teeth is 150 mm. These outer teeth had given no trouble; the ones that had broken off were all from the inner ring some 100 mm in diameter. In the failed gears examined, two or three had simply worn down until they no longer engaged with the mating teeth, which is why the gears had to be replaced.

At the time the original gears were made, all steel started off as ingots. In the as-cast state an ingot has no directionality but, as it is worked down to billet or bar, directionality appears as grains and inclusions are extended in the direction of working. This is a structural effect readily demonstrated

Figure 5.17   Flow lines in sectioned gears. Left: Satisfactory gear from blank made by upset forging. Right: Gear machined directly from slice of round billet.

by sectioning a wrought product, smoothing or polishing the surface, followed by etching to reveal the grain structure. The directionality is revealed as flow lines, which resemble the grain in timber. For any given quality of wrought steel, toughness and fatigue resistance are much better across the flow lines than parallel with them, just like timber. The effect is equivalent to chopping a piece of wood across the grain compared with along the grain, where it splits easily.

The flow line patterns of the old gear and one of the new were studied by sectioning across a diameter. The two photographs in Figure 5.17 show how their grain flow structures were distinctly different. The original gears had been upset forged before the teeth were cut, whereas the replacements had been machined directly from round bar. The flow lines reveal how the old gears had started off as a length of round billet, about twice the length of the gear but of smaller diameter. This had been hot forged to squash it down, so that the shape finished with a much larger diameter and shorter length than when it started. This was done specifically to develop a flow line pattern following the contour of the gear teeth so that all forces acting to bend the teeth would act broadly *across* the grain. The teeth were as tough as they could be for this type of steel and the inclusions were oriented in directions that imparted the maximum resistance to fatigue initiation and brittle fracture.

In contrast, the new gears had been machined from stock of the full diameter for the gear required. There was no upset forging, so the grain flow remained the same as the original billet, parallel to the gear axis. The result was that the flow lines in the teeth were in the most unfavorable orientation to resist fatigue and brittle fracture. This is why they broke off so quickly under service loads, despite having the same hardness — and tensile strength

— as the original gears. Failure had little or nothing to do with drivers' needing to double declutch when changing gear, or with the surface hardening heat treatment of the teeth. The manufacturer's insurers settled the claim and all the gears sent out were recalled.

This case demonstrates the importance not only of getting the shape of the item right, but also following the necessary manufacturing route to achieve optimum properties for the application. It was considerably cheaper to machine the gears directly from round bar rather than to first upset forge individual gear blanks, especially for the small batch numbers needed for spare-part manufacture.

5.7 Hooks and Keepers

An insurance company requested an investigation of the cause of cracking of high tensile steel wire hooks used at the ends of nylon straps for securing loads on vehicles and trailers. Several breakages had been experienced in service when equipment had fallen off vehicles and suffered damage and there had been serious road accidents, one causing death and serious injury. It was discovered that a number of unused straps with terminations made by the same manufacturer were also cracked although they had never been under any load and had been inspected prior to assembly. The terminations, described as "2.5 ton swan-neck spring and keeper," comprised a welded equilateral triangle at one end of the strap and a doubled hook at the opposite end that was put through the triangle before the strap was tightened.

Unused samples are illustrated in Figure 5.18. Both parts were made from 5-mm-diameter steel wire; the keeper was formed into a triangle and welded at the midpoint of one side, while the hook started off as a triangle but two limbs had been squeezed together and turned back to fit over the keeper.

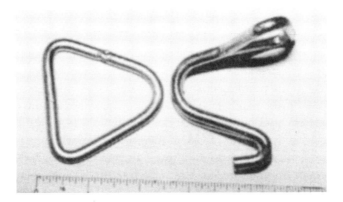

Figure 5.18 Hook and triangular keeper for nylon securing strap.

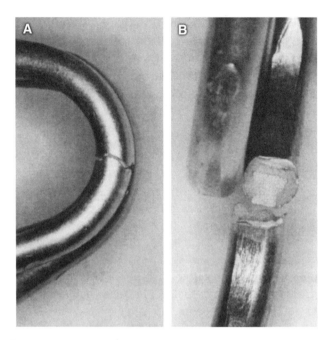

Figure 5.19   Broken hook with (A) fractured ends replaced and (B) fracture face exhibiting bright "fish eyes" characteristic of hydrogen cracking.

Both parts had been bright electroplated with zinc. Nylon webbing would be stitched over the straight limbs and the straps wrapped over the load on the vehicle, or sometimes attached to a large piece of machinery on a flat bed trailer and then tensioned with a specially designed grip.

By far the most likely cause of premature service failures of spring steel electroplated with zinc is hydrogen-induced cracking. Accordingly, a hook and a keeper from the unused samples were mounted in a vice and the jaws tightened so as to cause noticeable elastic deflection. The pressure was eased to check that no permanent plastic deformation had taken place. The jaws were then retightened to the same elastic deflection and left in that state at ambient temperature. Only one limb of the hook was tensioned in this way, the opposite limb being left unstressed. The triangular keeper was stressed by compressing one point against the opposite base, which imposed tensile bending stress on the inside face of the base. The stressed limb of the hook broke completely after between 48 and 60 h. Figure 5.19A shows the broken limb placed with the fracture faces almost in contact; while in Figure 5.19B the hook end is turned back so as to reveal the characteristic fish-eye feature on both sides of the fracture surfaces. This fracture is quite characteristic of hydrogen-induced fracture.

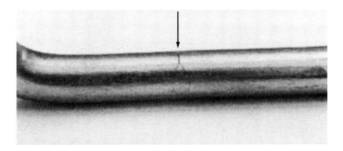

Figure 5.20   Crack in the middle link of the unbroken keeper.

The triangular keeper cracked after 36 h under constant stress. Figure 5.20 illustrates a single crack starting on the tension side of the elastic bend, branching into two just to form the Y shape above the neutral axis.

Vickers hardness tests (to HV30) carried out after locally removing the zinc coating gave values of 436 and 449 on the hook and 434 and 444 on the keeper. These indicate a steel having a tensile strength of the order of 1400 MN m^{-2}, typical of the normal range for springs. Hydrogen is easily picked up during electroplating and causes disastrous effects of delayed cracking if not eliminated immediately after products are removed from the electroplating bath, especially so in the higher strength steels. Most international standards give recommendations for stress relief treatments of formed products prior to electroplating and stipulate baking times and temperatures immediately after the components come out of the plating bath for avoidance of hydrogen embrittlement after electroplating. The time required depends on the hardness of the steel and the thickness of the electro-deposit. Because zinc acts as a barrier to the escape and high strength steels are particularly prone to embrittlement, for items like springs the baking times may be 24 h or more. Table 5.3 gives the minimum baking times recommended in BS1076.

The small company that made these hooks and keepers had never heard of hydrogen embrittlement and sent them out to a specialist electroplater to be zinc coated. The plating firm was fully aware of the heat treatment requirements but was not told the items were spring steel, and had assumed they

TABLE 5.3   Baking Times for Steels after Zinc Plating

Maximum Tensile Strength (MN m^{-2})	Heat Treatment
Up to 1050	None required
Above 1050 up to 1450	8 h minimum between 190°C and 220°C
Above 1450 up to 1800	18 h minimum between 190°C and 220°C
Above 1800	24 h minimum between 190°C and 220°C

were made from low carbon steel wire. They did not inquire and dispatched them as plated, without any baking treatment. However, the onus was on the plating firm to inquire before carrying out the process and this was taken into account when the respective insurers negotiated settlement of the substantial claims.

5.8   Rivet Failure in Multipurpose Tool

This case is a reflection of poor design specification that led to manufacture of an intrinsically faulty and unsafe product. Although quite a number of similar tools were discovered to have failed in the same way, this one came to light when a young man nearly severed an index finger when the knife blade suddenly folded as he was pressing hard.

The tools were essentially large pliers with hollow handles, into which a variety of implements such as knife blades, screwdrivers, spikes, hooks and even small socket spanners could be folded away. They represented a compact portable toolbox and were particularly popular with people following outdoor pursuits such as angling. For use, the chosen implement would have to be opened fully until it locked in place in line with the handle. It could be released only by partially opening any of the other implements in the same handle. This action lifted a spring locking tab that engaged in a slot behind the pivot in the handle of the tool fully unfolded. The security of any of the five tools mounted inside the handle was thus entirely dependent on the locking tab being fully engaged in its slot and the pivot reacting all the externally applied force.

The accident occurred when the young man had opened out a large pointed knife blade and was attempting to push it through a plastic cap on the top of a container. It was the first time he had used the tool, which had been given to him as a present. While he was pressing hard and waggling the blade from side to side to force the point through the plastic it suddenly folded, cutting his index finger to the bone. The head of the rivet, which served as the pivot, had separated and allowed the pivot to escape from its bearing in the handle and consequently disengaged the locking tab.

The head is a tapered plug that fit into a hole at one end of the rivet. The body of the rivet had been machined from bar stock and the hole extended about half way down. The manufacturer of these tools chose to assemble the five implements inside the handle and then press in the tapered plug, rather than use a solid rivet. Tapered joints are only suitable in applications where the external loads are compressive or place the joint in shear. They are easily broken if applied forces are, or occasionally become, tensile.

This type of failure could, and should, have been avoided if a solid rivet incorporating a shoulder or an external spacer had been used.

5.9 Scaffolding Guard Rail

This case does not strictly belong in this chapter but litigation was already in progress to recover damages from a manufacturer on the grounds of product liability, when a metallurgical investigation revealed that an allegedly faulty casting was not responsible for a serious accident. The circumstances were that an installation engineer fell from a scaffold tower and suffered serious injury while installing an air conditioning unit in the roof space of a shopping mall. He was working from a demountable scaffold. These are structures that can be erected quickly by snapping together lengths of aluminum alloy tubes and frames (Figure 5.21). The tubes have a C-shaped hook at each end and are locked onto the frames by a spring loaded claw, so all that has to be done to erect the scaffold is to press the hook over a crossing tube so that the claw springs shut and holds the tube in position. To dismantle, a trigger is lifted that opens the claw so that the tube may be lifted off.

The case pleaded was that the scaffold was defective in its material parts and was inadequate in that it was "of insufficient strength and made of unsound material," despite the fact that such scaffolds were, and still are, widely used. The specific allegation was that the end of a claw at one end of the guard rail above the platform had broken off as the engineer leaned against it, due to a manufacturing defect. As a consequence of this sudden fracture the guard rail swung outward pulling the claw at the opposite end

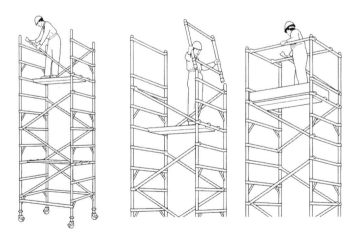

Figure 5.21 Aluminum scaffolding showing mode of construction.

Figure 5.22   Broken claw at the end of the scaffold guard rail.

off the side-frame. The tube followed him down to the ground, but the end broken off the claw casting was not recovered. Figure 5.22 and Figure 5.23 show two views of the broken claw as received, when a microsection had already been cut from the side of the fracture, and Figure 5.24 shows the unbroken claw at the opposite end.

The claws were aluminum alloy casting welded to a length of alloy tube, which would be of different composition as it had been extruded, not cast. The surface of both castings exhibited numerous pin holes, caused by gas porosity. This is a fault that should not occur with good foundry practice but which is nevertheless sometimes found in small castings for general engineering purposes. Unlike shrinkage cavities in a casting, porosity does not have a marked weakening effect unless it is present in excessive quantities

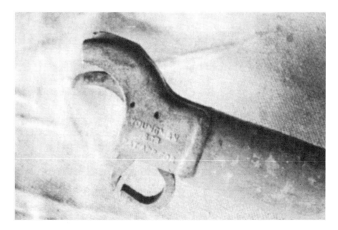

Figure 5.23 Side view of broken claw.

Figure 5.24 Unbroken claw at opposite end of guard rail.

within the section, because it exists as uniformly distributed tiny holes of rounded shape that do not exert any serious localized stress-raising effect likely to initiate fatigue.

A section had already been cut from the fracture for microstructural examination and presumably the evidence of porosity had provided the basis for the allegation of manufacturing defect. However, close study of the fracture revealed that the claw had broken in a sideways movement, forcing it to open it up as it was twisted off the frame tube. Shallow lips at the edges of the fracture indicated it had started where the microsection had been cut out and progressed across the section to finish at the opposite edge. Aluminum castings have low ductility, usually between 1 and 4% in the sand cast condition, even when they are free of gas porosity, so not much deformation is to be expected in a tearing type of fracture. Apart from the porosity there was no evidence of any significant internal fault. Nor was there anything to suggest this was a fatigue failure, where only a small area of metal had been holding the part together shortly before it finally broke. It is possible there may have been a lap or larger gas hole at the edge where the fracture started, which could account for why an investigator had cut the section from this region. Unfortunately, because the section was not produced and the opposite side of the claw had not been recovered after the accident, there was no way of establishing this from the evidence available.

The mechanism of the snap locking device is illustrated in Figure 5.25, the top view showing the claw in the locked position and the bottom view showing how it is released. Within the outer claw is an almost semicircular crescent-shaped piece (1), pivoted at P. The top sits in a recess inside the fixed claw so that the cross tube to which it is attached can be accommodated. In this closed position the bottom of the crescent holds the tube in place and prevents the claw from being lifted off. The crescent is locked in this position by a small step on its back face, which butts against a similar step on the finger pull (2), which is pivoted near the top at P. The finger pull is pressed against the crescent by spring S that is a U shape, having two legs that at all times press against the top of the housing.

To release the claw the finger pull is pulled back against the action of the spring until its step is lifted clear of the step on the back of the crescent. This allows the crescent to pivot as depicted in the lower diagram of Figure 5.25, allowing the claw to be lifted clear of the cross tube. The crescent will stay in this position, with its step above that of the finger pull, until the next occasion the claw is to be fitted. When it is pushed firmly down over a cross tube, as indicated in the sequence in the lower diagram, the top of the tube meets the top of the crescent and pushes it into the recess. As it moves to this closed position the step on the crescent pushes the finger pull back against the spring and the steps ride over each other to finish up as shown in the upper diagram. The spring is now holding the crescent in the locked position and the claw can only come out by drawing the finger pull backward, or if the end of the claw breaks off. The abutment steps are shaped such that there are two sloping faces in contact in the open position and two square faces in the locked position so that there is no cam effect.

If the guard rail had been pushed outward while both claws were attached, the bar should have bent in the middle until one of the claws broke as observed, but then the claw at the opposite end would have been visibly deformed and would have remained attached to the frame. The guard rail was, in fact, still perfectly straight and the other claw showed no sign of damage or having suffered any strain.

When the locking mechanism at the unbroken end was examined it was discovered that both legs of the steel spring were missing and the remaining

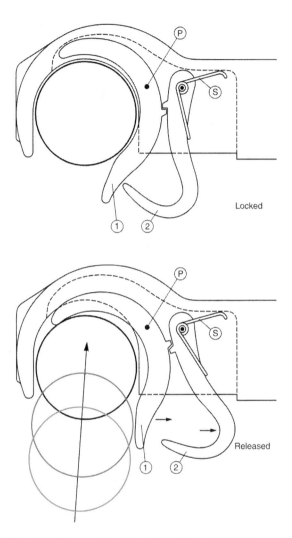

Figure 5.25   Claw locking mechanism. (Top) Claw locked securely onto frame tube. Crescent (1) pivots at (P) and is held in place by step abutment against finger pull (2) by spring S. (Bottom) To release claw: drawing back the finger pull against spring pressure allows abutments to override, enabling claw to be lifted off frame tube. To fit the guard rail the claw is positioned over the frame tube and pushed sharply downward, causing the abutments to ride over each other against the spring pressure and lock the crescent against the tube. The integrity of this position depends on the springs maintaining pressure against the back of the crescent to keep the abutments in the same relative positions.

part was heavily rusted. The legs had rusted away, as could be seen easily without magnification. Hence there could have been no pressure forcing the finger pull against the crescent. Without the spring the crescent could hang downward on its pivot and allow the locking steps to pass each other easily. Thus the claw could not have been gripping the frame tube as it should have done but was instead simply resting on top. The inability to lock the unbroken claw was readily demonstrated by placing it over a cross tube; there was no snap action as it was pushed down — the crescent just hung vertically — and it could be lifted off again without any resistance. In contrast the spring at the broken end was rusted but was still operative, so the two steps were able to butt against each other and exert their normal locking action. Hence at the time of the accident the unbroken claw would have been resting on the frame tube while the broken claw was clamped.

The cause of the guard rail coming off while the engineer was leaning against it and reaching upward thus had nothing to do with the weakness in the broken claw. What must have happened is that his movement lifted the unclamped claw off the frame and caused the rail to swing outward. This movement applied *bending* force to the claw at the other end, which was still clamped, and this caused it to break as the engineer was already falling. When the rescuers reached the scene the guard rail was lying on the floor and the piece broken off the claw was not recovered. But the freshly produced fracture had exposed the porosity in the casting and the initial investigators assumed this must have been responsible for the accident. They made no mention of the state of the claw springs or that the legs of the one at the unbroken end had rusted away and rendered the clamping action inoperative.

One other possibility was considered. The broken claw might have already been cracked, making it much more likely to twist off as the guard rail moved outward. Such partial fractures are often found when tubes are thrown to the ground as scaffolding is dismantled, instead of handing down the tubes to someone on the ground. If the claw lands on a hard surface end-on the impact may bend it inward with sufficient force to crack it or break it off. However, in this instance there was no staining or oxidation of the fracture surface to suggest that the claw had been partially cracked for some time and, unfortunately, the allegations in the Further and Better Particulars that the "hook" had snapped due to having insufficient strength were not substantiated. Because the broken end was not recovered it was not possible to discover whether this exhibited any witness marks from an impact.

The case did not go to court. The allegations that the hook had snapped due to a manufacturing fault and that was the direct cause of the accident could not be substantiated. Instead, the firm that had hired out the scaffold (who would have been the second defendant) settled the claim. They failed in their duty to inspect the scaffolding regularly to ensure all parts were in a safe condition. There was no case against the manufacturers of the scaffold. Despite the fact that the casting exhibited a degree of gas porosity, it was not a weakness that caused the accident. If it had been seriously defective, then failure would be expected almost the first time it came under load in service or, if not immediate overload, the fracture surface would have exhibited a progressive mode such as fatigue.

5.10 Gas Molding Problems

While injection molding is a well-known method for shaping polymeric materials, less well known is a technique referred to as gas molding. It is a method that allows retrofitting to existing machines and offers savings in material and speed of manufacture for existing solid products. Conventional injection molding is limited by product wall thickness because the hot product must be cooled to ambient temperature before removal from the tool is possible. Polymers are poor thermal conductors, so a large part of the molding cycle time is spent cooling the molten product. In addition, very thick walls require material that may not be stressed in service. Most common molded products thus have walls of 1 to 4 mm in thickness and thicker walls are deliberately eschewed by designers.

Gas molding involves overcoming the wall problem by injection of nitrogen gas at high pressure toward the end of the filling part of the cycle, the gas pushing the material to the tool surfaces and remaining after cooling to form a pocket within the product. The invention of the process in the 1980s encouraged some companies to use this method for existing products to save costs. Like all new technology however, care is needed to ensure that the method does indeed work as advertised, and that a hollow product is appropriate for the application. In the 1990s, a British company decided to use the method to make chair arms for a range of office chairs. The market had expanded with the introduction of the gas cylinder office chair, where the working position of the seat can easily be adjusted to suit the user. The company bought the technology from a large supplier of molding machines, who demonstrated the process on existing arm tools in their factory in Austria, apparently with great success. However, when it came to manufacturing on a commercial scale, serious problems arose. The process involved moving the gas nozzle within the molding machine by means of a simple lever outside the barrel (Figure 5.26). The steel lever failed by fracture across the hole about which it pivoted (top hole in Figure 5.26), was mended and failed again (at the same position). When we were called to investigate at a later stage, following initiation of court proceedings for failure of the contract, inspection of the fractured arm showed fatigue striations. Both failures had been caused by classic cyclic loading of an under-designed component. The attitude of the supplier was to reweld the broken lever, rather than determining the cause of the failures.

Figure 5.26 Intact steel lever for moving the gas injection nozzle forward within the barrel of the injection molding machine. The first arm fractured twice by fatigue from the upper pivot hole. Scale shown by British 2p coin at right.

Other serious problems had arisen with the gas-molded products. The new, lighter chair arms were much weaker than expected, mainly because the attachment points for the plastic arms to the steel chassis of the chairs proved very weak. They failed in routine quality checks, and entire batches had to be rejected. When sectioned, the arms showed that the gas pocket created by injection had not been formed evenly, but rather tended to be localized at the hotter parts of the tool. This was not at all surprising, because the melt will be less viscous where it is hottest, and the high pressure gas will naturally move to those zones in the melt, thus creating an uneven pocket in the final product. One of those zones was at the attachment points for the screws, and when in use, can be expected to experience high loading from the user when, for example, he or she lifts the chair to move it, or when simply pushing the arms sideways. It would have been disastrous if such arms were released into the market, and exposed to handling loads from the user. Failure could cause

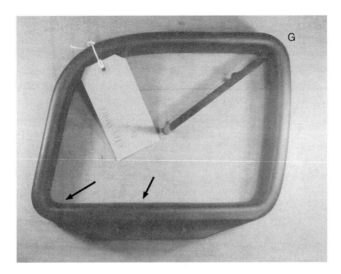

Figure 5.27   Pristine chair arm molding made by machine maker to demonstrate feasibility of gas molding, with gate (G) at upper right. Hesitation marks had been formed on the outer surface as indicated by the arrows.

personal injury, necessitate a recall of the product and certainly damage the reputation of the manufacturer to whom the chair arms were supplied for assembly into finished products.

The problem seemed intractable, and the company sued the machine maker for loss of production, machine time and the money invested in the new process. Experts on either side were divided and the dispute was set for trial in the U.K. Technology Court, a specialist division of the High Court, which tries technically complex cases with judges experienced in engineering cases. The court is an innovator in procedure, asking for experts to meet and prepare statements of agreement and disagreement so that argument in court is not wasted on spurious matters. The judge himself visited the factory and observed gas molding in action so as to be better informed about the nature of the problems.

A key part of the arguments concerned the first samples produced in Austria by the machine maker. They looked good externally, but there were now serious doubts as to their structural integrity following experience at the factory. Would the machine maker allow them to be sectioned to examine the gas pocket? The machine maker refused, so a nondestructive method was needed to solve the problem. We turned to x-ray inspection using soft x-rays as used by doctors to examine limbs for fractures. It would be ideal because flesh and bone are light materials of a density similar to the polypropylene of the chair arms. The chair arms might be thinner (3- to 5-cm diameter) than an adult human arm, but there would be a greater difference in density

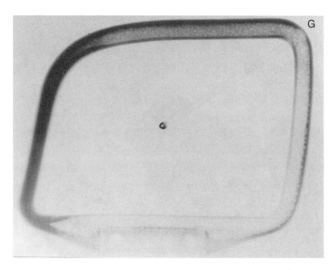

Figure 5.28   X-radiograph of chair arm showing serious internal defects caused by poor shape of gas pocket.

between a hollow interior and the solid skin. Under the watchful eyes of both experts, the samples were duly taken to a local hospital and exposed to the x-ray beam, one of the arms being shown in Figure 5.27 together with its corresponding x-ray negative (Figure 5.28). The x-ray image showed big differences in wall thickness, the inside walls tending to be much thinner than the outside (probably due to tool temperature variation). The gas pocket had penetrated the attachment zone at the bottom of the arm, while another side was solid and had not been affected at all. Thus the problems of the technique had been present from the start, which would have been apparent had someone bothered to investigate the trial moldings produced not by the client, but by the defendant machine makers. The additional problems with the lever on the machine seemed indicative of the lack of adequate backup, but did not appear directly connected with the product problems. Another chair arm showed the same kind of problem (Figure 5.29), and the x-radiograph was checked by sectioning the arm after the action had been settled (Figure 5.30). The case for the plaintiff was now very strong, but would it proceed to a long and expensive court trial?

Just before trial was due to start, lawyers for the two sides met and hammered out a surprising deal. The machine maker was suffering from a downturn in business and was storing a large number of new machines in warehouses. The plaintiff needed to reequip its factory and replace aging molding machines. So the defendants agreed to sell several new machines at a discount equivalent to the damages claimed by the factory for the failure

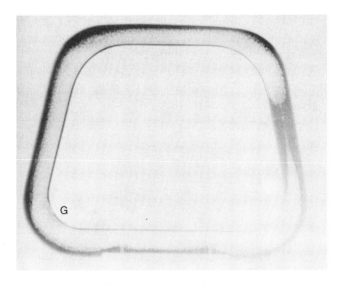

Figure 5.29 Radiograph of another design of chair arm showing inner defects. G is the gate where hot polymer enters the tool.

Figure 5.30 Sectioned chair arm showing defects.

of the process. The two parties settled the action then and there, saving the cost of a full trial and, more significantly, saving goodwill between the two parties. It is rare that such settlements are reached, but nonetheless encouraging that disputes can be settled amicably once the facts are established by expert evidence. Both companies will, in the future, be more circumspect about new technology, although it is also fair to say that gas molding continues to expand in its application, provided that thought is given to the intended use of that product, and careful control of the gas pocket is implemented. Thus it is far better to apply the method to brand new tools designed for gas molding, rather than retrofit existing tools, where control is much more difficult.

Fluid Transport

6.1 Introduction

Among the most demanding roles of any material is that of containing and transporting fluids. Why? Because escape of the contents due to failure of the wall can create far more serious damage than the initial break. Fuel spray from pipe leaks can cause devastating fires, while the damage from corrosive chemicals from leaking storage tanks can be extensive. Even small losses of water from supply pipes is serious if undetected, as many homeowners will know much to their regret from freezing water effects in winter. In supply systems to larger buildings, the effects are multiplied, and the losses far greater if equipment is damaged by the leaking water. Design, rather than manufacturing or assembly, defects in central heating systems (CHS) produce a multiplier effect of such severity as to seriously affect the credibility of major companies and corporations. So what are the requirements for containment materials?

6.2 Materials of Choice

The material of the wall must resist any kind of interaction with the fluid being contained, as well as the external environment. It thus implies resistance to corrosion and environmental degradation on both the inner and outer surfaces. In addition, the material must satisfy several other criteria and be capable of easy manufacture into both simple (pipe, cylinder) and more complex shapes (such as connections and joints). Because connections in piping systems are usually needed on site, welding the parts together is often a critical operation during construction. The integrity of such joints is often crucial to the integrity of the entire system, essentially because they are often weak mechanically when compared with homogeneous material of the pipe or container.

The mechanical properties needed in the materials of construction are also critical; they include

1. Resistance to crack growth (toughness)
2. Strength
3. Stiffness

Crack resistance is clearly needed when the containment system is loaded with a liquid, so that any small defects in its structure will not grow with time. The material must be strong enough to withstand all the anticipated loads on the system, sometimes over a wide range of environmental conditions. The material must also be stiff under load so that any distortion is strictly limited, although some applications such as fuel pipes on vehicles are highly flexible so as to allow ease of fit. These general requirements encompass a wide range of candidate materials, such as many metals and alloys, some glasses and ceramics, and many polymers. Because glasses and ceramics are clearly of restricted application due to their brittleness, metals and polymers are of prime importance for containment materials.

6.2.1 Design Criteria

The form of the chosen material is generally very simple: a pipe is simply a hollow tube of uniform circular section. Connections between pipes are obvious sources of stress concentration, either because of the change in section thickness or free ends left in the joint. They may be doubly at risk if there are any defects left over in the weld junction, a common problem in welding of all materials. More complex types of joints can arise at T-junctions or inserts for taps, requiring care in design to minimize the deleterious stress-raising effects of sharp corners, for example.

Special problems of stress concentration can arise in another perhaps unexpected situation, where pipe systems of different materials are present, especially where a local system joins the grid or external water supply, for example. Thus if the plastic pipe system in a factory is joined to the steel pipes of the supply system outside the factory, then any local load will be taken by the weaker plastic system, with potentially catastrophic results.

6.2.2 Corrosion and Environmental Degradation

One of the most common ways in which conventional materials, especially metals and alloys, fail in service is by corrosion. It may occur either from inside an enclosed system, as, for example, when steel is oxidized by dissolved oxygen in a CHS water supply, or externally by an aggressive environment. If dissimilar metals are used at junctions, as is common in soldering and in many joints, then the possibility of galvanic corrosion arises. Other types of corrosive attack will be examined in the case studies in detail, some arising from unexpected sources. Thus when a PVC tape was used to help seal a joint in a hot water system, thermal degradation of the PVC produced hydrochloric acid, which attacked the adjacent metal.

6.2.3 Case Studies

The case studies in this chapter include mainly metal and polymer systems, the former being well established for bulk transport and storage of a wide range of fluids for many years. The case studies demonstrate the problems that can arise in CHS systems, whether in a domestic or industrial environment. Failed connections in oil lines can cause serious environmental problems, and there is a study of the special problems of vehicle brake line failures. While metal alloys remain well used and familiar to all engineers, the recurrence of failures should act as a timely reminder of the dangers that can occur both in new installations and older products or systems.

Plastic materials apparently offer great benefits for water supply systems due to their great resistance to corrosion, the bugbear of steel and copper conventional systems, but have in recent years suffered a series of failures, especially in the U.S. There have been fewer problems with such systems in Europe, although failures have occurred from poorly made joints, for example, a topic discussed in detail in this chapter. Different types of failure are examined in relation to seals in systems. They are crucial but often neglected parts of a closed distribution network, such as in hydraulic braking systems, where failure can have immediate and catastrophic effects on users. In CHS networks, seal failure may be slow and undetected for some time, although consequential damage can be severe in financial terms, as one of the case studies demonstrates.

Flexible fuel pipes are common in vehicle engines, but once again, often overlooked as a potential hazard, perhaps because of their low cost and primitive function. However, if failure occurs, the results can be very serious, resulting in loss of the vehicle or worse. The investigation into a series of such fires in new cars in the 1970s surprisingly reappeared in the early 1990s as a direct result of a failure to learn the lessons from first failure. Indeed, the same kind of fuel pipe (nylon) was involved in an automobile accident that caused several subsequent accidents due to a fuel leak. The cause lay not so much in the nylon material, however, as in a small molded junction that connected three pipes together.

6.3 Corrosion Failures

Metals corrode because they are conductors of electricity. Thus when metal atoms are in a chemical environment that allows or causes them to give up electrons, they become positively charged ions that take part in chemical reactions, provided an electrical circuit can be completed. The net effect is that the metal component corrodes away where the electrons are given up and the useful cross-sectional area is reduced. This can be concentrated locally to form a pit or, sometimes, crack if a high level of tensile stress is acting, or it can extend across a wide area to produce general wastage. The load-carrying capacity is thus reduced and an eventual failure may occur simply because a load in the upper part of the normal spectrum exceeds the residual strength of the component.

The cause of accidents resulting from general wastage type of corrosion is usually obvious, for example, where the chassis or a suspension member of a vehicle has corroded away; there was one particular car where aluminum alloy shock absorbers exposed to road spray literally flaked away over a period of about 5 years in the British climate. Occasionally, however, the corrosion may be found to have occurred in an area that is concealed, such as the inside of a box section, or in an area that is inaccessible to routine painting or protection, such as a gap between two close fitting members of a structure. In a case some years ago, this was the reason for sudden collapse of a footbridge over a railway line.

Localized corrosion that leads to pitting may provide sites for fatigue initiation and, in addition, corrosive agents such as sea water may lead to greatly enhanced growth of the fatigue crack. Even rainwater can cause serious failures. Thus rainwater penetration of tubular cycle frames has caused corrosion-fatigue failures, resulting in serious injuries to the riders. The fatigue cracks had initiated at corrosion pits, although the immediately surrounding areas were less severely pitted and only lightly rusted.

Pitting corrosion also occurs much faster in areas where microstructural changes have occurred in welding operations. Some years ago an educational institute with several large buildings heated by hot water distributed through steel pipework from a single boiler house sued ten different subcontractors on the basis that the welds were faulty. The pipework had developed numerous pinhole leaks at the welds in pipes joined at different times by different contractors throughout the entire campus. The cause was not faulty welding but failure to control the boiler feed water, which had led to severe pitting corrosion inside the pipes at the edges of the weld beads.

Corrosion may be combated in a number of ways, ranging from cladding with a protective sheath, applying a protective film to the surface like painting, electroplating or hot dip galvanizing, to superimposition of electrical potentials on a large structure such as an undersea oil platform. Changing the battery connections on motor cars from positive earth to negative earth in the 1950s led to a tremendous reduction in the rate of what was then referred to as "body rot."

Some metals display an inherently greater corrosion resistance than others, but even those most resistant to normal atmospheric conditions have some reagent to which they are vulnerable. Stainless steels, for example, are virtually unattacked under oxidizing conditions because they have a built-in chromium content (at least 12%) which forms an electrically insulating and self-healing protective oxide film preventing most corrosive agents being able to set up an electrical circuit. If the oxide film is mechanically damaged it immediately re-forms and keeps the reactive agent away from the metal. However, if the environmental conditions reduce or exclude the oxygen necessary to re-form the chromium oxide film, stainless steels will corrode away almost as fast as nonstainless varieties. One excellent example of this process was when a family went away for a 6-week vacation and inadvertently left a pork chop on the draining board of their expensive new stainless steel sink unit. When they returned and scraped off the offending mess they discovered a mass of pinholes through the black stain of the chop's outline. Bacteria from the decomposing meat had established chemically reducing conditions and had consumed all the available oxygen, so there was none available to re-form the chromium oxide film. The family tried to sue the manufacturer for allegedly not making the sink unit out of stainless steel!

A tremendous variety of corrosion failures can lead to litigation, some in connection with causation of an accident and others concerning product quality and fitness for purpose. A corrosion expert is usually required to deal with these. However, here are three good examples to illustrate the forensic aspect when only "straightforward" corrosion mechanisms were involved.

6.3.1   Failure of an Oil Delivery Pipe

A food processing plant was fined a large amount for causing environmental damage due to long-standing leakage of oil from a pipe crossing a roadway. The plant had a large storage tank on one side of the road to which tanker deliveries were discharged, and a steel pipe carrying the oil through a duct under the road to their heating installations. The oil was a heavy, highly viscous variety that had to be heated in the winter months to keep it flowing at the rate necessary to keep all the heating units working. A heating element spiral was therefore wrapped around the pipe beneath the thermal lagging material. The duct was a concrete channel covered with steel plates to carry the normal road traffic.

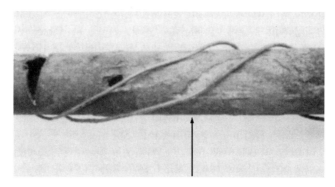

Figure 6.1 Failure of a heated oil pipeline showing how corrosion follows the line of the heating spiral.

When the environmental damage was discovered the source of the contamination was traced back to the channel under the road. Lifting the steel plates and removing the lagging exposed a series of holes in the walls of the pipe, following the line of the heating spiral, as shown in Figure 6.1.

A number of similar holes through the pipe wall were found and flaky rust could be lifted off to reveal extensive areas of corrosion following the line of the spiral. The heating element comprised a resistance wire running through the center of the copper-covered spiral. There was no intentional electrical connection between the spiral and the pipe, but in places the spiral had been touching the pipe.

Given that the standard electrode potential (see Table 2.1) of iron (Fe/Fe^{2+}) is +0.44 V and that of copper (Cu/Cu^{2+}) is –0.34 V, giving a corrosion cell potential of 0.78 V, how was the electrical circuit completed? Through the lagging material, which must have become damp and probably contaminated with brine that resulted from de-icing the roadway with salt during the winter months. The iron was the anode (gave up electrons) with respect to the copper (cathode) and moisture dissociation supplied the hydroxyl ions (OH$^-$) that produced the rust. The corrosion was most severe wherever the copper spiral made electrical contact with the iron.

There was nothing wrong with the materials or the method of heating the pipe to keep the oil flowing. The cause of the attack was that the thermal lagging should have been made impervious to water. Even though the duct was drained, over a period of time storm water and debris washed from the road would be likely to build up and block the drainage. Measures should have been taken to keep the lagging dry and there should also have been some thin, electrically insulating coating or wrap on the surface of the pipe to prevent any electrical contact with the spiral. It was easily foreseeable that a duct across a roadway would inevitably become flooded from time to time. So the blame rested with the architect and the subcontractor who installed the pipeline.

6.3.2   Vehicle Brake Pipe Failure

A second-hand car approximately 7 years old was purchased from a dealer with an MoT certificate (an official document based on vehicle tests carried out on all vehicles over 3 years old used in the U.K.) issued by an independent garage dated 1 week before the purchase. The new owner took the car back after a day or so, complaining that the brakes appeared to be "soft and spongy."

The dealer looked under the hood, noticed the brake fluid level was low and said air had probably got into the line. He promised to bleed the system and have the car ready within the hour. The brakes were working satisfactorily on the owner's journey home. The next day returning home from work the owner was fatally injured when his car ran out of control near the bottom of a steep hill and collided at speed with an oncoming vehicle.

The above information emerged at the inquest. Immediately after the accident a police vehicle examiner had taken possession of a brake pipe with a perforation that had clearly been the cause of the escape of braking fluid. He noted that the brake pads and linings were in good condition, consistent with having been renewed, and also that exposed sections of the brake pipes had recently been replaced. The pipe with the perforation followed the chassis from front to back for most of its length and was concealed by the exhaust system except in the one place where it was perforated. However, at the inquest the deceased's wife claimed that the pipe had been tampered with by someone dismissed for stealing from the firm where her husband, his foreman, had been the main witness. Deliberate damage to brake pipes by cutting or wrenching off to give the appearance of being the cause an accident is not as uncommon as might be thought; in one case the driver of a truck who had killed a child returned at night to where the truck had been parked and cut the brakeline with a pair of pliers.

For most of its length the brake pipe appeared to be in reasonable condition, with only one short length from the front exhibiting corrosion, apparently where it had caught splash from the front wheels. The perforation was in this portion, as illustrated in Figure 6.2. Notice that although the surface appears to be fairly bright and shiny there are numerous "freckles" around the large perforation.

Does this look like a hole punched from the outside or formed by mechanical means with some tool or implement? No. There would be some deformation of the surrounding metal if external force had been applied at this position. The crater-like appearance is characteristic of corrosion pitting from the outside of the tube wall.

The way this tubing is made has a lot to do with the way it has corroded. It was frequently used for the fuel and braking systems of motor vehicles and, in fact, is still used on many such systems. There is nothing intrinsically

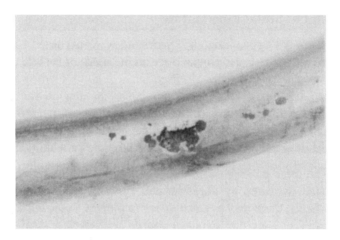

Figure 6.2 Perforation in the brake pipe.

wrong with the tubing and it does offer a cheaper way of making small diameter pipe that is ductile and easily formable compared with the more expensive cupro-nickel alloys. The tubing starts off as a long strip of low carbon steel of half the wall thickness of the pipe and a width of roughly twice its circumference, with scarfed edges. This is plated with copper on all surfaces and then roll shaped to form a double-walled tube, as indicated in Figure 6.3. It is then passed through a furnace which melts the copper, forming a brazed joint and also leaving a coating of copper on the outside. It finally goes through a bath of molten lead-tin alloy to produce a corrosion-resistant coating of "terne plate," rather similar to soft solder. The tubing is produced in long coils; to form a brake pipe the required length is cut off, fittings slid on and the ends expanded so as to make a secure fluid tight fixing to the brake cylinder or an appropriate union.

Figure 6.4 shows a section across the wall of the brake pipe, taken through one of the spotted areas evident to the left of the perforation. These spots were referred to earlier as "freckles," which is an apt description as they only appear to be surface blemishes. However, the terne coating has disappeared, and there is a cap of copper at the surface apparently following the original contour of the pipe; beneath it, a cavity has appeared extending almost half way through the wall. This is the result of the cell potential set up between the iron as anode and the copper, tin and lead cathodes in the coating. When the cavity reaches midway through the wall a further layer of copper will become exposed, causing the pit to penetrate rapidly to the inside wall. Figure 6.5 is a cross section through the perforation that shows how the center layer of copper braze had lined the developing pit as it approached the inside wall.

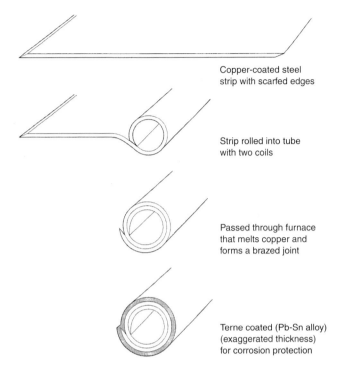

Copper-coated steel
strip with scarfed edges

Strip rolled into tube
with two coils

Passed through furnace
that melts copper and
forms a brazed joint

Terne coated (Pb-Sn alloy)
(exaggerated thickness)
for corrosion protection

Figure 6.3   Steps in the manufacturing process to make a cheap, small diameter tube with high ductility, suitable for forming into fuel and brake pipes of motor vehicles.

The terne coating on this short length of the pipe had been damaged by abrasion and spray from the road wheels, or there may even have been a pin hole in the terne metal coating that had exposed copper and possibly small areas of iron. Once the iron had become exposed at the outside pitting, the corrosive attack would have been very rapid. When the perforation first appeared the brake fluid would be ejected only when the brakes were applied and it would be squirted onto the road instead of dribbling down over the chassis or wheel hubs. The only warning sign to the owner would be the need to frequently top up the brake fluid reservoir.

Notwithstanding the unlikely possibility of the owner discovering the leak, the perforated pipe should have been detected in the MoT examination only a week before the accident. Fluid was being lost at every application of brake pressure because within a day of purchasing the car the new owner took it back to the dealer who immediately recognized the brake fluid reservoir was almost empty. Although the brakes were claimed to have been bled at this time, it was by no means certain that they were or that anything at

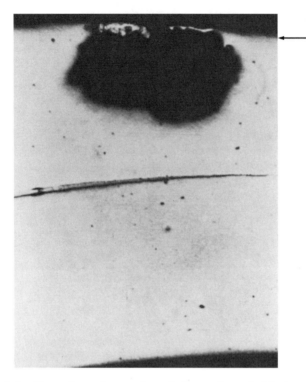

Figure 6.4 Cross through a section of pipe surface pit. Notice the cap of copper on the outside.

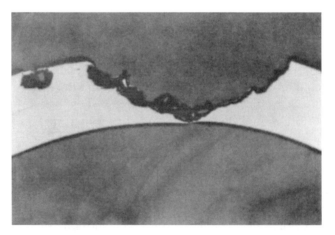

Figure 6.5 Cross section of pipe through spotted area. Notice thin flakes of copper braze resting inside of the hole toward the bottom. Terne plate provides very good corrosion resistance as long as it remains continuous over the outside of the pipe. Unfortunately, if it is not continuous or becomes damaged so as to locally expose a small area of iron, the subsequent rate of pitting corrosion can be very rapid because iron is anodic to all three metals in the coatings, i.e., the copper, lead and tin in the terne metal.

all was done apart from topping up the brake fluid, with the leak again going unnoticed.

The widow's claim that the brakes had been maliciously tampered with was clearly without foundation, but the dealer and the garage who issued the MoT certificate were prosecuted and fined heavily.

6.3.3   Stainless Steel Pipe Clamp Corrosion

Instructions were to ascertain the cause of failure of a pipe clamp that split open after a period of service on a pipe carrying pressurized hot water at 98°C, allowing an escape of water that led to extensive flooding damage. A large claim had been lodged against the firm who had installed the clamp and the firm, in turn, alleged that the failure had nothing to do with its fitting, but was the fault of the clamp manufacturers.

Figure 6.6 is a general view of the clamp, which is essentially a sleeve of thin (0.7 mm) type 316 stainless steel with a "T" junction, fitted to the pipe like a saddle, tightened by bolts passing through end pieces. It is lined with a soft gasket to make a water-tight seal. The T branch projecting from the side is not an off-take but rather it allows monitoring devices to be inserted without interfering with the flow of water. The clamp bolts were still tight at their original positions.

In what direction would the greatest tensile stress be acting when the clamp was attached to a pipe? It is the hoop stress, normal to the axis of the pipe.

The stainless steel had split from top to bottom, releasing the clamping force and allowing the water to force its way under the gasket and escape to outside. The bottom end of the split is shown in Figure 6.7A and at the top

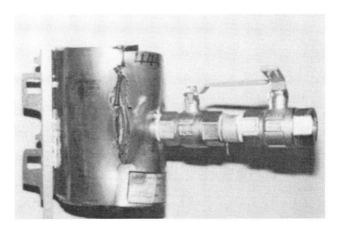

Figure 6.6   General view of the pipe clamp as received.

Figure 6.7 Closer views of the split. (A) Bottom of split. (B) Top of split showing PVC tape between the gasket and stainless steel.

of Figure 6.7B. In addition to the visible, surface-breaking multiple cracks, the slightly rumpled appearance is due to the fact that there are many more cracks part way through the wall, starting from the inside, that had not broken through to become visible on the surface. This myriad of fine branching cracks, all tending to lie at 90° to the tensile hoop stress, is characteristic of stress corrosion cracking, brought about by a combination of high levels of tensile stress within a metal exposed to a corrosive agent.

The gasket was made from a silicone elastomer because it is essential that it retain its elasticity for prolonged periods of exposure at temperatures up to 100°C. A different elastomer material is generally used on clamps for cold water pipes and compressed air lines. The gasket was made up from three pieces of material, held together with PVC tape while the cyano-acrylate adhesive was curing. The end of this tape can be seen at the top in Figure 6.7B and is visible behind the split all the way down to the bottom of the sleeve. It was immediately obvious that this tape had degenerated and become brittle in service and, most significantly, that the cracking of the stainless steel sleeve was confined to the immediate area in contact with the tape. No cracking whatsoever could be detected in the T junction or the rest of the sleeve, which exhibited no sign of surface staining or corrosion. Thousands of similar pipe clamps had been used on pipes carrying cold water and using a rubber gasket, most believed to be still in service, without any problems. A small number were fitted with silicone gaskets for hot water applications. The manufacturers claimed that PVC tape was used in all of these and no service failures had been reported to them. If this is true then it would suggest that the water in those applications was not as hot as that in the pipe where the failure occurred or it is also possible that the clamps were not done up so tightly.

Many alloys are susceptible to this type of attack, some of which otherwise have excellent corrosion resistance. It occurs when a high level of tensile stress exists or acts upon a component where there are traces of some specific chemical ion in the environment. In the absence of the particular ion or when the stress level does not exceed a particular threshold, there is no attack. For stainless steels the troublesome ion is chloride. The stress in this instance was derived from the clamps pulling the sleeve tight around the pipe, producing a tensile hoop stress. Cracks grow at right angles to the tensile stress, so this is why they all tended to lie parallel to the axis of the sleeve. The time taken to complete failure depends on the level of stress, the concentration of the aggressive agent, the wall thickness and the temperature where the process is taking place.

The source of the chemical ions was the strip of PVC tape used to temporarily locate the gasket inside the sleeve at the time of fabrication by the manufacturer. It served no purpose in the design or function of sealing action of the gasket. PVC degrades thermally at temperatures above about 72°C, one of the products being HCl (hydrochloric acid). The brittleness of the tape inside this sleeve shows that it had degraded under the service conditions on the hot water pipe. The chloride ions were thus present at the interface of the tape and the stainless steel, which allowed the stress to produce the stress corrosion cracks.

It would be only a matter of time in service on the hot water pipe before the failure took place. It is unlikely that routine inspection would have revealed the deteriorating state of the metal. At best all that might have been detected on the outside of the sleeve would be microscopically small cracks shortly before the catastrophic rupture took place.

This failure was clearly the responsibility of the manufacturer, who used PVC tape at the time the sleeve was assembled. It was not caused by the silicone gasket material, the adhesive, or the way the sleeve had been attached to the pipe. It was foreseeable that close contact at moderately elevated temperatures between PVC and type 316 stainless steel was likely to result in stress corrosion cracking. The problem with keeping the gasket in alignment during assembly could have been easily overcome in other ways, for example, using mechanical means or a jig. The failure would probably not have occurred, or would have taken very much longer to do so, if the pipe had not been carrying such hot water. Use of the PVC at temperatures approaching 100°C caused the rapid deterioration of the PVC.

A molybdenum-bearing type of stainless steel might have resisted longer, but it is unlikely any grade could have lasted for long under the high hoop stress applied in this instance.

6.3.4   Other SCC Failures

The same form of stress corrosion cracking that appears in the sleeve occurred in a fatal accident that involved failed stainless steel bolts from one of the early PVC manufacturing plants. The chloride ion on its own is a common cause of stress corrosion for some types of stainless steels, for example, fittings on ocean-going boats when an inappropriate grade of stainless steel for contact with salt water has been used. There was another case in which hollow spring pins used for hinges in a kidney dialysis machine failed by stress corrosion resulting from the salt solution used for cleaning the machine after dialysis.

Both a corrosive agent and a high level of tensile stress are necessary for stress corrosion. The stress either can be externally applied as in this instance or, quite frequently, it can be internal residual stress from a cold forming process. The mechanism of stress corrosion cracking was, in fact, first studied more than 100 years ago when brass cartridge cases were found to be cracking in humid monsoon conditions when traces of ammonia were in the atmosphere. The remedy was simply for the manufacturer to subject the (empty) cases to a low temperature stress relief anneal after the deep drawing process, which reduced the residual stress to a safe level.[1]

6.4   A Plumbing Problem

Chlorine attacks not just metal parts but many plastic materials, especially those used in plumbing systems. This actuality was not appreciated until relatively recently, when plastics were introduced on a large scale into central heating systems and other water supplies. The case study examined in depth here involved litigation, and occurred when a small acetal plastic junction failed suddenly one weekend in November 1988, in a sink in the Physics Department at Loughborough University (Figure 6.8). The subsequent flood of water from the cold water main into the Computer Department immediately below caused great damage to the equipment. The plumbing arrangement (see Figure 6.9) was the focus of attention by the loss adjusters and their expert. The acetal fitting was situated below the hot water tap, and was supported in a steel bracket, so that when the tap was turned on, cold water would be supplied to the large water heater. This in turn pushed hot water out to the tap itself.

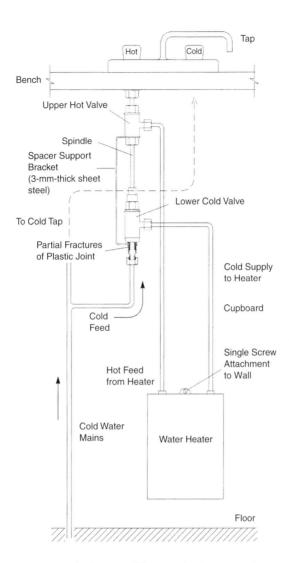

Figure 6.8 Pipework with direct cold water feed to tap. Hot water is fed from a water heater below the sink via a three-way junction, where the failure occurred.

The heavy water heater was attached to the wall by only a single screw, which had come dislodged from the wall, and placed the surrounding copper pipes under bending loads (Figure 6.8). The break in the plastic fitting was just below the lower bend in the steel bracket, where the rising main supplied incoming cold water to the system. Since the bracket was substantial, any extra load would have been supported by it rather than being transmitted to the plastic junction (Figure 6.9).

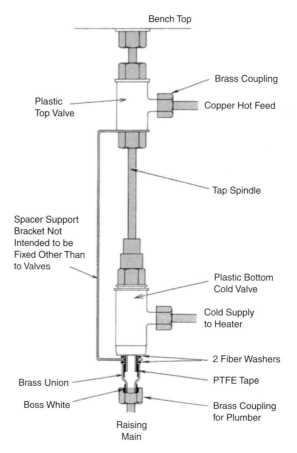

Figure 6.9 Details of the junction assembly showing the lower acetal resin thread where the fracture occurred.

6.4.1 Reasons for Failure

Clearly, there must have been another reason for the failure. The next suggestion was that the junction had been overtightened by the plumber. The system had been fitted during renovation work 4 years earlier. Now this is an interesting suggestion, because it seems to imply that the fitting *could* be overtightened, and might thus have been a faulty design in *allowing* overtightening. Nevertheless, overtightening is of course a common way of producing extra stress on a joint, but what did the evidence show? If screw joints are overtightened, there might be supporting evidence from the fiber washers used in the system. They bear any excess stress at the end of tightening, so if the joint had been overtightened, one might expect some damage to them. In fact, there was no evidence that the washers had broken or distorted excessively at all (Figure 6.10). But this is where the problem lay when it came

Figure 6.10 The washers on the failed joint showed little permanent set or cracking, so it was unlikely that they had been overtightened during fitment.

to assessing who would pay for the very substantial damages to the computers below the flood. The loss adjuster's expert blamed overtightening as the cause of failure, possibly exacerbated by the "faulty" screw attachment to the wall. Thus the loss could be recovered from the plumber or company who installed the system, and possibly the architect for planning the system in the first place.

The plumbing company and the architect (or rather their insurers) refused to accept the blame, and so proceedings were issued by the University against them. At this point, the defendants naturally needed their own expert to examine the failure and produce a report (preferably someone with expertise in the failure of plastics materials). The failed acetal fitting was critical, but had not been examined in detail by the first expert. Why not? The reason or reasons are not known. It seems so obvious that the evidence at the heart of a failure, the cracked fitting in this instance, should be subjected to detailed analysis. However, some experts fail, for one reason or another, to make the leap into detailed inspection, perhaps because they do not have the expertise or laboratory equipment, or perhaps because of casework pressure.

6.4.2 The Fracture Surface

The fracture surface of the acetal fitting is shown in Figure 6.11 with an interpretative map in Figure 6.12. The fracture surface showed several very old fracture origins, now concealed by debris deposited from the water supply, so inferred from flaps left by crack growth (Figure 6.13). The detail shown in the latter figure suggests that there were at least five different growth regions, with crack growth directions as indicated by the bold arrows. The

Figure 6.11   Side view of the broken fitting with the brittle fracture surface at right.

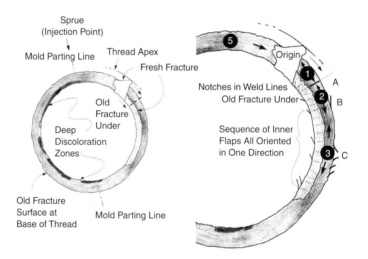

Figure 6.12   Fracture surface map to show multiple crack initiation and slow crack growth.

white areas represent the fresh fracture induced by the loss adjuster's expert when the sample rolled off his desk! When the areas adjacent to the fracture surface were examined in detail, one significant feature emerged: there were numerous subcritical cracks that appeared to have grown from weld lines in the threads and on the inner surface of the fitting (Figure 6.14). The weld lines appeared to be associated with flow lines in the outer surface of the molding, suggesting that the molding may have been faulty. Flow and weld

Figure 6.13 Close-up of side of the fracture surface with flaps due to crack branching, from which crack growth direction could be inferred.

Figure 6.14 Close-up of the crack tip showing weld lines ahead of the crack.

lines are indicative of cool tools, so that flow of molten polymer in the mold tool is inhibited. The fact that the fitting had been screwed tightly to produce a closure stress on the threads was indisputable as Figure 6.15 shows. So what effect would such weld lines have when the thread was screwed tightly by the plumber?

6.4.3   Water Pressure

Tiny weld lines could concentrate the tightening load if any were situated at the root of a thread. One common observation of failures from screw threads is that failure is often situated at the next-to-last thread, a feature confirmed by theoretical analysis of the stress-concentrating effects of thread forms. Thread failures are themselves rather common simply because threaded joints and connections are some of the most common ways of joining components together. However, there was no evidence of an excessive closure stress made by the plumber when finally tightening the joint, and the cause of the failure

Figure 6.15 Section of fitting showing closure strain at threads.

remained unknown at this stage of the investigation. What was clear was that there was no evidence supporting the proposal that the joint had been over-tightened (and that therefore the plumber was to blame).

One additional factor is the internal pressure from the water supply. Although it had not been measured directly, the specification of the fitting allowed for a pressure of up to 25 m head of water. The pressure will, of course, impose a hoop stress on the wall of the fitting, but what magnitude would it be? The pressure can be calculated using the simple equation:

$$P = \rho hg = 1000 \times 25 \times 9.81 \text{ Pa or Nm}^{-2}$$

So that

$$P \sim 0.25 \times 10^6 = 0.25 \text{ MPa}$$

Figure 6.16 Comparison of moldings showing different flow line patterns, none of which matched those of the failed fitting.

The hoop stress (the largest stress acting on the pipe wall from the water pressure) in the system is then simply given by

$$\sigma_H = PR/t = 0.25 \times 19/1.6 \sim 3 \text{ MN m}^{-2}$$

This stress is small compared with the "normal" tensile strength of acetal material, of about 70 MN m^{-2}. Although molding would reduce the strength somewhat, it was difficult to see how the combined effects of internal pressure and screw thread stress raiser could initiate crack growth and, ultimately, catastrophic failure.

6.4.4   Molding Features

What could have created the weld lines in stressed areas of the molding? A detailed survey was made of new moldings supplied by the manufacturer. The moldings were smeared with graphite powder to highlight the flow and weld lines, and it was determined that there were considerable variations between the 12 moldings examined (6 of which are compared in Figure 6.16). It was concluded that there was a pattern to the markings, especially in the flow lines. The set had probably been made in two batches, each producing a different flow line pattern. Weld lines did exist but were much less serious than in the failed sample. Moreover, the failed sample showed weld lines where none could be found on any of the new moldings, especially in the critical threaded areas of the lower inlet pipe. The failed sample had thus been made in a different batch, and may even have been a maverick sample.

6.4.5 Stress Corrosion Cracking

One failure mechanism that has been known for many years is environmental stress cracking (ESC). Certain fluids can cause brittle cracking of plastic products, even at very low imposed stresses. One of the first examples to be discovered occurred in polyethylene exposed to very strong detergents (such as an ionic soap known as Igepal). Stress corrosion cracking (SCC), where the fluid interacts chemically with the polymer surfaces to which it is exposed, was also an alternative cause of failure. In order for attack to commence in either form, there must be a driving force to open the crack. It can take two main forms:

1. Small stresses or strains imposed on the system
2. Frozen-in strain (oriented chain molecules)

It is also known that the more aggressive the attacking agent, the lower the critical strain needed to grow cracks.

6.4.6 Acetal Polymer

In its original form as polymerized experimentally, polyoxymethylene was not a useful plastic. The problem lay in its ease of degradation back to monomer, in this case formaldehyde (HCHO). This could occur simply when the material was heated (in an injection molding machine, for example). Two strategies were adopted to improve the stability of the material in order to offer it on the market: copolymerization with another monomer and end-capping every chain.[2] Since degradation unzips the chains from their ends, the latter strategy blocks unzipping. The former route allows very limited unzipping, because the second monomer cannot react and therefore halts further reaction. Both versions of the polymer are available commercially, the failed fitting being made from the latter. However, the commercial polymers are both susceptible to attack, especially by oxidizing agents. It was known, for example, that acetal could not be used in swimming pool plumbing, where chlorine levels can be very high. Chlorine is a very powerful oxidizing agent, which is why it is used for water purification (it attacks and degrades bacteria). Could the much lower levels present in potable water supplies have attacked the material?

6.4.7 A U.S. Problem

While the various expert reports were being digested by the several parties now in the action (university, plumbers, architects), we happened to come across a report in a technical newspaper that suggested that there could indeed be a problem with chlorine attack from the water supply. A news item in a U.S. journal[3] reported the settlement of a case (prior to trial) involving domestic hot water supply pipes, where polybutylene (also known as polybutene) pipes had been equipped with acetal copolymer fittings. The fittings had failed and caused floods, and the paper actually reported a class action, where many affected families sued the manufacturers and suppliers of the materials. Both the pipe and fittings had suffered extensive cracking on their inner surfaces, a problem expert opinion considered to be caused by chlorine and also probably by dissolved oxygen in the water.

A further class action in Texas came to trial in 1992, and resulted in a large settlement for the numerous plaintiffs (*Babb v. U.S. Brass, Shell, Hoechst-Celanese, DuPont*). It was this case that attracted our attention (acting on behalf of the plumbers in the U.K. case). Contact by the defendant's attorney with the plaintiff's attorneys produced not only copies of the expert reports in the case, but also the transcripts of the trial itself (when the expert evidence is tested in public). It was clear from those expert reports that even low levels of chlorine down to 0.3 ppm (parts per million) in the water could cause serious stress cracking of acetal copolymer.[4] Such levels can occur in drinking water, so it seemed as though the problem of the cracked acetal fitting may have been caused directly by chlorine. A check with the local water board produced extensive analyses, both from 1993 and 1988 (when the fitting failed). The records showed that free chlorine was very variable at different sampling points, but could rise as high as 0.9 ppm. One reason for high levels was given as the "slugs" of chlorine added when there were breaks in the pipes as a precautionary measure to prevent ingress of contamination.

A direct experiment was then carried out on the failed fitting using the EDAX facility of the scanning microscope. Analysis of the surface showed the presence of chlorine in significant quantities. Presentation of the new evidence to the other parties in the dispute produced a rapid settlement of the action, with the parties all walking away (and bearing their own costs). The U.S. actions were appealed, but the appeal was lost in the Texas Court of Appeal, and the many plaintiffs received full restitution of their damages. This was incidentally one of the largest class actions (outside automobile actions) in U.S. legal history and ultimately cost the companies many millions of dollars in damages awarded and the costs of the actions.

6.4.8   Aftermath

What did the Loughborough University failure show? There appeared to be no widespread failures of similar fittings (as far as is known), and it would thus be reasonable to conclude that the particular fitting was indeed a maverick sample. Perhaps the fitting was supplied by mistake, for the very same reason that a faulty radiator box was fitted to a new car (in the case discussed in Chapter 7). The failure could probably be attributed to low levels of chlorine in the water supply which led to rapid creep rupture at weld lines on the inner bore adjacent to the threads. The several cracks thus initiated eventually merged as they grew slowly. Crack growth probably slowed down as the closure stress was relieved by their formation. During this period, water leakage was slow and allowed deposits to grow on the fracture surfaces, helping to stem the leak. This helps to explain why the leak was not noticed, or if noticed, dismissed as insubstantial. Some stimulus over the weekend of November 6–7, 1988 caused the crack to suddenly jump open and a major leak resulted. Movement of the mains inlet pipe or "water hammer" (a sudden surge in water pressure often caused by valve closure or opening) could have provided the stimulus for the flood (Figure 6.17).

The results of the case show how important it is to be aware of problems that may have occurred in other countries using the same material in a similar way. The U.S. case also revealed (in the expert reports) how the manufacturing companies had actually tested the materials long before they were promoted as fit for water plumbing fittings, in low levels of chlorine. The laboratories in those companies had shown that levels as low as 0.3 ppm chlorine could cause cracking and hence destroy the integrity of the materials. Why that information was concealed when they launched the plumbing fittings and pipe remains unestablished. Polybutene has been withdrawn from the market by the makers as a direct result of the U.S. litigation, although acetal remains and is widely used for fittings both here and in the U.S. Now, however, manufacturers are (or should be) fully aware of the possible problems that can develop if low quality moldings are supplied to users. There is now a body of research that describes the rigourous testing on many other polymers for sensitivity to chlorine,[5] in addition to the results of our case study.[6]

6.5   Fuel Pipes

The case study discussed in this section involves extruded tubing used in car gasoline fuel lines under the hood of a particular brand of automobile (Fiat Mirafiori) in the late 1970s. The cars were brand new at the time the fires

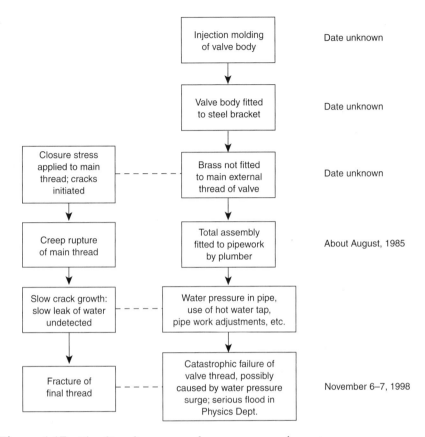

Figure 6.17   Flowline diagram to show sequence of events.

occurred in the late 1970s, and the incidents raised issues of consumer safety, quite apart from the warranty damage involved. One such fire occurred when a new car owned by the British actor Sir John Gielgud was traveling along the Embankment in London. Smoke was seen coming from the engine compartment, and although the fire was extinguished, substantial damaged had been caused (Figure 6.18). Examination of other fire-damaged cars by alert insurance inspectors showed that the fires were probably caused by a leaking fuel pipe near the engine.

The case was apparently solved with a recall, but reappeared in the late 1990s in a case before the High Court in Dublin. It raises the problem of dissemination of failure studies, especially in an international market where identical or very similar products are supplied to different national markets. It also focuses on the importance of quality control and assessment during product design and development, especially where consumer safety is paramount.

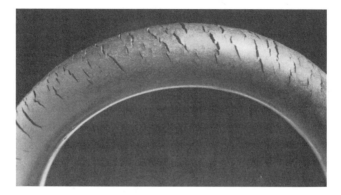

Figure 6.18 Ozone cracking in NBR rubber fuel pipe. The cracks have not yet grown to criticality.

6.5.1 Cracking and Abrasion

Ozone gas is extremely reactive and is produced in the atmosphere by the action of sunlight on car exhaust fumes, with the ozone levels rising in the spring and summer. However, the gas is also produced near electrical equipment, especially during sparking, so concentrations can be high under the hoods of gasoline engines. In addition, levels of atmospheric ozone rise during pollution episodes. Ozone cracking is easily initiated simply from bends in susceptible tubing. Examination of the material of the pipe from the fire-damaged cars showed it to be NBR (nitrile butadiene rubber), which is gasoline resistant, but an intact sample of pipe showed ozone cracks (Figure 6.19). Crack growth occurs laterally and at the crack tip, and will ultimately

Figure 6.19 The engine compartment of Gielgud's car showing the smooth rubber fuel intake pipe at T (below center) and the nylon return pipe at O (above center). The fire started at O.

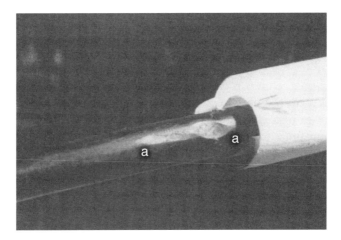

Figure 6.20 Abrasion marks on nylon return pipe where it came into contact with the hot metal of the engine.

penetrate into the interior of the tubing, resulting in loss of gasoline under pressure from the fuel pump. As soon as the liquid hits the hot engine manifold, it vaporizes, and any small sparks from the electrical circuitry can initiate an explosion followed by fire. In addition, a problem with another part of the fuel system revealed that a thermoplastic material had been used for the return pipe that passed over the engine, returning unused fuel to the gasoline tank. Due to its poor abrasion resistance, this pipe could also leak if any part contacted the engine manifold, where abrasion caused a hole to develop (Figure 6.20, a–a). The pipe was an extrusion of nylon 11, and possessed a melting point of about 176°C.

Since several cars had been damaged by such fires, it seemed clear that both unprotected NBR fuel pipes and nylon return pipes had been fitted widely, and so a recall of the model was carried out.

6.5.2   A Problem in Eire

The recall was carried out in the early 1980s, so it came as some surprise when the original investigator was approached by lawyers involved in a High Court claim for damages in the early 1990s. A serious fire in the Irish Republic in the late 1980s in a rather old Fiat Mirafiori had caused serious injuries to two young children who were strapped in the rear of their mother's car. She had been shopping, and upon arriving back home, had removed the ignition keys to open her front door. As she turned back to remove her children, the car interior burst into flames. Fortunately, the children were rescued by neighbors, but not before they had suffered serious burns. The resulting court action claimed substantial damages for their continuing care, as well as for the pain and suffering.

The accident was unusual in that the fire had occurred in the interior of the car rather than the engine compartment (where the original problem had been discovered). So what was the likely cause? Unfortunately, most of the evidence had been lost in the fire, because the car was nothing more than a burnt-out shell when it was examined later. There were two possible causes: a faulty heater near the dashboard, and the plastic return pipe to the gasoline tank at the rear of the vehicle. The seats were filled with highly inflammable polymer foam, but the rapidity of the fire suggested a gasoline leak and ignition from a spark. Ignition could have been from the faulty heater although it is well known that static sparks can easily ignite gas or fumes. The fuel return pipe passed through the interior of the car, and could have leaked gasoline just before the fire. It then only needed a small spark, perhaps when the woman left the car or closed the door, to ignite the fumes. A small fire became an inferno as the liquid gasoline caught fire, and the fire grew into the seats. Such a scenario seemed feasible, but lacked corroboration in detail.

6.5.3 *Murphy Infants v. Fiat Spa*

By the time the investigator's original report was requested, the case had reached an impasse. In personal injury actions, the plaintiff often faces the problem of discovering details of manufacturing processes, QC procedures and previous incidents, from the defendant companies. The problem of "discovery" from Fiat Spa in Ireland had led to a "striking-out" claim against the company, because Fiat either could not or would not release the required information to the claimants' solicitors. The latter thus pursued the information independently, and came across the public information of the recall in the early 1980s. The trail led to the insurance company, which had unfortunately deleted the original independent report on which the recall was based. However, the insurance company did have a record that the report had been commissioned, so it was able to make contact with the original investigator. Fortunately, the investigator had retained all samples and reports from the first accidents, and was able to supply them directly to the legal team in Ireland. The report was supplied as an affidavit to the Court, and the defendant witnesses (heads of litigation and engineering from Italy) were cross examined on the evidence of the fuel line problem.

Their answers were rather evasive and lacked credibility this was somewhat surprising because they had some time to consider the questions in court, since they were provided with a translator. On the flight from London the previous day, the investigator heard them speaking fluent English with their attorney! The claimants succeeded in their action, but the case went to appeal on the legal principle of striking out the defense. It effectively meant that Fiat could not succeed when and if the main claims went to full trial. Although Fiat won the appeal, the claim was settled before trial with a substantial award to the injured children.

6.5.4 Aftermath

Due to the extensive publicity in Ireland,[7] the case revealed a series of fires in this model, and further claims were lodged after the successful settlement of the Murphy children. In hindsight, it seems remarkable that greater care was not taken during testing of the new model. The radiator case in Chapter 7 shows how new car models are now driven in realistic conditions before launch onto the wider market, so as to reveal any latent or hidden defects that are not readily apparent to the design team. This is why FMEA methods are so important during development, and why it is important to know what previous accidents have occurred in such simple and low-cost items as fuel pipes. We followed up the original study by examining fires in new Ford Cortinas, for example. Car fires continue to plague many new models, perhaps because the engine compartment is so vulnerable. However, reinforced fuel hose made from resistant and strong materials is readily available to designers, and there is no reason why such hose should not be specified during the design phase. Elastomeric hose that is also ozone resistant is also widely available, so this particular problem is not insurmountable. Many synthetic rubbers, which do not possess vulnerable double bonds, have been made available commercially within the past couple of decades. Car fires are particularly distressing in their effects, and the wider problem was recently highlighted in the U.S., when the largest ever damages were awarded by a jury in Los Angeles.

The case study of the Fiat Mirafiori illustrates the importance of cooperation between regulatory bodies in different countries, so that they are all aware of design problems with specific products and can take appropriate action. It also illustrates why it is so important that the basic engineering message of choosing components fit for their function is taken seriously so that problems do not recur, and the consumer does not suffer as a consequence of pure ignorance by the design team and the regulatory bodies. An incidental issue is one of preservation of records and samples, so that the lessons of particular investigations are not lost forever. Indeed, publication achieves just this purpose, because then the information is recorded permanently for posterity.

6.6 SCC of Diesel Fuel Pipe Connector

This case study involved the failure of a diesel fuel pipe on a commercial vehicle. It was the immediate cause of a serious accident in Scotland, when fuel sprayed onto the road into the path of other vehicles.

The accident occurred on the morning of November 5, 1997, when the victim's car skidded on a patch of diesel fuel in the road and turned into the

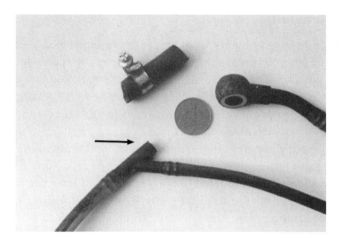

Figure 6.21 The failed Y molding (arrow) plus connecting pipe (at right) and repair tube as received from the Forensic Science Service.

opposite lane. The car collided with an oncoming truck, causing serious injuries to the driver. She subsequently spent considerable time in intensive care. The police followed the trail of diesel fuel some 5 miles to a local golf club, where the garage recovery vehicle was found. The spill had caused several other accidents, although none so serious as the first. A leak had occurred in the diesel return pipe, and the vehicle was quickly repaired. The remains (Figure 6.21) were examined initially by Strathclyde Police Forensic Labs in Edinburgh, which concluded that the line had been cut by a vandal. The case was referred to us to re-examine the remains, because the part concerned was extremely difficult to access in the engine compartment, and was thus unlikely to have been vandalized.

6.6.1 Remains of the Pipe

The parts of the pipe removed from the vehicle showed that the pipe itself had not failed, but rather a plastic Y-connection linking three pipes together (Figure 6.22). FTIR and DSC analysis showed that the connection had been injection molded from nylon 6,6 while the pipe itself was a nylon 12 extrudate. Although the break was flat and smooth, thus appearing cut, there were no traces of other failed attempts near the break. It is a difficult part to cut cleanly at one stroke, and why would a vandal try to cut the harder part? Traces of spray paint on the pipe and junction showed the parts to be original fittings (Figure 6.22). An intact return pipe from a separate wreck of a similar vehicle showed that the failure had occurred near or at the junction between the pipe and the nylon 6,6 fitting (Figure 6.21). Comparison also showed abrasion marks on the pipes at similar positions (lower arrows in

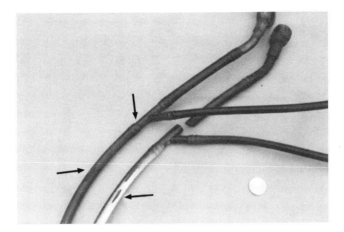

Figure 6.22   Comparison of failed and intact fuel lines from diesel recovery vehicles. The upper arrow shows one of the three junctions and the lower arrows show abrasion marks where the pipes made contact with hot engine parts.

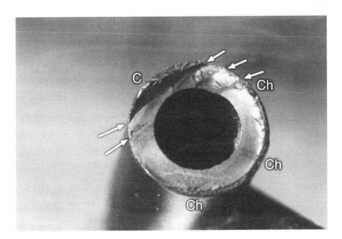

Figure 6.23   The failure surface from the nylon 6,6 molding showing eroded edge (chamfer, Ch) at the lower right, several crack arrest lines (arrows) and a cusp at top left of the sample (C).

Figure 6.22), a problem caused by wear against hot metal parts of the engine, itself a serious failure mode in car fires, as discussed in the previous section.

The failed surface showed several features that gave vital clues as to the way the junction had failed in service (Figure 6.23). Part of the outer edge showed signs of erosion in the form of a chamfer (Ch), followed by a smooth region and a set of crack arrest arcs (arrows). The final part of the surface showed a cusp of material rising above the plane of the surface (C). Detailed optical inspection revealed at least 11 crack arrest arcs, as shown by the lines

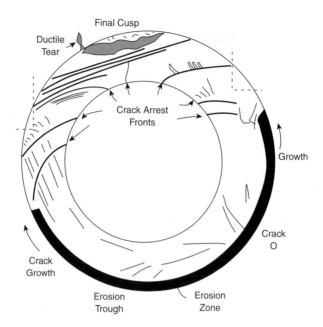

Figure 6.24 Fracture surface map showing detailed interpretation of crack features, with crack growth from eroded edge to final cusp.

in Figure 6.24, the fracture map of the surface. However several of the arcs represented single cracks separated by the central bore, and there were only seven major crack growth events. In the same study, some much smaller cracks could be seen growing parallel to the long axis of the tube. Interpretation suggested that the sample failed from an origin (O) in the eroded edge of the junction and grew in a series of steps to the final cusp. But what had initiated the sequence of events? The junction was just below the battery of the vehicle, and a possible cause of the erosion may have been attack by spilled battery acid.

6.6.2 Stress Corrosion Cracking

It is well known that nylon 6,6 is sensitive to attack by acids, especially sulfuric acid,[8] as indicated by Figure 6.25. A series of experiments with 40% sulfuric acid (battery acid) showed that a new junction failed suddenly by brittle cracking when exposed to acid, although only after several hours exposure under a very light self-load. The nylon 12 material of the pipe itself remained quite unaffected by the same fluid. It thus seemed feasible that acid had dripped onto the junction and attacked the edge. This degraded the material and allowed a crack to grow from the inner corner of the junction edge, growth which stopped at the first crack arrest line more than halfway down

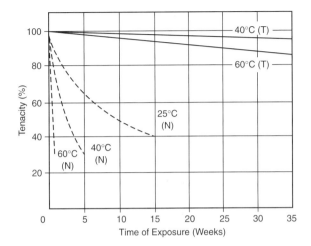

Figure 6.25 Loss of tenacity of Terylene PET fibers (T) and nylon 6,6 fibers (N) on continuous exposure to 10% sulfuric acid at various temperatures.[2]

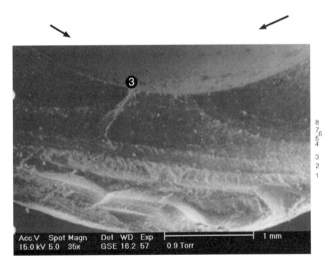

Figure 6.26 ESEM image of the final cusp on the fracture surface, with inner bore at the top of the picture. Crack growth direction is shown by arrows. Several major and minor striations are shown by the numbers at right.

the surface (Figure 6.24). Further intermittent growth then occurred in a series of steps until the final cusp was reached with the junction hanging by a thread. Further details of the fracture surface came with ESEM inspection. Much finer striations were seen between the large crack arrest lines in the ESEM (Figure 6.26). They showed that crack growth had occurred more slowly than expected, with the crack jumping intermittently under very slight loads. EDAX analysis showed traces of sulfur on the eroded part of the surface, supporting the acid attack hypothesis. However, the traces of sulfur disappeared further into the surface, suggesting that the crack grew mainly by simple strain of the pipe system later in the failure. So what loads led to crack growth?

6.6.3   Loading of the Return Pipe

The return pipe was not clamped to the engine manifold, but rather lay freely against it, as shown by the abrasion zone of Figure 6.22. Ties are normally available to prevent contact, but the present pipe examined appeared to have lost its ties some time ago. Flexible fuel pipes can move freely against rigid parts of the vehicle chassis, movement occurring when the engine is turned on and thereafter with driving. So what did the major and lesser striations represent in terms of the history of the vehicle? It was possible to suggest that the major crack arrest lines (Figure 6.24) represented start-up of the engine from cold, while the minor striations represented engine acceleration/deceleration during driving. Diesel fuel would thus have been leaking under low pressures (about 4–8 psi) from the return pipe with the engine running and the junction partially severed. The fuel lubricated points of abrasion, and reduced the load on the failing junction while the vehicle was moving. However, when stopped overnight, the diesel would have evaporated away, leaving a dry junction by the time the vehicle was started up again the next morning. Friction at such junctions would have been greatest during start-up. Such leakage increased with time as the hinged crack grew, with final separation just before the major spillage onto the road near Dundee.

6.6.4   Conclusions

The most likely explanation of the accident was therefore as follows. A small leak of battery acid occurred during routine maintenance of the recovery vehicle, with acid falling onto the nylon junction immediately below the battery. Chemical erosion of the edge led to stress corrosion cracking of the junction (Figure 6.27). One crack grew radially across the section, major growth occurring at engine start-up. The seven such major crack arrest lines represent seven engine start-ups from cold. Since garage vehicles are generally kept running through the day, each crack arrest front probably represents growth in 1 day, so the total sequence lasted about a week. Diesel fuel would have leaked slowly down the chassis and onto the nearby road, and would have been visible to a vigilant driver. Regulations in the U.K. stipulate daily checking of commercial vehicles for potential hazards, for example. Diesel fuel leaves a very slippery deposit on the driving surface, when the lighter

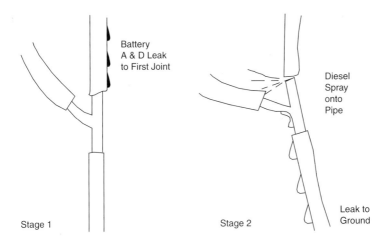

Figure 6.27 Failure mechanism of the pipe junction from SCC of nylon 6,6 by leakage of battery acid.

fractions of the liquid have evaporated away after a few minutes, equivalent to driving on black ice. The leak from the breakdown vehicle caused a total of four accidents that day, the most serious of which was experienced by the claimant in this action. Liability was denied by the insurers for the garage who owned the vehicle, but the injured woman driver received substantial damages for her very serious injuries. The new molded junction tested in our labs turned out on analysis to be acetal rather than nylon, a salutary reminder of the sensitivity of many engineering plastics to common chemicals found in car engines. Designers should be aware of the problem of stress corrosion cracking, and recommend appropriate materials for the function of the component parts of safety-critical products. Fuel lines are especially critical parts of engines, and the best possible materials are chosen for their construction. The consequences of poor design and maintenance of critical car parts can be devastating for the users.[9]

6.7   Sealing Materials

Design failures such as the acetal and polybutene cases from the U.S. are symptoms of new product development, despite the problems that had been foreseen to some extent by researchers. Tests carried out well before the widespread introduction of acetal resin had shown that the material could be sensitive to very low levels of chlorine in the water supply. However, the case considered in this section involved little or no direct testing of the product before widespread use in hot water systems. The case concerned one of the simplest products one can imagine: washers for hot water radiators.

Figure 6.28   Front view of the failed radiator with rust damage at the upper left air vent plug, and blanking plug at the lower right.

Figure 6.29   Plugs from the Stratford radiator showing brittle radial cracks.

At the time we became involved in the case, other investigators had already studied the extensive failures found in a wide variety of properties, with old people's homes and schools among the most common properties affected. Some domestic houses had also been affected. Plug and vent seals in thermoplastic polyester-polyether had failed and the leaking water had damaged floors and fabrics. The washers had been introduced in some cases only a few months before failing, the original intent being to improve washer lifetime (compared with older fiber washers). Failures were recorded from 1994 to 1996 before serious attention was paid to the problem. The engineer acting for the loss adjusters extracted several radiators (Figure 6.28) and examined the seals (Figure 6.29), concluding that the plugs had been fitted either too tightly or too loosely by the plumbers. This seemed unusual as many different plumbers had been involved, suggesting widespread incompetence at performing a very

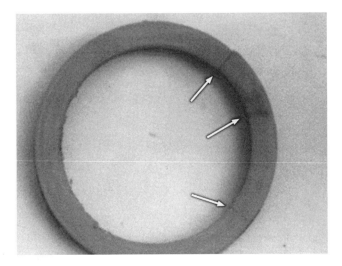

Figure 6.30   Failed washer showing several subcritical radial cracks (arrows).

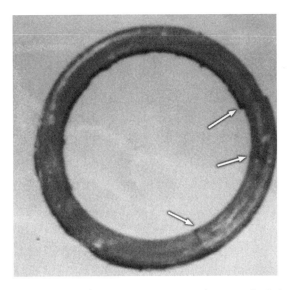

Figure 6.31   Same washer from Figure 6.30 rephotographed from engineer's report showing identity of crack paths.

simple task. The engineer's report to the insurers stated that one of the washers had broken during extraction from the radiator (Figure 6.29). Moreover, one of the photographs shown in that report exhibited traces of several radial cracks when inspected under a magnifier (Figure 6.30). Although the breakage had been mentioned in the report, the subcritical microcracks had been ignored. The state of the same seal was confirmed by rephotographing the picture in

Figure 6.32 Blanking plug from Benenden School with failed washer and evidence of extrusion on the outer side in the section at left (arrow).

the original report (Figure 6.31). Between our inspection and the original exmaination, a period of many months, there had been no change in the state of the seal. The conclusions of the initial report, therefore, effectively ignored vital evidence about the actual cause of the failures.

6.7.1 Failed Seals

The failed radiator taken from the Stratford old people's home (Figure 6.28) displayed rusting at the upper vent plug, showing the effects of long-term leakage. The plugs are shown in Figure 6.29, each with a single radial crack. Closer examination revealed many fine subcritical radial cracks visible as faint black lines against the red of the material (Figure 6.30), confirming their existence at the time of extraction (Figure 6.31). Other failed washers showed extrusion at the inner and outer edges, suggesting permanent set from exposure under compression loading when fitted (Figure 6.32 and Figure 6.33). The fracture surfaces showed crack growth from edge defects in the inner surface of the washers where they made contact with the steel of the radiator (Figure 34). Some of the cracks in the many washers examined showed the faint striations characteristic of fatigue growth (Figure 6.35). Other samples showed fast crack growth paths, probably induced when removing the washers.

6.7.2 Experimental Analysis

The infrared spectrum confirmed that the material was a polyether-ester elastomer, and DSC showed a melting point of about 220°C, a value consistent with the specification of Hytrel grade 7246. Comparison of granules, and new and failed plugs indicated a constant melting temperature, but

Figure 6.33   Air vent plug with cracked washer, showing traces of paint on the seal. Evidence of extrusion on the inner side is shown by the arrow.

Figure 6.34   Section of fractured washer with origin at upper right corner.

gradually increasing heats of fusion, from 32.3 mJ/mg for raw granules, 36.2 mJ/mg for new washers and 43.9 mJ/mg for failed washers.

Since the failed washers were all much stiffer than new washers, trial experiments were organized by an expert working for RAPRA in the U.K., to measure the set induced by exposure to hot water.[10] Five stacks of four new washers were compressed between steel plates, and washers fitted to

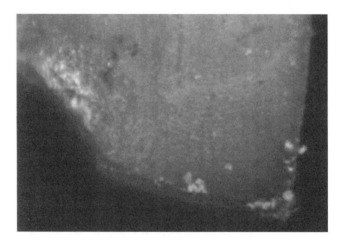

Figure 6.35   Close-up of lower right corner showing fatigue striations, probably produced by thermal cycling.

plugs using a torque of 27 Nm as recommended by the manufacturers. All were then exposed to 85°C for 3 weeks. After the experiment, permanent set of 90% was measured on the stack of washers. A torque of about 7 Nm was needed to unscrew the plugs, compared with about 2 Nm for a failed radiator plug. The hardness of the material had also increased by about 50% on average. The material possessed little sealing ability due to the lowered elasticity, the effect being comparable to that seen on failed washers exposed to central heating temperatures in service. Finally, the compression stress-strain behavior of new and exposed washers was compared. The new washers possessed an initial slope of 6 N/mm, while the failed washers showed a comparable result of 11.8 N/mm. The exposed washers were thus twice as stiff as new seals.

6.7.3 Discussion

Since the change in material properties observed on the failed washers could be reproduced experimentally, it was concluded that exposure to heat caused a critical loss of sealing ability of the material used in the injection molded washers. The temperatures to which they were exposed in service were not measured directly, but probably lay within the range 75 to 85°C, the higher temperatures being primarily used in old people's homes. CHS in those locations also tend to have longer hot periods, so the time to failure will have been lower, assuming a linear rate of material hardening. The loss of sealing capacity thus could be explained by material changes, probably by enhanced crystallization of the material at high water temperatures.[11] But how could

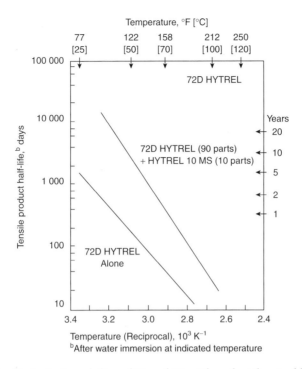

Figure 6.36 Hydrolytic stability of Hytrel 72 with and without added stabilizer as a function of time and temperature (DuPont).

cracking be explained? It is known from the commercial literature that thermoplastic polyether-ester elastomers are susceptible to hydrolytic degradation, stabilizers being available from the manufacturers.[12] Figure 6.36 shows the change in tensile product half-life as a function of temperature for a hard grade of Hytrel (72D), with and without added stabilizer (known as MS). It is clear from the lower curve that unstabilized Hytrel hydrolyzes fairly rapidly even at 60°C, having a half-life of only 100 days continuous exposure. There was no evidence that stabilizer had been added to the polymer washers.

More recent commercial literature[13] suggests that no grades of Hytrel are suitable for exposure to water temperatures greater than 50°C, so the radiator manufacturers should have been advised not to use the material as seals where temperatures were likely to be greater than this upper limit. The injection molders had previously developed washers for hot water taps in domestic supply systems successfully, but the temperatures of tap hot water are usually much lower, and exposure time is very much shorter than in CHS radiators. Washer breakage was probably caused directly by stress corrosion cracking, by hydrolysis, effectively confined to the crack tips.

Thermal cycling loads from expansion and contraction of the radiators would have been sufficient to cause fatigue crack growth. Chain degradation lowers strength and also enhances crystallization, another complicating factor in the failure equation.

6.7.4 Conclusions

The new material should have been tested thoroughly under expected service conditions before introduction onto the market, a conclusion agreed to by all the experts at a pretrial meeting. Ultimately, the substantial damages to property were paid by the insurers without a trial. The large production of several million unused washers was scrapped, and a new design using EPDM elastomer substituted. The case emphasizes the need to examine evidence objectively, and not to jump to hasty conclusions. If the first investigators get it wrong, the litigation machine is started and rolls blithely onward until halted by subsequent reinvestigations. Meanwhile, substantial costs have accrued, which must be paid by the losing side, usually the insurers. It is one thing to perform the research and development with new materials, and then ignore them (as in the case of the acetal fittings), and another thing not to perform routine tests at all.

References

1. Grimstone, F.S., Season-cracking of small-arms cartridge cases during manufacture, *J. Inst. Metals*, 39, 255–278, 1928.

2. Vogl, O., *Polyaldehydes*, Edward Arnold/Marcel Dekker, London, 1967.

3. Anon., Plastic pipe is expensive for industry, *Chem. Rep.*, March 18, 1991.

4. Armstrong, James and Duvall, Plaintiffs Exhibits in *Chris and Diane Babb v. Shell Chemical Co. et al.*, Matagorda County Court, Texas, 1992.

5. Lewis, P.R., Designing with Plastics, RAPRA-REVIEW Reports No. 64, 1993; e.g., Zhou, W., Chudnovsky, A. and Niu, X. SPE ANTEC 96, 3265.

6. Lewis, P.R., Degradation of an acetal plumbing fitting by chlorine, oral presentation, *Fapsig* session at ANTEC 2000, Orlando, 2000.

7. Anon., Court asked to strike out Fiat firm's defence in car fire case, *Irish Times*, October 12, 1994.

8. ICI Industrial Fibres Manual, 1981.

9. Lewis, P.R., Stress corrosion cracking of nylon 6,6, *Fapsig* session of ANTEC 2002, San Francisco, 2002.

10. Lewis, P.R. and Brown, R.P., Failure of TPE washers in central heating systems, *Fapsig* session of ANTEC 2002, San Francisco, May 2002.

11. Witsiepe, W.T., Thermoplastic polyether-polyester elastomers, *Handbook of Thermoplastic Elastomers, 2nd ed.*, Holden, G., Ed., Hanser, Munich, 1996, chap. 8.

12. DuPont technical brochure HYT-114, Hytrel 10 MS A Hydrolytic Stabilizer Concentrate, 1986.

13. DuPont Hytrel product guide and properties, 1997.

Failure of Storage Vessels

7

This chapter deals with the problems of storage vessels, which must be correctly designed in order to perform their function of containment of a fluid safely over a reasonable lifetime. The design problem is of course very similar to that of pipes, as described in Chapter 6. The consequences of failure can be catastrophic if the stored contents are released into the environment, as occurred in some of the examples described in this chapter. Historically, a variety of materials have been used to store fluids but the choice nowadays is narrow, with metals and plastics the main contenders. Large glass vessels, for example, were once very common, but they have been displaced by tougher materials capable of resisting imposed loads safely. Materials and manufacturing costs limit the choice further for mass-produced products such as domestic water storage tanks, where polypropylene has largely displaced galvanized steel. Widely different shapes can be produced quickly in plastics by injection molding or rotational molding, although manufacturing defects must be eliminated by effective quality control to prevent failure when the tank is put into service. Galvanized tanks suffer corrosion problems in time or through faulty installation, and can have equally dire consequences when failure occurs suddenly.

Composite materials have been widely used in specialty applications, such as header tanks for car radiators, the basis of the second case study in this chapter. Thermoplastic tanks have been in use in industry for a long period of time, at least from the early 1970s, and continue to expand in usage due to the ease of fabrication, the excellent resistance to corrosive chemicals and the low cost of the material. The speciality tanks are made individually to order by hand and are constructed with fairly simple equipment, so manufacturing costs are low. The increased usage has encouraged smaller companies to enter the field to provide competitive pricing, but the only standard covering their design, use and testing is German, and apparently not generally available to potential users.

Plastics materials are universal in specialist areas such as battery containers, due to their insulating properties and ease of shaping. However, problems have arisen when first introduced into safety-critical products such as miners lamps. Other problems have been caused during installation, as a case involving the Hong Kong transit system describes. Another problem arose when traction batteries for fork lift trucks failed prematurely due to UV degradation. Because thermoplastics can be shaped so easily, they are extensively used for domestic bathtubs, but problems can arise if the material is not capable of resisting applied loads. Two case studies show what can happen if either the material or the shaping process are not carefully monitored. Larger storage tanks are susceptible to much larger loads in service, and the consequences of failure are dire if the design cannot resist either external or internal loads. As in the last chapter, the failure of a conventional metal product is presented first.

7.1   Leakage of a Galvanized Tank

A previous chapter mentioned what is called the "galvanic series" in sea water, a ranking table setting out the common metals and alloys in order of decreasing tendency to corrode in sea water. Tables like this are useful for ascertaining which metals will be anodic and corrode when coupled to another metal. It stems from the ranking of electrode potentials of metals measured with reference to a hydrogen electrode in molar solutions of their ions at 20°C. Because real corrosion cells operate under less specific conditions, galvanic ranking tables are as good a guide as any with regard to which of two dissimilar metals is likely to be the anode and which is likely to be the cathode in a particular situation. If they are far apart the corrosion is likely to be rapid and if they are close it will be slow or may be overshadowed altogether by other effects.

The often quoted examples of the significance of the galvanic series are use of zinc and tin for coating protection of steel. From Table 2.1 the respective standard electrode potentials of the three metals are:

Zinc – 1.10 V   Mild steel – 0.58 V   Tin – 0.49 V

Because zinc is so much more electronegative than iron it will remain the anode in a corrosion cell and protect the steel. Even if a coating is damaged and exposes the underlying steel, zinc will still continue to protect the steel. After all, this is the basis for attaching sacrificial zinc anodes to the hulls of steel ships. Tin on its own is less reactive than iron in many chemical solutions and protects an article made of steel (i.e., tinplate) only while it remains a continuous coating. If it is scratched and the underlying steel is exposed then the iron becomes anodic to the tin and corrodes. As scratches are usually narrow the anode has a small area and the cathode has a large one, so the corrosion rate is rapid. That is why zinc is preferred to tin as a protective coating for steel articles in exposed situations. Galvanized steel tanks are widely used in common storage applications, although now plastic tanks are replacing them because of the susceptibility of steel to corrosion. Other unexpected problems can also arise in galvanized steel tanks.

7.1.1   The Failed Header Tank

The tank was a header tank for a heating system in a government laboratory in the U.K., and it was topped up from the public water supply when evaporation and loss from the system demanded. The tank was set high in the roof of the building at the gable end, double glazed from top to workbench level. It was painted black on the outside and faced almost due south. The tank was not shadowed by any other building. On the hot summer's day when an inspection was carried out in the early afternoon, the water temperature in the replacement tank had reached 76°C. It had failed suddenly, with water cascading into the workshop below and causing a great deal of damage. The workshop was packed with electronic equipment, so a large insurance claim was filed. When the seam of the old tank had given way, the mains water supply entered at full bore and, Murphy's Law acting as usual, the incident had occurred after work had ended on a Friday and went unnoticed until the following week.

It was a galvanized steel header tank which, for some unknown reason, had been painted with white gloss on the inside. This was still intact over most of the inside but corrosion was severe over an area of the base near one corner where the bottom had eventually perforated. The tank had not been mounted quite level, so this corner was the lowest point where any solid debris would tend to accumulate. There were particles of metal swarf projecting from the paint just beyond the corroded area. When the hole had been cut out for the downpipe fitting, particles of metal swarf had been left lying on the bottom of the tank and had been painted over but, as the swarf particles were thicker than the paint film, the tips were standing proud and had started to go rusty. These had initiated corrosion of the zinc, as some were still at the center of accretions of zinc corrosion product. The zinc coating had completely disappeared in the perforated corner of the tank, though there were still substantial areas of zinc coating in the surrounding area.

The explanation of the tank failure thus became clear. As the upstanding steel swarf particles in the paint rusted, the paint film was broken and exposed the galvanized coating, which then took over and acted as the anode. As the zinc surrounding these particles corroded away, the underlying steel was exposed, but this was still protected by the adjacent anodic areas of the remaining zinc for most of the year. However, every summer day when the water in the tank was heated to high temperatures by sunshine being absorbed by the black outer surface, the rate of corrosion here had increased dramatically and eventually corroded away the wall of the tank.

Basically it was the fault of the plumbing subcontractor when the heating plant was installed some 15 years or so before: first, for placing the tank high up in the gable end right against the window, painting it black and applying white gloss to the inside and, second, for not cleaning out the swarf when holes were drilled for the pipework. A plastic header tank would have been far better, but this system was installed in the days when galvanized steel tanks were still widely used in cold water systems.

7.2   A Radiator Failure

The problem of the quality of materials and manufacturing processes used to shape those materials applies to all systems in a car cooling system. Radiator reservoirs are products that must resist the high pressures and temperatures of the water, and the high temperatures to which they are exposed externally by the engine itself. New materials, such as glass-reinforced nylon, have become widespread for applications under the hood, and have proved themselves in applications such as inlet manifolds sitting directly on the engine. However, manufacturing standards, especially quality control by inspection, must be kept at a high level to eliminate defective moldings.

7.2.1   Material Requirements

High-temperature seals in CHS hot water systems (Chapter 6) must resist high-temperature degradation, and no less is true of new radiator materials. Radiator reservoirs in car engines, for example, must be capable of withstanding high water temperatures (about 80°C), high internal pressures and the high external temperatures of the engine compartment. New materials such as glass-reinforced nylon have become widespread for under-the-hood applications, and have proved ideal for inlet manifolds, for example. Such manifolds are lighter than cast metal equivalents, so that total engine weight is kept down and makes transport more efficient. A subsidiary bonus comes from greater ease of installation during assembly in the car factory. On the deficit side of the cost equation comes the greater capital cost of tool and machine investment than conventional materials, and the problems of development of such new materials.

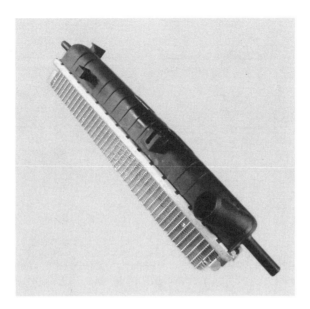

Figure 7.1   New radiator assembly showing the black composite tank attached to the aluminum heat exchanger vanes of the car cooling system.

Such developments have encouraged use of the same material, glass-filled nylon (GF nylon 6,6) for other car engine parts and, in the case examined here, car radiator header tanks (Figure 7.1).

7.2.2   Failure Investigation

As in so many such investigations, the critical failed part was the focus of initial attention, and was inspected macroscopically first. This enables the investigator to stand back from the actual failure zone, and place the whole component in its context. This in itself can prompt key questions that lead to the solution to the problem.[1]

The part failed by catastrophic failure of the tank, which was fitted to the cooling system, comprising just a half-shell (Figure 7.2A and B). The box was 41 cm long and 11 cm wide. Comparison of a failed product with an intact equivalent is always useful and, in this case, showed that the failed part revealed substantial distortion (Figure 7.3). The center part of the box had contracted significantly when compared with a new box. The same photograph also shows the way the part had been made, by injection molding from a central gate, leaving a remnant sprue in the center of the inside of the component. The sprue is circular and rather large because a wide gate is needed to allow the highly viscous molten polymer to penetrate all parts of the metal tool during molding.

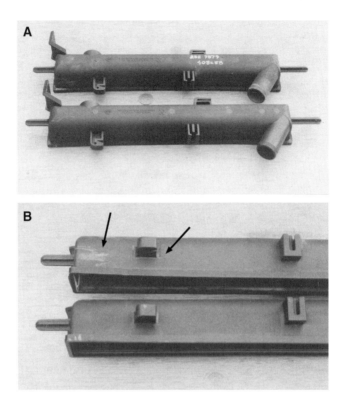

Figure 7.2 (A) Failed and new radiator tanks compared. The upper tank failed after only 500 miles in service. (B) Failure of the tank by slow leakage through a brittle crack (arrows).

Why should the distortion be important? It clearly distinguishes the failed box from a new box, so might be critical in determining the cause or causes of the failure. What then could cause such distortion? A problem common to all shaping processes is the problem of frozen-in stress or strain. When material is cooled from its molten state into the final product, such stresses and strains can be caused by overly fast removal of heat from the material. In polymers, the problem is one of frozen-in strain, which provides a driving force for crack growth, as well as causing distortion and hence mismatch with mating parts. In this case, the distortion had probably been revealed by exposure to the hot water of the cooling system, at a temperature not too far from the glass transition point of the nylon of about 79°C. The melting point of the material is about 265°C (as shown by the DSC curve of the material in Figure 7.4). Although there was no obvious connection between the distortion and the crack, it was an observation to keep in mind as the investigation progressed.

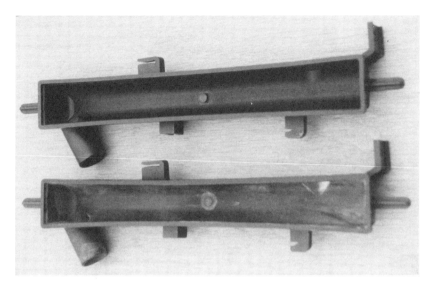

Figure 7.3   The inner surfaces of the new (top) and failed tanks (bottom), the latter showing severe longitudinal distortion. The failed tank appears lighter in tone due to treatment with chalk dust.

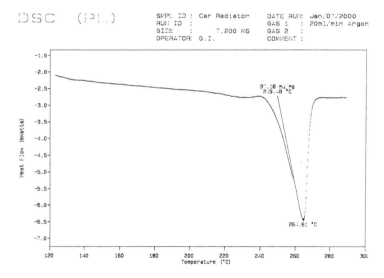

Figure 7.4   DSC curve of the glass-filled nylon 6,6 material used in the radiator tank, showing a melting point of 265°C and heat of fusion of 37.2 Jg⁻¹.

7.2.3   The Critical Crack

The critical crack was found at one end of the box, as shown by the arrows in Figure 7.5. It was a single brittle crack that adjoined a corner of an external

Figure 7.5   External view of the critical crack running along an external corner, the ends shown by arrows.

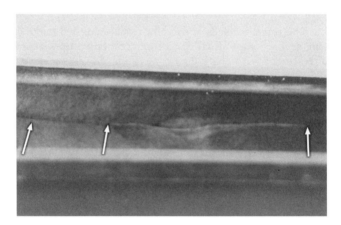

Figure 7.6   Internal view of the crack showing weld line at left.

bracket used for attachment of other engine parts. The arrow at left indicates the tide marks formed when the leakage occurred. Because they ran in one particular direction from one end of the crack, it could be inferred that the box was oriented vertically in the engine compartment with the lower end at the right in Figure 7.3. The crack was about 65 mm long, running through the wall of the tank. Inside the box, the crack possessed the same shape and dimensions as externally, but ran from or into a different feature known as a weld line (Figure 7.6). Weld lines are regular features found in moldings, normally where the molten polymer is forced around a core (to form a hole in the final product, for example) and the streams have to rejoin. The unusual position of this weld line is that it falls nowhere near such a design detail. The fact that the crack also lay very close to the weld line must surely provide some further clue to its origin.

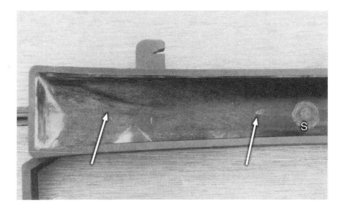

Figure 7.7   Inner surface of tank with sprue at extreme right with nearby cold slug (arrow), and weld lines at left (arrow).

Further information on the reasons for the weld line became evident when the material of the box tank was examined. It was important to see how the weld line had been formed and whether or not there were any more structural irregularities. Several methods were used to examine the failed sample, of which dusting of exposed surfaces with a white powder, chalk dust, turned out to be most useful, as Figure 7.7 shows. The reason is that molded composites often show great surface roughness due to the orientation of the fibers. The picture shows several prominent flow lines (precursors to weld lines) denoted by the arrow at the left, and a totally unexpected feature, a fragment of an original granule from the molding process (arrow at the right in Figure 7.7).

7.2.4   Microscopy

Of greater use where fracture surfaces are concerned is microscopy, initially at low magnification with a simple optical microscope, followed by SEM. It is always with some reluctance that one deliberately breaks a stable crack, but since all other methods had been exhausted, much valuable evidence could be shown by the fracture surfaces and this turned out to be the case.

Figure 7.8 shows one side of the fracture surface which, at first glance, seemed to show rather little in the way of a clear origin or other features that can often enable a picture of crack development to be reconstructed. Careful inspection, however, revealed tide marks left on the outer buttress. Since there were several such features, it was reasonable to suggest that several cracks had existed before the final catastrophic failure, probably small precursors to the final catastrophic failure. The evidence for that event lay in a much larger tide mark below, showing cooling water debris had collected there following a major loss of water. The second interesting feature seen at low magnification

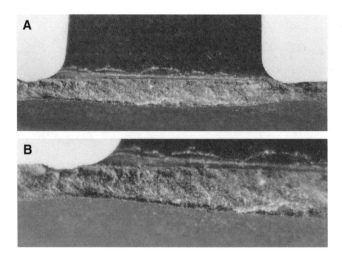

Figure 7.8 (A) Main crack near buttress corner showing witness marks from fluid spills and weld line visible on lower side of fracture. (B) Detail of fracture surface.

is a line of smooth material on the inner side of the fracture. This could represent unfused polymer present within the weld line already detected. Such indeed proved to be the case when the sample was examined in the SEM (Figure 7.9). Due to the much greater resolution of the method, vague or ill-defined features from the optical microscope could be seen with much greater clarity. The picture already shows substantial detail in the fracture, with a three-dimensional view unequaled by optical microscopy.

One hidden bonus of SEM, at least in this case, was the need to coat with gold to give a conducting surface (essential with polymers or non-metals) to bleed away electrons from the main beam. When the sample was reexamined optically, the contrast and definition was much improved, as Figure 7.10 shows. The weld line surface was now shown to be running for a large distance along the fracture surface. But more significantly, there were numerous visible cold slugs of partly melted granules embedded in the surface (shown by the upper arrows in the photograph). Their presence seemed to confirm a problem of "cold molding" in the sample. This occurs when the molding machine is started up ready for production. The barrel heaters are still warming up, and the polymer granules are not fully melted and homogenized before injection into the tool.

What about the mechanical strength of the material? It was important to test the material directly, and compare new and failed polymer samples. Tensile testing would provide basic mechanical properties, which could, for example, be used for comparison with the specification provided by the material supplier.

Figure 7.9 (A) Low magnification SEM picture of main crack near buttress corner. (B) High magnification shot showing weld line on inner surface and fiber pull-out.

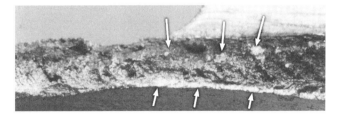

Figure 7.10 Gold-coated fracture surface showing cold slugs embedded in composite (upper arrows) and weld line (lower arrows).

7.2.5 Mechanical Tests

In a material showing orientation, it is standard practice to test samples both parallel and at right angles to any flow marks. Such tests could reveal any fundamental flaws such as weld lines, and so corroborate independent results from microscopy, for example. The results of analysis were as follows:

Sample No. 1 (new, lateral) $\sigma = 84$ MN m^{-2}

Sample No. 2 (new, parallel) $\sigma = 81$ MN m^{-2}

Sample No. 3 (old, parallel) $\sigma = 80$ MN m^{-2}

Sample No. 4 (old, lateral) $\sigma = 55$ MN m^{-2}

They show that the best results fell below the ideal suggested by a specification from the material supplier (84 MN m^{-2} compared with 140 MN m^{-2}). In one case the tensile test showed the sample to fall well below the ideal value when tested laterally to the flow marks in the sample. The material was brittle, although of high modulus. The results thus seemed to confirm that the product could be weakened seriously by flow or weld lines present. Could mechanical analysis shed any light on the reason or reasons for failure?

7.2.6 Mechanical Analysis

What stresses is such a radiator box likely to be subjected to in service? They can be calculated from the internal pressure of the system using standard formulae. A water cooling system is under internal pressure; one value suggested by the manufacturer was 25 psi. It produces a hoop stress of about 1.55 MN m^{-2}, a value well below the measured strength of the worst sample of about 55 MN m^{-2}. So what could cause the material to fail? There are four kinds of stress raisers that could initiate a brittle crack:

1. Geometric stress raiser at the buttress corner
2. Internal voids
3. Cold slug fragments, and
4. Frozen-in strain

The difficulty is attempting to estimate the net effect of all these factors working together. Using the known dimensions of the buttress corner, it was possible to use a stress concentration diagram[2] to estimate a K_t value of about 7.2. The model chosen to represent a void at a cold slug, for example, was that for a penny-shaped crack.[3] However, the evidence for the existence was rather weak, since distinguishing a void from a crack growth region was difficult from the micrographs. Nevertheless, a value of K_t of about 6 emerged from the analysis, so that a net stress concentration of about 25 could have been working to weaken the wall near the buttress corner. The final factor was the distortion in the box noted earlier. It was possible to calculate the effect it could have produced from a tensile curve made during mechanical testing, together with the observation of the widening of the crack in the whole failed sample box. The analysis gave the surprisingly large value of about 20 MN m^{-2}. Thus the net effect on the potential initiator was for a total stress of about 59 MN m^{-2}. This value is now comparable with the weakest sample tested, so it seemed reasonable to conclude that the combination of defects initiated one or, more likely, a series of cracks that created the final leak.

7.2.7   Aftermath

The results of the investigation were clear cut. The problem was caused by a combination of defects in the material of the wall of the box. They in turn had been mainly caused by faulty molding. One scenario by which they were produced has already been suggested: the failure box was made during start-up of the injection molding machine, when molding conditions had not been established. The failed box was therefore a single maverick. If this was the case, then several conclusions could be drawn.

In the first place, the radiator manufacturers could be reassured that the basic design was not at fault, and they could not expect to see widespread failures on new cars. Secondly, the suppliers could be asked to re-examine their quality policy. It is normal and good practice for molders to supply each operator on the machines a diagram of likely defects to look for in moldings as they are made. This is the first line of defense in quality, and perhaps the most important, because every component is (or should be) examined individually. The faulty box must have been mistakenly accepted as a good box at this stage, and forwarded through to the manufacturer. The molder should be asked to confirm that such quality checks were indeed in place, so that the user might be assured of specification-compliant products. The molder generally has responsibility to supply quality products, but it is also true that development designs supplied in short batch runs are not always examined as closely as is really necessary.

Several useful and practical suggestions to improve the situation were put forward for consideration by the investigation. Inspection could be improved at the audit stage in QA, by lightly dusting with chalk to show up any surface defects (such as cold slugs), which could indicate whether there was a problem in molding. The design could be improved by increasing the radius of the buttress corner. Sharp radii are easy to ameliorate by simply polishing the corners of the core which produce the corner in the tool. The effects are often dramatic, especially when the material of construction is brittle (as in this case).

7.3   Battery Case Failures

Thermoplastic materials have displaced many conventional materials such as glass and hard rubber for battery containers, essentially because they can be manufactured quickly and accurately by injection molding. The process also gives much greater freedom in designing cases of widely varying shapes. Plastics such as polypropylene are normally tough, able to resist impact blows during installation, and can be made stiff enough to withstand imposed loads during service. However, the strength of tough materials can be lowered substantially if poorly processed to shape, as the previous case study demonstrated. This comment applies across the range of polymers used in battery cases, including expensive but apparently tough materials like polycarbonate, as the case study below shows.

7.3.1   Miner's Backpack Cases

Speciality batteries are made for such applications as miner's safety lamps used during work underground (right-hand lamp in Figure 7.11). Because the cases are subjected to wear and impact blows by contact with rock surfaces, a tougher-than-normal insulating material is needed. Polycarbonate is a tough polymer that found widespread and successful application for this product in the U.S. when introduced in the 1960s. U.K. manufacturers had traditionally used ebonite or rigid vulcanized rubber, but that material is rather brittle and required very thick walls (approximately 4 mm) to resist imposed loads. The top was sealed in place after insertion of the battery plates, and a screw fitting was used on the front of the product to allow topping up the contents with distilled water. By contrast, polycarbonate would allow a transparent case to be injection molded, and could incorporate a leak-proof open vent to allow topping-up. To avoid design or patent infringement, the British battery case would be completely redesigned.

The first product (right center lamp in Figure 7.11) was developed with very little testing, and was unfortunately introduced into U.K. coal mines too rapidly in the early 1970s. Failures occurred very quickly, with the majority of new lamps failing within 3 months of introduction (Figure 7.12). Many mines had been supplied and their old stock completely replaced, with widespread failures bringing large coal mines to a halt due to the danger in which miners would be placed by loss of light underground. So what were the main failure modes? Cracks developed from several different areas of the sealed casing, including the leak-proof vents, the lid-case seal and at stress concentrations either present externally or within the case. Several leaks developed around the vents, where an organic solvent (a mixture of methylene and ethylene chloride) was used to create the final seal. Brittle cracks also developed at untreated parts of the case, such as a mold parting line on the side.

Figure 7.11 Various designs of miner's lamp battery cases, with the oldest at the right in aluminum (now banned because of the possibility of thermite sparks). The other lamps are made in polycarbonate, red filled at the right, and transparent at the center and left. The polycarbonate molding is at the extreme left.

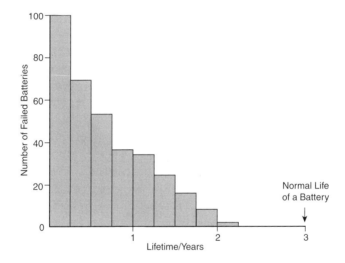

Figure 7.12 Failure records of first design of polycarbonate battery case in U.K. coal mines.

The crack here had started at the sharp corner at a small lip created by the joint in the tool surfaces. In other examples, cracks had started from no visible external stress raiser, but stripping the affected product showed that cracks could be initiated all too easily from very sharp internal corners (radii of curvature approximately 0.1 mm). What could be the cause of the several modes of failure?

Polycarbonate is extremely strong in the form of extruded sheet, finding use in safety shields and bullet-proof glazing. However, when it is injection molded into complex shapes, a lower molecular mass grade must be used in order to penetrate all the intricacies of the molding tool. It is almost universally true that polymer strength is very sensitive to molecular mass, falling

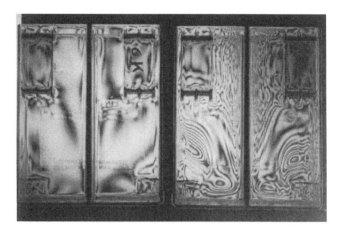

Figure 7.13   Strain birefringence produced in polarized light in a well-molded case (left), and a poorly molded case (right).

rapidly with lower chain length. Moreover, the material can possess a high degree of frozen-in strain, especially if the molding tool is cool. The polymer chains are effectively frozen into nonequilibrium shapes, frozen-in strain which will be relieved by crack formation if the part is constrained. Unconstrained parts will distort as shown by the maverick radiator tank in the previous section. The material manufacturers (General Electric Corp., U.S.A.) recommend that the tools be kept at a temperature of at least 80°C to minimize the problem. In addition, product strength will also be adversely affected by geometric stress concentrations like sharp corners, which can also be zones of high frozen-in strain as a result of constrained flow of the melt around them.

On further investigation on behalf of the National Coal Board, high levels of frozen-in strain were found at or near the crack initiation sites due to faulty molding practice. Figure 7.13 shows the high levels of chain orientation in the back of a cell, further increased during solvent welding. The solvent itself can initiate crazing and cracking because the polymer is swollen and weakened by absorption of the organic fluid. The existing design also possessed numerous serious stress raisers, which exacerbated the problem. Internal corners, for example, produced a severe stress concentration. Thus recommendations to the manufacturer included changes to molding procedure, adoption of a stronger transparent grade of material, quality checks using the procedure illustrated in Figure 7.13 (strain birefringence) and amelioration of sharp corners by tool modifications. The sharp corners could be easily modified by simply polishing the corresponding molding tool edges, a low cost way of improving product strength by an order of magnitude. The improved product is shown at the center in Figure 7.10. The failure rates experienced in many U.K. coal mines improved as a direct result of the

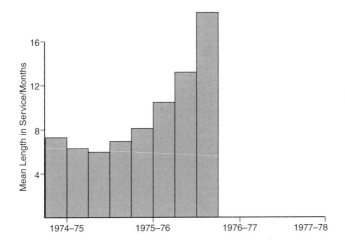

Figure 7.14   Failure record of polycarbonate battery cases after design modifications.

investigation (Figure 7.14). Although little coal is now deep-mined in the U.K., the product is currently licensed to several manufacturers in developing countries, such as India, where it has proved entirely successful.

7.3.2   Fire in the Hong Kong Subway

Fires in enclosed environments such as mines or underground railways are especially dangerous for persons in those environments. The danger from even very small fires is acute because the gases given off by combustion (such as carbon monoxide, CO) are extremely toxic. It is surprising how little combustion is needed to create very large volumes of such gases. It is therefore easy to see why underground fires are considered so seriously, and are investigated most thoroughly.

We were approached by a manufacturer of large lead-acid traction batteries for use on the Hong Kong subway system constructed in the 1970s. Fumes and smoke had been observed on an electrically powered locomotive while underground, and although the small fire had been successfully extinguished, the Transportation Authority wished to determine the cause of the problem in order to assure the safety of the system for travelers. The fire had started at the polypropylene base of one traction battery as shown in Figure 7.15. There was a small oval burn site with a brittle crack at the base of the hole, penetrating the wall (Figure 7.16). But what had created such peculiar damage? SEM using the EDAX analytical facility could provide more information to help solve the problem. Analysis showed traces of aluminum, silicon, lead and sulfur, which indicated that the crack had occurred before the fire and leakage of the acid contents. The aluminum peak in the analysis

Figure 7.15 Base of polypropylene traction battery case showing oval burn.

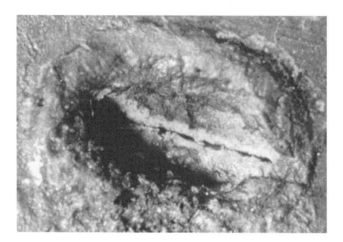

Figure 7.16 Close-up of hole with brittle crack in the bottom running through to the interior.

was quite unexpected, but could be explained by the presence of an aluminum-silicon alloy stud in the container holding the traction batteries. If the stud had been present when the battery was first inserted, it is likely that the base impacted the stud and initiated a brittle crack. When the crack penetrated the wall, sulfuric acid would have leaked and reacted with the light metal, igniting the plastic at the base (Figure 7.17). The small fire was quickly extinguished by the liquid acid, leaving the shape of the stud impressed in the base. The problem could thus be attributed to the installer rather than the battery maker. The design was not at fault, and greater care should have

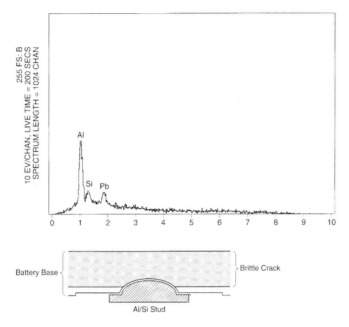

Figure 7.17   EDAX spectrum showing presence of aluminum and silicon with explanatory diagram of cause of fire below (schematic of probable failure mode from aluminum stud that impacted against battery base).

been used when installing large and heavy traction batteries to ensure that their containers were clear of any debris.

7.3.3   UV Degradation

Although polypropylene has been almost universally adopted for many different sizes of lead-acid battery, it can suffer degradation if exposed for long periods to sunlight. When plastic garden furniture was first introduced, users complained of surface cracking and crazing, which in some cases led to accidents when the largest cracks became critical under imposed loads (especially tables and chairs, Figure 7.18). Such deterioration is caused by the ultraviolet component, the most energetic part of the light spectrum, interacting with polymer chains at or near the exposed surfaces of products. The same UV light causes sunburn on exposed skin, which flakes away after continued exposure. Similar damage occurs with many polymeric materials, as many consumers are aware. Curtains, for example, will suffer by a process known as "phototendering" after long exposure to direct sunlight if the fibers are unprotected. The UV light is absorbed by the polymer chains and split, decreasing the strength of the product and encouraging brittle cracks to grow.

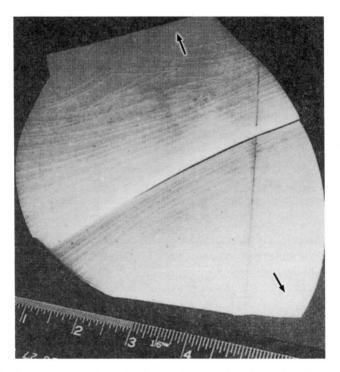

Figure 7.18 Network of cracks formed in flat surface of polymer table by ultraviolet degradation.

The problem discussed here occurred during one of the many military campaigns by the Israeli Army during the 1970s and 1980s. Fork lift trucks used during vehicle maintenance are often electrically powered, but the large lead-acid traction batteries must be recharged regularly to maintain their capability in service. Normally such charging would occur at night, but circumstances were such that charging occurred during the day, leaving the batteries exposed to intense sunlight. The tops of many such batteries suffered severe degradation as a direct result, creating much embarrassment to the battery supplier (Figure 7.19). It was observed that the heat-welded tops were most severely affected in the weld zone, the material becoming bleached by the suns rays (an effect known as "chalking"). The effect on the molecular mass of the polymer was confirmed using a special analytical method known as gel permeation chromatography (GPC), as shown in Figure 7.20. Polymer from the inside or hidden surface of a battery showed a much higher molecular mass than that on the upper exposed surface. FTIR spectroscopy showed the presence of oxidized chains (carbonyl groups) in the exposed material, precursors of chain cleavage. The fact that degradation was more severe in the thermally affected weld zone was caused by excessive temperatures used

Figure 7.19 Traction battery tops degraded by exposure to sunlight, with battery at left chalking in thermal weld zone.

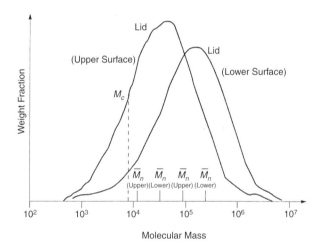

Figure 7.20 GPC curves of polymer from inner and outer surfaces of affected battery top.

during welding, and appropriate countermeasures were introduced on the assembly line at the manufacturers (checking of hot steel surface temperatures using a thermocouple, for example).

However, the polymer itself could also be protected by the incorporation of additives that can give protection against UV degradation, especially antioxidants and UV absorbers. The latter act by preferentially absorbing UV light and are used widely in sun tan lotions for skin protection. Such additives are now used extensively to protect a large range of susceptible polymers used in products that may be exposed to sunlight. One of the most common is carbon black, and only 1% will confer considerable degree of protection against UV light.

7.4   Domestic Bathtubs

One of the many post-World War II developments of plastics materials involved application of PMMA (Plexiglass in the U.S. or Perspex in the U.K.) to domestic baths. The material had been used for windshields and cowlings in fighter and bomber aircraft with great success, and it was only natural that its uses should be expanded during peacetime. Domestic tubs had traditionally been made from steel or cast iron with a surface glaze of enamel, producing a very heavy although durable product. During the post-war housing boom, lightweight PMMA baths were made by vacuum forming an extruded sheet, an extremely simple and low cost process. The sheet is heated by infrared heaters and then sucked into a cavity in a tool by a partial vacuum. The PMMA material possesses very high molecular mass (approaching 1 million), so the product is strong and durable, and the product is made by a casting process. Extra support is usually supplied to the undersurface in the form of hand-laid glass fiber mat in a cross-linked polyester matrix due to inevitable thinning of the wall in vacuum forming. If the fiber is not applied correctly, weakness in the reinforcement can have dire effects. The bath shown in Figure 7.21 failed suddenly when in use and flooded the room below. The family members affected were compensated fully for the damages.

During the late 1980s, one of the largest U.K. manufacturers decided to modify the material to save on the expense of the PMMA sheet and the subsequent reinforcement. A thin wall of PMMA can be co-extruded with a tough thick material such as ABS (acrylonitrile-butadiene-styrene), giving sufficient strength yet conserving the durability and polish of the PMMA that comes in contact with the bather. The results were unexpected after only little use in service on a housing estate in Glasgow (Figure 7.22). A network of cracks had formed in the PMMA surface film, the depth and severity increasing with time of use. Fatigue striations were detected in many of the fracture surfaces when opened and examined using SEM (Figure 7.23). What was the cause of the problem? A more detailed GPC examination of the clear PMMA layer showed the following molecular masses:

clear top layer from bath, $M_W = 71,900$

PMMA molding powder, $M_W = 66,200$

PMMA cast sheet, $M_W = 763,500$

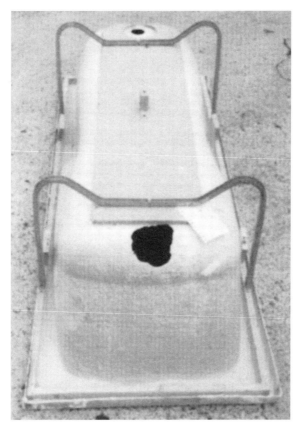

Figure 7.21   Failed bathtub showing large hole caused by stress from the user at the unreinforced zone of the plastic surface.

It was clear that a molding grade of PMMA had been used in the clear glaze applied to the ABS sheet, lowering the strength of the layer to such an extent that cracks began when the user sat in the bath. Further crack growth occurred at every session, probably exacerbated by extra thermal loads from the bathing water. Polymers have large coefficients of thermal expansion and even small rises in temperature will create stress in the layer. The strength of PMMA with cycling rate is shown in Figure 7.24, showing the difference in behavior between molded and cast PMMA, with a typical stress in a point-loaded zone of about 7000 psi (about 50 MN m^{-2}). The molded material would fail at only about 500 cycles compared with nearly 300,000 cycles for a cast high-molecular-mass material. There were several hundred fatigue striations, confirming the diagnosis. All the baths were replaced, and the process redesigned to incorporate a much higher molecular mass polymer.

Figure 7.22　Network of brittle cracks formed in new bathtub manufactured from coextrudate of ABS and PMMA (scale = 3 cm).

Figure 7.23　SEM of fracture surface showing fatigue striations.

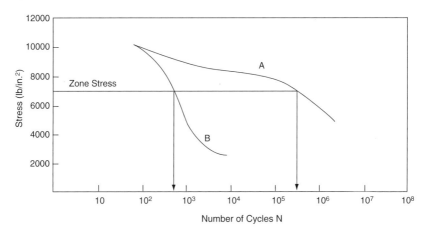

Figure 7.24 S-N curve for two cast and molding grades of PMMA with lifetimes for typical zone stress produced by point load from user.

7.5 Failure of Underground Storage Tanks

Product failure does not always result from fracture of a critical part, but can happen by distortion or creep if service loads are beyond that which was anticipated. The change in shape can cause loss of function, which is just as effective as fracture in causing product failure. The problem arose when an innovative rotational molder decided to expand his product range. He had started his company by making road cones and other road furniture using a method of shaping thermoplastics with low capitalization. It had been very good business in the U.K. because of the expanding motorway network, which used large numbers of such cones for maintenance work.

The process method works as follows.[4] Powder plastic of the appropriate final product weight is simply placed in a hollow steel container of the final external product shape. The molding tool is then rotated in an oven, when the polymer melts and forms a uniform film over the inner surface of the steel tool. On cooling, the plastic solidifies and the final product can be removed (a split tool is obviously needed for the final operation). Injection molding requires much more expensive tooling because the shape is created by two mating steel parts and the molten plastic injected into the hollow cavity between the two parts. The method was easily adopted for large products such as mancabs (for roadworker shelter) using a large enough oven. However, that market was limited, and the manufacturer sought to design other products to fit the large oven. He chose to design and make very large storage tanks for sewage plants, the tanks being buried below ground to accept the contents emptied into them. A few months after installation, such tanks were found to have distorted, with the side panels creeping inward

Figure 7.25   Buckled walls of large underground septic tank.

(Figure 7.25). The tanks seemed unfit for the purpose due to the reduced volume for the contents and potential interference with ballcocks and other control devices. So what was the problem?

Although thermoplastic products are easy to make, they need careful thought concerning the loads imposed on their walls over the lifetime of the product. With tanks buried below ground, the walls must be capable of resisting the external hydrostatic pressure from ground water present in the subsoil. The pressure, P exerted on the walls is given by the equation

$$P = \rho dg \qquad (7.1)$$

where ρ is the density of water, d the depth of any part of the tank wall below the top of the water table and g the acceleration due to gravity, a universal constant. When many existing installations were inspected, it became clear that those tanks that had been buried deep had suffered more internal distortion than those buried at shallow depths. Allowance was also needed for variation in the water table height as well as the time of exposure.

The tanks had been provided with very thick walls, so what was the problem? The material used was low density polyethylene, which creeps if subjected to a continuous load. Thus an exposure depth of only 3 m of ground water will impose a pressure of about 3000 Pa (about 3 kN m⁻²) on the sidewall. The walls had been given 12 buttresses around the perimeter, but they were about twice the thickness of the panels in between (Figure 7.26).

The solution to the problem lay in redesigning the tanks to give much greater resistance to hydrostatic loading, although many users reverted to fiberglass tanks, which provides a much greater wall stiffness and greater

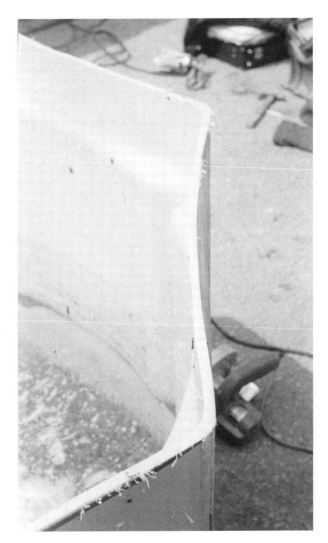

Figure 7.26 Sectioned tank showing inward creep on walls and thicker buttresses.

resistance to creep. The extra cost of the material and labor-intensive processing is more than justified by the longer life of a product, which could prove extremely expensive in replacing after fitment and collapse.

7.6   Failure of Large Storage Tanks

This case study is based on an investigation carried out after catastrophic failure of the virtually new tank that had been installed at the premises of a

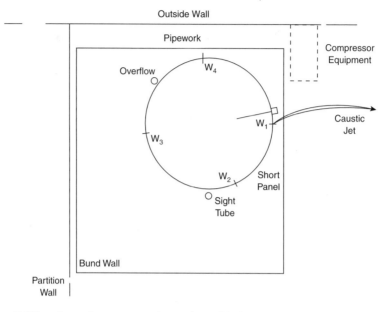

Figure 7.27 Plan of caustic soda tank welded together from polypropylene panels to form a 2.7-m-diameter tank. The jet of caustic soda emerged from the weld line of the lowest unreinforced panel and crossed the bund wall intended to inhibit escape of fluid from the tank.

small business manufacturing "dairy detergent."[5,6] This detergent is a dilute solution of caustic soda to which various other chemicals are added to aid the cleansing effect when flushing out dairy equipment on farms, for example. Concentrated (40%) caustic soda is the basic raw material for the final product, and just four deliveries had been made to the factory when the failure occurred in late 1994. Each delivery involved complete filling of the tank by a full load.

The failure fortunately occurred after the work shift had left for the day, and it was spotted by the production director, who was alone in the office above the factory floor. He heard a "bang" followed by the sound of "rain" and, looking out onto the factory floor, saw a jet of fluid shooting across the open space (Figure 7.27). The protective wall around the tank completely failed to constrict the fluid, which ran along the floor and into an adjacent unit that printed tachograph discs. Here the damage was extensive as specialist printing equipment was attacked and wrecked. The local fire department was called on to contain the fluid and prevent escape into the outer environment. Eventually a specialist recovery team company was hired to remove the fluid.

Figure 7.28   Face view of the failed panel with the large white arrow showing the origin of the brittle crack that eventually grew to the edges of the panel (small white arrows).

7.6.1   The Material Evidence

On inspection, the evidence of failure was actually very slight. The tank was intact, with only a small gap in the middle of a welded seam in the center of the panel to show that a very serious accident had occurred (Figure 7.28). The crack had been opened up (deliberately by other investigators), so that it traversed almost the entire panel when inspected several days after the accident. The crack also occurred at the dead center of the weld, where the panels had been joined together thermally (Figure 7.29).

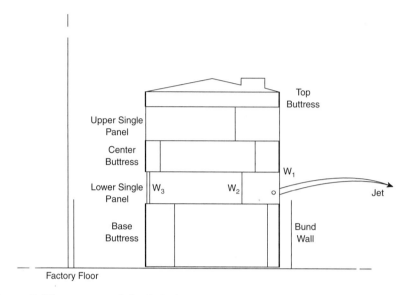

Figure 7.29 Section of the failed tank showing welded panels and position of critical crack.

Figure 7.30 Fracture surface of the critical crack showing four growth zones, each corresponding to complete fills of the tank after delivery by tanker. The origin is at a small pin hole in the weld.

It was clearly vital to examine the fracture surface, apparently the only piece of forensic material evidence available after the incident. It had to be removed using a circular saw (a rather lengthy procedure with such a large tank, although cutting the soft polymer was like slicing cheese), and the key

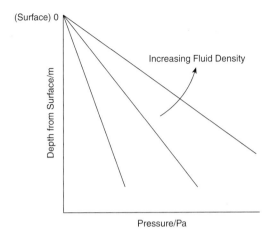

Figure 7.31 Variation of hydrostatic pressure acting against the walls of a container as a function of depth, for liquids of increasing density.

fracture surface is shown in Figure 7.30. So what did it show? The fracture surface was very simple, with:

1. Four distinct zones
2. A very clear origin
3. Vertical flutes across all the surface

It was easy to suggest that the boundary to each zone represented a period of slow crack growth following each complete fill of the tank. Notice also how the size of each zone increases with each fill, a feature one would expect from a growing crack, where the stress concentration at the crack tip becomes larger as the crack depth increases. The origin (O_1) appeared to be a small, elongated pit, or pin-hole, in the outer surface of the panel.

7.6.2   Subcritical Cracks

The interpretation of the fracture surface was of a weld failure, but did this mean that the weld itself was faulty, or was the material substandard, or perhaps the material had been attacked by the caustic soda? The design of the tank might also be at fault.

Further inspection of the tank was needed to check the other welds, especially those welds at the same level on the overall structure. The reason for examining those welds is that the pressure in a tank is given by an equation similar to that applicable to buried tanks:

$$P = \rho hg \qquad\qquad (7.2)$$

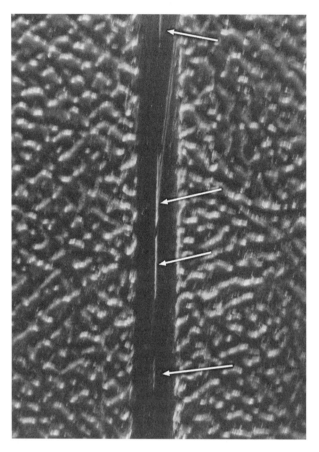

Figure 7.32   Close-up of subcritical cracks that have developed in weld W_4 at the same vertical position of the tank as the critical crack.

where P is the hydrostatic pressure of the contents, ρ the density of the fluid, h the height from the top fluid surface and g the acceleration due to gravity. Thus the pressure should vary with depth as shown in Figure 7.31 for fluids of varying density. In this case, since the density is fixed, and g is a constant, the only factor controlling pressure is the distance from the top level of liquid. In other words, if a vertical weld had failed at a particular height, then there could be evidence of other cracks at nearby welds at the same height if failure had been caused by the internal pressure of the contents.

The hunch proved correct, but only in one of the four possible welds (W_4 as shown in Figure 7.27). The weld was obscured by its position, making inspection very difficult (looking for a dark crack on black material in the dark), although when fine talc was used to dust the weld, it revealed several subcritical cracks (Figure 7.32). What did it indicate? It might show that the welding was faulty, but it did not explain the uncracked welds (W_2 and W_3).

Were there any other clues to the cause? Another factor could be overstressing: was there any distortion visible in the tank? After all, the distortion visible in the radiator box was a significant clue to that problem. If Figure 7.28 were re-examined, such distortion does indeed exist, best seen by tipping the page and viewing the edges of the far side and the crack at a slanting angle. Both features can be seen to be bowed outward, in a convex manner, the cracked weld showing the greater effect. The distortion in the wall was confirmed by direct measurement of the circumference at several heights, a difference of 20 mm in a total of 7.55 m being measured for the center of the cracked weld compared with a higher panel. Although the effect was very small, it could be indicative of overstressing, producing creep of the panel material.

7.6.3 Material Testing

The quality of the welds and the sheet material also needed to be assessed independently. Samples from both intact and cracked welds were sectioned, and the sections polished and etched to show any internal structure (Figure 7.33). No serious problem with weld structure could be found, apart from the presence of tiny pin holes. The tensile strength of the welds also proved reasonably consistent with one another and manufacturer's figures. Chemical analysis of the weld and bulk materials using DSC proved negative, the melting points all being close to one another. FTIR showed no obvious anomalies (such as an oxidation peak).

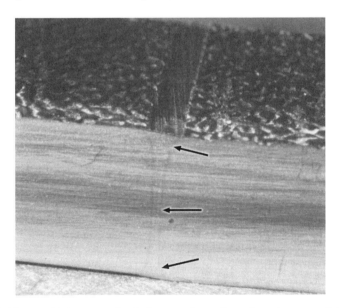

Figure 7.33 Weld design in final closure of panels to form hoop, with hot blade inserted between panel edges. The weld forms when the two ends are pressed together.

7.6.4 Weld Defects

Although weld strengths appeared reasonably high, there was a small difference of about 4% between the tensile strength of welds from intact and cracked panels. Could mechanical analysis be used to check the stress-concentrating effect of the pinholes? The first point to check was the appropriate formula needed to calculate the hoop stress in the vessel. Fortunately, the stress situation in a static pressure vessel is very simple. Where the ratio of tank radius to wall thickness is greater than about 10, then the tank can be treated as a thin walled vessel.[7] The ratio is in fact $1.35 \times 10^3/12 = 112.5$, so the hoop stress, σ_H is given by the equation

$$\sigma_H = PR/t \tag{7.3}$$

where P is the hydrostatic pressure, R the radius of the tank and t the wall thickness. Knowing R and t, and calculating P using Equation 7.2 with a known density, then the hoop stress at the failure crack was evaluated as

$$\sigma_H = 3.4 \ MNm^{-2}$$

It was now possible to calculate the stress concentration (see p. 50) that would have been acting at the critical pinhole,[8] prior to the first growth of the crack, since

$$K_t = \text{weld failure stress/actual stress at origin} \tag{7.4}$$

Hence $K_t = 20.4/3.4 = 6$.

Thus, from mechanical tests of welds, it was possible to calculate that the real stress acting at the pinhole in the center of the lower single-thickness panel was about six times the nominal hoop stress from the hydrostatic pressure of the contents.

7.6.5 Tank Structure

There appeared to be no serious problems with the material, processing or fabrication, but could the design of the tank be questioned? The structure shown in section in Figure 7.29, is composed essentially of single thickness (12-mm) panels, which have been buttressed by three extra hoops of material at base, center and the top of the structure. But is this the best way of resisting hydrostatic load? Equation 7.2 shows a simple linear relation between hydrostatic pressure and height for a given fluid (Figure 7.31). If that is the case, then should not the thickness increase gradually with distance from the top? Thus a dam increases

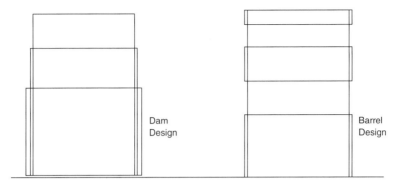

Figure 7.34   Schematic sections of two contrasting tank designs; at left, a dam design with increasing wall thickness to resist increasing hydrostatic pressure from contents and at right, the barrel design of the failed tank.

in thickness from top to base to resist the water pressure, and the same principle should apply to any fluid reservoir.

By adding hoops, the top band could be redundant, and the lower bands might not be sufficient to resist the much greater pressures toward the base of the structure. Such a hypothesis would explain why the failure occurred in a lower, unreinforced panel. It would not explain why only two welds failed from pinholes, but the calculation of hoop stress above shows that the single-thickness panel is having to resist a large hoop stress. Doubling the wall thickness would halve the applied stress, while having three panels here would give a stress of only about 1.15 MN m^{-2}. Even if pinholes occurred in the weld, failure would be much less likely with such substantial lowering of the hoop stress. The general conclusion of the stress analysis was that the design itself was faulty: in order to resist hydrostatic pressure, the tank should have been designed like a dam wall, rather than like a barrel (Figure 7.34).

But why should just two of the four welds have shown cracks? The answer to the problem came when the welding stage was inspected directly. The hoop of panels for such tanks is made sequentially by hot fusion welding, that is, by melting the surfaces of two panels and pushing them together. This is fine for three of the welds where the flat panels are joined, but difficult for the final joint when the ends have to be brought together by bending the sheet into a cylinder (Figure 7.35). It would certainly explain the lower quality of one weld, and the low quality of another weld was probably caused by similar problems in bringing two large flat sheets together. The quality of such welds is tested for through-the-thickness holes using a spark tester, a method that will not detect partial pinholes. One rather disturbing aspect of the process is that the hoop so formed is under a bending stress, so the outer surface of the final wall will be in tension. This will of course make failure much more likely, and is akin to the frozen-in strain problem of the radiator box already

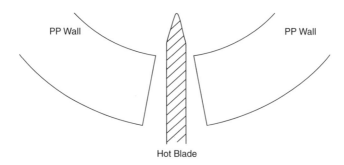

Figure 7.35 Adjacent barrel tanks holding acidic and alkaline contents at a wire-making plant.

described. In this case, however, there was a frozen-in stress rather than strain. It was possible to calculate the effect from simple bending theory.[7] The effect probably added about 1.5 MN m^{-2} to the hoop stress, so that the above calculation underestimated the stress.

7.6.6   Aftermath

We concluded that the basic design of the tank was faulty, having been made like a barrel rather than a dam. Failure was inevitable, and the shape explains why failure occurred so early in the life of the structure. Because the walls were exposed to excessive stresses, it was inevitable that the tank would fail quickly. The stress would seek out the weakest welds in the most exposed panel, and failure was not caused by faulty welding at all. That is not to say that the welding process could not be improved, for example, by controlled bending of individual panels thermally before final welding.

But the failure should never have occurred in the first place, because there was a standard for such thermoplastic tanks, published by the German Welding Institute, DVS 2205. Only partial translations existed in published form at the time of design of the tank, but the design philosophy was perfectly clear. The design procedure[6] makes allowance (using safety factors, or derating factors) for holding dangerous chemicals, pinholes in welds and so on. The manufacturer of the tank, a small business man with entrepreneurial skills, had hired an engineer to check and approve the design. The engineer unfortunately performed misguided calculations, leaving the insurers to shoulder the considerable expenses of the clear-up.

Having explained the failure, what were the consequences of the investigation? As is usual, several investigators had been instructed by loss adjusters acting for the two injured parties. The above investigation was carried out on behalf of the tank manufacturer, and since liability was accepted, their role was limited but other investigators agreed with the general analysis. A much more serious problem (which arises whenever design defects

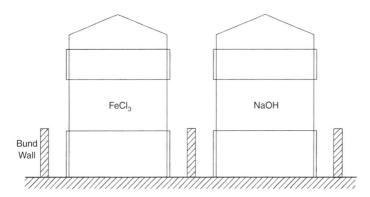

Figure 7.36 Storage tanks for water treatment chemicals. Tank leakage could have caused a fire.

are discovered) was the state of other tanks made to the same design. How many had been built and installed? What fluids were they holding? For how long had they been installed?

7.6.7 Inspection of Other Tanks

A range of tanks built to the same principle had indeed been installed, but only shortly after installation of the failed tank. The original investigator was asked by the manufacturer and insurers to inspect all such installations, which ranged from tanks for fruit juices, soap solution and ferric chloride ($FeCl_3$), an acidic fluid used for water treatment.

Although the tanks were relatively new, few were found with microcracks, essentially because none of the tanks had been filled to capacity. The cracks in the welds that were found were far from critical, being only millimeters in size. The economy at the time was depressed, and the companies concerned had been on short-time work. Some of the other tanks inspected were much smaller than that at Warrington, and this had not been stressed to the same extent. The most serious potential problem was found at a steel wire works in the Midlands, where there were two tanks adjacent to one another (Figure 7.36). One held caustic soda, the other ferric chloride. If the tanks had split, the two chemicals would have reacted together with great evolution of heat, probably causing a fire. The tanks were in a confined space, close to manned equipment, so the consequences of failure would have been more serious than at Warrington because of the enclosed space. The bund walls had only been designed to accept the contents from a floor leakage, and would have been no help in a crisis such as the Warrington failure. No microcracks were found, however, because the tanks had never been more than half-full since installation, due to the fact that the tanker could not approach the site. The factory was set in a narrow gorge and the only access

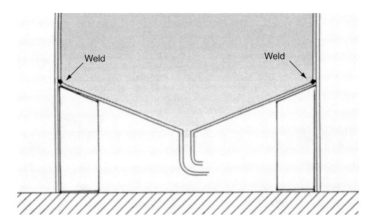

Figure 7.37   Tank with internal cone for holding raw paint. It collapsed because of the poor support for the inner cone. The base of the tank was supported by the main weld and four vertical panels, two of which are shown. A steel support frame should have been used instead.

to the tank building was over a small bridge incapable of carrying a full tanker. Needless to say, this and many other tanks had to be replaced by tanks of the correct design.

7.6.8   Other Tank Failures

Such tanks continue to fail, however; one recent failure in 1998 involved a paint tank. It had been designed with an inner sloping floor, as shown in Figure 7.37. This was essentially to allow all the contents to be mixed within the tank and then drained away for further processing. The tank failed the first time it was used, collapsing in a misshapen heap on the factory floor, the contents draining away over the factory floor. The weakness of the design shown is that all the mass of the contents is taken by a single weld, with support for the inner cone only provided by four plastic panels. They failed quickly and the weld had peeled away, failing progressively, so that almost all the weld had disappeared. The design was again at fault, with the absence of reliable support recommended by DVS 2205, such as a steel frame resting on the ground, and bearing the weight of the cone and contents. Fortunately, the design was a one-off, made by a small company for a specific contract, and had not been repeated elsewhere.

Thermoplastic storage tanks have displaced not just metal or alloy equivalents but other polymer types, especially glass fiber–reinforced vessels. Although much more expensive, the reinforcement from the glass fiber makes for a much stiffer wall, a factor that allows tall silos to be constructed. Nevertheless, failures have been reported by Meyer Ezrin,[9] some of which have actually been caused by the glass used. In another case reported by Derek

Hull, a large milk tank failed catastrophically after 10 years of reliable service.[10] The collapse demolished an electricity substation and created substantial physical damage to its surroundings. It was used for storing milk products, and was made from random mat GRP fitted with a polypropylene liner. Failure started at a butt weld in the latter, from a combination of cyclic loading (filled and emptied daily) and nitric acid attack, suggesting stress corrosion fatigue. The slightly acidic contents seeped into the GRP and caused further SCC, ultimately leading to the sudden failure.

7.7   Conclusions

The case studies in this chapter have highlighted the critical role of materials and their use in containment products. Although plastics materials have found extensive application for storing fluids, their use requires a considerable degree of caution both in terms of design philosophy and installation. When changes to conventional and traditional designs are made, allowance must be made for any changes in the material of construction. If the properties are quite different, then substantial alterations must be made to the design geometry. Thermoplastics, in particular, possess much lower tensile moduli than steel and most structural metals (by a factor of about 100, or two decades) as well as lower strengths. On the other hand, they do offer considerable resistance to hazardous chemicals, and they can be used for chemical storage, for example. They can also be processed to shape very easily, using methods such as injection or rotational molding or even by simply hot welding flat panels together. As with many structural designs, the zones where subassemblies fit together are usually the weakest parts of the structure and will fail from here if overloaded. For structural integrity, all design work must start at the weakest parts, and make allowance for any unpredicted problems at these zones.

The importance of testing prototypes before release into the market is a recurring theme in this chapter. There is no substitute for testing products under realistic conditions to assess lifetime before launch, rather than relying on the user to suffer the consequences of hasty marketing. It is especially true for storage tanks holding dangerous fluids, where the results of failure can endanger life and property. A simple water test on the large storage tanks of the last section would have shown very quickly that the walls would creep outward very rapidly. Testing underground tanks would be more difficult, but could have exposed the problem of variable wall thickness. On the other hand, no amount of testing would have shown the weakness of maverick and faulty radiator header tanks. Here the problem is one of quality control, assuring the user that all products are structurally sound and fit for their intended purposes.

References

1. Lewis, P.R., Premature fracture of a composite nylon radiator, *Eng. Failure Anal.*, 6, 181–195, 1999.

2. Pilkey, W., Ed., Notch in bending, Chart 2.29, *Peterson's Stress Concentration Factors*, 2nd ed., Jossey-Bass, San Francisco, 1997.

3. Pilkey, W., Ed., Penny shaped void, Chart 4.71, *Peterson's Stress Concentration Factors*, 2nd ed., Jossey-Bass, San Francisco, 1997.

4. Crawford, R.J., *Rotational Molding of Plastics*, Wiley/Research Studies Press, New York, 1992.

5. Lewis, P.R. and Weidmann, G.W., Catastrophic failure of a polypropylene tank. I. Primary investigation, *Eng. Failure Anal.*, 6, 197–214, 1999.

6. Weidmann, G.W. and Lewis, P.R., Catastrophic failure of a polypropylene tank. II. Comparison of the DVS 2205 code of practice and the design of the failed tank, *Eng. Failure Anal.*, 6, 215–232, 1999.

7. *Roark's Formulas for Stress and Strain,* 6th ed., McGraw-Hill, New York, 1989, p. 516.

8. Pilkey, W., Ed., Stress concentration diagram for elliptical hole in infinite panel in tension, *Peterson's Stress Concentration Factors*, 2nd ed., Jossey-Bass, San Francisco, 1997.

9. Ezrin, M., *Plastics Failure Guide*, Hanser-SPE, Munich, 1996, pp. 346–349.

10. Hull, D., *Fractography*, Cambridge University Press, London, 1999, section 10.4.3, p. 335 ff.

Accidents in the Workplace

8

Despite rigorous safety standards and practices applied in industry, accidents still occur from time to time, either due to workers disregarding safety procedures or to some exceptional and unforeseen circumstance arising during routine operations. It is sometimes found that a faulty tool or machine setting was responsible. Serious accidents are usually subject to an inquiry by a team of experts and attract nationwide publicity, as well as likely prosecutions of management; smaller accidents are dealt with by local management teams with their insurers usually insisting on inclusion of independent experts with knowledge of the process operations and materials involved. The cases in this chapter are presented as representative examples illustrating the wide diversity of investigations requiring the skills of a forensic engineer.

8.1 Explosion in a Foundry

Two workmen operating a small furnace in a nonferrous foundry suffered severe burns and one also lost an eye. This was typical of the kind of incident that occurs when liquid metal comes into contact with water, which results in a violent explosive ejection of the molten metal. The cause of this particular accident was quite clear; the lawyers acting for the injured workmen were instructed to establish the cause of the eruption and determine who was at fault.

8.1.1 The Accident

This accident involved a low-frequency electric induction furnace melting baled copper scrap, consisting of miscellaneous clippings, stampings, odd lengths of tube and various offcuts arising from manufacturing processes, all compressed into rectangular bales. The melting unit was a low-frequency induction furnace, a type that can never be allowed to become completely empty because it relies on a continuous loop of liquid at the bottom to act as the secondary coil of a transformer. After a cast is poured, there must still remain sufficient residual liquid to maintain the loop. Subsequent additions of cold bales have to be charged gradually into the residual liquid. If the furnace were filled to the brim with fresh, cold charge melting would cease or become inefficient due to the energy transfer characteristics. A furnace full of cold, solid metal would be disastrous for the foundry and put the melting out of action for several days, if not weeks.

On the occasion of this accident the charge was mainly baled scrap, with small additions of virgin metal to adjust the alloy composition just before casting. Scrap was stored outdoors under a roof covering, but there were no sides to the structure and in windy, wet weather rain was known to blow under the cover and form puddles on the floor. Because of this risk of moisture, bales of scrap were brought into the warm foundry and weighed into stillages several hours before they were due to be charged. To charge the metal into the furnace the bales were tipped from the stillage onto a mechanical conveyer, which carried them some 2 m up to the charging platform. The furnaceman's job was to stop and start the conveyer, so that only one or two bales were fed into the furnace at a time and allowed to melt before the next bales were added. In this way any residual dampness was dried off by the heat from the furnace before the bale dropped into the liquid metal. Despite this procedure it was quite normal for occasional spitting and sputtering to occur as nonmetallic contaminants such as paint, grease and volatile materials in the scrap bales came into contact with the liquid metal.

Metals melt at much higher temperatures than water boils: aluminum alloys at around 650°C, copper and brasses at 800 to 1100°C and steel at 1550°C, compared with 100°C when water becomes steam at atmospheric pressure. When water vaporizes its volume increases substantially; if this volume is suddenly raised to the temperature of molten metal there is a further rapid increase. For example, 2 mL of water (about 1 tsp) forms 3.17 L of steam at 100°C; moreover, when this is raised to 1100°C in a bath of liquid copper it rapidly expands to 13.6 L. Hence, if even a small amount of water finds its way into a bath of molten metal a violent explosion usually ensues, ejecting quantities of liquid metal. With reactive metals such as aluminum there may also be chemical reactions with the steam that not only further increase the volume but also produce hydrogen and give rise to further explosive reactions.

The furnacemen and others working in the foundry were provided with protective clothing, boots, gaiters, gauntlets, helmets and face shields, which all conformed to the safety requirements. The materials for the clothing were of a type that if a splash of hot metal landed on them, a gaseous reaction ensued, which actually blew the metal away, so it appeared to run off like rain dropping from a waterproof jacket or trousers. All safety equipment was kept in a locker room at the side of the foundry, about 20 m from this particular melting furnace. Prominently displayed warning notices were on the walls of the foundry and on the charging platform of each furnace. At the opposite end of the foundry building to the locker room was a two-story suite of offices for the foundry manager, foreman and clerk at floor level and three rooms above housing an analytical laboratory. The manager, foreman and laboratory staff frequently went into the melting area and the foreman, in particular, often assisted the furnacemen at busy times. If their visit was brief and not directly onto the furnace charging platforms they would wear hard hats and safety spectacles only. The foreman usually wore his protective trousers but would not put on the jacket and face protection unless he intended to work on the charging platform.

The accident had occurred in mid-morning as the furnaceman began charging for the second cast of his shift. The scrap bales had been brought into the foundry approximately 2 h earlier and rain water was said to have run out of some of the bales into the bottom of the stillages. The furnaceman upturned a stillage onto the conveyor and ran the first bales up toward the furnace platform, but stopped the load just short of the furnace mouth to allow any moisture to dry off. He went behind the furnace to stamp numbers on test bars for the laboratory from the previous cast. The furnace had a fume extraction canopy, but this had been swung aside to allow access for charging.

The foreman had been outside in the stockyard and as he returned through the foundry he noticed that the metal level in the furnace was low and getting very hot, and he was surprised to see bales waiting at the top of the conveyor. Thinking that the furnaceman might have gone to the wash-room, he started the conveyor. He was not wearing his protective jacket. The noise of the conveyor alerted the furnaceman, who came toward the charging platform from the opposite side to the conveyor. As it would be some time before he was due to pour the metal he was not wearing his protective jacket and had taken off his face shield because, he claimed, he could not see clearly enough to stamp numbers on the test bars. It is believed that two or three bales had dropped into the furnace when a violent explosion blew metal "all over the place." A partly melted bale of scrap was found over 10 m from the furnace. Both men suffered severe burns to their upper bodies.

8.1.2 Investigations

An investigation was carried out by the Factory Inspectorate the day after the accident. The inspector was unable to establish the precise reason for the eruption but he pointed out that neither of the injured men had been wearing suitable eye protection or molten metal jackets. He wrote to the firm drawing attention to two sections of the U.K. Health and Safety at Work Act, namely,

> *Section 2*, which imposes general duties on the employer to ensure as far as is reasonably practicable the health and safety of his employees and that this duty extends to the provision and maintenance of safe systems of work, together with the provision of information, instruction, training and supervision that is necessary to ensure/fulfill this obligation; and
>
> *Section 7*, which imposes duties on an employee while at work to take reasonable care for the health and safety of himself and other persons who may be affected by their acts or omissions while at work.

After serious consideration, it was decided not to instigate legal proceedings against the company and the individuals concerned in this instance, but a strong warning was given should a similar incident occur in future. While conducting the investigation, the factory inspector had observed procedures that required changes in working practice. The main recommendation was that the dust and fume extraction hoods should be modified so that they could remain in place while the furnace was being charged with metal.

8.1.3   The Pleadings

People injured in industrial accidents are entitled to state benefits but, if negligence can be proved, additional substantial damages can be obtained through actions in the civil courts. The foreman and the furnaceman's trade union instructed lawyers who initiated proceedings against the employer, whose defense was taken over by its insurance company's lawyers.

The two plaintiffs were individually represented and submitted separate claims but these were largely similar, the differences being in the nature of the injury and their role in the incident. The independent expert was called in to explain how and why the accident occurred, most of the findings already being included in the above account of what happened. The plaintiffs' case was that the accident was caused by reason of the defendants' breaches of statutory duty and/or negligence inasmuch as they:

1. Failed to keep and maintain a safe place of work.
2. Failed to provide the plaintiffs with proper and adequate clothing and/or equipment.
3. Failed to ensure the plaintiffs were wearing proper and adequate clothing and equipment.

4. Failed to set a proper example by management and other staff to wear proper safety clothing and equipment when in the vicinity of the furnace.

5. Caused or permitted the hood to be absent from the furnace while molten metal was contained therein.

6. Caused or permitted scrap metals destined to be used in the furnace to be stored in the open air where they became wet.

7. Failed to organize an adequate system of drying of such scrap before it was placed in the furnace.

8. Exposed the plaintiffs to the risk of accident in the knowledge that the danger of water becoming present in molten metal is a well-recognized cause of explosions.

9. Caused or permitted the plaintiffs to follow an unsafe system of work.

10. Failed to have any or sufficient regard for the safety of the plaintiffs.

Both claimed general damages for pain and suffering, and the furnaceman claimed special damages in respect of loss of wages and of future earning capacity due to loss of an eye.

In their defense the employers admitted the plaintiffs were employed by them as experienced foundry workers and that the accident occurred on that particular date, but they denied all the allegations and counter-claimed that the personal injury and damage sustained were wholly caused or, if not, materially contributed to, by their own negligence, namely, that the furnaceman:

1. Caused or permitted the furnace to become or remain overheated.

2. Caused or permitted an excess of scrap metal to be fed into the furnace at one time.

3. Failed to ensure the scrap metal was allowed to warm up sufficiently to dry off moisture before charging to the furnace.

4. Removed the canopy hood from the furnace while the same was in use.

5. Failed to heed or observe the absence of the canopy hood (both claimants).

6. Failed to wear the protective clothing and equipment provided. It was the defendant's case that an ample supply of molten metal clothing, gauntlets, foundry boots, safety helmets and full face protection was provided and that fellow employees were instructed and exhorted to wear the same. Moreover, it was a term of both plaintiffs' contracts that they should wear the equipment provided and notices stating that such clothing and equipment should be worn at all times were clearly posted in the vicinity of the furnace. Notwithstanding this, the

plaintiffs negligently chose not to wear the jacket and helmet visor provided on the occasion of his accident.

7. Failed to exercise reasonable care for their own safety and unnecessarily exposed themselves to the risk of such injury as actually occurred.

When the parties are represented by equally experienced legal advisers, they recognize the strengths and weaknesses of each other's cases and usually reach some agreement by negotiation. It is only when they cannot agree, or if they agree on liability but cannot agree on damages, that the case actually goes to trial before a judge.

8.1.4   Outcome

In this instance a settlement was reached by negotiation. While it was agreed there was a degree of contributory negligence on the part of the plaintiffs, the employers were held liable on the grounds that they failed to exercise proper management supervision and control and failed to adopt safe working practices. It was in the contract of employment that safety clothing and equipment had to be worn in the furnace areas, yet the employers failed to exercise discipline in that respect. Indeed, they condoned the disregard of this regulation by the acts of senior management and laboratory personnel in frequently visiting the furnace areas without wearing the specified clothing. In addition, their working practices were open to question as, indeed, the factory inspector had pointed out, they were not written down and they relied on the experience of furnacemen as distinct from any formal training. If the fume hood had been in position over the furnace, the shower of metal droplets would have been contained. They could and should have exercised more rigorous control over the storage of scrap and the elimination of moisture and condensation before it could be charged into the furnace.

This outcome may appear surprising because, at first glance, it seems the injured men were the architects of their own misfortune (to use an expression much loved by those giving legal opinions), as they had been provided with all the necessary equipment but had chosen not to wear parts of it despite prominent notices posted all around the foundry. But it is not as simple as that.

It is the management's responsibility to see that protective clothing is worn and to exercise their rights under the terms of contract if an employee willfully disregards safety instructions. Unfortunately, people become familiar with the processes with which they are involved and recognize the greater hazards and guard against them, but they tend to relax when everything is proceeding normally. It is also true in this instance that molten metal clothing and foundry boots are cumbersome to wear all the time and face shields do become smeared. The problem is that if something unusual occurs or if there is an emergency, there may not be time to do anything about it — that is the nature of an accident. It is one of the responsibilities of management to recognize the possibility of such situations and insist on the observation of all safety procedures at all times.

8.2 Accident with a Pressure Die-Casting Machine

Pressure die-casting is a process widely used for the mass production of accurate small to medium sized castings in aluminum or zinc alloys, having good surface finish, sometimes incorporating inserts of other metals such as steel pins and screw threads. It is a process similar to injection molding of plastics. Essentially, the machines comprise a set of water-cooled metal dies and cores that are clamped firmly together while a measured quantity of the molten alloy is injected under high pressure. The clamping force has to be sufficient to prevent any liquid from escaping. A short time is allowed for solidification, during which period the dies have to remain clamped. When the casting is solid and able to support itself, the dies are opened and the casting ejected. After cleaning the opened mold, the faces of the cavity are recoated with a release agent and then clamped together again ready for the next casting. Different sizes of casting require different time cycles that have to be set according to the mass of metal injected and the time necessary for the heaviest section to solidify. It is a mass production process, so in order to achieve maximum output the cooling part of the time cycle is absolutely critical; too long a time slows down the production rate, and if the time is too short for complete solidification, castings either break up when the dies are opened or become distorted by the ejector pins.

In some pressure die-casting processes the liquid metal is drawn from near the bottom of the reservoir and injected with minimum turbulence, in order to eliminate dross and avoid air entrapment. In other processes the metal is ladled out of a large melting pot and a "shot" sufficient to make the casting poured into a receiver and then injected. Castings made in this way are very likely to carry air into the mold and, although the outer skin of the casting may be free of porosity and well formed, the air and any other gases evolved during solidification end up within the thicker sections. The internal gas pressure thus set up may sometimes be sufficient to cause parts of the casting to swell when first taken from the mold while the outer skin is still soft and relatively weak.

8.2.1 The Accident

This particular accident occurred when two men were operating a machine of the latter type making castings in an aluminum alloy. Both were experienced

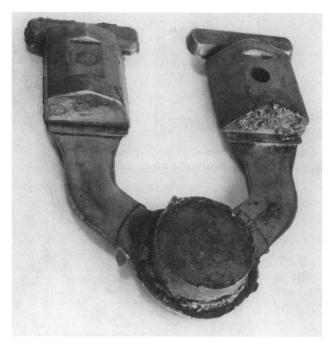

Figure 8.1 Pair of aluminum alloy die castings on common sprue, as removed. Notice the broken skin in the end face at the right-hand side where liquid metal has burst out after dies opened.

workers, very familiar with the machine, so much so that they were left to work on their own, virtually unsupervised, during a night shift. One of them suffered severe facial burns when liquid metal squirted out from between the dies as he was waiting with tongs ready to remove the finished casting as soon as the dies opened. He and his colleague who had poured the shot into the injector reservoir claimed he was wearing a visor, but a jet of metal struck his clothing just below this and ricocheted up into his eye.

The casting in question, illustrated in Figure 8.1, was to form a pair of matching spacers for a motor mount, the general view with the injector sprue shown at the bottom. The spacer at the right shows where liquid alloy had burst out from the face at the sprue end. The narrow blocks at the far end are "sinks" to catch any dirt or residues swept before the liquid as it is injected. These would be broken off the finished casting and put back into the melting pot, along with the sprues. A microsection taken through the casting revealed extensive voids due to air entrapment within in the body of the casting. This was confirmed by x-radiography before sectioning, as illustrated in Figure 8.2. The metallographic structure revealed the pressure of this entrapped air had forced liquid alloy through the skin of the casting. For this to occur the dies must have been partially opened in order for the internal

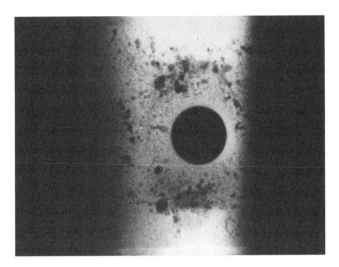

Figure 8.2 X-radiograph of right side casting showing excessive porosity caused by air entrapped as liquid metal was injected.

air pressure to rupture the unsupported skin. This was clearly the source of the liquid metal that squirted out as the dies were unclamped. The position of the dies where this metal was ejected would have been just below the eye level of someone standing at the side of the machine waiting to remove the finished casting as soon as the dies opened.

On the morning after the accident it was discovered that the timing cycle on the machine had been altered from the setting when these particular dies had been installed the previous day. The number of castings made up to the time the accident occurred was about 10% greater than what should have been possible in the number of hours the two men on the night shift had been working. It appears that they had decreased the cooling time of the machine cycle in order to produce their expected quota of castings in less time and thus take a longer break. It was the first time they had make this particular casting. In view of the evidence of the way the skin had burst open it seems they were unlucky with this particular casting in that more air than usual had been carried in by the turbulence as the metal was injected and the dies had opened before the skin was thick enough to withstand the internal pressure.

8.2.2 Outcome

As in the previous case, the operators were to blame for the cause of the accident but the management was held responsible on the grounds that:

1. The two workers were inadequately trained and had been left on their own to work unsupervised for the entire 8-h night shift.

2. The time cycle setting controls should have been locked or otherwise made tamper-proof so that adjustments could only be made by authorized personnel.

8.3 Eye Injuries

A variety of accidents may occur during working processes. It is mandatory that machines are provided with guarding that prevents flying splinters from reaching the operator, although it is by no means unknown for those using the machine to offer some reason (or excuse) as to why they were working with the guard out of position at the time something went wrong that caused a tool to shatter. For example, in one case a toolsetter was called to realign tools in a power press when an allegedly uncovenanted stroke brought the punch down while it was still misaligned with the die. Many personal accidents result from pieces breaking off hardened corners of hand tools, pneumatic chisels, etc. flying toward the user's face or someone nearby, causing a penetrating injury. Loss of an eye is particularly sad for a young person, as there are cosmetic effects and an artificial eye can never respond like a real one. It is therefore particularly important to discover where a particle came from, what caused it to break away from its parent body and, particularly for an insurance company and litigation purposes, who was at fault.

Contributory negligence is likely to reduce substantially any damages awarded by a court, for example, a craftsmen who continued to use tools that had gotten into an unsafe condition, like the mushroomed head of the chisel shown in Figure 8.3, or skilled workers who take short cuts or cannot

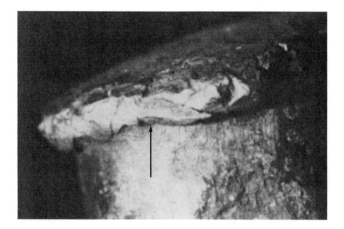

Figure 8.3 Head of chisel. The triangular eye splinter has been replaced in the mushroomed edge in the center field. A diagonal line left of center at about 80° is one edge of the splinter; a diagonal line in the center at about 170° is another edge, coming down to just right of center to meet at a sharp point.

be bothered to follow safe working practices with what to them seemed a simple, straightforward job.

8.3.1 Eye Injury While Replacing Clutch Plate

Replacing the clutch plate on a motor vehicle is a commonplace garage workshop operation that requires separating the gearbox and clutch assembly from the flywheel at the back of the engine. Replacement requires the new clutch plate to be centered on the flywheel before the outer cover is bolted into position. To center the new plate a dummy gearbox shaft has to be used and removed after the bolts have been tightened. The splined end of the gearbox shaft may then be passed through the new plate and located in the flywheel bush bearing when the gearbox is refitted. The gearbox bolts are then inserted and tightened to hold the gearbox to the engine.

The dummy shaft should be a purpose-made tool that is soft enough to be safely tapped with a hammer, but frequently a shaft taken from an old gearbox is used, similar to that illustrated in Figure 8.4. As it is the real thing, the teeth and splines will have been case hardened, which means they will have a skin that is extremely hard and brittle. So any hammering or tapping to center the new clutch plate on the splines should be done with a soft-faced hammer.

The striking faces of engineer's hammers are surface hardened. Hence, as a glancing blow against the corner of one of the gear teeth would bring the hammer face forcibly into contact with a case hardened steel, there is a foreseeable high risk of one or the other splintering. This will usually be the harder and more brittle of the two, in this case the gear tooth, as its corners are not rounded and the case hardness is in the region of 850 HV compared with the hammer face of 600.

An experienced garage mechanic who had already done a normal day's work was working overtime to complete an urgent job fitting a new clutch

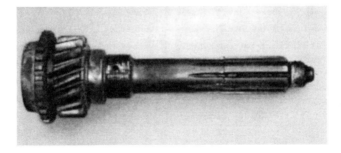

Figure 8.4   Old gearbox shaft used as dummy for changing clutch plate. The splined portion fits through center of clutch and the spigot end must locate in the flywheel bearing.

Figure 8.5 Open-ended spanner used to tighten bolts around clutch cover.

plate to a light commercial vehicle; although fatique may not have been a factor, he was keen to finish work for the day. Working from beneath the vehicle he was using an old gearbox shaft as the dummy to center the clutch plate. He needed to extract the dummy shaft before refitting the gearbox and started to do so by tapping the projecting portion with an open-ended spanner. Figure 8.5 shows the end of this spanner, exhibiting several deep, angular indentations similar to the profile of the teeth of the gear. He was looking toward the back of the engine, with his face close to where he was striking, and swinging the spanner toward his face. He was not wearing any eye protection. He suddenly felt a blinding pain in his right eye.

A particle was removed from his eye at the hospital, described as a "sharp flake of metal" (magnetic, therefore steel). He eventually lost the sight of the eye and commenced litigation. His lawyer sent the particle to a local college seeking a report. Unfortunately they lost it while taking photographs. (There is a moral here: when manipulating such a small item of evidence, it should never be moved or turned during visual examination except when held with a magnetic probe or tweezers over a piece of white card with the edges folded up.) Fortunately, the college's investigator had measured it and was able to describe what it looked like. Instructions from the insurers of the man's employers were to examine the gearbox shaft he was using as the dummy and establish whether the particle might have flown from one of the teeth and, if so, what caused it to break away.

Close examination of the outsides of the gear teeth on this dummy shaft revealed several chipped teeth; a recent one is illustrated in Figure 8.6. The size of this cavity matched the dimensions of the particle insofar as these could be relied on. However, several possible cavities were found on the outsides of other teeth in a similar position. Quite clearly the corners of several teeth had been caught by glancing blows and small fragments had been broken away. The scalloped form of the cavities is characteristic of a

Figure 8.6   One of several chipped teeth on dummy shaft.

hard brittle case broken by an oblique impact. As the outer corners of these gear teeth were extremely hard (>900 HV), under relatively light blows the exposed corners would be likely to emit tiny, sharp edged particles at high speed.

Such a small flying particle would not have caused a penetrating eye injury if eye protection had been worn. The injured man had been issued safety glasses but he claimed the glasses did not stay in position when he was working beneath a vehicle and spots of oil and greasy finger marks smeared the glass and made it difficult to see what he was doing. There was a foreseeable risk of eye injury given the tools he was using and the way he had to work with his face so close to the object he was striking. However, no amount of legal argument about whether or not the risk of injury was *reasonably* foreseeable could ever compensate for the loss of his eye, although damages awarded would be substantially reduced on the grounds of contributory negligence.

The sad fact is there would have been nothing wrong with using the old shaft as the dummy and the injury need never have occurred if the case-hardened gear teeth had first been softened by tempering.

8.3.2   Lath Axe

A self-employed building contractor was reslating a roof, using a tool called a lath axe, illustrated in Figure 8.7. This has an axe head at one end and a square-faced hammer head with serrations on the striking face at the other. Since purchasing the tool several weeks before his accident the contractor had noticed the outside of the hammer head had chipped in places, but he had continued to use it, because it "was one of the best tools he had ever

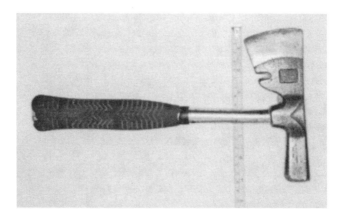

Figure 8.7 Lath axe.

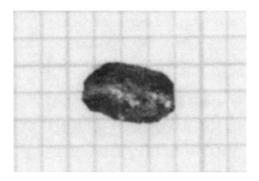

Figure 8.8 Fragment of metal removed from eye resting on a 1-mm-square grid.

owned." He was on the roof using the hammer end to trim brickwork when he felt something hit his eye. Thinking it was a piece of the brick he rubbed it and continued working but the pain became so intense he had to stop working.

The tiny fragment of steel removed from his eye at the hospital, measuring 3.5 mm × 2 mm, is illustrated in Figure 8.8. It has a sharp rim and the uppermost face exhibits what is referred to as a conchoidal (shell-like) fracture, characteristic of a piece of hardened steel displaced by a gouging impact. The other faces resting on the graph paper were worn and bore features consistent with the outside of this worn hammer head. The confirmatory test is to place the particle in likely cavities on the suspect tool and see how well the surface features match the surrounding ones on the tool. In this instance, not only did the suspect location provide a good physical fit in the cavity, but it also displays conformity of external contour

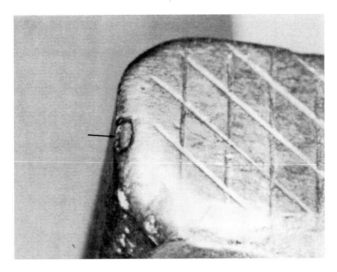

Figure 8.9   Eye particle replaced in suspect cavity on hammer head.

and surface markings. In Figure 8.9 the particle is shown resting in the matching cavity at the top of the head of the lath axe.

The tool had been manufactured overseas and, although well finished externally, the hardness of the striking face was considerably above the range specified in the British Standard 876 for hammers. This standard specifies hardness in Rockwell numbers, but because a Rockwell test cannot be carried out on such a tiny particle the Vickers hardness test has to be used instead. The converted Rc hardness range is equivalent to 520 to 640 on the Vickers scale. The rim of this hammer was 880 HV and a test on the particle gave a value of 900 HV. At this level any steel will be brittle and the striking face of a hammer is likely to splinter.

The brittleness on its own would have been enough to account for the rim splintering under a heavy, glancing blow, but in this instance there was another dangerous fault. A microsection cut from the striking face exhibited a network of cracks produced during the heat treatment used to harden the rim. A group of these is shown in the etched microsection of Figure 8.10. The way they follow grain boundaries is characteristic of cracks formed in medium and high carbon steels when the cooling rate from the hardening temperature is too fast. In this instance it suggests that the hammer head had been quenched into water instead of oil. Quench cracks form at the surface and clearly account for the way numerous pieces had flaked away from this hammer head before the accident.

Unfortunately for the injured man, who owned and had been the sole user of the tool since new, there had been ample warning of its dangerous condition in the way several pieces had broken off the outer rim during

Figure 8.10   Microsection of hammer head showing quench cracks. Polished and etched section (×50 magnification).

previous use. The risk of further splintering was therefore foreseeable; so the hammer should have been taken out of service long before the accident. A further difficulty for the injured man was that he had purchased the tool from a market stall and had no receipt. It appeared to have emanated from China, a fact that raises formidable problems in litigation.

8.3.3   Printer's Drying Frame

A young man working for a small printing firm lost an eye while helping carry a drying frame up a narrow staircase. The frame consisted of a tall stack of 50 hinged trays mounted in a steel frame with castors. The individual trays were flat and made of steel wire mesh, so that sheets of paper coming from a silk screen printer could be laid on them one at a time while the color dried. Each tray was hinged so that it could be stacked practically vertical until needed, and then folded down to a horizontal position when a fresh poster came from the printer. Coil tension springs at the pivot ends held the trays in the raised position and were stretched when the tray was pulled down. Figure 8.11 is a photograph of the upper trays in two adjacent dryers: the one at the left has the trays in the horizontal position, the one on the right has them in the raised position. Attention is drawn to how far the springs are extended when the trays are horizontal.

The side handrail of one of the six drying frames on the first floor of the building had been damaged, so the frame was sent to a local fabricating firm who formed a new tubular handrail and welded it into position. The top of

Figure 8.11   Side views of two drying frames to show how far the springs extend when the trays are folded down to the horizontal position. In the frame at the left all but the top two trays are down, whereas in the one at the right every frame is still in the "up" position.

this handrail and the weld attaching it to the back frame can be seen in the left-hand drying frame of Figure 8.11. Notice how far the spring is stretched when the top tray is in the raised position and also how close this spring is to where the welding was carried out. When the frame came back from repair it had to be carried up a narrow staircase to the first floor as there was no elevator in the building. One man pushed from the bottom, while the young man was pulling at the opposite side, so at times his face was quite close to the top weld. As they reached the turn near the top of the staircase, the uppermost spring suddenly broke and the hooked end shot into the young man's eye, injuring him so severely that his eye had to be removed.

The fractured spring was sent for examination to establish the cause of its sudden breakage. As it had necked down at the point of fracture it was clearly not a fatigue failure, confirmed by examination of the fracture that exhibited all the features of a ductile overload. Even if it had been fatigue it would have been difficult to explain why it had broken in the middle of the straight portion rather than where it was bent. Springs of this type are formed from cold drawn patented steel wire, which have a strongly oriented fiber structure in the longitudinal direction and, significantly, have a carbon content of the order of 0.8%, which puts them in the range of steels that respond to heat treatments.

The polished and etched longitudinal section of the length removed from the injured man's eye is shown in Figure 8.12, with the fracture at the left. This reveals localized areas where the steel has undergone heat treatment;

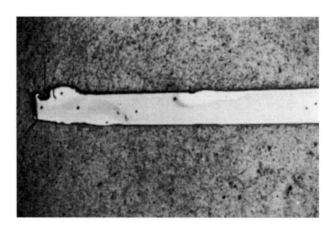

Figure 8.12   Polished and etched section of spring adjacent to fracture. The wire diameter is 0.9 mm.

some appear as white areas, having a high hardness, surrounded by a shaded heat-affected zone, while immediately adjacent to the fracture there is a knob of light-etching metal with a crack in it and the underlying metal is soft. (The black diamond shapes are Vickers hardness indentations; the larger they are, the softer the metal.)

Obviously, this end of the spring had been affected by inadvertent heat treatments, highly localized and related to the welding. Weld spatter droplets had fallen onto the spring and transferred enough heat to raise the surface locally to transformation temperatures. Adjacent to the fracture can be seen where a molten droplet has bonded to the spring and transferred enough heat to soften the center section. The weld droplet itself has a hot tear at the outside caused by contraction stress as it was solidifying. Farther along, smaller spatter particles have heated the metal to a hardening temperature but only carried sufficient heat to affect the microstructure in a shallow zone immediately below the surface.

As a consequence of these microstructural changes resulting from the weld spatter, the spring was unable to withstand the bouncing up and down of the trays as the frame was manhandled up the stairs. The unfortunate young man's eye must have been directly in line with the spring when it suddenly broke under what was, in effect, a mechanical overstress of the softened region while the spring was under tension. The firm that did the welding accepted liability; they were well aware that spatter always occurs when arc welding with flux-coated electrodes and should have taken precautions to cover the springs and/or remove the top few trays.

8.4 Ladder Accidents

Ladder accidents are one of the most common kinds of domestic and industrial accidents because ladders are such widely used pieces of equipment, and the user is exposed to a high level of risk unless safety rules are obeyed strictly. Both of the accidents described here occurred because one or more of the rules was broken, with serious personal injuries as a result. There are several standards dealing with ladders, of which the most important in the U.K. is the British Standard.[1]

One of the accidents occurred on a dry, summer morning, just after the homeowner had erected the two-stage extension ladder (which had just been purchased) against the back wall of his house to clean the upper windows (on the first floor of a two-story detached property). The ladder was supported on the level concrete paving slabs of the patio adjacent to the back garden of the house. According to the witness statement, the owner was at or near the top where he was washing a fanlight above an upper window. As he moved down the ladder to clean the pane below, the ladder suddenly slipped from the sill, and "walked down" the wall, and he fell to the ground where he sustained very serious injuries. The ladder ended up at right angles to the wall. One of the plastic tips to the ladder had broken (Figure 8.13A, B and C), but the feet were intact. There was no damage or visible defects to the metal ladder itself. It was thought that the broken tip could have caused the fall, by allowing the ladder to slip down the wall, so the owner, who was also the injured party, initiated litigation against the ladder manufacturer. Following funding from legal aid, the lawyer approached an expert for a report.

8.4.1 The Material Evidence

The key evidence was thus the broken tip (Figure 8.13). It showed a brittle fracture in an unidentified, relatively rigid plastic. The fracture surface was very fresh, and there was no sign of old or subcritical cracks. FTIR analysis showed that the material was in fact a copolymer of polypropylene, which should normally be tough and resilient. But what did the fracture reveal, and were there any obvious features that could represent defects exposed in the surface?

The central void is clearly a stress concentration with a stress concentration value of at least two. However, analysis of the crack surface itself showed the origin to lie elsewhere, at an external corner produced as a feature of the design of the tool used to injection mold the component, known as a mold parting line. It is simply where two mating parts of the steel tool meet, and often show a mismatch owing to mold tool wear (Figure 8.13B). The

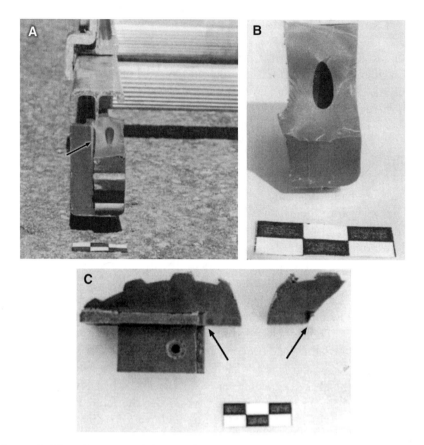

Figure 8.13 The parts of the accident ladder. (A) End of ladder. (B) Fracture surface of ladder tip. (C) Intact and broken tips compared.

conjunction of this small corner and the larger external corner thus produced a stress concentration larger then elsewhere on the corner. Although only one of the two tips had broken, both showed severe abrasive damage to the parts in direct contact with the brick wall against which the ladder had been leaned just before the accident.

The possible causes of the fracture at this stage of the investigation were:

- Poor material
- Faulty manufacture
- Poor design

But there was little support for poor material, such as degradation, from either DSC or spectroscopic analysis. Although the void represented poor design and molding practice, it did not initiate the crack that broke the tip.

The sharp corner in the molding had initiated the crack and it represented a possible design defect if it had failed and caused the accident. Sharp internal corners are commonly present in many molded products, but are not necessarily defects unless it can be shown that these features cause product failure and hence accidents.

8.4.2 Ladder Stability

How was the ladder being used at the time of the accident? The key variables are the angle of repose of the ladder and the coefficient of friction between the feet and the ground. A visit to the site of the accident was essential, so the witness statement could be checked, and any further evidence that could clarify the circumstances could be examined directly. The visit showed visible evidence of the intermittent contact between the tips of the ladder and the wall below the window, and the traces of an impact with the small sill above the patio doors. The trace contact marks corroborated the witness statement, showing how the tips and hence the ladder structure itself had oscillated from side to side as it slipped down the wall. No traces of marks from the feet on the concrete slabs of the patio itself could be found. The angle of repose and coefficient of friction of the feet remained unknown, however. A reconstruction of events was essential to measure or calculate the data using the actual ladder itself.

8.4.3 Reconstruction

Although the injured user attempted to guess the information requested (especially the angle of repose and degree of extension of the ladder), it is always best to measure independently. After traumatic injury, an individual is more likely to forget such information, even if, in normal circumstances, they could recall such details. The ladder had not been photographed *in situ* just after the accident. There were no trace marks of the feet on the patio, from which the extended length of the ladder could be inferred. However, there were some key bits of information that seemed indisputable: the tips of the ladder were resting on the sill, at about 16 ft (3.69 m) from the ground (as measured directly during the site visit).

The events were reconstructed using the ladder fitted with new tips, and started by assuming the ladder was fully closed since this fitted the known facts. Another ladder owned by the investigator was placed by its side for the purposes of comparison and safety during stability tests. The aims of the test were as follows:

1. To estimate the static coefficient of friction of the feet

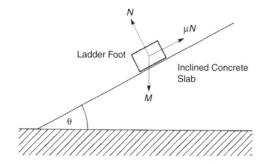

Figure 8.14   Coefficient of friction of ladder feet on an inclined slab.

2. To establish the angle of repose
3. To determine the footprint of the rubber feet
4. To load the ladder statically at the estimated height of use
5. To examine dynamics by simulation of movement

8.4.4   Coefficient of Friction

The first task was to estimate the static coefficient of friction (μ) of the polypropylene feet.[2] A simple way of doing this for very light loads is simply to place the feet on a surface similar to that being used for the real ladder and tilt it until the feet just slip (Figure 8.14). In this case, the surface is simply a concrete slab. Theory shows that the critical condition for slip on the inclined plane is

$$\mu = \tan \emptyset \qquad\qquad (8.1)$$

where $\emptyset$ is the angle of inclination of the slab to the level ground. Two experiments established that the coefficient of friction for the feet (mass about 100 g) was

$$\mu \text{ (feet)} \sim 1.00$$

Such a value is typical for the elastomeric polymer concerned acting on smooth concrete. But would the feet as fitted to a ladder exhibit the same value? Direct determination from the (unladen) accident ladder showed that it slipped at an angle of about 40°, so that neglecting friction at the tips, the coefficient of friction is about 0.6, considerably lower than the value estimated from an inclined plane experiment. There are several reasons for this situation. In the first place, the coefficient of friction of polymers is known to be dependent on load, *decreasing* as the load *increases*. Secondly, the feet of the accident ladder had been designed for a repose angle of about 75°

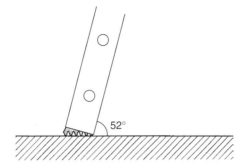

Figure 8.15   Fixed attitude ladder feet (schematic).

(Figure 8.15), any other angle lowering the contact area of the serrated surface against the ground. This was demonstrated by recording the footprint of the feet at several angles of repose. The edge in contact with the ground thus becomes even more heavily loaded over a much smaller area of contact.

8.4.5   Repose Angle

The next question to be addressed was the likely angle at which the ladder had been leaned against the wall. The claimant thought that it had been leaned against the sill of the upper window, so that then the angle of repose could be calculated for two situations: an unextended ladder and the ladder extended by one rung. Greater degrees of extension would create progressively lower angles of repose. As a working hypothesis, it was thus assumed that the ladder had been used either unextended, or with one rung extended. Leaning the ladder against the sill would be given by

$$\sin \emptyset = \text{vertical height to sill/ladder length} \qquad (8.2)$$

With the known length of the unextended ladder being 4.46 m, extended by one rung being 4.71 m and with the adjacent sill being 3.69 m from the level ground surface, then $\emptyset = 56°$ (unextended) or 52° for an extension of one rung. The situation for the ladder is shown schematically in Figure 8.16 and Figure 8.17, with the plastic tips leaning against the window sill. In this position, a slight movement of the ladder would allow the ladder to jump-down onto the adjacent wall, where either the aluminum tips of the lower section of the ladder or the plastic tips on the upper section would make contact with the brick wall. Both sets of tips showed abrasion, most visibly obvious in the case of the plastic tips (Figure 8.18). In addition, matching the ladder to the wall with known lengths and heights showed that the unextended ladder had most likely been used. The angle of repose of 56° was well below the recommended angle of repose of 75° for this design of ladder.

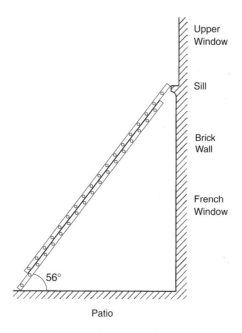

Figure 8.16 Side view of unextended ladder leaning against window sill (schematic).

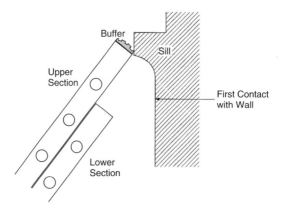

Figure 8.17 Close-up of tips against wall (schematic).

But what could explain the curious set of marks below the window and the comment about "walking down the wall"?

8.4.6   Stability Experiments

The final phase of experiments involved simulating the weight of the user when working near the top of the ladder. Both the actual weight and height

Figure 8.18 Top of failed ladder tips showing wear on surfaces, with contamination by brick dust (arrows).

of the user were known, and it was most likely that he was standing on the fifth step from the top when the ladder slipped. The user could thus be simulated by simply suspending a fixed mass of 72.6 kg (726 Newtons) to represent his weight on a rope from the upper rungs. The mass of the ladder of about 20 kg (200 N) was leaned at an angle of 56° against the wall, representing the unextended ladder (Figure 8.19). The exact position of the suspended mass was also important, because when ascending or descending a ladder, the user shifts his weight from foot to foot. The user could not remember which rung he was standing on at the time of the accident, but it was likely that the fourth, fifth and sixth rungs from the top were in use at the time. Since the user was cleaning the right-hand pane of glass, his left hand was probably holding the left-hand part of the uppermost rung. By leaning over, his weight will have shifted to the right-hand part of the rung he was standing on, so the right-hand part of the fifth rung was initially chosen as the point of attachment of the suspended mass.

Figure 8.19 Reconstruction with weight hanging from ladder rung (safety ladder at left).

One feasible stimulus for the accident could have been momentary loss of contact of the left-hand tip with the sill against which it was resting, by reaching over to the right, for example. A spring balance was used to determine how much force was needed to pull the left-hand stile at right angles from the sill (about 10 kgf). The torque at the top of the ladder simultaneously pulled the left-hand foot out of contact with the ground, and the loss of contact causes the right-hand tip to slip down to a slightly lower position against the wall. Repetition of the effect led to progressively lower positions against the wall until the whole ladder became dangerously unstable

Figure 8.20 Stick-slip marks made on white board by ladder tips after uncontrolled slipping of the ladder. It occurred with the user mass hung from the fourth rung down from the top.

and the experiment was halted. The effect is known as "stick-slip" motion (Figure 8.20).

So what did the reconstruction show? First, it suggested that the ladder had been leaned against the wall at an angle of a maximum of about 56°, well below the recommended safe angle of repose. Second, it confirmed that at relatively low angles of repose of this particular design of ladder, stick-slip motion could occur after momentary instability (even if the angle of repose was above the critical angle of repose). That instability was produced by a torque load that moved one of the tips of the ladder from contact with the wall. Provided the user was near the top of the ladder, catastrophic and uncontrollable loss of the ladder was inevitable.

8.4.7   Conclusions

The reconstruction of the accident showed that the user initially leaned the ladder at too low an angle for a reasonable safety margin. Although it was above the critical angle of repose, it was susceptible to stick-slip instability when the user was near the top of the ladder. The visible contact evidence from the wall confirmed stick-slip movement of the ladder tips. But the question of the fractured tip remained unanswered. It could still have caused the accident if the tip had broken at the sill, and initiated stick-slip motion. However, both the broken and intact tips showed abrasion against brickwork, so it is more likely that it survived for some distance down the wall. The final piece of evidence was an impact mark on the small wooden sill above the patio doors. This was probably caused when the tip hit the sill, and the tip broke from its weakest point. The fracture was thus the result, and not the cause of the accident.

Given this conclusion, it was decided that the case had no chance of success at trial. The victim of the accident did not receive any compensation. The moral of this forensic story is that initial perceptions of failure may not always survive critical scrutiny. Investigation should always examine the circumstances surrounding a product failure: the fracture is just one more piece of evidence to build up a picture of events based on the most reasonable interpretation of *all* the evidence. Ladder accidents are very common, and a site visit is essential to gather more evidence of the incident. In this case, the contact evidence on the wall was important for construction of working hypotheses to explain the accident. In addition, practical reconstruction of the accident using the failed ladder demonstrated stick-slip motion above the critical angle of repose, and helped explain the contact evidence. However, the answer to the problem lay not in the tips but the feet of the ladder, since it is the feet that play the crucial role in the stability of ladders.

8.4.8   Workplace Accident

The second accident occurred when a painter was working alone in a factory, painting the interior walls. He was found lying on the ground partly on the fallen ladder, unconscious and with severe head injuries. There were no witnesses, so the reconstruction was vital in establishing what had happened. Unlike the previous case, the ladder had marked both the floor and the wall during the fall. It had slipped back perpendicular to the wall, so it was essential to determine original the angle of repose. Marks had been left by the feet on the quarry tile floor (Figure 8.21), showing exactly where it had originally had been leaned. The exact ladder length was also known. It turned out to be at an angle of about 75°, the correct angle for safe work, a fact established by reconstruction shortly after the accident by his supervisor. It was also clear that the painter had been near the top, as shown by the extent of painting that had been completed (Figure 8.22).

What had caused the accident? The marks on the floor provided the clue to what had happened (Figure 8.21). When soft rubber slips against a hard surface, the only marks should be from abraded rubber, but the marks were gray. Examination showed them to be more likely to have been formed from the aluminum feet of the ladder. Replacing the accident ladder as in Figure 8.23 showed that the rubber feet had worn to such an extent that they were pushed into the hollow aluminum feet by the weight of the ladder above. A user on the ladder would exacerbate the situation. The coefficients of friction between aluminum or rubber and quarry tile were measured by direct experiment and turned out to be about $\mu \sim 0.4$ and 1.0, respectively. Static analysis shows that the stability of any ladder decreases as the user ascends,

Figure 8.21 Fallen ladder on quarry tile floor with mark from foot at center of picture.

and is most unstable when the user is near the top. So the painter had used the ladder successfully at least once, as shown by the painting near the top of the wall (Figure 8.22). At the second attempt, the ladder became unstable when the painter was at or near the top, and started to slip uncontrollably, perhaps when he was reaching out on one side to paint the wall. As the ladder slipped the painter lost his balance and fell, his head hitting the floor and the fallen ladder.

The painter won substantial compensation for his injuries because employers have a responsibility to provide employees with safe and reliable equipment needed to perform their work. The amount of compensation was reduced by an element of contributory negligence, however. The painter should have checked the state of the ladder, and he should not have used it without someone footing the ladder to provide extra stability. All such points

Figure 8.22 The accident scene showing the unpainted wall above (top arrow) and the slipped ladder (lower arrow). Note damage to the duct in center of wall caused by the falling ladder.

would have been discussed at trial, but the substantial costs of trial were saved by the agreed settlement before the case proceeded.

8.4.9 Ladder Accidents and Design Improvements

After car accidents, one of the most common causes of death and serious injury both in the U.K. and the U.S. is accidents in which the victim falls.[3,4]

Figure 8.23 Reconstruction with ladder feet placed on floor mark. The ladder was erected at the correct angle, but the rubber feet have been pushed into the ladder recesses.

So what can be done to lower the accident rate? Informing users of the dangers of ladders and the best way to use them is one way of warning the user of the potential dangers. Indeed, new ladders have some of the most elaborate warning notices posted on any product. Due to the instability of lean-to ladders, they should be stabilized wherever possible, by tying the feet or tips to a solid support, or by having a colleague standing on the feet to prevent slip. Ladders should never be used when the floor is wet, as this lowers the coefficient of friction, and the floor should also be level so that both feet are in contact. Ladders must be inspected at regular intervals, and the critical feet and tips renewed when worn or damaged, a service many ladder manufacturers actually provide for free. But can ladder design be improved so as to lower the chances of slippage accidents of the kind considered here?

One of the problems of the accident ladders is that both possessed fixed attitude feet, so that any deviation from a repose angle of 75° lowered the contact area with the ground. Since the feet are the key to the stability of ladders, one solution is to provide feet that adjust as the angle of repose is changed (Figure 8.24). Such articulated feet are thus always in complete contact with the ground and provide an extra margin of safety. The design of the plastic tips and feet can also be improved for ladders of the specific design considered here. Although the tip broke during the first accident rather than causing it, the design possesses several stress concentrators: one by design (sharp corners), the other from manufacture (internal void). Both could easily be eliminated, the first by simply smoothing the corners of the metal molding tools, the other by more careful control of the molding process. Both procedures would increase the strength of the

Figure 8.24   Articulated ladder feet.

product substantially. In the second case, regular maintenance of the work ladders would have prevented the accident. A ladder with articulated feet would also have helped because this design is such that the rubber foot pads are very visible and users have adequate warning of their state of wear.

References

1. Specification for portable aluminum ladders, steps, trestles, and lightweight stagings, BS 2037, 1994.

2. Hepburn, H.A., Portable ladders. I. The quarter length rule, *Br. J. Industrial Safety*, 4, 155, 1958.

3. Goldsmith, A., The role of good design and manufacturing in preventing ladder accidents, *J. Products Liability*, 8, 127, 1985.

4. Betzen, F.E. and Jones, P.L., Potential of ANSI safety requirements for portable metal ladders, *J. Products Liability*, 6, 7, 1983.

Failure of Medical Implements

9.1 Introduction

In society today access to adequate health care is considered paramount, with extensive use being made of state-of-the-art technological methods, novel instruments, medical aids and biocompatible implant materials and devices. Such technological support has spread to almost all sections of medical science, together with areas as diverse as prevention, diagnosis, therapy and rehabilitation.

The introduction to Chapter 2 likened the work of the forensic engineer to the medical pathologist, drawing analogies between failed mechanical components and the human body. This relationship can be further reinforced when considering the relatively new and fast developing area of *engineering in medicine*. Here, engineering/mechanical principles are employed to solve problems that arise in areas of biology and medicine. In short, engineered components are being designed and used to replace parts of living systems in the human body. The range and variety of engineered components utilized in medicine are enormous and include devices such as turbines to pump blood, heart pacemakers, drug delivery systems, joint replacement devices, etc. Materials used for the fabrication of such components are designed to operate in intimate contact with living tissue and have minimal adverse reaction with the body system. However, there are only limited ranges of materials that exhibit characteristics desirable for *in vivo* service and these materials have been termed biomaterials. There are ranges of relevant standards (ASTM, BS and ISO, for example) that describe required material characteristics and mechanical response, with the focus firmly on corrosion resistance of metallic materials. Nonetheless, biomaterials are not limited to metallic systems: polymeric and ceramic materials are also utilized for *in vivo* service. Components or devices engineered from biomaterials are referred to as biomedical or implant devices.

9.2   The Body as a Working Environment

As a working environment, the body can be deemed an extremely hostile setting. Body fluids are essentially an aerated solution containing approximately 1 wt% NaCl at 37°C. It will also contain other salts and organic compounds, but in relatively minor concentrations. Consequently, for metals, body fluids are very corrosive and lead not only to uniform corrosion, but also to crevice attack and pitting. In addition to corrosion, particulate debris will be generated by the articulation of bearing surfaces of devices such as hip prostheses. As the articulating surfaces wear against one another, debris will be generated and accumulate in surrounding tissues, releasing enzymes that result in the death of surrounding bone cells (osteolysis). With time, sufficient bone will be resorbed from around the device, eventually leading to mechanical loosening.

A further consequence of corrosion is that by-products are transported rapidly throughout the body and may segregate in specific organs. Even though some species of corrosion product may be excreted from the body, they may nevertheless still persist in relatively high concentrations by virtue of the ongoing corrosion process.

9.3   Design and Performance Criteria

In addition to corrosion issues, the choice of which material to employ must take into account:

- In-service loading of the implant device, prosthesis or instrument
- Biocompatibility with any surrounding tissues or body fluids
- Friction and wear of any articulating surfaces
- Fixation methods, such as bone cement or osteointegration (the extent to which bone will integrate into, or grow next to, an implant)

By their very nature, these considerations are minimum requirements to provide design confidence in the structural integrity of a device.

When assessing surgical instruments and equipment, identical attributes to those of biomaterials are required. Whether manufacturing an implant device, surgical instrument or equipment, the design engineer will invariably be working to an intended performance criterion along with a set of design requirements to meet in-service demands. Minimum performance and design requirements can be described as follows.

9.3.1   Performance

The intended performance of a medical device or tool can be described by addressing its

- Functional characteristics
- Intended in-service conditions of use

Account has to be taken of any published standards, clinical and scientific literature and any *validated* test results.

9.3.2   Design Attributes

To meet performance benchmarks, the development of applicable design attributes has to consider the following points as a minimum:

1. Physical, mechanical and chemical properties of the instrument materials; microbiological and particulate contamination levels; the ease of use, cleaning and maintenance
2. The potential deterioration of the material characteristics due to sterilization and storage
3. The effect of contact between the instrument and body environment, or the implant and other instruments
4. Shape and dimensions, to include their possible effects on the body
5. Wear characteristics of materials and the effect of wear products on the instrument or body
6. Insertion, removal and interconnecting parts
7. Extent of fluid leakage and/or diffusion of substances into or out of instruments; leaching of chemical species out of the implant
8. The accuracy and stability of instruments with a measuring function
9. The ability of the implant, instrument or fragment of an instrument to be located by means of an external imaging device

Application of performance and design criteria is intended to minimize any likelihood of premature failure. Needless to say, any design solution will be evaluated prior to introduction (preclinical) in addition to in-service (clinical) assessment. As with any engineered artifact, the critical engineering issues applicable to premature failure in a medical device or tool are design, material selection and biocompatibility.

The contribution of engineering to the advancement of health care and quality of life has been substantial and will increase further as technology advances. Nevertheless, as with any artifact, failures can and do occur. The first case reviewed in this chapter will show how device design and material selection becomes subject to change. As *in vivo* experience of device behavior accumulates with time, the knowledge gathered can be fed back into required performance and design attributes.

9.4   Hip Joint Failures

A short historical review of design and materials used in a replacement hip joint is appropriate to introduce the topic of hip joint failures. The story began in 1961, when Sir John Charnley revolutionized modern total hip replacement with the introduction of his "low friction arthroplasty." Some 40 years later, current designs continue to be based on his principles of using a relatively small metallic femoral head and a polymeric socket. However, materials utilized for device fabrication have changed with the advance of time. There has been a movement away from surgical grade 316L stainless steel to a range of more exotic alloy systems. In his first designs, Charnley used PTFE as the socket-bearing material, but he soon found that wear levels were unacceptably high. Ultra-high molecular weight polyethylene (UHMPE) produced much better lifetimes, and it is the most common bearing polymer in use today.

Today, the device "parts" are a ball, which is inserted into the top of the femur, with a stem for stability (see Figure 9.1). The stem may be composed of titanium or a cobalt based alloy and the ball or "head" is generally cobalt chrome or ceramic. The stem is often inserted with a bone cement but may also have a sintered porous surface coating which allows bone ingrowth (osteointegration) for mechanical locking.

The socket is composed of a metal shell (usually titanium or cobalt chrome) which bone grows into, and a plastic (ultra-high molecular weight polyethylene) liner, which articulates with the new ball.

Whether due to a manufacturing fault or unforeseen service conditions, the consequences of medical device/instrument failure can have a far-reaching effect as demonstrated by the following case study.

9.4.1   Fatigue Failure of Prosthetic Hip Components

When a patient has been diagnosed with a diseased or damaged hip joint, total hip replacement is accepted as a standard method of treatment. However, complications may arise from in-service (usually fatigue) failure of the

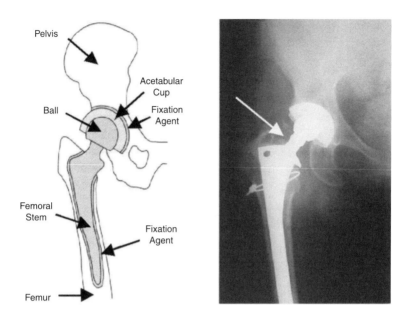

Figure 9.1 Total replacement hip device. Sketch of device (left) and x-ray of device *in situ*, with expected location of fracture arrowed (right). The wire was added during the surgical procedure to prevent the femur from splitting.

femoral component. Fatigue is known to depend on factors ranging from design and material of the device, through the surgical technique employed during implantation, to the weight and level of activity of the patient. In order to illustrate the complexity and *reality* of fatigue failure in implant devices, an illustration based on the work of Rimnac et al.[1] will be introduced as an initial case study.

A metallic total hip component was developed in the early 1970s. It had a trapezoidal cross section to its stem and neck, which was intended to impart improved mobility, stability and stem strength over previous hip designs. The femoral component was fabricated from 316 surgical grade stainless steel in a hot forged and lightly cold-worked condition. At one New York hospital, 805 patients received this implant over a 6-year period prior to 1979. Of this population, at least 21 patients had to have remedial treatment for a fractured femoral component. This represented a failure rate over four times higher than that reported for other femoral component designs.

To investigate the reason for such high failure rates, a failure analysis was conducted on all 21 fractured parts. Fracture generally occurred within the proximal third of the stem (arrowed on Figure 9.1). Optical microscopy revealed a dominant crack initiation site at the posterior corner on the medial side of the stem. A second crack had initiated on the lateral side of the stem,

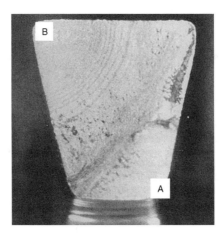

Figure 9.2 Optical micrograph of fracture surface on femoral stem of total hip device. Crack growth from medial corner (A), and clamshell markings emanating from lateral corner (B).

and exhibited clam-shell markings typically found on fatigue fracture surfaces (Figure 9.2). The boundary between the two crack fronts was identified by a step near the central portion of the trapezoidal cross section.

Based on microscopic observation and stress analysis, Rimnac proposed the following sequence of events to explain the fracture of the femoral stem. Residual tensile stresses induced by large compressive overload on the medial side of the stem resulted in the growth of a fatigue crack prior to a second crack nucleation on the lateral side. With crack growth, there is a progressive reduction in residual tensile stresses, along with an increase in the extent of crack closure, ahead of a fatigue crack subjected to cyclic compressive loads. As a result, the medial cracks slowed down or stopped after a certain amount of crack advance. The nucleation of medial cracking increased the stress level to which the lateral side of the stem was exposed. With time and cyclic loading in service, the two crack fronts eventually met up. This coalescence of crack fronts produced a step on the fracture surface. Rimnac et al. concluded that the failure of the femoral stem was a consequence of the combined effects of the trapezoidal cross-sectional design and of the materials properties of the stainless steel used to fabricate the component.

9.4.2   Failure in Femoral Stem of Total Hip Prosthesis

Total hip prostheses do have a finite lifetime within the body environment and will therefore simply wear out with time. This can be aptly demonstrated by the following case where a person falling had apparently caused breakage of a total hip prosthesis.

An elderly woman had a fall when she went to answer the front door of her council house. Her foot went through a floorboard that had been weakened by dry rot, causing her to tumble. When help arrived, it was quickly recognized that the woman had damaged her right hip and required urgent medical treatment. At the hospital, it became apparent that the patient had been the recipient of a total hip replacement some 10 years earlier and the device had broken. A surgical procedure was promptly undertaken to retrieve the broken prosthesis and insert a replacement device. After a full recovery, the patient instigated legal proceedings against her landlord (the local council) for her injury and suffering. Although the woman stated that her fall had not been particularly heavy, she believed that her injury was a direct result of the fall. The legal action was for a claim of negligence in maintaining her floor to a reasonable standard, resulting in a fall that broke her hip prosthesis.

The broken femoral stem of the device was submitted for investigation Figure 9.3A, and is shown with the surgical extraction tool having been left *in situ*. Figure 9.3B, shows an optical micrograph of the fracture surface, where striations associated with a fatigue failure mechanism are clearly visible. Fatigue is a mechanism that often involves many hundreds, if not thousands, of loading cycles to reach the point of failure (Chapter 2, Section 2.4) and is *not* an overload mechanism. If, as claimed, the hip prosthesis had suffered an overload failure resulting from a fall, the loading pattern would present a totally different fracture surface (Chapter 2, Section 2.3).

To date, the life expectancy of a total hip prosthesis is approximately 10 years. When the age of the device in question was taken into consideration and combined with evidence of failure resulting from fatigue, it was determined that the device had simply reached the end of its useful service lifetime and failure was *not* a direct result of the fall. The loading experienced at the instant of impact would in all probability have been withstood by the device if it had not been considerably weakened by the presence of a growing fatigue crack.

However, the woman *had* suffered a fall that was a result of poor maintenance practice by her landlord. The litigation was settled out of court by the landlord's insurers, with the woman receiving substantially reduced damages for the incident.

9.4.3 Manufacturing Contamination of Acetabular Hip Shells

On December 8, 2000, an orthopedic device manufacturer announced the recall of a specific range of acetabular shells that formed one part of a hip replacement device (Figure 9.4). The reason given for the recall was that a mineral oil lubricant residue on the outer porous surface might have contaminated a small number of the implant shells. The porous coating on the shell was intended to allow bone tissue to grow into the surface, thereby

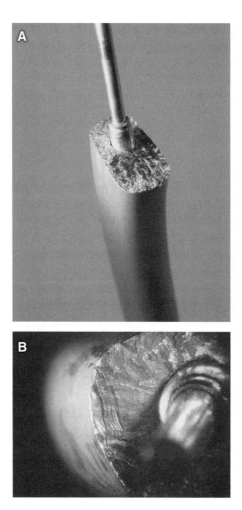

Figure 9.3 Broken femoral stem of total hip prosthesis. The extraction tool protruding vertically out of fracture surface (A), and fracture surface clearly showing fatigue striations (B).

providing a more secure bond. Oil residue that was thought to have originated from the manufacturing process had not been completely removed prior to the total hip replacement surgery.

The shell is implanted into the upper part of the hip (acetabulum) and under normal conditions, the bone would form an integrated bond with the shell. However, when surface contaminants are present, bone does not always bond with the shell.

With mineral oil as the contaminant, small amounts of the residual lubricant will be broken down and eliminated by the body. At the time of this writing, the only known problem resulting from such contamination is

Figure 9.4   *In situ* acetabular ball and shell of a total hip replacement device (center).

the inability of the bone to bond with the affected hip implant. However, the result of such a deficiency is a device that will come loose from the bone. Reported symptoms would include severe groin pain and the inability to bear weight on the affected leg. The only solution that would provide effective relief for the patient is revision surgery.

At the time of the recall, it was anticipated that some 17,500 patients had been fitted with the suspect shells but that there were only some 61 reported cases of patients experiencing loosening of the shell. However, in June 2001 it was reported that the number had increased to more than 1,850 revision surgeries.

Thus a simple process failure, machining oil contamination at the production stage, can have far-reaching and dire consequences for a large number of individuals. What was initially considered *possible* contamination of a small number of implant shells was subsequently found to be a major failure of performance and design attributes of the device. Although this case had not been resolved and not all the facts have been made public at the time of this writing, to the inquiring mind it does raise some obvious questions concerning product integrity. Furthermore, this type of failure must also bring into question the reliability of quality control procedures in place on the production line.

9.4.4   Corrosion of a Polished Titanium Alloy Femoral Stem

A particular modular cemented total hip replacement system was launched in 1979 with a monobloc (one piece) matte-finished titanium alloy straight stem. In 1987 the stem of this device was changed from monobloc to a modular separate stem and head configuration, and in 1989 the surface finish of the stem was changed from matte to polished. During 1992 the product range was extended to include the option of a polished conventional stainless steel stem, and a polished high nitrogen stainless steel stem was added to the range in 2001.

In the U.K., the Medical Devices Agency (MDA) had become aware of 28 revisions, due to recipient pain, where corrosion was confirmed in the polished titanium alloy femoral stem. The incidence of these revisions was spread across nine different centers, and represented a confirmed failure rate of 0.14%. In addition, the MDA became aware of eight additional possible cases, of which five were considered by the clinicians involved to have been resolved without the need for further surgery. Since 1999 the number of reported cases of corrosion of the polished titanium stem has continued to increase.

The most common clinical symptom signaling potential problems was severe atypical pain at 2 to 5 years post-implantation, along with an absence of overt infection or femoral loosening. However, it would appear that pain relief could be achieved upon movement. Additionally, corrosion has been seen along the full length of the explanted stems, but in some cases it is focused on the distal half of the stem.

A most interesting aspect of the problem is that extensive testing in five independent biomaterials laboratories has failed to establish categorically why the polished titanium alloy modular femoral stem sometimes corrodes in this manner. Furthermore, the MDA has no information of any case of corrosion in the original matte-finished titanium alloy stem or in either of the stainless steel variants. Although presenting manufacturing difficulties, titanium alloy is generally considered to be highly corrosion resistant *in vivo*. One probable answer is that the matte surface would bond better with the bone and resist any physical actions that would damage the TiO_2 surface film. It is this film that gives titanium its corrosion resistance, as the metal itself is highly reactive chemically.

In addition, the elastic modulus of titanium is a closer match to that of bone than the range of alternative bio-alloy systems. Consequently, from a purely mechanistic view, titanium alloys are gaining popularity for implant device fabrication. Nevertheless, this particular case does raise questions as to the performance attributes of polished titanium prosthetic devices.

A review of the published literature[2–4] describes sporadic cases of corrosion of other models of polished and unpolished cemented titanium alloy hip implants. However, the polished stem in question is currently the only *titanium* alloy hip implant repeatedly exhibiting this corrosion problem in the U.K. Accordingly, the MDA issued a device alert —— MDA DA2002 (04), dated May 2002 — for the device in question.

9.5   Catheter Failures

Since the catheter is one of the most common articles in use in medical practice, its failure can have serious consequences. Those consequences are much more serious in the case of catheters implanted into the human body, or in use during surgical intervention. Incidents of both kinds of catheter failure are discussed in this section.

9.5.1   Fracture of a TPE Catheter

A nylon/polyether TPE catheter fractured during the final stages of childbirth in a British hospital.[5] The failed product in question was a 1-mm-diameter catheter, one end of which had been sealed and provided with three small holes for infusion of drugs into the patient (the "distal" end), as shown in Figure 9.5. The other end (the "proximal" end) was fitted with a socket into which a hypodermic could be inserted to provide the appropriate drug. After administering an epidural anesthetic, the catheter failed on withdrawal. The distal end had sheared off at the proximal side hole and a small fragment was left in the patient's spinal fluid. It was decided that there were far more risks in attempting to remove the fragment than leaving the piece where it was. The fragment was small, sterile and apparently presented no further risk to the patient.

This case presented many of the problems faced by investigators not just in medical cases, but also more generally. When a hasty attempt is made to study surviving evidence, it can often point to misleading conclusions. In this instance, an expert made an initial examination of the failed catheter tip with a hand lens and produced a mistaken inference that the device had failed by being cut, despite the evidence of brittle behavior elsewhere on the tubing (Figure 9.5 and Figure 9.6). In addition, the catheter sample had not been well preserved between the accident and later investigations. The failed catheter tip was badly contaminated with debris, and no attempt had been made to store the device under dark conditions so that no further deterioration could occur.

The catheter showed brittle behavior (Figure 9.7), and our research showed that it was probably caused by a combination of UV and gamma radiation of the polymer, initiating chain degradation. Environmental scanning electron microscopy (ESEM) of the cut surface showed no cut marks, as initially suggested by another expert witness (Figure 9.8). Fourier transform infrared (FTIR) microscopy showed traces of esters near the fracture, confirming degradation. The catheter was on the edge of complete disintegration, but still possessed enough residual ductility to allow its use before the final failure occurred.

Figure 9.5   ESEM image of failed distal end of TPE catheter. The failure surface cut across the drug infusion hole nearest the proximal end shows both brittle behavior and ductility.

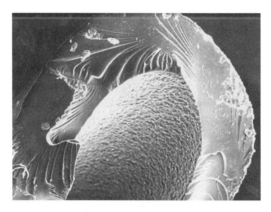

Figure 9.6   ESEM micrograph of fracture surface at the proximal end of the catheter, showing completely brittle and ductile behavior.

The requirements of regulatory bodies (such as the MDA in the U.K.) are stringent, and maverick products should not enter the supply chain. The patient sued the hospital and the manufacturer, and the case was settled by mutual agreement between the three parties just before trial. The hospital paid its own costs, and the manufacturer paid damages to the injured person.

9.5.2 Fracture of a Breast Tissue Expander

Extensive reports of breast implant failures arose in the U.S. in the late 1980s. Most of the failures occurred from permanent implants made from silicone rubber filled with silicone gel. In the case we were asked to investigate, a silicone breast tissue expander failed suddenly after several infusions of saline solution,

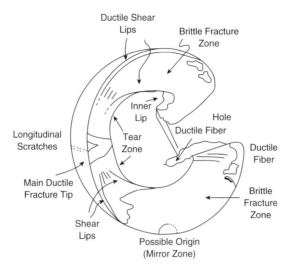

Figure 9.7 Fracture surface map of failed distal end of catheter, describing main surface features and possible origin (sketch magnification: 50×).

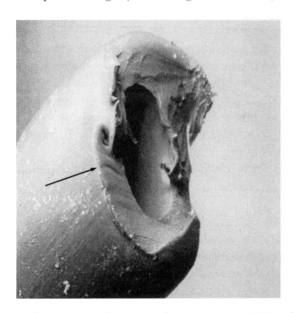

Figure 9.8 SEM fractograph of a cut surface on a new TPE catheter, the cut being deliberately made with a Tuohy needle (a hollow steel needle with sharp tip for insertion into the back). Defects in the edge of the needle leave striations in the catheter surface.

causing great distress to the patient.[6] The device in question was designed to stretch muscle and other chest tissues prior to implantation of a permanent prosthesis. The operation is commonly performed after mastectomy for

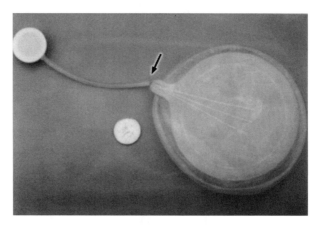

Figure 9.9   General view of breast tissue expander, with dome at the left for filling via hypodermic needle.

removal of cancerous bodies and, following implantation, the tissue expander bag is inflated in a series of steps with saline solution over a time period of some 40 days. The chest tissues are thus strained progressively, as the bag becomes larger.

In simple terms a tissue expander can be likened to a balloon (bag), with an attached tube (catheter) through which saline solution is passed to expand the balloon (Figure 9.9). Failure of the device under consideration occurred during the fill sequence, with total loss of bag volume occurring some 40 days into the procedure (Table 9.1). Since the surgeon appeared to have over-filled the bag, the sequence of events thus raised the issues of possible medical negligence as well as product liability.

Closer inspection of the fractured tissue expander showed a simple fracture in the catheter tube where it connected to the bag (Figure 9.10). There were no outstanding features on the fracture surface, the tube having broken by growth of a single brittle crack (Figure 9.11). There were no traces of fatigue striations to show crack arrest typical of cyclic failure, the fracture surface appearing smooth and clean. The origin lay at the edge of the catheter wall where it joined the shoulder of the bag, a zone of maximum stress concentration. ESEM examination of that zone revealed much finer cracks at the interface of the tube and the shoulder (Figure 9.12). The cracks extended around the periphery of the joint and had grown catastrophically in a single event that broke the tube entirely, fracture morphology indicative of failure in the *adhesive* used to join bag to catheter. The bag was also examined and showed large salt crystals contaminated with traces of blood, indicating cross leakage while still implanted, as well as the presence of some residual saline after removal from the patient's body. As the catheter was found to have completely broken away from the

TABLE 9.1 Tissue Expander Saline Fill Notes

Date of Fill	Volume of Saline Added, ml	Comments
Aug. 8	250 cc	Operation with 550-ml capacity bag inserted by surgeon
Aug. 22	50 cc	
Sept. 5	100 cc	Total 400 cc added
Sept. 19	170 cc	Total 570 ml added
Oct. 3	100 cc	
Oct. 10	150 cc	Total 650 cc [*sic*] added (expander is probably leaking)
post-Oct. 17	—	Patient experiences total loss of fluid from bag

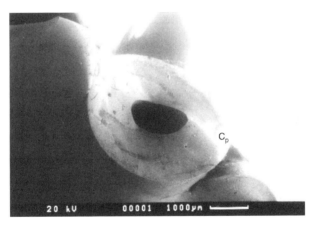

Figure 9.10   Fracture of catheter tube at bag connection point (ESEM).

expander bag, it was surmised that all saline fills after this event would simply have leaked into the chest, and been dissipated into the patient's body (Table 9.1).

This appeared to be a clear-cut case of product liability, with a faulty device unknowingly being implanted by the consultant. However, medical cases where liability seems at first sight to be straightforward tend to become less clear as the cases proceed through litigation. In particular, defendants will usually allege that medical negligence was involved. In this case, it might be claimed that the consultant had wrongly placed the device, putting excessive load on the device. There was no evidence in fact for this allegation.

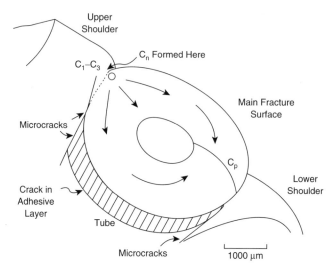

Figure 9.11   Fracture surface showing single brittle crack growth.

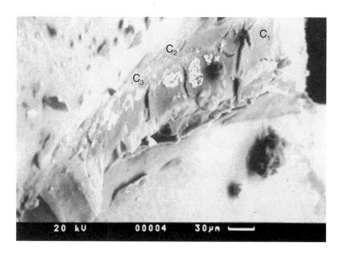

Figure 9.12   Finer cracks at the interface of the tube and the shoulder (ESEM).

Nevertheless, it was determined that the consultant had made a simple arithmetical error in her notes (Table 9.1). Furthermore, the consultant was apparently unaware of any lack of expansion of the bag, even when the added saline exceeded the nominal fill volume, some 21 days prior to termination of the procedure. However, the patient had developed a strong relationship with her consultant, and refused to accept the implications of the facts of the case as shown by the hospital records. The case thus did not proceed, and the patient received no compensation for her undoubted trauma.

Nevertheless, it is important to recognize the significance of designing such devices. Allowances have to be made for an inherently low strength of material, and provision has to be made for a higher factor of safety than that presently used for this type of device. Relating this case back to "intended performance and design attributes," it can be seen that the breast tissue expander in question failed in both its design attributes and in its service performance, thereby compromising any structural integrity of the device, along with compromised health and safety of the patient. The device was manufactured in California by Meritor, a company that has received considerable help from Federal authorities to improve its quality management, design and manufacturing methods following a large number of complaints about failure of its products in the U.S. market.

9.6 Examination of Needle Recovered from Upper Thigh

The remains of a badly corroded needle were removed from the upper thigh of a generously endowed female patient. Her doctor suggested that the needle might well be of a surgical variety, originating from a prior procedure undertaken on the patient some 2 years earlier. The woman immediately took advice from her lawyer, and initiated legal proceedings against the hospital and the surgeon who had performed the initial surgery. The purpose of litigation was monetary compensation for her perceived injury.

X-rays prior to removal showed the needle in one piece, but subsequent removal or handling caused failure across a waisted section (Figure 9.13A). Comparison between the rust-stained flesh tissue coating the outside surfaces and the tiny area of bright clean fracture surface revealed that it could not have been in contact with body fluids. Figure 9.13B shows the threading eye at the left and a tapering point of circular cross section at the right. The

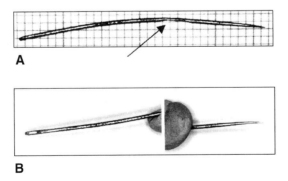

Figure 9.13 (A) Recovered needle with waisted section arrowed. (B) Closer view of threading eye and tapering point of circular cross section mounted on Blu-Tack.

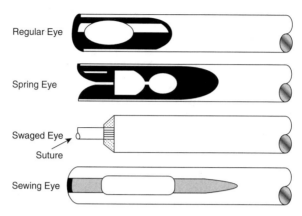

Figure 9.14 Morphology of different needle eyes. Regular, spring and swaged are of a surgical variety, and sewing is the variety used by seamstresses.

extreme tip was slightly bent, and external surfaces had originally been coated with a bright metal; patchy areas of corrosion were visible all along the body of the needle. X-ray analysis in the SEM revealed the needle to be unalloyed, plain carbon steel, with no chromium or nickel within its bulk that would classify it as a stainless variety. However, there were patches of a nickel electroplated surface coating commonly used to form bright, protective coatings on articles made from plain carbon and low alloy steels. This was a surface coating, and not a significant ingredient in the steel from which the needle was made.

Surgical needles are invariably made from stainless steel. Many are curved and some are semicircular. Points are usually of a triangular cross section to produce razor sharp edges having a cutting action for piercing tissue. The needle in question had none of these features.

Suturing threads in surgical needles are usually single filaments secured by swaging into the end of the needle, although some do have eyes (Figure 9.14). The needle under observation had an elongated eye with grooves on either side to minimize the effect of the double thickness of thread when passing through material. Eyes of surgical needles that do not have swaged threads are far less elongated, almost circular, as they only have to accommodate a filament as distinct from a woven thread. Also, the surfaces on either side of the eye are ground flat so that the thickness of the eye is less than the full diameter of the body of the needle. Again, the needle in question did not exhibit the features associated with a surgical needle.

Since surgical needles are made from stainless steel, there is no need for any protective coating. However, unalloyed plain carbon steel rusts rapidly in moist air and so ordinary sewing and darning needles are electroplated with nickel to maintain their bright appearance. It has to be emphasized that stainless steels retain this property only when there is a free access of oxygen to the surface; after a lengthy period exposed to non-oxidizing conditions in the human body stainless steels will start to corrode. However, the fact that this particular needle shows only patchy areas of corrosion and was not stainless steel suggests that it had not been buried within human tissue for more than a few months.

The needle recovered was an ordinary sewing needle, manufactured from carbon steel. If the needle had been of a surgical variety, it would have been manufactured in stainless steel. Furthermore, the needle displayed none of the physical characteristics associated with surgical needles.

For an ordinary carbon steel sewing needle, the degree of breakdown observed in the nickel coating along with associated patchy rusting in the underlying steel are not consistent with having been in the patient's body for several years after an operation.

9.6.1   Outcome

In the first instance, it had been suggested to the patient that monetary compensation for her perceived injury would be in the region of £50,000 (ca. 1998) – sufficient motive to confuse an ordinary sewing needle with the surgical variety. However, when reviewing this case, it became perfectly clear that design attributes required of surgical needles were a decisive factor when clarifying the exact nature of the needle in question. As a final afterthought to the case, it transpired that the female patient had been an enthusiastic seamstress for a number of years, thereby providing a possible scenario as to how a sewing needle could have entered her thigh.

9.7   A Defective Breathing Tube

A recent court case was concerned with litigation proceedings regarding a medical product that allegedly did not meet its intended design attributes or in-service performance criteria. More specifically, it was claimed that the product had been poorly made, did not conform to the dimensional require-ments specified in an engineering drawing, and apparently could not perform its intended in-service function. The component involved was a transparent sight tube for a breathing apparatus (Figure 9.15), for which the design drawing had specified a polysulfone plastic for a production molding process.

The suspect batch comprised over 100 samples, and it appeared that faults contained in the finished product could be directly attributed to a defective molding tool. It was this tool that the manufacturer blamed for his difficulty in making acceptable moldings. An independent expert appeared to suggest that the tool was at fault, so the manufacturer of the apparatus then sued the toolmaker, claiming that the molding tool was the direct cause of such manufacturing faults.

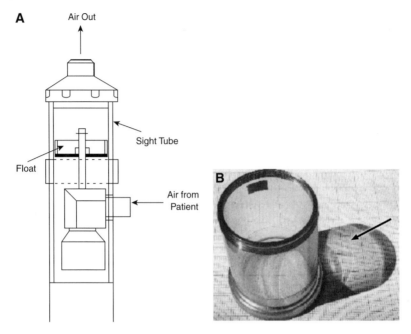

Figure 9.15 Cross section of the breathing apparatus (A), and transparent sight tube (B) showing molding defects in shadow.

We sought a second opinion from the defendant toolmaker, with the opinion based on one or two samples released by the manufacturer. Inspection revealed mainly molding defects, and possibly some damage which could be attributed to the tool itself. Inspection of the remaining 100 units also revealed variable molding conditions in the finished product. This observation indicated that the molder had experienced problems with handling the polymer. It is well known that polysulfone is a difficult polymer to mold easily and, for example, a very hot tool must normally be used (>100°C).

Subsequently, it was determined that the molder had been using water-cooling and, because of low processing temperature, could not mold at all. However, he had managed to retrofit an oil unit for hot molding, but thermal control was suspect. It was not difficult to suggest these manufacturing limitations as the root cause of inherent faults observed in the finished product.

9.7.1 Outcome

Two main conclusions were established:

1. Sample taken from the large batch showed that all of the defects were caused by variable molding process conditions.

Figure 9.16   Markings on site glass.

2. Some marks on the molding could only have been caused by a blunt instrument (such as a screwdriver tip) levering against the precision tool surfaces (Figure 9.16). However, these markings could in no way be responsible for the variation of process conditions observed.

The expert for the plaintiff refused to consider evidence contained on the sample moldings, and reiterated his original views. The case collapsed after the plaintiff was cross-examined on the witness stand on the third day of the trial.

9.8   Failure of Surgical Tweezers

Two cases of the failure of medical tweezers are considered in this section. Both problems were encountered before introduction of the products onto the market, showing the intense effort that goes into research and development before taking the substantial risks of premature failure.

9.8.1   In-Plane Cracking of Surgical Tweezers

After specializing in production of steel-based surgical instruments, a manufacturer decided to introduce a new range of titanium microsurgical tweezers. The production lines were installed and commissioned, and the new instrument range introduced to the market place. Fabrication of the tweezers required an initial stamping of blanks from sheet stock, followed by a pressing sequence to form a dog-leg (double bend) toward one end (Figure 9.17A). This dog-leg section was then riveted to a mirror image blank, to form the final tweezer profile. In addition, a dog-leg geometry provided the "spring" necessary for normal operation.

Production and sales went well for the first year and, in order to increase output, it was decided to introduce larger titanium sheets for the initial blanking process. Although this pressing operation had been undertaken on

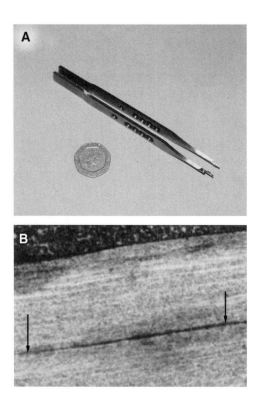

Figure 9.17 (A) Press formed double bend on part fabricated titanium surgical tweezer blanks. (B) "In-plane" crack in the arm thickness of the partly fabricated tweezers.

many occasions over the previous year, and with no unforeseen problems, blanks from the larger titanium sheet cracked in an in-plane mode during the pressing operation (Figure 9.17B).

A through-thickness section, taken at the region of cracking on one of the tweezer blanks, revealed the microstructure to be typical of heat-treated Ti-6Al-4V alloy. The location and extent of cracking can be seen in Figure 9.17A. Cracking was limited to within the confines of a double bend and approximately midway through the material thickness. Bands of oriented beta (β) structure were visible over the section (Figure 9.18A), and the in-plane cracking had occurred along one such band (Figure 9.18B).

At some point in its history, the initial billet, from which the Ti-6Al-4V sheet had been rolled, was held for too long at a temperature above its alpha/beta (α/β) transus. This resulted in formation of large β grains. Subsequent working (forming the sheet stock) had rolled the β grains into long pancakes. The Widmanstatten basket weave structure of the β grains became oriented in the rolling direction, causing planes of weakness. As such, a β structure has low ductility/formability and the double shearing mechanism,

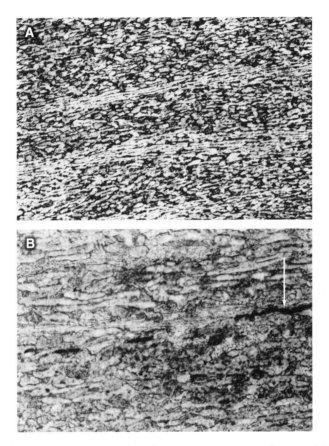

Figure 9.18   Optical micrographs of titanium tweezers showing (A) bands of oriented beta and (B) cracking along a beta band.

imparted by pressing of the "dog-leg" profile, had caused in-plane cracking to occur.

Under normal circumstances, cracking of the type observed would only be regarded as cosmetic in that the crack would not cause failure of the component. Nevertheless, when considering the in-service application of the tweezers (surgical procedures), it could be argued that, in addition to aesthetic issues, there was a possibility of bacterial ingress into the cracks. This could well engender future repercussions when considering product liability issues. On the other hand when considering fabrication of the tweezers as a whole, it could be contended that cracks are "manufactured-in" at the fabrication stage, in the form of a riveted connection where the two halves are joined.

In summary, the material in question was of the specified composition. However, past thermomechanical history of the sheet introduced planes of weakness in the form of large pancake β grains. It was the shearing action of the bending process that introduced in-plane cracks within the partially fabricated tweezers.

From a general engineering viewpoint, the observed cracks could be considered cosmetic and would be unlikely to lead to failure in normal use. However, when considering the intended performance and design characteristics, in addition to product liability, it was considered prudent to scrap any partially or fully formed tweezers that had been fabricated from the titanium sheet in question.

It transpired that the tweezer manufacturer had not specified a desired material grain size to his stockist. It may well have been that he had no knowledge of the need for such a specification. However, had the manufacturer requested the stockist to advise and provide appropriate material for such an application-specific use, he might have had cause for complaint in that the sheet supplied was not suitable for his particular purpose.

9.8.2 Production Failure of Titanium (Ti-6Al-4V) Ophthalmic Tweezers

A small manufacturer had marketed a range of high value ophthalmic surgical instruments. Due to limited production facilities, rough machining of the instruments had been subcontracted, with only final grinding and surface finishing operations undertaken in-house. Unexpected failures started to occur during the final surface grinding operation on a range of titanium (Ti-6Al-4V) ophthalmic tweezers.

Tweezers were taken for observation from both a good and a brittle (the manufacturer's terminology) batch. Both pairs of tweezers were in a partially fabricated condition, with the problematic tweezers having fractured into two at a change of section some 7 mm from the jaw end (Figure 9.19). Intricate internal profiles had been machined by traveling-wire EDM (electrical discharge machining), and had been undertaken as an integral part of the subcontractor's duties. In addition to EDM, flat sections on the legs and tips of the instruments had been surface ground.

Observation with the naked eye clearly revealed a color difference between the two EDM machined surfaces, characteristic of surface roughness differences from differing machining parameters. The broken tweezers had an appreciably rougher surface finish than the unbroken tweezers.

At no point did the bulk microstructure give cause for concern. In both instances it was typical of Ti-6Al-4V alloy that had been annealed for 2 h at approximately 704°C, and air-cooled. However, the broken tweezers displayed a thin white band concentrated at the surface of the specimen (Figure 9.20A), suggesting contamination from gases such as oxygen or

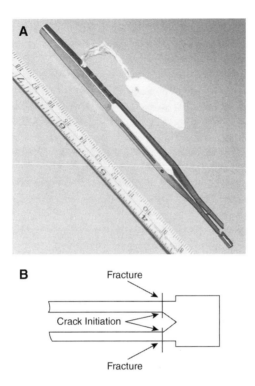

Figure 9.19 (A) Part fabricated ophthalmic tweezers broken at section change. (B) Sketch of crack initiation points and propagation paths.

hydrogen, and could be directly related to contamination pick-up during the machining (EDM) process.

To gain an idea of inherent ductility, one leg of the fractured tweezer was bent back to an angle of almost 90° (Figure 9.20C). No fracture occurred and, in addition, there was no obvious cracking at and around the bends. This would suggest that the material was not inherently brittle (as the manufacturer had suggested) and, in all probability, the cause of crack initiation that led to failure was a localized event.

The major part of component lifetime is usually necessary to grow a crack in service. That lifetime will be severely curtailed in an artifact that contains a crack *prior* to entering service. With respect to the broken tweezer, surface cracking caused by EDM machining had been propagated by the action of surface grinding. Failure is inevitable once a crack initiates — it is only a matter of time and the service conditions. Forces acting at the time of failure are almost immaterial. In this instance a crack had been initiated by the machining conditions during profiling and had gradually developed to the point of failure during grinding (i.e., fatigue).

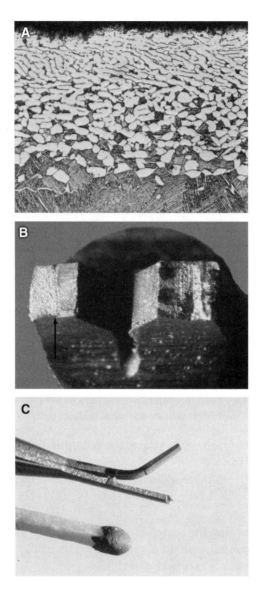

Figure 9.20 Contamination forming a brittle surface layer at point of fracture (magnification: 750×). (A) Facture surfaces showing fatigue striations (arrow) (B) and deliberately bent leg (C) to demonstrate high level of inherent ductility away from fracture site.

In summary, the material used for fabrication of both sets of tweezers was Ti-6Al-4V alloy, and the bulk microstructure of both units under investigation gave no cause for concern, with no inherent brittleness within the bulk of the broken tweezers. The broken unit had failed by a fatigue mechanism, with crack initiation at a discreet point on an EDM profiled surface.

Surface indications suggest that EDM machining parameters in operation at the time of profiling were different between the two units. The broken unit had experienced more abusive (roughening) conditions than its intact counterpart, producing areas that were brittle and prone to cracking. As discussed in Chapter 2, Section 2.4, once initiated, a crack would fatigue to failure from minor defects resulting from surface grinding. However, the root cause of failure was that the tweezers contained a crack in the first instance.

The simple remedy for this manufacturing problem lay in a return to initial traveling-wire EDM parameters that were in operation at the time of production of the uncracked batch of titanium tweezers. In an attempt to explain why EDM parameters were altered, a final discussion with the fabricator revealed that the workforce had only recently transferred to a piece/part working practice. A probable scenario then became clear: in an attempt to increase individual throughput, fabrication line operatives had taken it upon themselves to increase EDM cutting speed in order to reduce machining time.

9.9 A Failed Crutch

An elderly woman suffered trauma and injury when one of the pair of crutches she was using to support herself suddenly broke at the junction of the aluminum handle and the main shaft. The woman was recovering from an operation to remove the lower part of one of her legs, and fell onto her stump. Each crutch consisted of an aluminum tube into which was fitted an aluminum telescopic arm, the telescopic action being utilized for height adjustment to suit the individual user's needs. The crutch in question had fractured near the junction of the two tubes, inside a plastic insert (Figure 9.21) that connected them. The fracture surface itself was not very revealing, but did show brittle behavior. This feature was considered somewhat unusual for the plastic, a polypropylene copolymer.

Examination of the interior of the polymer tube under magnification revealed several subcritical cracks or crazes close to the edge of the fracture surface. These were a strong indication that service loading had exceeded the tensile strength of the plastic. There was no other visual evidence of excessive loading or misuse on the exterior of the crutch tubes. However, there were signs of defects on the plastic inside the metal tube, at a point below the subcritical cracks. This combination of features observed on the plastic insert was indicative of material degradation, and that the part had become defective. The wear pattern on the aluminum tube showed that the failed crutch had been used more heavily, consistent with the greater support needed for the user's amputated leg (Figure 9.22).

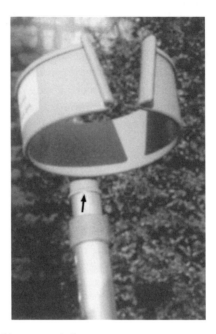

Figure 9.21   Site of fracture of plastic connector near junction of two aluminum tubes.

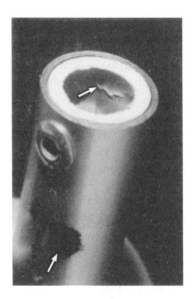

Figure 9.22   Defect in plastic connector (top arrow) and wear pattern (lower arrow) on aluminum crutch tube.

The injured woman received compensation for the trauma and injury after the manufacturer accepted the findings of our investigation.

9.10 Failure of Nerve Probe during Surgical Procedure

A female patient underwent circumferential reconstruction surgery on her lumbar spine at a private hospital in the U.K. During the procedure effective monitoring of motor pathways was undertaken, with specifically designed electronic nerve stimulation equipment. Such equipment is used during this type of surgical procedure to reduce the risk of nerve damage by effective monitoring of motor nerves. However, toward the end of the operation, a nerve stimulation probe failed while being removed from the patient's leg; an operating room doctor had attempted removal by pulling on the lead of the probe. The probe in question was of a straight needle variety, and failure was by way of lead detachment from the probe at its soldered connection leaving the probe *in situ* within the patient's leg. A decision was made to complete the spinal surgery and remove the needle probe at a later date. This was accomplished 7 days later, requiring additional surgery recuperation and scarring. The patient sought compensation from the hospital for her injuries and, in turn, the hospital authorities sought to pass responsibility for failure on to the equipment manufacturer.

The probe and lead in question were not available for examination because they had been disposed of prior to any investigation. However, similar units had a needle length of some 35 mm with leads attached by soldering with a lead-free alloy system (Figure 9.23). Quality control procedures for the solder joint were somewhat antiquated, relying on gently pulling the cable lead to ensure the joint had been properly made. This was a rather ambiguous quality control method, leaving itself open to question when considering the integrity of a newly formed solder joint.

Strain relief is a term to describe methods used to ensure that loading is not transmitted to vulnerable parts of an assembly. Strain relief methods used

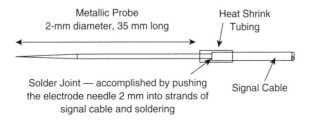

Figure 9.23 Needle electrode schematic, showing heat shrink tubing over a soldered joint between needle probe and signal cable.

to protect the solder joint were minimal, relying on polymeric tubing that had been heat-shrunk over the rear of the needle and approximately the first 20 mm of lead wire. As a solution to the problem of strain relief, it could be considered minimal. There are far more efficient mechanical routes for negating the transmission of load to a solder joint.

When considering soldering as a fabrication route, it should be remembered that the process has been in use since Roman times. More recently, the 1950s saw the start of an explosion in the use of soldering as a fabrication process — it was the advent of today's electronics industry. The point being made here is that soldering is a tried and tested manufacturing process. Furthermore, when working as a designer or manufacturing engineer, training will develop awareness of the normal or expected location of a failure — in any type or part of the system (the weakest link principle). Any deviation from the normal or expected location will have been caused by additional (unknown) factors. When considering design and manufacture of the needle probe, the weakest link will be its soldered joint, this being true for virtually all assemblies having soldered connections. It would be safe to say therefore that the probe failed at an expected location.

9.10.1 Outcome

The defense by the manufacturer was based on the so-called "development risks," where new technologies carry an increased probability of "unknown" effects or failure. Without this form of protection, manufacturers would not be willing to shoulder the burden of introducing new technologies to the market place. However, although the technology of magnetic nerve stimulation may be considered novel, it was not the technology that failed, and therefore the technology was not at issue. What was at issue was a design or manufacturing failure. The crux of the matter was whether or not the solder joint failure could have been foreseeable.

As a soldered joint should be recognized as a "weak link" by both designer and manufacturer, the needle failure would be considered a foreseeable event. It was not the technology of nerve stimulation that failed during the surgical procedure; rather, it was the tried and tested manufacturing route of soldering that was victim to failure. Based on these observations, any defense focused around "development risk" was considered null and void. The manufacturer conceded, paying the majority of costs involved before the case went to trial.

References

1. Rimnac, C.M. et al., Failure analysis of a total hip femoral component: a fracture mechanics approach, in *Case Histories Involving Fatigue and Fracture Mechanics*, Special Technical Publication 918, ASTM, Philadelphia, 1986, pp. 377–388.

2. Willert, H.G. et al., Crevice corrosion of cemented titanium-alloy stems in total hip replacements, *Clin. Orthopaed. Relat. Res.*, 333, 51–73, 1996.

3. Schöll, E. et al., Osteolysis in cemented titanium alloy hip prosthesis, *J. Arthroplasty*, 15(5), 570–575, 2000.

4. Shahgaldi, B.F. et al., Effect of corrosion on tissue in contact with orthopaedic implants, *J. Bone Joint Surg.*, 82-B, 2000; Orthopaedic Proceedings Supplement II, 122.

5. Lewis, P.R., Fracture of a TPE catheter, oral presentation, Failure Analysis and Prevention Special Interest Group of the SPE, ANTEC, Dallas, 2001.

6. Lewis, P.R., Fracture of a breast tissue expander, oral presentation, FAPSIG at ANTEC, San Francisco, 2002.

Component Failure in Road Traffic Accidents

10

The usual reason for investigating the failure of a component found to be broken after a road traffic accident is to ascertain whether the componet was broken in the trauma of collision or had suffered some kind of prior mechanical failure that caused the vehicle to go out of control. In the first instance, driver error or freak road and weather conditions might be held responsible. In the second instance, it is essential to ascertain the mode and cause of failure in order to establish where and with whom responsibility might rest. For example, failure might have resulted from a manufacturing or assembly fault, or mechanical malfunction due to wear, or some progressive weakening such as fatigue or corrosion. If the cause turns out to be mechanical, then it is essential to take into account the recent servicing history of the vehicle and what adjustments might have been made shortly before the accident occurred, for example, overtightened wheel bearings, loose unions and a whole gamut of faults stemming from careless or unskilled maintenance.

The case histories that follow have been selected to represent the variety of modes of component failure. Unfortunately, these have to be limited to interpretation of the fractographic evidence in relation to the circumstances of a particular accident. Supporting details of the accident such as usually provided to the failure investigator, e.g., police "scene of accident" photographs and road measurements, statements of witnesses, reports on the damage from vehicle inspectors and insurance engineer assessors, etc., have been omitted except where they directly relate to the findings.

Figure 10.1 Four exhibits from the inquest showing damage to the truck and one of the wheels.

10.1 Steering Arm from Truck

Prior component failure accounts for only a very small minority of road traffic accidents, the vast majority resulting from collision. Human nature being what it is, a driver almost invariably seeks to blame someone else's mistake or malfunction of some vital system like steering or brakes for loss of control, yet the experience of forensic investigators tends to support the cynical remark that the most likely cause of an accident is "the nut who holds the steering wheel."

10.1.1 The Accident

An articulated truck with a flat-bed trailer was traveling along a two-lane highway in the late afternoon, when it veered off the road as it was approaching a slight bend, rode over a steel bridge parapet and plunged onto a country road beneath, narrowly missing a small car driven by a mother with three children. The driver of the truck was killed. He had left his depot at 6 A.M., driven 160 miles to deliver a load and was returning with the vehicle empty. Vehicle inspectors found the front tire to be torn and punctured and the wheel rim buckled, which they attributed to damage sustained as the wheel struck the steel parapet (Figure 10.1). They also found the steering box sector shaft was broken (Figures 10.2 and 10.3) and pointed out this could have accounted for loss of control. The fracture surfaces were smooth at the

Figure 10.2   Side view of steering box with broken end of sector shaft resting in position.

Figure 10.3   Side view of steering box with broken end of sector shaft removed.

outside with a roughened area at the center (Figure 10.4) and the break had occurred immediately below the bottom bush in the steering box where bending forces would have been greatest. Figure 10.5 shows how the steering box was mounted on the chassis. Otherwise the vehicle had been well maintained and was in a fully roadworthy condition prior to the accident.

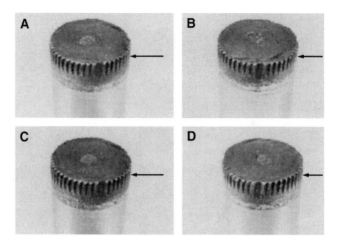

Figure 10.4 Fracture surface of splined shaft seen from four different directions, showing distortion of every spline at edge of fracture.

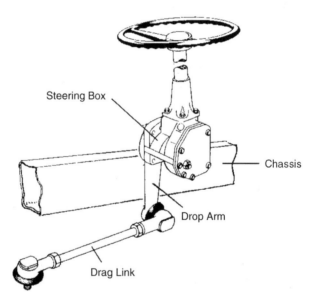

Figure 10.5 Arrangement of linkages and drop arm when steering box is mounted on chassis. Notice the drop arm and drag link project below chassis.

The driver's father stated that his son was 29 years old and had worked as a heavy truck driver for 5 years, during which time he had never been involved in any serious accident or had any convictions. The day before he made the trip he had played in a cricket match but had gone to bed early because he had a long journey the next day. He occasionally drank a pint of beer for refreshment, but was not a heavy drinker and valued his license too highly to drink excessively. He had no physical ailment or illness and appeared to be in good spirits when he left home on the day of the accident. There was no reason to suppose he would have attempted suicide.

The director of the driver's firm stated the deceased was regarded as one of his best men and had a good record. He had never been involved in any serious accident other than minor scrapes. He undertook most of the firm's long distance hauls, and was sometimes away overnight. The vehicle involved was 18 months old and had logged 70,000 miles. It had passed mandatory inspection only 1 week before the accident and had satisfied all the requirements.

A medical pathologist found no indication of anything physically wrong that could have affected the driver's performance. Chemical analysis of his blood had revealed a small amount of alcohol but this level was well below the legal limit.

Another witness was a telecommunications engineer, traveling in the direction opposite to the truck, when he saw it veer off the road and fall over the parapet of the bridge. He stated: "Although difficult to estimate, I would reckon its speed to be 55 to 60 miles per hour. It was just a truck coming towards me until I heard a bang that I thought might be a tire blow out, but it could have been metal breaking. I realized something was wrong when I saw the truck had left the road and was straddling the crash barrier. It then went over the bridge parapet." This witness then went on to describe another accident in which the steering system of his own car failed; on that occasion he remembered hearing a cracking sound just before he lost control. He thought a similar thing might have happened in this case and that the sound he heard could well have been metal breaking.

10.1.2 Investigations

The only technically qualified engineer witness called was from the police traffic department; he had 11 years' experience examining crash vehicles. He had arrived at the scene of the accident about 35 min after it occurred. After describing the damage outlined above, his comments were that "the steering box shaft had sheared, but the rest of the steering system was properly coupled up with no excessive wear on the linkages; most of the oil had leaked from the steering box after the collision. The vehicle had been generally well maintained although two of the trailer tires were worn close to the legal limit. The road at the time was dry and the weather clear. Tyre markings on the soft shoulder indicated the truck had left the carriageway shortly before it mounted the crash barrier. There was no sign of a tyre blow-out and the damage to the front tyre was consistent with the wheel striking the crash barrier." He then pointed out that the road starts to bend slightly at the scene of the accident and if the steering shaft had failed by fatigue this could account for the vehicle leaving the road as the driver would have had no steering control. If the braking system had been damaged by collision with the crash barrier it would not have been possible to stop the vehicle before it reached the bridge. There were no tire marks to suggest the brakes had been applied prior to collision with the barrier.

A legal representative of the vehicle manufacturers questioned this witness and asked if he had noticed any twisting of the splines of the steering shaft. The witness replied that he had observed they were bent noticeably on both sides of the fracture (see Figure 10.4); if the splines had been in this condition before the accident they would have altered the position of the steering wheel in the "straight ahead" position. When asked if it was likely that this shaft had been twisted for months or weeks, the witness replied that if it had, he would have expected someone driving the vehicle regularly to have noticed it, unless the steering had been completely reset immediately after the splines had been bent.

This witness was further questioned about the possibility that the shaft might have been cracked before the accident. He replied that if the shaft had been held together by the small area at the axis he would have expected it to have failed suddenly on the road, even if the vehicle were unladen. He would not expect such a small segment of metal to be able to withstand heavy steering loads such as those experienced in maneuvering a fully laden vehicle. Subsequent to his examination at the scene, he had taken the wheel and tire to the forensic science laboratory for expert examination, along with the steering box and broken sector shaft.

The forensic scientist was a highly qualified chemist with 20 years' experience in forensic science and an expert in tire examination. He had examined the parts submitted to the laboratory. He stated his findings could not possibly support the theory that premature failure or deflation of the tire caused the accident. This witness had also examined the steering box and sector shaft. The extract from his report read to the court was as follows:

> *Rocker shaft. The fracture surfaces of the two pieces were examined and found to exhibit characteristics typical of fatigue failure. It was apparent the components had been operating for some time on the central quarter-inch of metal, but after a cursory examination it is not possible to state whether the final failure was spontaneous or the result of impact.*

A verdict of "accidental death" was recorded. The witnesses' statements all supported the view that the driver lost control because the steering arm suffered a fatigue failure.

10.1.3   Alternative Explanation

However, at this stage the reader may find it helpful to list the points that support this hypothesis, and it is strongly urged to refer back to Section 2.4 of Chapter 2, particularly those parts dealing with fractures, before continuing with the technical evidence in the present case. Considerable significance may then be attached to the question put to the vehicle inspector at the inquest by the legal representative of the manufacturer.

Bear in mind most people who witness a serious accident usually form a view as to why it occurred and they become more convinced of this view each time they recall the event. Not much credibility can be attached to the telecommunications engineer's evidence about hearing a sound like metal breaking and likening this to a failure of a steering shaft on his own car when he was inside a vehicle on the opposite roadway and must have been approaching the truck at a closing speed of something over 100 mph.

The first thing to do when parts such as these are received is to look at them, with the aid of a low power microscope where necessary, particularly the position of the fracture and its path across the section, as well as the nature and extent of damage present on adjacent components. If the parts have not been cleaned or dismantled, the distribution of road dirt and damage to paint are useful pointers to what might have caused the damage. If enamelled or electroplated items, such as bicycle forks, have been deformed in a collision impact, a pattern of fine, parallel cracks will often be found in the brittle film on the surface. This provides a clear indication of the way the underlying metal had stretched and hence the stress system that caused the deformation. It is virtually the same effect as in the brittle lacquer technique used by stress analysts to study strain and stress distribution when complex shaped components are loaded. However, in this instance, the parts received had all been cleaned and there was no brittle coating on the surface.

The steering box mounted on the vehicle chassis has an internal mechanism where a line of hardened steel balls circulates in the threads between a worm screw and a nut, to give a low-friction movement. When the steering wheel is turned the worm rotates within the nut. As the nut moves up and down the thread, the forked end of the sector shaft follows it, turning the sector shaft backward and forward. A drop arm mounted on the splined end of the shaft transmits the motion to the steering mechanism of the vehicle (Figure 10.5). The arm is fastened onto the sector shaft over tapered splines, held in place by a nut and lock washer.

It is clear from Figure 10.2 to Figure 10.4 that the fracture path is perpendicular to the axis of the shaft. It exhibits a pip at the center (referred to by the forensic scientist) and a smooth area around the outside. There is no obvious initiation site, or sites, where fatigue fracture might have originated and no crack arrests or beach marks. Furthermore, a fatigue fracture in a

ductile material in torsional shear would tend to follow a helical path at 45°
to the axis, not at 90° as this one does (see Figure 2.17B).

In contrast, a circular shaft broken by mechanical overload in torsional
shear would display a degree of ductile deformation (twisting) all around the
periphery before the fracture started (hence the bent splines). The fracture
surface would appear as a series of concentric rings, like smears, finishing as
an area of tensile fracture near the center as the two pieces finally came apart,
thus leaving the characteristic "pip" (see Figure 2.7). Hence, from these
observations alone, the fracture was caused by torsional overload and not
bending or any other form of fatigue.

In this particular investigation the independent metallurgist appointed
by the insurers of the manufacturing company carried out an exhaustive
examination of the failed shaft and associated components to ascertain
whether they departed in any way from their material and manufacturing
specifications. None did, but when the other components inside the steering
box were examined, clear evidence was found of a massive impact against
the steering arm which had forced several of the recirculating balls so hard
against the worm that the case-hardened raceways had been indented.

Hence the shaft did not fail by fatigue, and should not have been held
responsible for the loss of steering control at the inquest. It was almost
certainly broken as the vehicle ran along straddling the crash barrier before
it went over the bridge parapet. Sadly, this is typical of the kind of accident
that results when the driver falls asleep at the wheel. The vehicle drifts off its
path and there is no evidence in the tire marks on the road of any braking
or steering correction prior to the truck falling over the bridge parapet, which
there surely would have been if the driver had remained alert.

10.1.4 Further Examples of Steering Shaft Failures from Motor Vehicle Accidents

Figure 10.6 shows the bottom of a splined steering column where it entered
the steering box in a small family car. It was, unfortunately, not an isolated
case. Several broke in this manner when the cars were getting old and the
majority of these vehicles were found to have tight swivel pins on the front
axle due to lack of greasing. This is a complex fracture caused by cyclic
torsional loads, where fatigue initiated at the outside of every one of the
individual splines. The cracks started by following a helical path across each
spline and when they entered the main cross section below the splines they
continued as individual cracks toward the axis, all maintaining an orientation
at 45° to the axis and producing the star-like appearance in the final fracture.
However, just before they met up at the axis torsional overstress on the last
remaining cross section produced a small pip of ductile fracture at 90° to the
axis. The stress on a circular shaft subjected to torsion varies as the *cube* of

Figure 10.6 Fracture surface of splined shaft failed in torsional fatigue (right), alongside one that failed in bending (left).

the radius so that, when there is only a small area of sound metal near the center, the stress level under normal loads is much greater than when the cracking is still in the outer, splined region. It could be argued that these failures were the result of poor design, in that the shafts were not strong enough to withstand foreseeable loadings for the life of the vehicle; however, the age and uncertain history of the vehicles by the time such fractures began to be experienced, together with the evidence of poor maintenance, did not provide a case strong enough for a successful claim against the manufacturers.

Splined shafts with square section splines follow a similar pattern but the width of the splines gives the final fracture a more block-like appearance and, because some of the first splines start to fatigue in two positions the blocks are sometimes pulled out of line when the final, ductile torsional overload occurs at the axis.

The fracture of the steering shaft at the left in Figure 10.7 is a bending fatigue failure of a long shaft that directly connected the steering wheel to the steering box on a vintage car (from the days when a frontal collision could drive the steering column like a spear into the driver's chest). When restoring the car the owner had managed to obtain a steering box and shaft from a similar vehicle that was being cannibalized for spares. He fitted the parts to his car and subsequently exhibited it at meetings and took part in road rallies. In one of these the steering column suffered a fatigue fracture while rounding a bend at the bottom of a hill. A spectator was badly injured. The shaft must have been slightly bent when fitted, with the result that every time the steering wheel was turned through more than 180° the middle of the column went through a cycle of compression and tension. Eventually the inevitable fatigue failure occurred.

Figure 10.7   Steering shaft failed in bending fatigue.

10.2   Wheel Detachments

On the road wheel detachments may result from both fatigue failure and mechanical overload. When wheels are held on to the hub by means of nuts with conical seats tightened onto studs in the hub or brake drum, the sequence of failures can be readily deduced from examination of the individual fractures. The first ones to fail will display the greatest area of fatigue cracking and the later ones the least, often with severe erosion of the stud on the last ones to break due to the wheel moving about as it became increasingly loose. By identifying the first studs to fracture it is then a fairly straightforward matter to investigate the cause. The fatigue cracking invariably starts at the root of the first thread below the nut, as this is the smallest cross-sectional area and subject to the greatest stress when the nut is tightened. One of the reasons that wheel nuts are now tending to be replaced by conical seating bolts with a long, reducing taper into the threads is that these reduce the stress concentrations significantly compared with nuts that screw onto a uniform thread profile. The root of the first thread in engagement is the most highly stressed and is consequently where fatigue cracking is most likely to initiate (and where a torsional overload fracture will occur if the nut is grossly overtightened).

Wheel detachments have also been found to occur by the wheel center itself disintegrating due to the joining up of fatigue fractures around an individual bolt hole. Such detachments are usually attributed to incorrect mounting of the wheel on the hub or failing to tighten the nuts.

Another common cause of wheel detachment as a result of fatigue is when a stub axle carrying the wheel breaks away from the suspension, as illustrated in Figure 10.7. Such failures usually occur when the vehicle is maneuvering or moving slowly, when the bending loads on the inboard end of the axle are considerably greater than when it is traveling normally on the road. A typical fracture surface of a steel stub axle shows two fatigue crack initiation sites, a larger area radiating from the bottommost fiber and a much smaller one radiating from the uppermost fiber. The final break is a ductile fracture occupying a band across the middle.

The reason for this unequal development of the fatigue cracking is that tensile stresses acting on the bottommost fibers are caused by the weight of the vehicle tending to bend the axle upward plus cornering forces acting to push the bottom of the wheel outward. Both are of a cyclic nature when the vehicle is traveling on the road but the cornering force only becomes significant when the weight of the vehicle is transferred to the axle as it changes direction. However, the stresses on the uppermost fibers are always lower, because there is no external gravitational force bending the axle upward as there is along the bottom of the axle; rather it is the opposite effect — gravitational force produces compressive stress in the uppermost fibers and so tends to counteract tensile forces when the vehicle is cornering. The net result is that the fatigue initiates first at the bottom of the axle and propagates upward and it is only when the cross-sectional area has been reduced and the applied loads generate higher stress levels that the cornering forces are able to initiate a fatigue crack at the top of the axle. This is also the reason why the final break almost always takes place when cornering, usually at low speed, because the upward bending forces are greatest when a heavily laden vehicle is maneuvering.

Torsional overstress which twists the retaining nut off the end of an axle is a common cause of wheel detachment when the vehicle is traveling at high speed and usually occurs shortly after wheel bearings have been adjusted during servicing. In the majority of motor vehicles wheels are mounted on their axles by a pair of taper roller bearings that must to be critically adjusted to allow a small amount of free play without becoming sloppy. Some front wheel drive vehicles are fitted with a pair of ball bearings separated by a tubular spacer clamped tightly together and the only provision for adjustment is to place shims at the ends of the spacer. The retaining nut has to be tightened to a high torque. Some wheel detachments have occurred simply because a mechanic has mistakenly tightened taper roller bearings.

Taper bearings are retained on the axle by a washer and castellated nut which has to be carefully set to allow a small amount of free play and is prevented from coming unscrewed by a cotter pin or "C" clip passing through a hole in the screwed end of the axle and lining up with opposite castellations of the nut. The method of making this adjustment is to fit the roller bearings and tighten them until they bind, then release the nut by one sixth of a turn and check that the wheel turns freely with minimum end float. The nut is

Figure 10.8 Torsional shear at end of stub axle.

then locked in this position, or the nearest pair of castellations in the *unscrewing* direction, by inserting the cotter or spring pin through the castellations.

When disc brakes are fitted to a vehicle the friction pads and associated parts may be examined without removing the wheel bearings. However, in order to inspect the friction linings and expander of drum brakes the drum must be removed. On small cars this is usually integral with the hub as a single casting, which necessitates taking off the castle nut and withdrawing the outer taper roller bearing. After the brakes have been attended to, and usually the bearings regreased, the hub/drum unit is replaced and the bearings have to be adjusted to the required amount of free play. This is where the problem is likely to arise. If the mechanic replaces the nut and turns the castellation in the tightening direction to line up the castellations with the hole in the axle (or, as has been known to happen, tightens them fully as if they were ball bearings with a spacer), then the bearings will heat up when the vehicle goes back on the road. Within about an hour or so of high-speed driving, the bearing on the right side of the vehicle seizes and twists off the end of the axle to produce the torsional shear failure illustrated in Figure 10.8.

The reason that it is the wheel on the right-hand side of the vehicle that detaches is because the direction of rotation in forward motion tends to tighten the castle nut as the bearings expand under frictional heat. This quickly results in the castle nut binding tightly as the free play is reduced and the friction may then cause the castellations to shear through the cotter. When this happens the bearing locks solid, the threaded end of the axle shears under torsional overload and the wheel detaches, carrying the hub with it.

Although similar frictional heating may occur if bearings on an axle at the left side of the vehicle have insufficient free play, the direction of wheel

Figure 10.9   Frictional heating close to bearing.

rotation as the friction increases acts to unscrew the nut, which tends to relax the frictional force compared with positive tightening on the right axle. The driver feels no immediate effect as the wheel detaches but first becomes aware of the problem when a wheel overtakes the side of the car! A loose wheel rolling into the path of another vehicle traveling at high speed often has fatal results, certainly in countries that drive on the left side of the road. The clues as to the cause of the axle shearing are readily apparent in the state of the outer bearing, the nut and cotter and the signs of frictional heating in the vicinity of the bearing, as illustrated in Figure 10.9.

Wheel detachment on both right and left sides of the vehicle may also occur if worn or faulty bearings fail and pieces of a broken roller or parts of the cage jam and cause seizure. This can usually be traced by careful examination of the debris to a worn out or damaged bearing. The detachment illustrated in Figures 10.8 and 10.9 occurred on a small car that had undergone a 20,000 mile service only the day before, and this had required removal of the rear brake drums to inspect the linings. The young mechanic who had carried out the work was not supervised so full liability for the accident was accepted by the garage's insurers.

10.3   Brake Pipe Failures

By far the two most frequent causes of accidents resulting from failure of the braking system are loss of hydraulic fluid due to either corrosion or fatigue of the pipework. In both cases the loss begins as a slight ooze at the site of a perforation or a fatigue crack penetrating the wall and, if this passes

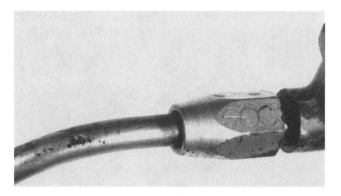

Figure 10.10 Pipe connecting brake expander inside front brake drum to hydraulic circuit.

unnoticed, all the fluid eventually escapes and the brakes become inoperative. The brake pipe failure discussed in Chapter 6 (Section 6.3.3) was an example of corrosion-initiated failure. Figure 10.10 shows another example of external corrosive attack. The following case is an example of fatigue failure.

10.3.1 Brake Failure by Fatigue

The failure mechanism outlined in Section 6.3.3 was due to a corrosion cell being set up between metals of markedly different electrode potentials. This problem may be overcome quite simply by making the pipe from a homogeneous alloy with substantially better resistance to corrosion and thus needs no protective coating. Such an alloy has been used for many years in upscale cars and is as formable as Bundy pipe (see Figure 6.3), although rather more expensive. However, this alloy is just as vulnerable to fatigue, with failure usually occurring where the ends of the pipe are swaged within couplings to fixed components in the braking system, such as expander cylinders and the pistons of disc brakes. Fatigue is likely to occur if there is relative movement, which sets up cyclic bending or torsional stresses at the root of the flange inside a union where the pipe is connected.

Figure 10.11 shows a short length of pipe from a "buggy"-type vehicle used for towing strings of luggage trailers at an airport. The brakes suddenly failed, causing severe injury to one of the loaders and some damage to an aircraft. It was found that all the hydraulic fluid had been lost from the reservoir during the 72 h since the level had last been checked. The maintenance log at that service recorded the level to be slightly low, so a minor top up had been required. Cursory inspection of the underside of the vehicle at that time had revealed no signs of leakage.

After the accident it was discovered that fluid had been escaping between the pipe and the union connecting it to the brake expander mounted at the

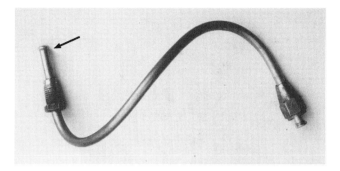

Figure 10.11   Swaged end of brake pipe with fatigue crack beneath coupling.

Figure 10.12   Close-up of swaged end with crack just below the curved bulb.

top of the brake plate of the front wheel. The escaping fluid had simply run down the pipe and dripped off the bend at the bottom, so there was practically nothing to show how much fluid had been lost. The escape had occurred through a circumferential crack in the pipe immediately below the swaged flange, as marked by the arrows in Figures 10.11 and 10.12. The crack extended approximately 240° around the circumference, exactly following the ridge left by the swaging tool when the flange was formed at the end of the pipe. A section along a diameter was removed as shown in Figure 10.13, which enabled the completely cracked part of the flange to be separated. The fracture face exhibited characteristic features of fatigue, showing the mark left by the swaging tool to be the initiation site. On the other half of this section still attached to the pipe, the lower limb in the figure is cracked right through but the opposite side shows the end of the crack penetrating only about 15% of the wall.

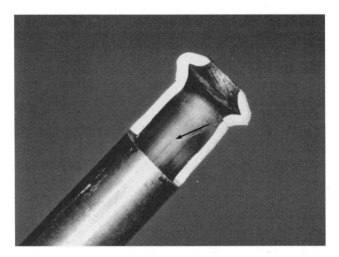

Figure 10.13   Section through fatigue crack. It can be seen as a faint line below the bulb running across the wall.

When the expander cylinder mounted on the inside of the brake plate was inspected it was discovered that the retaining nut was loose. This caused the cylinder to be twisted sideways every time the brake shoes came into contact with the rotating brake drum, whether the wheel was rotating forward or backward. Cyclic stresses on the pipe were concentrated at the groove left by the swaging tool directly behind the flange. A fatigue crack was initiated and began to propagate, following the groove. Although the stress cycles would have been essentially torsional in nature at first, the sharp change in section immediately below where the flange was clamped dominated the direction of crack propagation. Later on, as the one-sided crack development continued, bending stresses from the internal hydraulic pressure would cause build up of axial stress and accelerate the rate of crack propagation.

The fatigue cracking must have started some time before the accident, but brake fluid would only have begun to escape when the crack penetrated the wall. Gradual reduction in the cross-sectional area of the pipe wall would result in ever-increasing stress levels, causing the crack to propagate faster and an ever-increasing escape of brake fluid. As it was a power-assisted braking system the driver would have been unable to detect any difference in the feel or movement of the brake pedal. Hence the loss of all the hydraulic fluid from the system only 3 days after topping up the reservoir is entirely consistent with the way the fatigue cracking had propagated. The only prior warning would have been if fluid had been noticed underneath the vehicle but with continual use day and night this most probably would have been spread all over the loading and baggage handling areas of the airport.

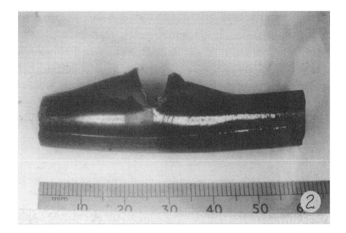

Figure 10.14   Two views of bubble in wall of thermoplastic brake pipe.

10.3.2   Failure of a Plastic Pipe

An example of brake failure not involving a metallic component is illustrated in Figure 10.14. This short length of thermoplastic pipe from an air braking system on a commercial vehicle burst and led to a serious accident. A new vehicle had been purchased with a bare chassis and was sent to a specialist auto body worker to have a side loading unit installed. This work had necessitated some welding above the longitudinal chassis members. The work was finished and the vehicle was being driven out of the shop and onto a busy road. The driver applied the brakes to stop before entering the road but they failed, allowing the truck to continue forward into the path of oncoming traffic. The driver reported hearing a pop like a cork coming out of a bottle as he pressed the brake pedal.

As Figure 10.14 shows, a bubble had developed in the pipe wall and had split open at the top. Only this one short length of the pipe had been affected. The bubble was found to be on the top of the pipe a few centimeters directly below where one of the welds had been made. Clearly what had happened is that heat from the welding operation had softened the thermoplastic and expansion of residual air inside the system had blown the bubble and thinned the wall to a fraction of its original thickness. The first time the full air pressure built up inside the pipe, the bubble had burst, which would account for the 'pop' heard by the driver.

10.4   Lamp Filaments

When accidents occur after dark it may be alleged that one or another of the vehicles involved did not have its lights on. It thus becomes very important to establish whether or not this allegation can be supported by physical evidence and, if it can, which filaments were incandescent and which were cold at the time of a collision. When faced with a wrecked vehicle this seems a daunting task but if the lamp filaments can be recovered, the the investigation is fairly straightforward because of the way tungsten behaves when subjected to mechanical shock at high temperature compared with when cold, and also by the color and volatility of its oxide.

10.4.1   Failure Mechanisms

Tungsten has the highest melting point of all metals (3410°C), which is why it is universally used for the filaments of incandescent lamps. It is brittle at temperatures below 340°C but above this it becomes ductile and can be worked like other metals. These difficulties are overcome in processing and it can be drawn into fine wire for filaments. Low voltage lamps, such as those used in motor vehicles, need robust filaments, so the wire is formed into single coils suspended between two posts of a metal having a somewhat lower melting point. In house lamps, which are powered by a mains supply, the filament wires need to be much longer and of smaller diameter so they are formed into coiled coils, a configuration that gives a superior light output compared with a single coil of the same wattage.

In addition, when heated to incandescent temperatures tungsten readily combines with oxygen, so this must be excluded from the immediate environment of a lamp filament. Evacuating all gases, however, is not a solution, because this would cause the tungsten to volatilize, which would not only waste away the wire over a short period but the evaporated metal would condense on the inside of the glass envelope and reduce the light transmission. So the glass envelope is filled with an inert gas or mixture of gases such as argon and nitrogen that do not react with the tungsten and the tungsten does not volatilize significantly over the lifetime of the filament. If the envelope is broken when the filament is cold, then the air that enters does not oxidize the tungsten but, if the filament is incandescent, it will react rapidly and give off copious fumes of tungsten trioxide. This gas is volatile at temperatures above 800°C and condenses to form a yellowy film over the all nearby cooler surfaces. Such volatilization only occurs if the filament was incandescent when the glass envelope was broken.

Figure 10.15A to Figure 10.15D, taken under a scanning electron microscope, show breaks in four single coil filaments from 12-V vehicle lamps that failed under three different conditions. Two of the four, (A) and (C), both show blobs and ripples characteristic of wire that has melted and quickly resolidified after breaking the electrical circuit. These are typical of what happens when an incandescent filament is subjected to traumatic mechanical shock, causing the wire to stretch and locally neck down so that it melts like

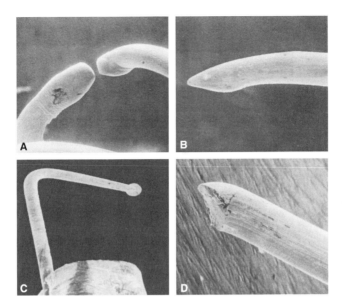

Figure 10.15   SEM photographs of broken lamp filaments. (A) Incandescent failure in inert atmosphere. (B) Incandescent failure with air access. (C) Incandescent failure at filament post, slightly oxidized. (D) Brittle fracture at temperatures below 340°C.

the end of a welding rod. Quite often the filament may not be stretched enough to fuse like these examples but, instead, the filament is thrown forward or backward and distorts because it is so weak and ductile when incandescent. Consequently, a filament that is found to be badly distorted after a collision, although not melted as illustrated above, must have been incandescent at the moment of impact because otherwise, if it had been cold, it would not have possessed the necessary ductility to deform plastically.

Filament (B) in Figure 10.15 exhibits a wasted, tapering end, as distinct from a fracture of the full cross section or a molten blob, and there is a tiny white particle adhering near the point. This is a fragment of glass that has fritted onto the surface. A color photograph would show this end of the wire to be coated with a yellowish-white film of tungsten oxide. It is typical of a filament that was incandescent when the glass envelope was broken and allowed an ingress of air.

One small part of the filament begins to react and the oxide instantly volatilizes, reducing the cross-sectional area carrying the current. As a consequence this small area gets hotter than the rest of the filament and so oxidizes ever more rapidly. The oxide condenses on some nearby cooler surface, but meanwhile the filament continues to waste away faster at this one spot until eventually all the metal has been converted to oxide, producing these characteristic conical-shaped ends on each side of the break.

The particle of fritted glass is also evidence that the filament was hot enough to fuse it to the surface after the glass envelope had broken.

Figure 10.15D exhibits a characteristic brittle fracture when the filament is below its brittle/ductile transition temperature. When the filament is broken in this way the coils are undistorted and there is no sign of melting, oxidation or any reduction in cross-sectional area at the point of fracture. Longitudinal score marks from the wire-drawing process extend right up to the edges of the fracture. Hence when this filament was broken there was no current flowing and its temperature must have been below 300°C. It was certainly not incandescent when the lamp suffered some kind of mechanical shock. When filaments have been in service for a long time grain growth occurs, which makes the filament more susceptible to mechanical shock; in some old filaments a single grain may occupy the entire cross-sectional area.

10.4.2 Motorcycle Accident

Figure 10.16 and Figure 10.17 show the filaments from bulbs from a motorcycle headlight and a car involved in a fatal accident. In her statement to the police the female driver of a large car said she had paused at the gateway at the end of her driveway to check that there was no approaching traffic on the poorly lit urban road. Seeing nothing she pulled out into the road but was almost immediately struck at the rear by a solo motorcycle. The rider was thrown onto the back of her car and killed instantly. The motorcycle was wrecked. She claimed that it must have been traveling very fast and could not have been showing lights or she would have seen it approaching.

Figure 10.16 shows the main beam and the dipped beam filaments inside the broken bulb of the motorcycle headlight. The dipped beam filament has a brittle fracture adjacent to the terminal post, but is bowed and stretched to a limited extent. The main beam filament is broken and bent into a much more pronounced curvature. There is light oxidation adjacent to the ductile fracture, which has rounded blobs at the ends, but no significant wasting away of the cross section. A tiny particle of glass, visible as the white spot (arrowed), was fritted onto the filament.

The above evidence clearly establishes that the main beam filament was incandescent when it was subjected to a force that caused it to bow into a broad horseshoe shape. The filament fractured while it was still hot but the glass envelope must also have been broken at the same instant. This allowed ingress of air which oxidized the tungsten but, as the temperature of the filament was falling, it was by then too low for extensive volatilization of the oxide. It was however still hot enough to fuse the fragment of glass to the surface. The brittle fracture of the dipped beam filament shows it was not incandescent when it experienced the force but the middle part of the coil must have been above 340°C for it to bend in a ductile manner. The center

Figure 10.16 Bulb from motorcycle headlight showing fragment of glass adhering to filament.

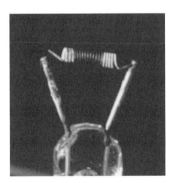

Figure 10.17 Bulb from rear headlight of car.

part of this filament must have been heated above this temperature in the middle of the coil by radiation from the main beam filament but the junction at which it connected to the support post where the fracture occurred had been below the ductile/brittle transition temperature.

The above evidence thus establishes conclusively that the motorcyclist had been riding on main beam when the collision occurred.

Figure 10.17 shows the bulb from the rear headlight of the car, found not to be working when the lights were tested after the accident. This is photographed against a black background in order to show up the yellowish/white tungsten tri-oxide coating toward the ends, but there is also dark blue di-oxide over the center left-hand side. This evidence shows that the filament had been incandescent when the glass envelope was cracked and air entered, but the filament cooled rapidly and did not break until its temperature had fallen below 340°C. Inertia force from the collision had caused the coil to fracture in bending at the stress concentration point where it was attached to the support post. Hence the tail light had been working immediately before the collision when the motorcycle ran into the back of the car. The woman was clearly mistaken about the motorcycle lights, but the insurers settled the claims in full.

10.5   Tow Hitches

Loss of a trailer being towed on a busy road is likely to have serious consequences for oncoming traffic, especially if the trailer snakes and overturns in freak weather conditions or as a result of poor driving. The critical part when seeking to find the cause of such an accident is the ball and socket of the towing hitch, or tow pin if the coupling is a simple ring and yoke type. If there is extensive deformation on both the vehicle side and the trailer side of the hitch, then quite clearly an overload force must have acted and this leads inevitably to the conclusion that the hitch itself could not have been the initial cause of the trailer breaking away, especially so if there are ductile fractures in the linkages. On the other hand, if there is no evidence of mechanical overload of the linkages then the answer will usually be found in the form of a fatigue failure of some vital part in the hitch. The following two cases illustrate these features.

10.5.1   Trailer Accident

The director of a small building firm was driving a short wheel base Landrover towing a single-axle trailer loaded with scaffolding frames and tubes on a main road. The trailer was wider and longer than the Landrover. It had just rounded a bend and started to descend a gentle gradient. The driver of a following car said it was not traveling very fast as he had been seeking an opportunity to overtake when the road was clear. However, he held back when he saw another car approaching. He stated that he saw the trailer appear to swing into the path of the oncoming car and there was a violent collision as a result of which the driver was fatally injured. The front offside wheel of the car was pushed backward and there was extensive damage to the bodywork. Loose scaffolding on the trailer had flown forward and gone through the windshield. The driver of another vehicle a short distance in front of the Landrover confirmed the road was dry and visibility was good. He estimated his speed to have been about 40 mph. He made a statement to the effect that he heard the noise of a collision and when he looked into his driving mirror he saw that a car had run into a trailer in the middle of the road. He thought this might have been because the trailer had separated from the Landrover just as the other car was approaching. He estimated the speed of this car as it

Figure 10.18 Damage to the front of the car caused by collision with the trailer.

Figure 10.19 Extension bracket and side arms to which the towball was attached at the rear of the towing vehicle.

passed him to have been in the region of 60 mph and was well toward the middle of the road, although on its own side of the central white line.

Figure 10.18 is a view of car showing its position immediately after the collision. Figure 10.19 shows the tow ball mounting on the back of the Landrover. This was an extension bracket from the main chassis member to bring the tow ball level with the bumper and there were two side supports of steel angle section, now hanging loose. The tow ball itself had been bolted onto the extension bracket by the two high tensile steel bolts shown in Figure 10.20. It will be noticed that both bolts are bent but the bracket itself was only slightly deformed. The left side link seen hanging loose in Figure 10.19 was found to be buckled when the extension bracket was removed.

Figure 10.20   Bolts from the towball plate showing remains of threads stripped from nuts. The arrow shows a piece of sheared thread.

At the inquest a police vehicle examiner said he believed the tow ball had broken away because the bolts were of high tensile steel and had been grossly overtightened, causing them to strip the threads in the mounting bracket (Figure 10.20). These finally pulled out under the normal slewing action of the trailer as it was being towed with an insecure and unevenly distributed load. The trailer wandered over the centerline and the oncoming car was unable to avoid a frontal collision. Figure 10.21 is the underside of the head of one of the bolts, showing sharply defined, unrusted witness marks from the teeth of the lock washer. The other bolt displayed similar marks, thus establishing that both must have been tight before the accident. Slivers of machined threads referred to by the vehicle examiner are noticeable in the roots of the bolt at the right-hand side in Figure 10.20. A complete section of a thread from the plate can be seen five turns below the head in the lower bolt.

However, an independent investigator, while agreeing that the high tensile bolts had sheared threads from the softer steel bracket, disputed this explanation for the cause of the collision on the grounds that if the forces

Figure 10.21 Witness marks (arrows) from the lock washer on the underside of the bolt head.

had been solely side-to-side slewing when the bolts finally pulled out, this would not account for the way the plate itself and one of the side links had buckled, nor for the bending of both bolts in the same direction just under their heads. Many other Landrover vehicles (including those operated by the same police force for recovery purposes) were fitted with this same type of towing bracket and no similar failure had ever been encountered. He considered this damage could only be accounted for if the front corner of the trailer had been pushed back violently while still coupled to the towing vehicle and reasonably in line with the direction of travel.

This was the view accepted in the subsequent litigation between the insurance companies, where the major issue was whether or not the trailer had detached before the collision and had veered across the road into the path of oncoming traffic. It was agreed that because the trailer was 40 cm wider than the towing vehicle the front corner would have been projecting almost to the middle of what was a fairly narrow main road. The oncoming car was traveling fast and its front wheel collided with the corner of the trailer, pushing it back violently and tearing the tow ball plate off the bracket. This accounts for the buckling of the left side arm and why both bolts bent in the same direction as they ripped threads of the nuts retaining the towball. The collision forces must have been greater than any previously applied up to that moment of impact. The damage to the car was all along its offside, none near the center of the hood as would have occurred in a frontal collision. Loose scaffolding on the trailer had been projected through the windshield on the driver's side only. The offside wheel of the trailer had been torn from its axle but there was no significant damage to the tow hitch still attached at the front.

In light of this evidence it was decided that the driver of the car had been primarily responsible for this accident. There was a suggestion he might have been using a mobile telephone as he went by the vehicle in front of the Landrover.

10.5.2   Tow Bolt Fatigue

The second case concerns a large twin-axle skeletal trailer carrying a portable workshop that was being towed by a long wheel base truck on a motorway. (A skeletal trailer is a flat chassis frame fitted with tow hitch and the normal road-running equipment, onto which box-shaped containers may be attached by means of turnbuckles.) Witnesses stated that the trailer was traveling at about 60 mph when it began to swing violently from side to side, detached from the truck, overturned, slid across the roadway on its side, overturned again as it struck the crash barrier and came to rest in the overtaking lane of the opposite roadway. Two cars collided with it, one caught fire and there were several fatalities. The cause of the detachment was that a high tensile steel bolt inside the hydraulically damped hitch had broken, allowing the socket end clamping the tow pin to pull out.

Maintenance records revealed a history of problems with this particular trailer. On three separate occasions cracks found in the "A" frame had been repaired by welding. These were attributed to twisting and "bottoming out" of the trailer as it was towed over rough ground on building sites. The owners had been warned that the truck used for towing this trailer was unsuitable as it had a long overhang behind the rear axle that placed excessive forces on the tow hitch, as illustrated in Figure 10.22. A new tow hitch had been fitted only 10 weeks before the accident, yet 6 weeks later two of the bolts attaching it to the frame were found to be loose and wearing and had been replaced by drilling out the holes and fitting a larger diameter bolt. Even more dis-

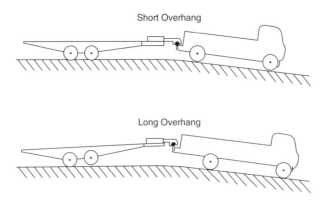

Figure 10.22   Diagrams showing how tow ball overhang affects loading on the tow hitch when traveling over uneven ground.

Figure 10.23 Parts of the hitch involved in the accident. The socket end still clamping the ball on the tow pin had pulled off the damper tube in the hitch body.

Figure 10.24 Closer view of parts that separated. The fractured end of the bolt is visible through the hole in the damper tube at right, which fit into the tube at left. The nut and missing end were not found after the accident.

turbing was a report that one of the bolts inside the hitch had broken and had been replaced on site.

Figure 10.23 shows the hitch and tow pin as recovered after the accident. The bolts which can be seen at the right are those that held it to the trailer frame and those at the left were from the towpin attached to the truck. Attention is drawn to the "as-new" appearance of the aluminum castings and the bored-out holes for the larger bolts at the right-hand side. The tow pin is dual purpose in that it has a ball at the top for a socket clamp and a pin below for attaching a trailer having an eye ring. There are two other bolts in the socket end of the hitch, marked by the large arrow, which pulled out at the time of the accident. These two components are shown in Figure 10.24 and were held together by two high tensile bolts, one vertical (at the right) and the other (at the left) horizontal. The nyloc nut (a locking nut with nylon insert) is still present on the horizontal bolt but the vertical bolt has broken level with the inner surface of the tube and the slightly rusted fracture is just

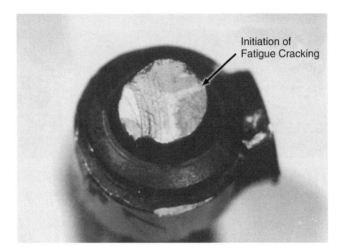

Figure 10.25   Closer view of fatigue fracture of bolt.

visible inside the hole. Figure 10.25 is a closer view of this fracture and reveals the characteristic form of double bending fatigue initiating at the right-hand side with secondary initiation at the left.

The interpretation of these fractures is that both bolts had been subject to cyclic shearing forces as the trailer was being towed. The vertical oscillations of the hitch led to fatigue cracking across the threads of the vertical bolt, which eventually broke completely and the nut was lost. The head portion was loose inside the damper tube, so all the towing forces were now transferred to the horizontal bolt. This could act as a pivot in the vertical plane but side-to-side movements in the horizontal plane caused it to bear alternately against the holes in the steel tube and gradually wear them away. Eventually there was so little section left that a penultimate tug tore through one side and the final tug as the trailer swayed in the opposite direction pulled through the other, allowing the socket end of the hitch to pull off the damper tube. Thus the trailer detached and the exposed end of the damper tube (Figure 10.26) revealed the tearing of the holes on both sides caused by the horizontal bolt having to take over the work of the fatigued vertical bolt, both manifestations that the hitch had been persistently overloaded and was indeed unsuitable for towing this trailer by a truck with a large overhang.

Much has been omitted from the findings of the investigation into the cause of this accident; for example, checks on the trailer after the accident revealed that the nose weight on the towbar was nearly twice what it should

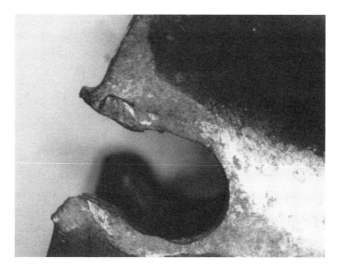

Figure 10.26 Tearing of hole in damper tube as horizontal bolt was pulled out (close-up of lower center part of the damper tube shown in Figure 10.24).

have been and no proper record had been made of the bolt replaced only 3 weeks earlier, presumably the vertical one, and no attention whatsoever was given to discover why it had failed so soon after the new hitch had been fitted. The trailer was an accident just waiting to happen. There was no suggestion there was anything wrong with the hitch. It was unsuitable for the particular type of trailer and the way it was being used.

Fraudulent Insurance Claims

11

It is possible to insure against almost every kind of loss. The terms of an insurance policy are, however, carefully worded so as to specify precisely what risks are covered and the conditions under which liability will be accepted by the insurer. Where risks are foreseeable the policy clearly sets out the responsibilities of the insured to prevent such losses. Many people fail to read the "small print" and assume that their policy will pay out for all kinds of loss or damage. Only after making a claim do they discover they did not observe their part of the contract. For example, a homeowner returned to his house after taking a long winter vacation to find the central heating boiler had failed and, as a result of a particularly severe frost, several radiators had split open. In addition, a water supply pipe had burst during the frost and had flooded the ground floor of his house when the thaw came. Unfortunately, he found that it was a requirement of his household insurance policy that he should have had his heating system serviced annually. It transpired that it had not been serviced or inspected since it was installed more than 6 years before the incident.

People who suffer loss usually assume that it will be covered by insurance, but when they read the terms of their policy before filling out the claim form they often find that it is not. Human nature being what it is, a few are sometimes tempted to deliberately introduce damage or describe circumstances that simply could not account for the damage or loss described. Occasionally, claims that are clearly spurious or fraudulent may be submitted in order to obtain money from an insurance company.

One do-it-yourself homeowner claimed for the cost of redecorating two rooms in his house, allegedly necessitated by water escaping from an upstairs radiator on his central heating system. By the time the loss adjuster inspected the premises, the redecoration had been completed, new carpet laid and a new, larger radiator fitted. The homeowner produced the original radiator, which had a hole near the bottom on the side facing the wall. The hole was part way up the rear panel of the radiator, well above the bottom section where sediments collect and pitting corrosion eventually leading to a perforation tends to occur. Suspecting that this was not a genuine failure, the loss adjuster sought a metallurgist's opinion as to the origin of the hole. A piece was cut out so that the inside wall of the radiator could be examined. The wall exhibited a degree of internal corrosion consistent with several years' service, but there was no significant pitting. The damning evidence, however, was that the way the metal had deformed revealed the hole had been made using a 3-mm-diameter punch with a sharp point, almost certainly an engineer's center punch. In addition, although the punch had penetrated the wall at an angle it would not have been possible to drive it in while the radiator still hung on the wall. Not surprisingly the claim was rejected and the insurance policy canceled.

11.1 Car Keys

Modern cars and commercial vehicles are fitted with sophisticated electronic remote door locking and immobilization systems, although generally all still have a metal bladed key that is inserted into a barrel-type ignition lock to start the engine. While most locking and immobilization systems can be overcome by an expert with the right kind of apparatus they defeat the casual, opportunist thief. Nevertheless, a large number of cars are still stolen, usually when left parked or taken from garage or gas station forecourts when the driver leaves the vehicle for a few moments to pay for gas, etc. The owners invariably claim that they locked the cars before leaving them parked or, if the vehicle was in a garage forecourt, that they took the keys with them when they went to pay. When the claim is subsequently made, the insurance company usually asks a loss adjuster to interview the insured and collect the keys. Quite frequently the insured is only able to surrender one set of keys, claiming that he or she had lost the second set or had only been supplied with one set at the time of purchase. (This is sometimes claimed even when the car had been purchased new only a few weeks before the theft!) Some claim that the spare keys were kept inside the stolen car, without apparently realizing that this defeats the whole object of having a second set of keys.

   The forensic engineer is thus presented with one set of keys that are claimed to have been the sole keys in use for the length of time the insured owned the vehicle and for whatever mileage it is estimated to have covered, sometimes running into tens of thousands. Often it is found that the keys surrendered fail to exhibit a degree of wear commensurate with the use claimed. In many cases the wear is so slight that the keys can only have been the spare set that had never, or hardly ever, been used. In such cases the insurers substantially reduce the settlement of the claim on the grounds that the insured failed to secure the vehicle.

All the necessary observations can usually be made by visual examination, supplemented by use of moderate magnification of the critical areas. It is sometimes helpful to compare the surrendered keys with a set for the same make and age of vehicle with a similar mileage by visiting a dealer for the make of car. The critical areas for assessing the degree of use are:

1. Finger grime and dust in the crevices around buttons and icons, particularly in the small lettering molded into the plastic case. General dulling wear on the areas rubbed by the fingers. Light scratches on the exposed rounded corners. Scoring of the key-ring slot and rounding of its sharp edges caused by sliding along the metal key ring.

2. Effects similar to those listed above appear on the plastic finger grip of the key. It is useful to check whether it is a manufacturer's original or a copy key, which will bear a different name and logo integrally molded into the plastic. The metal blade is particularly revealing. If it has milled external edges, the peaks soon wear and become rounded by pushing against the spring loaded plungers inside the lock barrel. If the key has a profile machined into the sides, similar rounding on the internal corners soon develops. Lock barrels are greased internally. When a vehicle is new this is a clear, golden color but with use it gradually becomes darkened by fine wear debris that collects in the crevices along the key blade. After very many insertions into the ignition lock the electroplating on the outside of a key begins to flake or wear away, particularly near the entry nose.

3. Many sets of keys are mounted on a split steel ring attached to a leather fob. When new the leather has square cut edges that do not always line up, so the mismatch may soon begin to curl and become rounded. The stitching is tight when new but, after a period of use, strands begin to break and the stitching around the outside loosens. A leather fob that has been carried about in a pocket or purse for a lengthy period loses its original firmness and the edges in particular develop a rounded and worn appearance. Transfer lettering may also have worn off, leaving only faint indentations on the leather.

Figure 11.1   Hole in the bottom of an oil filter.

11.2   Perforated Oil Filter

A fruit farmer submitted a substantial claim for replacement of a clutch/gear-box assembly on a large tractor. He stated that he was grubbing out fruit trees in an old orchard when the clutch burned out and, upon dismantling, he found that the gearbox had seized due to complete loss of oil. There was a small hole in the bottom of the external oil filter, mounted on the side of the gearbox. The claimant stated, "This must have been pierced by a tree pruning kicked up from the ground. Everything was satisfactory when the oil was changed only three weeks ago." The insurance inspector was some-what dubious, so he submitted the filter for examination.

Figure 11.1 shows the hole in the bottom of the filter. It had been formed by a penetrating object 8 mm in diameter entering at a slight angle and making an elliptical hole with smoothly turned-in edges. There was slight denting around the hole in the bottom of the filter but no signs of scratching

Figure 11.2   Hole in the end plate of a filter cartridge showing a piece of wood trapped between outside folds. (A) View of base where hole is exactly in line with that on outer case (Figure 11.1). (B) Side view of piece of wood showing it is the edge of a planed board, not a piece of tree pruning.

of the paint or abrasion. After the bottom of the canister had been sawn away, it could be seen that the flap of metal pushed inside had an indentation at the center, consistent with the canister having been pierced by an 8-mm-diameter conical steel punch with a nose 1 mm in diameter. The same tool had continued through the space between the canister and the filter cartridge and punched a circular hole 8 mm in diameter in the end plate, as illustrated in Figure 11.2A. A sliver of wood was trapped between the folds of the paper filter but no shreds of this could be found on the sharp edges of either hole. Instead of following the line of the two holes, the sliver of wood had entered through the hole in the canister but then changed direction and passed through the space between the inside of the canister and the top of the cartridge, to finish up trapped between the paper folds on the outside, as can be seen in this photograph. When this sliver was examined it was found to be a strip some 5 cm long broken off the edge of a machined tongue-and-grooved floorboard. It was of roughly square cross section and could be passed through the hole in the canister without touching the edges.

The substantial claim was initially rejected by the insurers as fraudulent and they threatened prosecution, but were impressed by their insured's genuine distress upon learning how the hole had been made and that he had only guessed that it was caused by a piece of tree pruning. (Laboratory tests had shown the thickness of the steel was such that all attempts to drive a wooden dowel into the end of the filter case resulted in the wood splintering and only causing a slight dent in the steel.) He said the tractor had been left in the orchard overnight and he had only been running it for about 20 min when the clutch failed. He had gotten off the tractor and had seen the hole in the filter and a train of oil leading back to where he had started that morning. There were no metal punches or anything similar that could have formed the hole in the tractor toolbox. The insurance inspector made inquiries of the local police who said several instances of malicious damage to machines and tractors left out overnight had been reported in that vicinity but they had been unable to find the culprit(s). Accordingly, the insurance company met the claim in full.

11.3   Major Engine Damage, Allegedly Due to Loss of Oil

An insurance company received a substantial claim on a motor policy. The six-cylinder engine of a 12-year-old car was beyond economic repair due to extensive damage caused by the connecting rod of the No. 3 cylinder breaking and punching a hole in the side of the engine block. The insured driver stated:

> *I was driving home from work along a dual carriageway road in a stream of traffic moving at about 40 miles per hour when we came to a section where one lane was coned off for road repairs. The road had been dug up on the inside lane and there were piles of material between the cones, which included some large pieces of what looked like reinforced concrete with steel wire sticking out. To my horror a lorry in front of me brushed one of these piles and a piece of concrete rolled into my path. I could not stop or slow down because the traffic was a continuous stream, so I just steered the car so that the lump would*

go between my front wheels. As I passed over I heard a loud bang and it had obviously hit the underside of the car, but I could not stop. I had to keep moving until I came out of the coned off section, which was another 1/4 mile (about 400 metres). As soon as I came clear I pulled over to the side but just as I did so I heard a loud bang from the engine and then a terrible hammering noise as the engine lost all its power. A friend was a few cars behind and he pulled over behind me, but there was nothing we could do. The engine was wrecked. There was a stream of oil along the road behind the car. I had a tow rope in my car so we hitched up and he towed me home. When I got back I could see there was a big dent with a hole in the front of the crankcase in line with where I had steered the car over the concrete. The oil must have all run out before I could pull over to stop, so the engine seized and the big end broke and knocked a hole in the side of the block.

A staff engineer of the insurance company took possession of the perforated sump and the pieces of the broken crankshaft and submitted them for forensic examination. Three different features emerged proving that the story had been concocted to justify a claim for accident damage whereas in fact it was mechanical breakdown resulting from "wear and tear," not covered by the insurance policy.

Figure 11.3 is a view of the fracture face at the bottom of the connecting rod. Figure 11.4 is of the lower part of the broken connecting rod, big end cap and the two bolts. Figure 11.5 is the oil sump from the bottom of the crankcase, showing the dents, holes and scratches allegedly caused by running over the lump of reinforced concrete.

The fracture is a fatigue failure at the bottom of the connecting rod that had been developing over a period of time. Consideration of the load transfer path establishes that when the crack reached completion and finally broke, the big-end cap tilted sideways and the forces from normal rotation of the crankshaft bent the bolt on the opposite side that was still intact. The bolt at the broken side was not subject to these forces, so it remains straight. The loose connecting rod flaying about inside the crankcase would quickly punch a hole in the side of the engine block.

There was no evidence of overheating, which would have been inevitable if the lubrication system had failed due to oil starvation. Moreover, if the engine had run out of oil the components at the bottom of the engine that are splashed by oil in the sump would be the last affected. The valve gear and

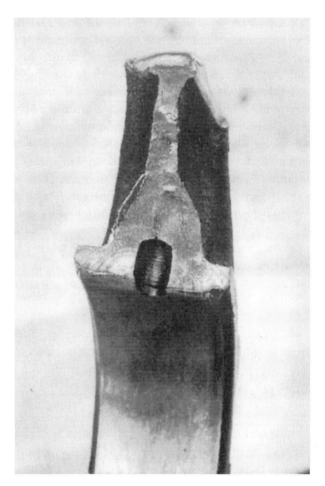

Figure 11.3 Fatigue fracture of connecting rod big end, initiating at the oil passageway hole.

combustion zones would be the first to suffer and, again, there would be blueing and galling wear over the sides of the cylinders swept by the piston. None of the signs usually associated with oil starvation could be found.

Turning to the front of the crankcase cover, Figure 11.5, the hole and the nearby indentation look more like they have been made with the end of a screwdriver blade than with a piece of steel reinforcement wire sticking out of concrete. There are several wavy lines scratching the paint in different directions behind the hole. How could these random scratches have been produced if the car was moving forward over the piece of concrete at 40 mph? They would obviously have been straight and parallel or, at most, exhibit only slight differences in direction.

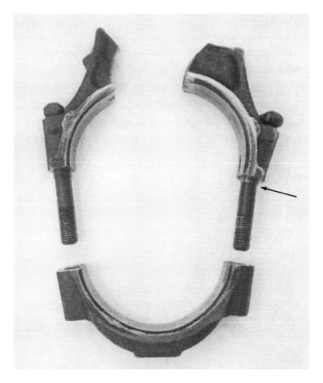

Figure 11.4 Side view of broken big end. Notice the right-hand bolt (arrow) is bent, the other straight.

Figure 11.5 Holes, dents and scratches on underside of sump cover.

The owner's handbook for the vehicle gave the engine oil capacity as 11 pints (5.75 L). The leakage rate through the hole was tested by pouring 2 L of hot engine oil into the sump and measuring the time for 1 L to run through the hole. This was found to be 22 sec. Hence assuming the sump contained

5 L at the time of the incident, the engine could have run for over 110 sec before experiencing significant distress. During that period the car running at 40 mph would have covered just over 1 mile, so the engine could hardly have been starved of oil if the sump was perforated only about $1/4$ mile before the car was brought to rest, as the plaintiff stated.

The claim was rejected. Although the insurance company could have taken legal action it canceled the policy and advised the insured that he would need to obtain coverage in the future from a different underwriter.

11.4   Three-Car Road Accident

Three insurance companies received "write off" claims, two of them very substantial, for three vehicles involved in a collision at dusk on a wet evening. The accident was said to have occurred at a 'T' junction on country roads having no curbs and with wide, soft margins. The major road had a white centerline but the minor road, and another almost directly opposite, had only stop lines. There was no street lighting. Car A was a small family sedan, car B a large, luxurious sedan and car C a high performance sports convertible with a soft top. Figure 11.6 represents what is supposed to have happened and summarizes what all three claimants told their respective insurers. (This incident happened in the U.K. where cars have right-hand drive and keep to the left of the road.)

Car B had pulled up at the stop line on the minor road and was intending to turn left. Car A had been following some distance behind but the driver said that although the road was straight it was undulating and, because it was raining the windshield kept steaming up and he was fiddling with his headlight switch, so he did not realize car B had stopped until it was too late to avoid a collision. He said he panicked and accidentally pressed the accelerator instead of the brake and ran into the back of car B, pushing it into the major road.

Car C was traveling fairly quickly along the major road from the right, rounding a slight left bend lined by hedges that did not allow a clear view of any vehicle turning out from the minor road until almost upon them. However, drivers of both cars B and C were familiar with this junction and, indeed, traveled these roads frequently because they were members of the same golf club nearby.

The plaintiffs' descriptions of what happened were consistent. Car A had run into the back of the much heavier car B and pushed it more than half-way across the major road. The driver of car C said he was unable to avoid a collision and his car struck the driver's door of car B and then bounced up into the air, turning over and landing upright on its wheels on the right side grass verge further down the road. The driver of car A said he saw the sports

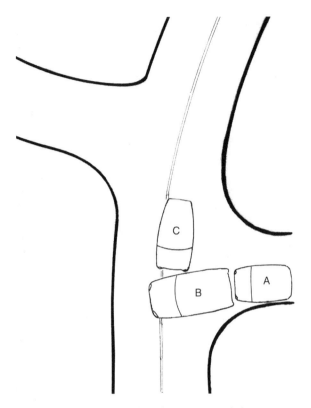

Figure 11.6 Road plan showing alleged positions of three cars in collision.

car somersault at least once, but saw it had landed on its wheels so he ran over and released the driver from his seat belt. The driver was dazed, but able to walk. The driver of car B said he realized another vehicle was approaching because he could see its headlights, but he could do nothing to warn the oncoming car as he was sideways on to it. After the collision he telephoned for his daughter to come out in her car and she drove all three to their respective homes. Her husband was in the motor repair business and he went out with a recovery vehicle and took the three damaged cars to his premises, where they were later classified as "beyond economic repair" by all three insurance companies. Since no one was injured the police were not informed.

A staff engineer for the insurers of car C inspected the damage 4 days after the accident. His suspicions were aroused so he visited the scene but could find no marks on the road or the soft verges, nor could he find any debris such as broken glass or plastic. However, a claims inspector for the insurers of car A visited the scene 3 weeks later and found several pieces of headlight glass and the entire rear bumper and light cluster from car B, conspicuously present on the grass verge.

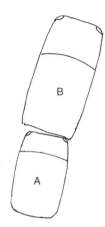

Figure 11.7 Positions of car A and car B at the moment of collision, recon-structed from bodywork damage.

An independent engineer and a crash reconstruction expert later exam-ined all three vehicles together and compared the damage to the circum-stances described in the drivers' statements. Many discrepancies were found. The most significant were:

1. With car B set to make a left turn into a narrow road the steering would have been turned to the left, but the rear damage caused by car A was concentrated toward the right-hand side and indicates the relative positions at the moment of contact must have been as illus-trated in Figure 11.7. Moreover, the trunk top of car B appears to have been open, as its edges had left clear impressions on the front hood of car A. The most severe compression of the brackets securing the rear bumper to car B was at the right-hand side and the left side bracket appeared to have been broken by pulling away the bumper with an upward twist.

2. Car C had registered two separate frontal impacts against the driver's door of car B about 25 cm apart. This evidence is clear from the photograph in Figure 11.8 (top) showing the front door (driver's side) of car B taken in the recovery breaker's yard. The front crash-resisting bumper structure of car C had dented the sill below the door in two places. (It was this deformation of the floor pan and buckling of the side members that necessitated car B being written off.) In the first impact the rim of the right side headlight of car C had lightly dented the middle of the door panel. This shows toward the right side of the photograph where at the 1 o'clock position there is paint damage showing that a single break in car C's headlight glass had cut into the door panel (Figure 11.8, bottom). The second impact a little nearer

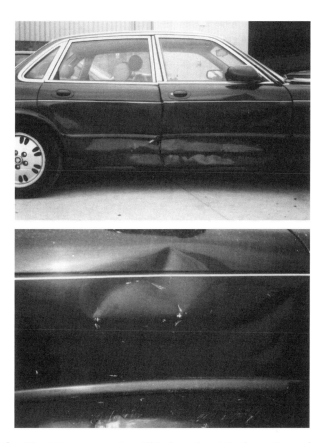

Figure 11.8 (Top) Damage to the sill below the right front door of car B revealing two separate impacts by the bumper of car C, the second below and slightly to the rear of the first. (Bottom) Indentations in door caused by broken glass in the headlight of car C. In the first there is only a slight mark from broken glass near the 1 o'clock position of the headlight but in the second the glass is broken around the entire circumference and the indent in the door panel is deeper.

the rear of car B had made a deeper indent in the sill slightly below the first, and the door panel paintwork is now marked by broken glass in a complete circle the same diameter and the same height above ground as the headlight rim, revealing that all the headlight glass must have been broken when this second impact occurred. A specialist in crash reconstruction estimated the closing speed for the first impact would have been approximately 12 mph and the second 16 mph.

3. There was hardly any damage along the left side of car C, not even at the front as would be inevitable if it had struck car B as shown in Figure 11.6. Its right wing was buckled by compression from the broken headlight back almost as far as the driver's door and the glass windshield flattened and completely shattered. The roof was

Figure 11.9   Roof and windshield damage to car C. Notice the left wing exhibits very little damage and the headlight glass is unbroken whereas the right wing is compressed and the headlight glass broken.

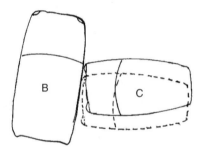

Figure 11.10   Relative positions of cars B and C at first impact (full outline) and second (dotted outline) as reconstructed from damage.

compressed, as can be seen in Figure 11.9. Despite this extensive damage there were no marks of abrasion from the road surface anywhere on the bodywork or the windshield frame, nor was there any sign of turf, soil or other vegetation in crevices or jammed between the wheels and the tires such as usually found when a vehicle has overturned onto a grass verge. When the frontal damage of car C was matched against that on the right side of car B, both impacts indicated that the vehicles must have been in the relative positions shown in Figure 11.10 at the time of collision, the dotted outline representing the second, more violent impact.

4. Other features inconsistent with the drivers' descriptions were that on all three cars the windshield wipers were in the parked position, despite the drivers' statements that the crash occurred at dusk on a wet evening. The driver of car B said he knew there was another vehicle coming around the bend to his right because he could see the

road lit up by its headlights, yet the filament of the headlight in the offside of car C exhibited a brittle fracture, showing it was not incandescent when it broke. (See Chapter 10, Section 10.4.)

The physical evidence thus demonstrates overwhelmingly that this accident did not happen as claimed. It had clearly been staged somewhere other than the road junction in order to justify substantial insurance claims. The drivers had colluded in drawing up their statements. The crushed windshield and soft top of car C were more consistent with having something like a mini rubbish dumpster dropped onto it than rather than having rolled over on the road, and it is difficult to believe how the driver could have escaped very serious head injury if he had been strapped inside the vehicle at the time this compression of the soft roof had occurred.

At the trial it transpired that there had in fact been a close business relationship between the drivers of cars B and C, far from their previous claim of being casual acquaintances at a golf club. Furthermore, the write-off values they were claiming for their respective vehicles were substantially more than the purchase prices. However, no connection could be established between them and the driver of car A, although it is difficult to believe that he was not part of the conspiracy, inasmuch as he claimed to have seen car C turn over and land on its wheels yet when he ran to open the door the driver climbed out a little dazed but otherwise uninjured.

Criminal Cases  12

Evidence in criminal cases is usually presented by government-recognized forensic science laboratories on evidence and submitted by police forces. Such laboratories are usually staffed by scientists and various specialists such as handwriting experts who, although generally quite experienced and skilled in their respective fields, seldom have experience in manufacture and general engineering. Occasionally, investigating police officers may instruct independent experts in such fields but, more commonly, independent experts are called in by lawyers acting for the accused in order to challenge or expand upon the evidence given to the court by scientists. In addition, insurance companies may have an interest in the outcome of a case so they too may wish to have material evidence examined by an independent expert and, if necessary, to challenge the interpretation given to the court. The cases that follow are selected from the authors' experience in this field and, not surprisingly, have a strong metallurgical bias.

12.1 Counterfeit Coins

No matter what the currency there will always be forged notes and coins in circulation. Government departments and forensic science laboratories quickly determine how the currency is made and many of the counterfeiters are caught, but not before the public has suffered. When the U.K. first introduced the gold-colored £1 coin counterfeits soon appeared that had been crudely made by casting in solder and electroplating with brass. These coins had a dull ring and as soon as the plating wore off the edges they marked paper like a pencil. At the time of this writing much better counterfeits are in circulation, made from the correct alloy, and their only "give-away" is the quality of the lettering around the milled rim (Figure 12.1). The milling marks of this £1 sterling coin are themselves very irregular, but who

Figure 12.1   Edge of a counterfeit coin above a legally minted coin, showing irregular milling marks and poorly formed lettering.

examines such details in their loose change? The face patterns are excellent although many do not match known patterns and dates. Metals are heavy compared with paper so the more manufacturing processes the forger has to use to make good copies, the less the "profit." The tendency has thus been to cast the coin by an investment casting technique, using the "lost wax" process in which many wax patterns copying the genuine coin are set in a refractory mold and cast at the same time from the correct alloy. The tiny area on each coin where the pattern was joined with others onto the "tree" inside the mold is easily removed by polishing to match the rest of the rim.

However, some very good counterfeit "silver" (actually cupro-nickel alloy) coins were produced by casting when decimal coins were first introduced in the U.K. Coins were physically larger than they are now and the value of currency and the cost of living were such that there existed a stronger motive for counterfeiting the 50p coin; the pound at that time was still a paper note. The first 10p coin weighed 11 g and the 50p coin weighed just over 13 g. It did not require any great proficiency in mathematics to work out that, with some means of melting and casting, £1–30 worth of 10p coins could be converted to £5–50 worth of 50p pieces. Molds containing upward of 30 or so impressions of 50p pieces were mounted in a small centrifugal casting machine, the 10p coins melted and then forced into the investment. It was a job that could be done in a few minutes when the boss wasn't around. There was no record of any purchase of the cupro-nickel alloy. When solidified the individual castings were broken off the sprue and the tiny area where they had been connected was polished. Such castings of course are not quite

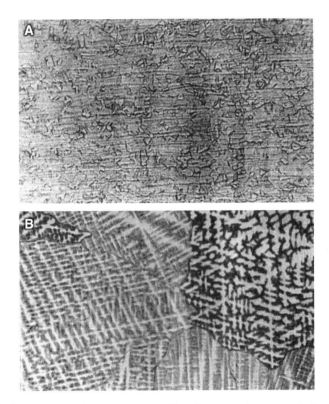

Figure 12.2 (A) Etched microsection of legally minted coin made from wrought copper nickel alloy showing recrystallized grains with directional coring from original cast billet from which the coinage strip was rolled (magnification: 75×). (B) Etched microsection of counterfeit coin made by casting, revealed by large irregular grains having nickel rich cores merging into copper rich matrix due to nonequilibrium cooling from the liquid state (magnification: 75×).

so sharply defined as a coin made in a coining press from solid metal, but they were practically impossible to detect visually in normal transactions.

There were, however, physical ways of detecting the counterfeits. Legally minted coins start off as cast slabs that are rolled down to thin strip and the coins then blanked out and stamped in power presses with machined dies. This is sometimes followed by milling the edges. The counterfeit coins were as-cast so they had a different microstructure, as illustrated in Figure 12.2A and Figure 12.2B, which are etched sections of the wrought and the cast cupro-nickel alloy, respectively. The cast structure (Figure 12.2B) exhibits large grains that are cored (that is a compositional segregation due to the first solid to appear being higher in nickel than that formed near the end of the solidification process), which is especially pronounced in copper-nickel alloys. Figure 12.2A shows a longitudinal section of a minted coin that has been rolled from a 125-mm billet to a 3-mm-thick strip. This exhibits smaller equiaxed grains that are drawn out in the direction of working and the coring segregation is oriented in the direction of rolling.

A microstructural examination requires a section to be cut from the suspect coin and to be polished and etched. Once it had been established that the counterfeits were being made by casting, then physical tests that do not require such preparation could be devised to quickly sort them. However, as the value of the currency fell and the size of the coins was later reduced, the risk and surrepticious effort were unjustified, so the quantity of forged coins in circulation fell.

12.2   Shotgun Pellets

A drug dealer was murdered, shot with a double-barrelled shotgun. Two cartridges had been discharged at close range, the pellets from the first shot hitting him in the chest and those from the second in the lower abdomen. A week or so before the murder he had received a threatening letter about defaulting on payments to which had been taped 10 shotgun pellets, found to be the same size as those of the 48 recovered from the chest wound. Pellets recovered from the lower wound were larger. The prime suspect arrested was found to own a double-barrelled shotgun and there was evidence to suggest this person was the sender of the letter, although this was vehemently denied.

The 10 pellets on the letter were individually weighed and analyzed very accurately for 12 elements, including impurities usually present at low levels in lead shot as well as the principal alloy elements, antimony and arsenic. Both harden the shot but the arsenic also increases surface tension of the molten metal so that it will form spherical droplets in the shot-making process. These results were compared statistically with similar analyses of 20 pellets from the chest wound. Mean weights of these two batches were found to be 0.1107 and 0.1088 g with standard deviations of 0.0077 and 0.0083 g, respectively. The forensic science laboratory that conducted this investigation had built up a database of over 600 analyses of shotgun pellets covering the full range of commercially produced shot sizes. The laboratory reported there was a closer match between the pellets from the letter and the ones recovered from the chest wound than could be found when matching either group of these pellets with its database. On this basis the laboratory concluded that the murder pellets were from the same cartridge as those on the letter. At trial this conclusion was challenged by three different experts.

A metallurgist pointed out that the various alloys are prepared and their compositions adjusted in a furnace holding between 50 and 100 t of metal. This is cast into 25-kg ingots and sent to various shotmakers. The shotmakers remelt the ingots and pour the molten metal through a sieve at the top of a tower and, as it falls, the streams break up into droplets and solidify. Although considered individually, quantities of impurities were close in the two groups of pellets analyzed; when certain critical ratios were compared there were significant differences. For example, while the lead alloy is held in the molten state, copper, being completely insoluble and less dense than lead, tends to rise to the surface and will be higher in the first ingots to be cast than the last, whereas bismuth, being soluble in the liquid lead and having no tendency to segregate, will tend to oxidize near the surface and will thus be higher in the last ingots to be cast than the first. Individual ingots from the same cast will thus vary slightly, particularly when their analyses are reported in parts per million. The average copper/bismuth ratio in the 10 pellets was slightly more than twice that in the pellets recovered from the wound. This suggests that even though these two batches of pellets might have originated from the same cast in the refining furnace they had been poured at different times during the shot making process and could well have been made by different shotmakers who had purchased their ingots from the same refiner.

A single kettle of liquid alloy at the shotmaker's would hold typically 30 to 50 t of metal and would be continually replenished with additional ingots as liquid was drawn off. A total of 50 t of alloy would be enough to make 500 million pellets if each pellet weighed 0.1 g. Under cross-examination the analyst agreed that his data showed that the two samples of pellets most probably came from the same source but not necessarily from the same cartridge.

The firearms expert explained that although there would be no difficulty in uncrimping the end of a cartridge, removing the wadding, taking out 10 pellets and then recrimping, he did not believe the chemical analysis did, or could, prove the 10 pellets were taken from the same cartridge as the other 20. He pointed out that the statistical mean weight of the two batches differed slightly despite exhibiting almost identical standard deviations and that there appeared to be two distinct groups even within the batch of 20.

The retired manager from the shot manufacturing firm explained how the shot is made by melting 50 t or so of ingots in a kettle (so called because the metal poured is drawn from the bottom), and is poured through a screen at the top of a tower. The streams of liquid metal break up into droplets and solidify as they fall down and finish up in a water bath that quenches them. They are then polished and rolled over a series of sloping plates that reject the pellets that are not truly spherical, which are returned to the kettle to be remelted. Ingots of different alloys are segregated in their stockyard, but there is no certainty that all the ingots charged to the kettle on the same day will have come from the same supplier or have been delivered at the same time. Finished pellets are sent as small orders to various cartridge makers and they sell boxes of cartridges to a wide variety of outlets. Thus sportsmen thousands of miles apart could be using shotgun cartridges containing pellets made from the same kettle of metal in the same shot manufacturing plant on the same day.

As the Crown's case against the accused depended almost entirely on the analyst's conclusion that the pellets on the letter were from the same cartridge as those in the fatal wound, the jury not surprisingly reached a verdict of not guilty.

12.3   Metal Theft

Nonferrous metals are of considerable value and many small enterprises make a living by collecting scrapped items at source and selling them to scrap merchants who sort and regrade them before sending them to refineries. At the very bottom of this pyramid are individuals who ask no questions about the source of their scrap and who make their living by selling it to the highest bidder. This case concerns one such individual who made a gross mistake.

An electroplating firm ordered 9 t of copper cathode from a copper refinery. This is a pure form of copper that is produced only by electrolysis; the cathodes are somewhat irregular, 5 to 10 mm thick, with a smooth surface on one side and numerous tiny nodules standing proud on the other, as illustrated in Figure 12.3. This sample is a piece of cathode of similar size to

Figure 12.3   Piece of copper cathode approximately 30 mm², ex-refinery. Notice nodules on the surface and along the right-hand side, which formed the edge of the cathode in the electrolysis bath.

those stolen and is much larger than the guillotined pieces that it was to have been cut into for the electroplating process. It is included here to show the characteristic nodules on the surface as well as along the edge at the right-hand side. Freshly produced cathode is a bright salmon pink color when it leaves the refinery but oxidizes to a dull brown after a few weeks. For use as anode in barrel electroplating the cathode has to be reduced to small pieces about 25 mm^2, so the electroplating firm needed to send its metal to another firm that had a powerful guillotine. The electroplating firm arranged to have this done on a Monday but, because the consignment arrived late on Friday afternoon, the truck was driven inside the plating firm's yard and the gates locked. It was not visible from the outside. On Monday morning when the gates were opened up the truck was gone, and with it 9 t of copper worth more than £9000.

The nonferrous metal trade has a system of notifying all dealers and metal merchants of a theft and the nature of the material stolen. Some 4 to 5 days after the theft a small van drove to a scrap dealer 250 miles away from where the truck was taken. The driver offered to sell a quarter ton of scrap copper, saying he had more if the price was good enough. The scrap merchant realized that in the load of mixed copper — a few old hot water cylinders, pipes, wire, and so on — were pieces of cathode, so he purchased that load and offered to buy all that the driver could deliver. He also notified the police. Within an hour the driver was back with another quarter ton, most of which was cathode. He was arrested and the police accompanied him back to a small yard where they found the stolen truck containing just over 8 t of copper cathode.

The man arrested claimed that he was just a small-scale scrap dealer, who had bought all the metal in small lots from local housing estates and small industrial units. It hardly needed a metallurgist to identify it as ex-refinery cathode, which is totally different from swarf or clippings arising from manufacturing processes, or discarded items from plumbing systems and electrical wiring. The thief was obviously unaware that the only uses for cathode copper are in electroplating and for remelting and alloying with other metals. In no way could the metal in his possession have been collected from housing estates and light industry. It was particularly incriminating that the total amount was 9 t and was just starting to develop the brown oxide coating. It could only have emanated from the one refinery still operating in the U.K., and its color was consistent with it having been produced some 3 to 4 weeks before it was recovered. Further inquiries revealed that the man arrested had been living with his family in a caravan not far from the refinery at the time of the theft.

Another case of theft that required examination of coarse pieces of swarf found in the soles of a suspect's boots has already been referred to in Chapter

2. The suspect was accused of breaking into a factory and stealing metal bars from the side of a large lathe. Pieces of swarf picked up from the floor around the machine were compared with pieces dug out from the accused's boots. Not only was the composition of these pieces, as shown in x-ray scans obtained under the scanning electron microscope, practically identical — aluminum brass containing copper, zinc and aluminum — but the serrations produced by the cutting tool matched exactly when the suspect chip was compared with the swarf from the scene. As a cutting tool wears it develops ridges and cavities that are unique to that particular tool, an effect similar to the way the rifling of a gun barrel marks a bullet fired from it. The piece picked up was large enough, and recent enough, to identify as having been machined with the same tool as the one found in the boot.

12.4   Chain from Murder

A woman abruptly left her group of friends in a bar, allegedly because she was being pestered by a man. She walked home and locked her door, securing the chain, but the following day she was found raped and brutally murdered. The chain was hanging broken from the door handle. The man who had been pestering her was known to her friends and lived in the same district. He was questioned by police and claimed that he had walked home soon after the woman left and had watched a late-night movie on television. The police searched his premises and found a small crowbar under sacking at the side of his house with four links of brass chain twisted tightly round the hooked end, shown close up in Figure 12.4. Figure 12.5 shows part of the broken chain that the woman had used to secure her door alongside the four links twisted round the end ofthe crowbar.

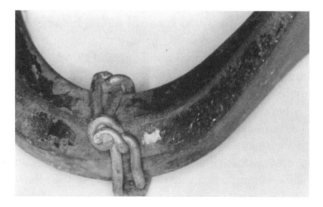

Figure 12.4   Links of brass chain wrapped around a crowbar.

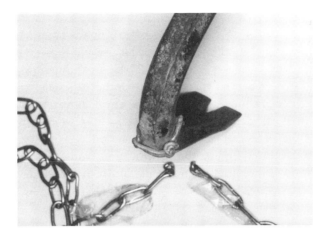

Figure 12.5 Twisted links of ornamental brass chain used to secure door.

Forensic examination revealed that the chain was composed of welded links made from brass wire. The diameter of the wire and the pitch of undeformed links away from the fractures of both exhibits were practically identical. The chemical compositions of one link from the chain on the door and one from the crowbar were not identical but were both within the specified range for 70/30 copper/zinc alloy.

The man was arrested and charged with murder. DNA tests later confirmed that he had raped the woman. At trial, the defense sought to claim that the scientific tests had not established beyond all doubt that the links on the crowbar were indeed from the same length of chain used to secure the door. At this point an independent engineer was called. He found that the links had been electrically welded on the same type of machine, but the damning evidence was that the torsional fracture surfaces where the wires had been twisted to destruction were perfect matches to the crowbar and the chain still hanging from the door.

12.5 Coin Box Busters

For security reasons it is not possible to give a full description or include photographs of the items referred to, but this case is a good example to show the role of the engineer with experience in manufacture in the criminal forensic field. Essentially they were three ingenious, though crudely constructed, devices for breaking open coin boxes in gaming machines, public telephones and similar situations.

A police detective produced the first device, found in the trunk of a car seen driving away from a broken telephone box that had been kept under observation. The driver was found to be in possession of a large quantity of small coins and a device of the type described below, so he was arrested and charged with criminal damage and theft. Suspecting that he was one of a gang systematically breaking open coin boxes in different areas of outer London, the police searched the vehicles of other suspects and found two other similar devices concealed in the spare wheel compartments. Both suspects claimed the devices were used in car repair work and denied any knowledge of each other or of the person arrested.

The detective in charge of the investigation wanted to know whether there was anything in common in the design of the three devices and the way they had been constructed.

There certainly were similarities. All three devices were of similar design, based on a hydraulic car jack widely obtainable from automotive accessory stores. In this instance all three were of the same make and had the same color paint on the body of the hydraulic cylinders. Parts of the jack had been removed and replaced by two steel bars of square section, slightly bent in the middle and with sawn-off ends to which were crudely welded the cutting ends from two cold chisels. These formed a pair of claws capable of piercing the sides of the coin boxes. Surface score marks from the manufacturing operation on the bars of all three devices were an exact match and the microstructures and hardnesses were the same. The bars had obviously all been cut to the same length from the same bar stock and had been bent to the same angle while heated with a gas welding torch, which had oxidized the surface to a blue-gray color. The chisel ends were slightly different, but all had been cut to the same length from 1-in. (25-mm)-wide cold chisels. As each chisel has only one cutting end, six would have been required to construct three pairs of claws.

Another part of the device was a length of M18 screwed steel rod. Such rods are readily available from DIY stores in 1-m lengths. On each device these rods were 0.5 m long and had an M18 nut welded on one end so that they could be turned with a spanner to open and close the jaws. The hydraulic ram had been converted into a punch by welding on a stub cut from the top of a high speed steel twist drill. All three were of slightly different diameters, increasing consecutively by 1/32 in. apparently taken from a sized set of HSS twist drills, but they were cut to similar lengths and rather poorly welded to the rams.

It was clear that all three devices had been constructed in the same workshop using the same design concept — it is unlikely there would have been a drawing or a materials specification — and with parts obtained from the same sources. On each device, one pair of welds had been made with a gas torch and the others with electric arc welding equipment, using flux-coated mild steel electrodes. All the welds exhibited similar imperfections and looked as if they had been executed by the same person, who was by no means a skilled welder.

The police had established that a considerable number of coin boxes in different localities had been broken into with these particular devices, mainly because the holes in the sides matched the claws formed by the cold chisels and the locks had been pushed in by a circular object of similar diameters to the twist drills. The engineering evidence proved complicity in their design and manufacture and led to the conviction of all three suspects found with the devices in their cars.

12.6 Remelting Beer Barrels

A number of public houses in a large city had experienced a spate of thefts of aluminum beer barrels. Whole batches of empty barrels placed in their yards awaiting collection by the brewery had disappeared in the early hours of the morning. In a suburb of the same city a large warehouse and yard was occupied by small firms in the metal recycling trade, among which were vehicle dismantlers, one of whom had a small metal melting unit used for separating assemblies that contained aluminum alloy parts. As a vehicle was taken apart components containing alloy were placed onto a sloping hearth under oil burners so that the aluminum alloy melted and ran down into a bath while the iron and steel were left on the hearth to be raked out from time to time. The molten alloy was cast into ingots and sold to a metal refiner.

The police suspected this warehouse yard might have been the destination of the stolen beer barrels, so they kept watch in a number of ways, including helicopter surveillance, but were never able to observe any barrels on vehicles entering the site. (It was later learned that the reason for this was that the barrels were carried in closed vans and the sheet metal gates of the yard were always kept locked "to prevent entry by nosey parkers and casual passers-by.") Although most of the firms on the site were car dismantlers, one of them ran a one-man business stripping old electrical cable to recover lead and copper. He owned the lease of the site and lived a prosperous lifestyle, despite the small throughput of his business. Early one morning the police raided the site and found the beer barrel melting process in full swing, with a closed van still partly filled with barrels backed up to the door and five men, including the cable stripper, apparently engaged in operating the furnace and casting 50-kg ingots. All five were arrested, ordered to strip and change their boots, and the burners were shut down by the cable stripper. However, the cable stripper claimed he had nothing to do with the melting process but had merely attended to open the yard and carry on with some cable stripping in a different part of the building while the others were

Figure 12.6 Beads of aluminum alloy in the heel of a boot, picked up by walking on a floor close to metal casting operations.

working. He admitted that he did this from time to time but had no idea where the barrels came from and said this job was usually done at night because the furnace was in use by the other firms for car parts during normal daytime hours.

His association with the beer barrel melting became clear after forensic examination of metal particles found on the soles of the boots and on the clothes he was wearing when arrested.

All the suspects' clothes were brushed and a number of tiny particles of metal were collected. In addition, there were numerous particles in the soles of their boots, such as illustrated in Figure 12.6. Examination under the SEM revealed that all were rounded particles characteristic of splashes and droplets such as those emitted by molten metal running into open molds. Every one of 20 samples taken from boots and clothing of all five men were found to be aluminum alloy containing low percentages of magnesium and silicon. This composition spread would include the alloy used for beer barrels, but not the ones commonly used for automobile castings, which usually contain greater amounts of silicon. Most significantly, no particle recovered from the cable stripper's clothing or boots was copper or lead but, even if there had been any from this source, they would have taken the form of mechanical slivers or clippings, not solidified droplets

The clothing exhibited numerous holes formed by hot particles landing on them, particularly below the trouser knees. Figure 12.7A shows two holes joined together in the side pocket of a nylon jacket worn by the cable stripper. These had been formed by one, or possibly two, splashes of hot metal striking the fabric and melting through the nylon. Figure 12.6B shows the lower leg of corduroy trousers, where small hot particles had landed. These particles

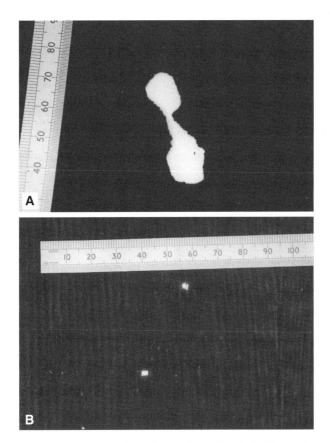

Figure 12.7 (A) A hole melted in the pocket of a dark blue nylon jacket and (B) a hole burned in the lower leg of corduroy trousers, both caused by proximity to splashes and hot droplets of metal emitted during the pouring and casting of molten aluminum alloy into ingot molds.

appear to have been still adhering when the trousers were removed but had been torn away when the trousers were brushed, judging by the torn fabric.

Although most of the above observations are essentially scientific, the engineering dimension becomes important in identifying the particles and clothing damage as typical of that expected when workers are standing close to foundry operations. Few scientists have ever observed the splashing that occurs and the distance droplets may carry when a stream of molten metal poured from a furnace first strikes a launder and then runs into an open ingot mold, or the fine spray of droplets that are thrown up as it solidifies when the metal has picked up hydrogen due to being melted under reducing conditions. In this instance, the damage to the clothing worn by the cable stripper clearly established that he must have been standing very close to the stream of molten metal as the ingots were being cast.

Intellectual Property Cases

13

13.1 Introduction

Intellectual property is an area in which many forensic engineers become deeply involved. Forensic engineers are employed because courts need to arbitrate between parties who dispute some aspect of new technology or engineering. Indeed, many practicing engineers also become involved because they will need to protect new ideas or devices that they conceive or make either for themselves or for their employers. Disputes commonly involve inventions or designs where priority must be established, especially in technologies where development is rapid.

The subject essentially deals with the creation of new devices and machines, or ideas that take some practical form. An essential attribute is thus novelty; the device must be unknown before its creation. A second attribute is that the device has a bodily form and can be applied in some useful way. The new device receives legal protection in the form of a document that establishes the owner, the period for which the document is valid, the nature of the right protected and the exact definition of the device. In the most important example, the document is a patent, but it can also be a registered design (in the U.K.) or a design patent (in the U.S., for example). Other forms of intellectual property include written words (copyright) and marks of approval placed on devices (trademarks and tradenames). Confidential information, such as a secret formula, can also be protected. The rights established are like property rights, such as ownership to land established by a title deed. However, the property is virtual rather than real, and has a strictly limited life, 20 years for a patent and varying periods for other rights. Although different rules apply in different countries, there is reasonable compatibility between the major industrialized countries especially with regard to patents (as established by international treaties such as the WTO).

13.1.1   Patents

Close examination of the concept of a patent shows that it has a much wider range of application than might at first glance appear to be the case. Since protection is by a written description, the document protects an inventive concept of which the practical device is just one manifestation. In other words, the patent protects an inventive concept, rather than just one machine built according to that idea. If a competitor copies a machine and hopes to avoid prosecution by changing the material or design in some way, he or she still risks the chance of litigation because a patent protects the concept and not a particular embodiment of that concept.[1,2]

So "designing around" patents is a key skill, but fraught with danger because everything depends on the words used in the claims of a patent to define the inventive concept. This is where the expert evidence of a forensic engineer is often crucial, because he or she helps the court to reach an understanding of the words and technical terms used in the claims. The court will then be able to determine whether or not a particular device actually infringes those claims, when those claims are interpreted correctly. The forensic engineer will also be able to give a court some idea of the "state of the art" at the time the patent was awarded, and make comments about the originality of the concept. This is often the most difficult hurdle faced by a patentee, because the concept must not be an "obvious" development of something that exists already in the state of the art.

13.1.2   Case Studies

Several cases from the U.K. and Europe will be examined in some detail in this chapter, but all have an international flavor because patent law itself has many transnational implications. This reflects the nature of invention in the modern world: once an idea is conceived, it can be applied in many different countries. Since the basic reason for granting a patent is to protect new ideas, it follows that there must be tests for gauging exactly how new that idea really is in the light of what has been conceived previously (anywhere in the world). Although these tests are first applied by the government agencies that initially review a patent application, deeper investigation is inevitable if a dispute arises. Thus, for example, a forensic engineer will be asked to carry out a search for prior art to determine the originality of a specific design. This search is more detailed than the official search, simply because the net will be much more extensive in scope than government searches.

The cases we will describe arose because one patent owner sued another over a potentially infringing device. Since a patent gives a monopoly right of manufacture of a specific design, and if another manufacturer produces a product that appears to fall within the ambit of the patent, court proceedings may be initiated to resolve the issue. In the first case, a manufacturer of rubbish bins in Germany established a large business by providing plastic-bodied containers that offered greater security for, and ease of disposal of, the contents. When the firm began manufacture in the U.K., an entrepreneur spotted that the design could just as well be made in a more robust material, steel. By redesigning the bin, the patent could be avoided, but the patentee felt rather differently, and court proceedings were initiated.

In the second case, the holders of a patent for the design of lawnmower casings decided to sue another lawnmower maker because they felt that the lawnmowver maker infringed their patent. The case is significant because, after examining the patent in great detail, the court decided, in light of previous patents in the same area, that the patent could not have been valid at the time of granting.

The final example shows how it is possible to circumvent patent claims by a careful analysis of the way a specific device worked, and indeed, how it could be improved. The residual current device (RCD) protects consumers by isolating the main electrical supply if a fault is detected, so that if a lawnmower user (for example) accidentally cuts the power cord, he or she will not be electrocuted because the RCD quickly breaks the circuit.

13.2   Wheeled Containers

One example of a wheeled container is the so-called "wheelie bin" (Figure 13.1 taken from German petty patent no. 7611603). The container is now so widespread in the U.K. that it is easy to forget the problems of rubbish disposal that confronted the country only a few years ago. The per capita volume of waste rose over the years, and the original small plastic or steel bins of the 1960s and 1970s were not capable of meeting demand. One interim solution, to use simple plastic bags, created more problems than it solved, mainly because of the insecurity of such containers, which can easily break and spill their contents. The wheelie bin was invented in Germany in 1975–1976, and the product has spread gradually into the U.K. The main buyers are local authorities, who are responsible for rubbish collection. The investment makes great sense, because

1. The amount of rubbish that can be collected at one time is much greater compared with plastic bags or conventional bins.
2. The rubbish is sealed better in bins, so spillage is minimal.
3. Emptying the bins is more efficient, with specially designed disposal vehicles.

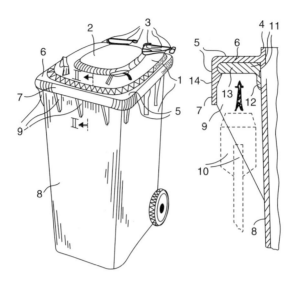

Figure 13.1 Early version of a domestic wheelie bin of 250-L capacity. The diagram at right shows a metal bar under the rim to support the lifting fork.

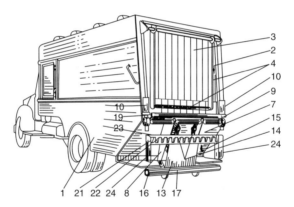

Figure 13.2 Rear view of garbage truck showing the lifting bar with forks (22) used to raise the bins, from GB 1 383 036 of 1972.

The critical technical step in the design of the wheelie bin is the creation of a reinforced lip at the front of the bin that enables it to be hoisted automatically by a hydraulic lift onto the truck (Figure 13.2 and Figure 13.3). The critical patent is Schneider, dating from 1976 (GB 1 588 932).

13.2.1 The Lifting Lip

Part of the design problem with using a thermoplastic material is ensuring that the bin is rigid enough to withstand the critical lifting phase. If the

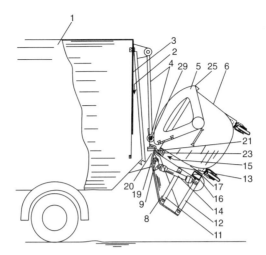

Figure 13.3   Section of the truck rear to show the lifting operation.

product is subjected to severe mechanical loads in service, then the strength or stiffness of part of the product subject to the most load becomes the critical part of the product. Since the wheelie bin will be full of rubbish (under maximum fill conditions), the lifting lip takes the whole load of the contents of the bin. In other words, the lifting lip is the critical part of the load path from bin contents to comb bar.

The lifting lip must not deform too much, and the material of which it is made must also be tough enough to resist crack propagation. Much effort is put into careful design of the lip to maximize its stiffness and strength. This is why claim 1 of the original patent devotes considerable space to defining the lifting lip in some detail. The first claim in a patent is critical because it aims to define the inventive concept concisely yet accurately, as widely as possible to catch infringers but not any prior art, and without ambiguity, so that the breadth of the monopoly it is clear to the reader:

What We Claim Is

A container for refuse, comprising a body of substantially rectangular cross-section having a cover therefor, a depending flange which extends along one side wall of the body in the region of an upper edge of said wall and is stiffened by substantially vertically arranged struts connected to the body, and a rib which extends substantially parallel with the body between the body and the depending flange; and wherein a reinforcing member is provided for said flange, said member extending along and projecting laterally from said flange and being adapted and arranged to serve as an abutment for said container during emptying thereof.

As with many patent claims, it is much easier to rearrange the long sentence into subclauses so that the sense of the inventive concept can be seen more easily. The above claim then becomes:

What We Claim Is

1. *A container for refuse, comprising*
2. *A body of substantially rectangular cross-section having a cover therefor,*
3. *A depending flange which extends along one sidewall of the body in the region of an upper edge of said wall, and is stiffened by*
4. *Substantially vertically arranged struts connected to the body, and*
5. *A rib which extends substantially parallel with the body between the body and the depending flange; and*
6. *Wherein a reinforcing member is provided for said flange, said member extending along and projecting laterally from said flange and being adapted and arranged to serve as an abutment for said container during emptying thereof.*

The "depending flange" (the third clause in claim 1) is the lifting flange or lip, and the claim defines how it is constructed in considerable detail. For example, the lip extends along the whole length of one of the side walls, so that the full load on the lip when it is being lifted is spread over the maximum area. Figure 13.4 shows just how the metal forks (or comb bars) of the lift on the truck are designed to mate with the cavity below the front depending flange in order to empty the container (they are shown by the lower set of dotted lines). Another important feature of this claim is that no dimensions are provided in the claim; this is typical of mechanical patents. In fact, there is a variety of such bins, ranging in enclosed volume from 250 to 350 L and up to the large industrial bins of 1100-L total capacity. The former type is usually supplied to domestic premises, the latter type to shops and businesses in the U.K.

Clearly the volume of the large 1100-L bin is much greater than the volume of the standard domestic bin, so extra reinforcement of the lifting flange is needed. The ribs, which are a key design detail of such bins, provide the extra stiffening where it is needed so as to resist the bending loads imposed during the lift. Irrespective of the kind of material used, the use of ribs is a universal design strategy for controlling product stiffness. On a larger scale, for example, ship hulls made from steel are reinforced internally by providing ribs and stiffeners both laterally and longitudinally. They are welded to the structure during construction.

However, plastics are much less stiff than many metals (including steel), and much more extensive reinforcement of critical parts is needed for small products, such as bins, than for steel products. Internal ribs are

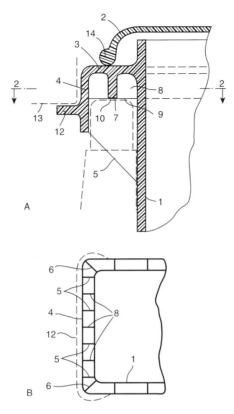

Figure 13.4 Section and plans of the Schneider lifting rim with the forks shown by the dotted lines in the upper diagram.

thus commonplace in many plastic products, and often can be used for a secondary design function.

13.2.2 Plastic Bins

What is the material of choice for the wheelie bin? When first developed in Germany, wheelie bins were injection molded in HDPE (high density polyethylene), a low-cost but very tough thermoplastic. This makes for a light product capable of withstanding much mechanical abuse, an essential feature of the product specification. The product is manufactured in a single operation, with hot polymer injected via a single gate in the center of the base. The process requires considerable capital investment both in the large molding machines and the precision tools needed to create the shape. The molding process itself exerts influence on the geometric design of the product. One such constraint, the re-entrant angle problem, is imposed by the need to withdraw the core of a molding tool at the end of the molding cycle. Effectively it means that all reinforcing members in a plastic molded design must allow withdrawal of the metal core of the tool from the hot product. Thus all ribs must point in a certain direction governed by the direction of withdrawal. This is why the preferred embodiments of the Schneider bin have ribs and struts that are primarily oriented down the main long axis of the structure (Figure 13.5). There are no re-entrant ribs in the structure so that the product can be removed easily at the end of the molding cycle.

13.2.3 Growth in Use

To lower production cost it is an essential aim to keep injection molding machines working continuously and, because tools for large products are very expensive, it is important to ensure that there is a market large enough to absorb production. In the U.K., the use of wheelie bins is decided by local authorities, and this has been a slow, stepwise process. The local authority has a large investment, not just in the bins themselves but also in the trucks fitted with the lifting forks. The old rubbish bins could not cope effectively with the increasing volume of rubbish that was being generated. With the advent of recycling schemes, several wheelie bins are often provided for domestic sorting of the rubbish. At the collection sites designated by progressive authorities, large capacity bins are dedicated for specific materials (glass, paper, etc.).

Another factor that has helped stimulate the growth in the use of such bins is the growth in the number of domestic residences, with an increasing number of single-parent and smaller family units. All residences need bins for rubbish disposal, and the net result is a burgeoning market for these products.

However, the large wheeled rubbish container is a product exposed to problems not usually encountered by the smaller, domestic bin. They are situated outside business premises in many public places, and durability can be a problem. Fire can be a specific problem, especially fires started by vandals. Polyethylene burns fiercely when the rubbish inside is ignited, so there is a need for an alternative material of construction. Metal is the obvious alternative, with sheet steel or aluminum the preferred material of construction, but how does one make the metal in the volume needed? Injection molding is inapplicable to steel, and the existing design with extensive ribbing is simply too complex for extra fabrication operations. Sheet steel is commonly welded to make large structures, and it is now automatically mass manufactured in a factory environment. Robotic manufacture of car bodies, for example, is commonplace in the automotive industry.

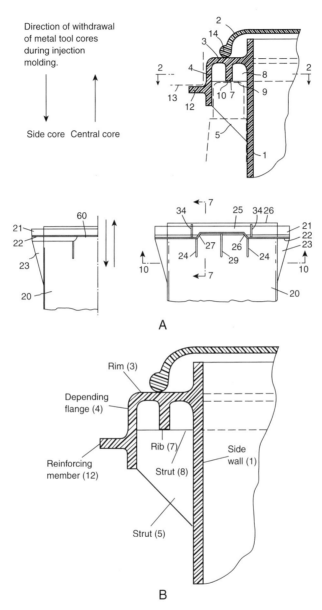

Figure 13.5 (A) Manufacture of the Schneider bin showing the withdrawal direction in the injection molding tool, assuming the gate lies at the center of the base. (B) Key parts of the Schneider lifting rim labeled according to claim 1 of the patent.

13.2.4   The Steel Bin

During the 1980s, an entrepreneurial company (Egbert H Taylor Ltd) based in the British Midlands decided to enter the market with a sheet

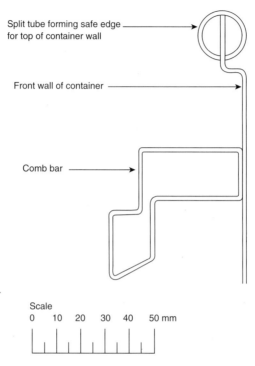

Split tube forming safe edge
for top of container wall

Front wall of container

Comb bar

Scale
0   10   20   30   40   50 mm

Figure 13.6 Section of the Taylor 1100-L bin with a hollow steel bar as the lifting lip.

steel 1100-L wheelie bin. Manufacture of the basic box shape was not difficult and could be achieved by a small number of welding steps on preformed sheet steel. But the critical lifting flange needed redesign: multiple ribs and flanges are critical in improving the stiffness of low modulus thermoplastics, but would be excessively expensive on a steel lifting lip. In any case, the much greater stiffness of steel (210 MPa compared with about 2 MPa for HDPE) implied that a much simpler design could be introduced. The Taylor company came up with the idea of using a tube welded to the chassis (Figure 13.6). The concept exploits the monocoque idea, where the load is supported in the shell of a hollow member, a principle widely used in general engineering. The flange, or comb bar as it is called, could be made using the same dimensions needed for the plastic version so that the forks could engage easily, and the mechanical properties of steel would easily accommodate the lifting loads. An intrinsically strong and tough product, it would also be more resistant to crack growth.

Naturally, the product when made and sold into the market attracted the attention of the patentee of the plastic equivalent, and a dispute arose, which eventually came to trial in the Patents County Court in London in 1996. The large steel 1100-L bin made serious inroads into a market dominated by a single manufacturer, and the competition harmed the sales of the plastic equivalent. The problem faced by the patentee was simple: was claim 1 infringed by the steel product? As usual, the legal problem starts with the claim and its technical interpretation by a skilled reader.

The difficulty the patentee faced was considerable because of the rather narrow way in which the claims had been drafted, with several engineering terms of inevitably narrow definition. This is a perpetual problem for patentees (or the patent agents who usually draft such documents). Draft your claims too widely and you run the risk of catching not just infringers but also the prior art (in which case your patent is obvious and hence invalid). Draft the claim too narrowly and the claim fails to give you the protection you desire for a complete monopoly of your particular product.

13.2.5 The Trial (*Schneider v. Taylor*)

The trial came before the Patents County Court in London in July 1996. The trial lasted 3 days. Virtually all of the oral evidence was presented by three expert witnesses: two were experienced in design and use of refuse equipment, and the third (the author of this chapter) was experienced in design of polymer products. The plaintiffs' case rested on a wide interpretation of claim 1 to catch a lifting rim of quite different structure to that claimed by the preferred embodiment. As usual, the defense attacked the validity of the Schneider patent, using examples from the prior art to show how the device developed in an apparently logical way from antecedents.

13.2.6 Meaning of Terms

The thrust of the counterattack by the defendants was not, however, very convincing, mainly because the immediate prior art did not include the specific reinforcement elements claimed by Schneider in claim 1. In other words, the inventive concept was original and novel, and so could not be attacked for being obvious to a skilled reader.

The main defense then shifted to construction of claim 1, and the infringement issue. The principal integers were the focus of attention, and the specific problem for the claimants was how a bent steel tube without conventional ribs could be construed to include ribs. The exact meaning of several terms in claim 1 were thus crucial to the infringement issue. Those terms included

depending flange
strut
rib

Here are some technical definitions from the 1964 edition of *Chambers Technical Dictionary*, a popular technical dictionary in the U.K.

> flange = a projecting rim, as the rim of a wheel which runs on rails, the top and bottom members of an I-beam

> strut = any light structural member or long column which sustains an axial compressive load

A general definition of rib was not satisfactory, but the *Oxford English Dictionary* states

> rib = a raised band, a prominence running in a line

The components are shown in the preferred embodiment of Figure 13.5B.

13.2.7 Alternative Interpretation

In order to bring the Taylor lifting rim into the claim, some flexibility in the meaning of the key terms was needed by the plaintiffs in the case. One of the experts appearing on behalf of Schneider labeled the components of the Taylor bin as shown in Figure 13.7. There are a number of problems with this interpretation. Let us look at the common identities first: the sidewall and struts are clearly not controversial, and cannot be confused. The problems arise with the identification of the rib, flange and reinforcing member. Thus the rib is identified with part of the outer flange, and the reinforcing member is divided into two separate parts, and flank each side of the rib.

In this case of identity of parts it is necessary to refer to the description of the invention in the patent-in-suit. The relation of the parts is described generally first at line 87 on page 1 of the patent:

> *Conveniently, the impact bar, the reinforcing member and the flange together define an assembly of U-shape in cross-section, opening towards the base of the container*

The structure is described in more detail on page 2 of the Schneider patent from line 45 onward. From line 65 on, the patentee describes the function of the various components thus:

> *Where the refuse container is provided with a device for suspension in a so-called comb bar, the spacing between the individual struts 5 is approximately uniform as illustrated in Figure 13.4. The intervening space is however divided up by smaller struts 8. The lower edges 9 of these*

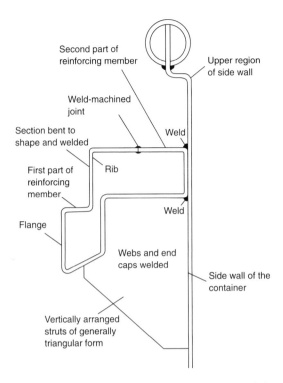

Figure 13.7   One interpretation of the parts of the Taylor lifting rim.

> *struts are flush with the lower edge 10 of the rib 7. It has been found that the flange 4 might be deformed between two struts 5 and 8. As a result of such deformations the area enclosed by the body part, the struts and the flange 4 can be reduced, and this will continue until the teeth of the comb bar will no longer find sufficient room for penetration with the result that the refuse container will no longer be capable of being hung in the garbage truck and will therefore become useless.*

What the patentee is describing here is the problem of inadequate reinforcement of the lifting rim. The pocket in which the forks or teeth of the comb bar sit is defined by the reinforcing member 12, depending flange 4, the lower edges of the rib 7 and small struts 8 and the sidewall of the container 1 (Figure 13.5A). The situation of Figure 13.7 shows a rib that

1. Does not have the properties of a rib, with a free end
2. Does not form a surface against which the teeth of the comb bar abut during lifting

It also seems clear that the structure of the lifting rim the patentee claims is not just the structure shown in the preferred embodiment in Figure 1 of the patent, but a whole range of structures, variants of the same basic principle. It will be noticed that all have structures that are capable of being injection molded, with a withdrawal line oriented along the main axis of the container (Figure 13.5A).

13.2.8   Standard Dimensions

Another important issue that arose during the course of the trial was the question of what dimensions should be chosen for the lifting lip. After all, the patent claims or specification nowhere state dimensions of the lifting rim, and the rim could be of any reasonable size, provided it was capable of performing the desired function of bearing the imposed load of the rubbish within it when lifted onto the truck. This is a common situation in patent claims, because the patentee wants the widest possible definition of the invention claimed so as to deter direct copying or other kinds of imitation.

However, it seems reasonably clear that the dimensions of the lifting pocket on the Taylor bin are designed to accept the standard forks or teeth of the lifting comb on the truck. After all, the Taylor bin only appeared after the Schneider bin, and Taylor could not sell its design on the market if it did not fit comb bars already fitted on rubbish trucks. Standardization of components is of course commonplace with engineered products and a problem that recurs when a new idea suddenly appears and several manufacturers enter the field with sometimes only slightly different designs. The consumer is tied to his supplier because only the supplier's spare parts are made to the exact dimensions of the device originally supplied to the consumer. This was the problem faced by car exhaust makers that wished to supply replacements for existing cars, and it is known as the "must fit" criterion. The current British law (Copyright Design and Patents Act, 1988) excludes protection of "must fit" dimensions for new designs (as protected by the new "design right," the replacement for copyright in design drawings). Thus it seemed clear that Taylor had copied the existing dimensions of the Schneider pocket, but without necessarily infringing any intellectual property (IP) rights held by Schneider.

13.2.9   Judgment

At trial, all the witness evidence consisted of testimony from the three experts involved. Despite attacks on credibility of some of the experts, and strained attempts to define a rib in rather unusual ways, the patent was found to be "valid but not infringed." The patent survived attacks on its validity, but the attack from the prior art failed, and a clear inventive step was identified.

From the expert evidence provided by the polymer expert, the judge decided the patent had been written for a designer skilled in plastics injection molding, and it was difficult to see how a steel flange could have been envisaged by the patentees. It was thus difficult to see how a steel rim could fall within the normal construction of claim 1. Since no serious attempt had been made at trial to attack the validity of the Schneider patent, it was held to be a legitimate invention. The final verdict clearly justified the Taylor company in the defense of its very successful product.

13.2.10 Afterword

It is interesting to note that the Taylor steel bin was itself patented, and used to pursue alleged infringers of the concept. The company has proven the commercial and technical quality of its bin, and competed very successfully in a large market with its plastic equivalent. The smaller plastic bins of the domestic market remain safe for the original patentees, but much of its trade in the large bins has been lost to a product that offers extra advantages in terms of longevity, safety and security to the user. Whether or not steel bins enter the domestic market remains to be seen, although it seems unlikely in the immediate future.

There are several factors involved. Small plastic domestic bins are lighter and more user friendly than steel. On the other hand, they are more susceptible to damage (especially of the lifting lip), and they are also combustible. Brittle cracks at the corners of ribs are quite common and, if they reach a critical size, they will propagate catastrophically. This could cause the loaded bin to fall while being loaded onto the rubbish truck, so damaged or cracked bins should be replaced as soon as the damage is detected. However, the manufacturing costs for a steel domestic bin will be higher *pro rata* than for larger containers, and corrosion may occur after some time in service. Although rusting can be inhibited by galvanizing and painting, such bins receive a great deal of mechanical abuse in service, creating impact craters, for example, from which rusting can develop.

The case study is a good example of how materials displacement can legitimately be pursued by designers, especially if the original patents are too narrowly worded.

13.3   Lawnmowers

Many intellectual property actions are settled before any trial, especially if the potential liability in costs awarded against the losing party could exceed the cost of a court trial. The costs of full trials are considerable, especially if common and well-known products are the subject of patent disputes. There will be much court time devoted to examining the prior art and the validity of the patent-in-suit, largely because it is a common defense in such actions to challenge the very basis of the patent being used to catch an infringer. On the other hand, the resultant judgment can create severe financial problems to the losing side. The reason for this state of affairs is that a product found to infringe may have to be removed from the market, or alternatively, a royalty on all sales (past, present and future) may be imposed by the patent owner. In fact, the largest damages ever awarded in any court action worldwide were awarded against Kodak for infringing Polaroid's instant photography patents, a case that had severe effects on Kodak's cashflow for several years.[3]

The case study analyzed in this section ended with a High Court trial, and was not appealed. There were no fundamental points of law that could be challenged, and the case was so definite in its conclusion that the plaintiff's patent was declared invalid on no fewer than three different counts. Patents that do come to trial are subjected to rigorous forensic analysis, and it is only those patents that are fundamentally inventive that survive. In many consumer product areas, patenting is extraordinarily extensive (especially by larger manufacturers), but any particular patent faces a severe problem in that it may be difficult to distinguish it from the many similar patents in the prior art. The case study presented here involves an area of great commercial activity: gardens, and specifically, lawnmowers.

Although the materials of construction are rarely specified in new inventions (so as to give much wider claims), a significant aspect of the case study involved the use of materials, and the specific advantages of thermoplastics for lightweight consumer products. Choosing one class or indeed a specific member of that class of materials necessarily entails consideration of the manufacturing method used to make the shaped product (as seen in the previous case study). There are substantial differences between the ways in which different materials are shaped, and such methods can limit the shape used in the actual embodiments of a new idea.

13.3.1 History of Development

The idea of using a mowing machine to trim lawns dates back to the Victorian period, but the irresistible rise of the internal combustion engine produced numerous examples of powered mowers in the early part of the 20th century. The cylinder mower was (and to some extent, still is) the principal way in which rotary power was applied to cutting grass. The blades in such mowers are set lengthways on a cylinder spaceframe, and, as the cylinder rotates at the level of the lawn, it cuts through the sward. The quality of finish is high because the blades can cut very finely, and the sward can also be cut very close to the ground, producing a smooth and level finish. This is the traditional way of cutting grass, and the art of cylinder mower design has reached a high state of perfection, especially for ornamental and recreational lawns, as well as sports surfaces such as golf links, cricket greens and bowls pitches. However, cylinder mowers are mechanically complex, and the machines are, as a result, expensive. The manufacturing companies also tend to be long established and hence rather conservative in their design attitudes.

With the growth in leisure time since World War II, the demand for gardening products in all countries of the developed world has increased at a high rate, with a correspondingly high demand for innovative new products that can be produced at much lower cost.

13.3.2   The Hover Principle

It is always inspiring to see the development of new ways of applying ideas to achieve practical ends, and the principle of the hover machine is no exception. The idea was developed in the 1950s from crude prototypes on the kitchen table of Christopher Cockerill: he used a blast of air directed downward onto a solid surface to lift a platform and so reduced the frictional force needed to move the platform in any desired direction. Since a mass of material must be lifted bodily above the ground, a high velocity air stream is essential and it must be spread over a large area. The force is simply the product of the air pressure and the area over which it is applied, so that a large area is preferred. The lifting force increases with the square of the air velocity, so that the higher the air velocity, the greater the lift. A high speed motor to drive the fan blades is thus needed to produce the blast. The idea was patented and developed by Cockerill into large vehicles, hovercraft, which are now in regular use for transportation across both land and water (for example, by the U.S. Marines). They have the advantage of not needing a conventional harbor, and they offer more flexibility to transhipment. The carrying speed is much higher because of the very low frictional force opposing lateral motion.

13.3.3   The Hovermower

The hovermower is another way in which the principle has been applied to practical problems, in this case, by simply cutting grass, but without the need for a wheeled vehicle. The invention has a priority date of October 1, 1964, when the concept was first patented (Figure 13.8). The central idea is that the motor that powers the fan to produce lift also powers a cutting blade. The machine must be lightweight, and various materials were used in the prototype hoods.

There are several possible material solutions to meet the property requirements of the hood. Indeed, the first prototypes explored many such possibilities (such as glass-reinforced thermoset plastic), although the ultimate choice was tough thermoplastics. Not only could thermoplastics meet

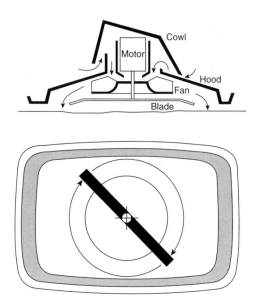

Figure 13.8   The hovermower shown in section and plan (U.K. 3 338 038 of 1964).

the strict property needs, but the hoods could be mass manufactured using injection molding. This method is ideally suited to long production runs (for large product numbers for a mass market) because of the high capital investment needed to make the metal tools needed to create the product shape. Quality control is of course vital to ensure that the final product meets the property specification, but when well controlled, this manufacturing method gives exactly identical products for production runs of hundreds of thousands, and even millions. Injection molding is also a method that is less labor intensive than manual fabrication or pressing of metal shells (for example), and the process can be automated relatively easily.

Although there are several plastics that can meet the demanding property specification, one in particular has been widely used: ABS (acrylonitrile-butadiene-styrene). It is tough and crack resistant, relatively easy to mold and available in a wide range of grades and colors. This is the material of choice for the structure of the Dyson vacuum cleaner (1996).

The hovermower has been manufactured by several companies since the expiration of the 1968 patent, and it is available to European gardeners at low cost. For reasons of product liability, the hovermower has not been widely adopted in the U.S. While various improvements have been made to the basic idea, there are still several intrinsic problems with the way the machine works.

13.3.4   Wheeled Rotary Mowers

One problem with hovermowers is the lack of control over the cutting height, and hence the quality of the final lawn finish. The width of the cut is limited and so the mower is less efficient when large areas of lawn need cutting. A conventional wheeled design overcomes such problems since the height of cut can be controlled simply by lifting or lowering the wheels (often each one separately). Grass collection can be a problem with hovermowers, a solution easily solved by incorporating a collection box at the rear of a wheeled mower. Width of cut is no problem since the hood can be made in a variety of sizes. Rollers can also be incorporated at the rear to provide that striped finish close to the hearts of British gardeners. So what effect does the design change have on the property specification?

The addition of wheels to the mower makes the overall product weight less of a problem, and traditionally, designers used sheet steel and cast aluminum for the hoods. However, metal gives much less design freedom compared with plastics materials, especially in detailing. The complexity possible in injection-molded hoods makes detail such as wheel arches and height adjustment much easier to incorporate into the hood, and the internal ribs needed to support the motor can also be made in one operation. This has long been a strong advantage for injection molding: good design can incorporate many separate functions into a single product, the hood. The number of separate parts is minimized (a design philosophy known as "parts consolidation"), thus saving on assembly costs during manufacture.

13.3.5   Monocoque Mowers

Until about 1990, design of wheeled rotary mowers was restricted by numerous patents that had been taken out by many companies for various design concepts. Flymo, the original hovermower company, introduced two new designs using plastic hoods, and was sued by Black & Decker for infringement of one of its patents. The patent (U.K. Pat 1 601 039 or U.S. 4 1994 345) deals with a mower in which the hood is formed by encapsulating the motor and blade by a plastic hood. The model originated in Germany, where it was known as the Rasenkatz or lawn razor. The two key parts are (1) the "dish-like body" and (2) the "dome-like cover," which when joined together form a monocoque of much greater stiffness than either separate part (Figure 13.9). The principle is well known in patent case law because it is an important feature of the invention of the thin wall battery container (now universally used in all large batteries).[4] The principle follows naturally from consideration of the great stiffness of the Catnic lintel when compared with partial shells.[5] The complete shell supports any load much more efficiently than a partial shell, because the load is spread

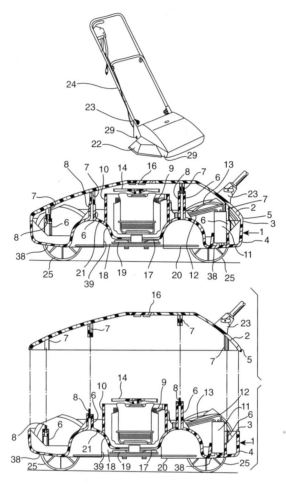

Figure 13.9   Sections of Rasenkatz lawnmower to show mating parts of base and lid (from U.S. 4 194 345 of 1980).

over a greater area, and that area is linked together so that all parts of the shell contribute to load bearing.

13.3.6   The Rasenkatz Patent

What does the patent-in-suit specify and, critically, what is the width of the claims? Claim 1 of the patent (filing date June 16, 1977), which was the basis of the infringement case against the Flymo products, reads as follows:

What We Claim Is

A rotary lawnmower comprising: a dish-like body defining the chassis of the lawnmower and having a substantially continuous bottom wall, at least a portion of which is substantially in the plane of a cutting blade of the lawnmower, and a wall extending upwardly from the bottom wall to define the outermost peripheral sidewall of the body; a motor equipped with an output drive shaft having a free end, said motor being mounted in said body so as to cause said free end to penetrate said bottom wall for carrying the cutting blade thereon; and, a cover co-extensive with the uppermost edge of said outermost peripheral side wall and engageable therewith to define, conjointly with the dish-like body, a housing enclosing said motor.

The claim can be subdivided as before:

What We Claim Is

1. *A rotary lawnmower, comprising*
2. *A dish-like body defining the chassis of the lawnmower, and having a substantially continuous bottom wall, at least a portion of which is substantially in the plane of the cutting blade, and*
3. *A wall extending upwardly from the bottom wall to define the outermost peripheral sidewall of the body;*
4. *A motor equipped with an output drive shaft having a free end, said motor being mounted in said free body so as to cause said free end to penetrate said bottom wall for carrying the cutting blade thereon;*
5. *And, a cover co-extensive with the uppermost edge of said outermost peripheral sidewall and engageable with to define, conjointly with the dish-like body, a housing enclosing said motor.*

The specific embodiment of the claim is shown in Figures 1 to 3 of the patent (Figure 13.9), and the shape of the body seems to be reasonably included by the claim. But the key term used to describe the shape of the base chassis is "*dish-like.*" This does not seem like a technical term, so what exactly does it mean? A sensible interpretation of the term dish would be a saucer or shallow plate, but does this interpretation also include the Flymo shown in Figure 13.10?

Moreover, does "dish-like" also include the shape of the Zundapp mower shown in Figure 13.11? If the definition can be stretched to include both the Flymo and the Zundapp (which date from December 11, 1969 and so predated the patent-in-suit by a substantial margin), then problems regarding the validity of the Rasenkatz patent could arise. If a wide meaning for the term "dish-like" could be demonstrated by evidence at trial, then the patent would be invalid because the idea was already known at the priority date of the Rasenkatz patent.

13.3.7   Design Development Sequence

One way of defending an attack of infringement is to show that the basic concept of a patent is obvious at the priority date of the patent, and hence

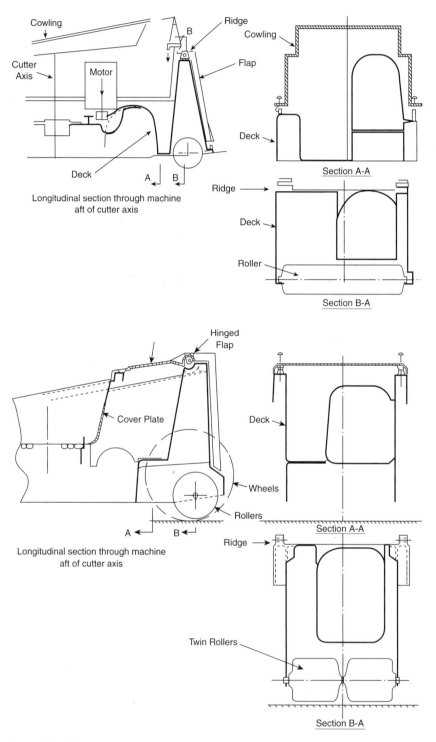

Figure 13.10 Sections of two Flymo rotary mowers, the 350S and the 420S.

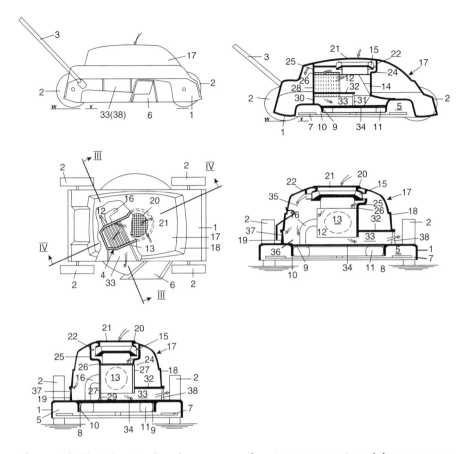

Figure 13.11   The Zundapp lawnmower showing construction of the outer case with base (1) and mating cover (17) (D 2 030 848).

it is obvious in light of prior art, and invalid. This is normally the task of an independent expert witness, who can advise the court in its approach to interpretation or construction of the patent. The witness was asked initially to propose a design sequence for a lawnmower based on general engineering principles, ending with the design in question. One aim of such a task is to pinpoint the steps in the sequence that are either commonplace or unusual (and thus potentially inventive). The argument proceeded as follows; the summary is taken from the more extensive expert report presented in evidence at the trial.

1. The first step is to consider the design for function, i.e., cutting grass using a motor-driven blade. The motor and blade must be supported safely and rigidly, and there must be a partly open space at the base of the mower for the action of the blade on the grass.

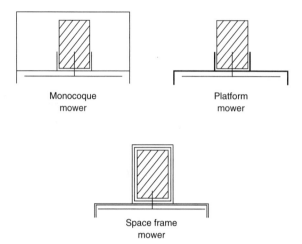

Figure 13.12 Conceptual development of mower case, showing three alternative design options (stage 1).

2. There are three design options (Figure 13.12; stage 1):
   monocoque
   platform
   space frame
   The shell bears the load in the first two options, while the struts support the load in the space frame.

3. What are the loads imposed on a mower? There is the static load of the motor and blade acting vertically down when the mower is in use, or perhaps at right angles if the mower is hung up for storage. There may be dynamic loads when the blade is rotating (normally not a problem if the blade is rotating true and in balance). There will be dynamic loads on the body when the mower meets obstacles on the lawn, or if it jams under large obstacles. The body of the mower must remain rigid in use so that when steered, the mower will move in the desired direction and not deform when it cuts the grass. Impact loads will also be important, especially those from stones thrown up by the blade from the lawn. However, the body must withstand being dropped or hitting large obstacles in the garden, and also resist large objects dropped onto it. All these requirements argue against a space frame, because objects might penetrate the body, hit the blade and be ejected. Likewise, stones on the lawn might be thrown up through the body to injure the user.

4. The need for a tough enclosure to the blade suggests such materials as steel, aluminum alloy, GRP composite or a tough thermoplastic. An electrical insulating material might be preferred for safety reasons,

so metals are excluded. The polymer options are also favored from another viewpoint: vibration damping or attenuation. Vibrations from the motor and blade could cause resonance in the body, thus making the mower noisy in use. It could also cause fatigue cracking in susceptible areas of the body. Polymers are favored here because they tend to absorb or damp vibrations, while metals tend to transmit them freely (like a bell).

5. Thermal resistance is important when the mower is in use: the motor will develop moderate temperatures of up to about 70°C. Metals will easily resist such temperatures, but polymers could be affected. If a polymer is chosen it should be able to remain rigid above this temperature to give a safe margin.

6. The loading criteria are critical, and a stiff material is demanded. Polymers are generally less rigid than metals, so care would be needed in choosing the wall thickness. The greater the wall thickness, the greater resistance to bending and torsion. The importance of torque and bending stiffness are directly related to the safety of the user; if it were too low, the part of the shell next to the blade could be distorted and make contact with the blade, causing catastrophic failure. Monocoque construction is favored because the overall product stiffness is much greater than that of individual shells. In addition, an external flange could increase the local stiffness of the critical outer edge of the mower to resist external blows. The options thus become as shown in Figure 13.13; stage 2. The favored option would be the monocoque mower because it provides a cover for the motor, shielding it from the user.

7. The final set of criteria deal with the manufacture of the device: it must be capable of mass manufacture with few assembly steps. Injection molding was well known before the priority date of the B&D patent, and tough thermoplastics such as ABS can be molded easily into very complex shapes. Some complexity is needed because wheels may be attached, a handle is needed to connect the user to the body in order to steer the device, the motor needs to be fixed securely to the body, the cable feeding electricity to the motor needs to be fixed securely and bosses for screw fixtures will be needed during assembly. The material is tough (impact resistant) and resistant to the environment, is thermally stable to about 100°C and can be made stiff enough for the function of the mower.

8. If injection molded, a single, closed monocoque is impossible to make by molding since the method involves injection of hot polymer into a metal tool with a shaped cavity. The cavity is produced by two mating halves that must be capable of separation at the end of the

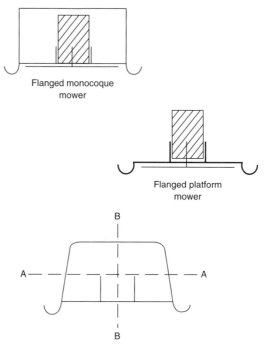

Figure 13.13 Stage 2 of development of flanged monocoque lawnmower.

molding cycle. This means that reentrant angles cannot be used in the shell design. So how is the monocoque divided? The various options are shown in Figure 13.13, Figure 6, by two possible dividing lines. Option AA is feasible while BB is not because of the reentrant properties of the external flange. A gate situated in the center of each part would represent the best design solution.

9. Option AA gives the model shown in Figure 13.14; stage 3 (top), which itself could be further modified by moving the bond line so that the external flange is incorporated into the shell, as shown in the lower part of the figure. In the opinion of the independent expert, this design option would have been obvious to any designer working before the priority date of the B&D patent.

As is the practice in all actions, the expert evidence was exchanged before trial so that both sides could see what arguments would need to be developed and explored. The expert for Black & Decker, a distinguished design engineer, generally supported a wide interpretation of the patent-in-suit with the two Flymo mowers indeed infringing claim 1 (and probably other claims as well). As is also common in many patent actions, the parties did not meet to discuss their positions, and focus on the points of agreement and disagreement. It

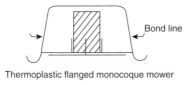

Thermoplastic flanged monocoque mower

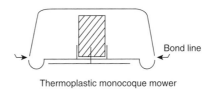

Thermoplastic monocoque mower

Figure 13.14   Final stage of design development of a thermoplastic-cased rotary lawnmower.

is now common for experts instructed in many U.K. product liability cases to meet before trial starts. Those points should already be clear to the legal teams without the need for expert interpretation, especially with a simple mechanical patent.

13.3.8   Pretrial Litigation

In important civil actions, there are often subsidiary issues which are tried separately before the main trial. This dispute did give rise to a prior action, and was concerned with the process of "discovery." This is the process whereby each side provides information to the other that is relevant to the dispute. In IP trials, such information includes design data (e.g., plans of various models, and even real products) and internal reports concerning design philosophy and implementation, etc. The action was important because it set a precedent for all future actions and widened the basis of discovery. The question at issue was simple: should a new Black & Decker lawnmower about to be launched (and mentioned specifically in a witness statement) be shown to the Flymo legal team?

13.3.9   Discovery

Discovery is the process of finding evidence not already revealed in a case as it proceeds to trial. Thus a manufacturer will or should keep voluminous documentation concerning product quality, dates and times of manufacture, as well as financial records of sales, and components and materials purchased for manufacture of the product concerned. In product liability cases, records of customer returns for particular batches or products will also be important for checking whether or not there had been a problem with the batch from which the failed product came (especially if a design defect is suspected).

There may also be material evidence in the form of actual failed products which had been kept or returned to the manufacturer by other consumers. If they do exist, it is important that they be inspected for the nature of the failure mode and should be compared with the actual failed product for any parallels. All such evidence will normally be confidential to the manufacturer, and is said to be "privileged." The process of discovery is thus a normal part of pretrial proceedings, and it is a two-way process, with each side exchanging discovery documents and any other evidence that is directly relevant to the case in hand. An expert will be asked not only about the nature of the evidence which should be disclosed before discovery, but he or she will also be asked to examine that evidence after discovery has taken place for any clues that might shed light on the actual failure at the heart of the case.

13.3.10 The New Model

Although many documents or, in this particular case, actual products are privileged, when they are mentioned in a witness statement they should be revealed to the other side in a dispute. One of Black & Decker's witnesses mentioned in his witness statement a new model about to be launched for the 1991 mowing season, and which apparently fell within the inventive step claimed in the Rasenkatz patent at the heart of the dispute. Such new models are normally kept under wraps until the launch so that the competition does not know what to expect until the model is publicized, and its various apparent advantages demonstrated to the buying public. Such secrecy is of course notorious in the car industry, where competition for new buyers is extremely fierce. Just such secrecy is endemic in many other consumer product markets. Black & Decker refused to release the product for discovery by Flymo, pleading commercial secrecy, until the dispute was brought before Judge Hoffmann sitting in the Chancery Division of the U.K. High Court.

The judge decided that, since the new model had been mentioned in a disclosed statement, it should be made available to the defendants for inspection. A report of the short action[6] has become important because of the significance of the result for unrelated disputes. This is thus an example of case law not just for patent actions but for any other action involving discovery in the U.K. Inspection duly occurred in a meeting at the patent agents acting for Flymo, and in fact the very same model was used by the plaintiff's counsel to open the case in the Patents Court.

13.3.11 Main Trial (*Black & Decker v. Flymo I*)

The action between the two companies occurred over 6 days in the Patents Court. The two witnesses of fact, the chief designer at Black & Decker and the chief designer at Flymo, gave evidence in turn. Most if not all the design documentation was presented as a result of discovery between the two parties, and some of it (actually a very small fraction) formed the basis of cross-examination. One basic aim of such questioning was to determine to what extent the inventive concept of the Rasenkatz was actually exploited by Black & Decker in their new model, only just then revealed to the defense. For the Flymo designer, questioning focused on the step-by-step evolution of the design of the two Flymo mowers accused of infringement.

13.3.12 Infringement

There are several issues that a court needs to consider in patent trials:

> How are the patent claims to be interpreted?
> On a reasonable construction of the claims, do the defendants' products infringe?
> Is the patent valid, when considered against the prior art?

The question of infringement really depended on how the court interpreted the term "dish-like," and the prompt given by the figures and diagrams from the patent-in-suit. It was difficult to describe the alleged infringing products as "dish shaped" (one of the key integers of claim 1 of the Rasenkatz patent), because the Flymo models in fact have wedge-shaped bodies. It seemed difficult to believe that the Flymo models could infringe the patent on simple interpretation of the words. However, because the words could have a wider meaning, it was necessary to question Flymo's designer to see what steps were taken when the two Flymo models were being planned and made.

Figure 13.15 shows the actual development sequence at Flymo, from the initial hovermower to the two models alleged to infringe the B&D patent. The chief difference of the Husqvarna model from 1974 was the existence of a closed cell at the front end of the RE 350 and 420 models. This was a kind of submonocoque but it may not have been inventive since the principle was already well established in earlier mowers. One interesting point that did emerge from cross-examination, however, was that the stiffness of the Flymo models derived not so much from the lid attached to cover the motor but from the grass-collecting duct at the rear of all the Flymo models (Figure 13.10). In fact, the mower operated perfectly well when the top was not attached at all! This demonstrated quite conclusively that the stiffness of the complete body derived mainly from this duct rather than from attachment of the lid.

Since a Gillette defense was used by Flymo in its pleadings, it was also important for the barrister for the plaintiff to question the chief witness-of-fact for Flymo, its chief designer, about the sequence. The so-called Gillette defense stems from case law of 1913, when the Gillette company sued a British

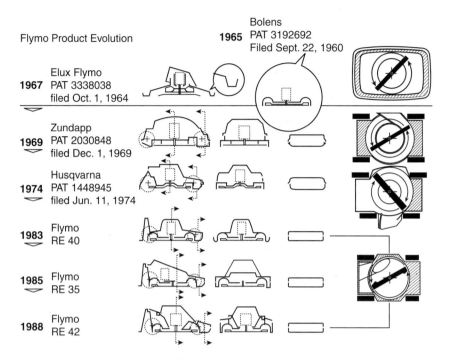

Figure 13.15 Development of the Flymo wheeled rotary lawnmowers from the hover mower.

manufacturer of safety razors. The defendant argued that his device was obvious and only used a sequence of noninventive steps. He won the case but Gillette swept the market with its product.[7] At the time of design of the models, the Flymo designer had used the Husqvarna as a model, and had not even seen the Rasenkatz patent at all. Each step that the designer took in developing the range of models may have been noninventive and thus the Gillette defense could succeed at trial.

13.3.13 Validity

The next question that arose concerned the validity of the patent. The patent had been challenged by the expert acting on behalf of Flymo as being obvious, in that a simple design sequence using well-known principles would arrive very easily at the patent mower. This was not enough in itself to destroy the patent, because, for example, the expert admitted that he was not a lawnmower designer. However, the similarity of the structure of the Zundapp to his preferred design was very clear, and this could support the inference that the patent was indeed obvious. So the Zundapp patent was clearly worth examining in some detail for its principles of construction.

The general design principles of the Zundapp mower have been briefly mentioned above, but there were numerous other mowers of very similar design (such as the Husqvarna shown in Figure 13.15) in the prior art. However, for practical convenience, arguments at the trial revolved mainly on the Zundapp patent. It was useful to have the device before the court for direct examination, but a Zundapp mower itself could not be found. The defendants therefore asked a prototype modeler to make a model of the casing of the Zundapp, using the design ideas presented in the Zundapp patent and the diagrams of the preferred embodiment (Figure 13.11). It showed a base and cover modeled to approximately the same size as a real mower, and constructed from sheet plastic bonded together. The model was then available as a court exhibit so that the principle of construction could be examined in detail. The point about whether or not the Zundapp cover and base could be injection molded was discussed. The base of the model showed a re-entrant angle in the base or chassis part, a feature that the modeler had included in the prototype, but which appeared not actually to be present in the Zundapp diagrams (Figure 13.11). As the witness explained, the re-entrant to the base chassis could, however, be molded using sliding cores.

The design sequence discussed above was presented by the expert instructed by Flymo in court and tested by cross-examination. The expert for Black & Decker was not called to present his evidence. It was attacked vigorously by the barrister acting for Black & Decker. However, several other issues emerged during the course of cross-examination, including the meaning of words in the specification.

13.3.14 Wording of Claim 1

As in the previous case, the meaning given to specific words in a patent claim are crucial to the size of the claim. If the key terms of the claim are interpreted in a narrow sense, then the patent will not catch infringers, but if they are given a wider meaning, then the size of the claim widens and catches infring-ing products (Figure 13.16). However, a wide claim poses a dilemma for the patentee, because if too wide, the claim will catch the prior art. If this happens, the patent must be invalid because it describes an idea that is already known in the art. Such a problem is known as a "squeeze" argument, and is central to the problem of successful patenting.

What terms of claim 1 of the patent-in-suit were important at trial? Few of the terms of claim 1 of the Rasenkatz patent could be called technical, apart from

output drive shaft

Terms like "sidewall" and "chassis" have a technical connotation, but "dish-shaped body" is not a word found in technical or engineering dictio-naries!

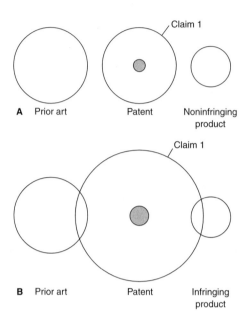

Figure 13.16 Boundary marker model to illustrate the patentee's dilemma. (A) A narrow reading of the claims isolates the invention from the prior art but does not catch infringers. (B) A wider reading of the claims catches infringers but also catches the prior art, so the patent is invalid.

Another word that was chosen for interpretation was

spiral

The reason why the word "spiral" was potentially important was that it was mentioned by the Rasenkatz patentee as being an alternative design configuration for the lower hood cutting chamber (to a simple annular chamber). Cut grass could be dumped outside the main area of the hood, as shown by Part 22 in the figures from the patent (Figure 13.9). The actual grass duct in both Flymo Chevron models was in fact helical. The outlet for the grass lay well above the base of the moldings at the rear rather than at the side of the chassis (Figure 13.10), so that cuttings are thrown up into the rear collecting bag. Counsel for Black & Decker thus wanted a more general definition of the term, rather than the narrow mathematical definition of a planar figure with regularly increasing radius. The expert resisted the suggestion, even when asked about the use of the term

spiral staircase

The expert agreed that the term was used in everyday parlance, but that it was not a rigorous use of the term. Moreover, there was no hint of helical ducts in the Rasenkatz patent.

Another point that arose during the trial concerned the strict requirements of claim 1: nowhere in the claim is the need for wheels mentioned. Although wheels are well known and thus an obvious feature, the claim could be interpreted in such a way as to include within its terms a hovermower hood!

13.3.15   Judgment

The judge asked the Catnic test questions in deciding infringement, in attempting to construe the patent claims in the light of the evidence.[5] His interpretation of claim 1 was straightforward: a dish-like body was essential to the invention, and the alleged infringing models bore no resemblance to a dish, being more sledge-like due to the rear grass collecting unit. He also felt that the cover and body did not produce the clam-like (monocoque) effect described by the patentee. The cover could be removed and the mower would still work. In addition, the motor output drive shaft in the 350S is not directly connected to the blade, but offset, so does not comply with this essential integer of claim 1 (Figure 13.10). The rear wall of the same model extends downward, so the "substantially continuous bottom wall" was not present in the alleged infringing model, an additional feature that put the model outside claim 1 of the patent-in-suit. All these variants produced quite different effects on the way the mower worked, and this would have been understood by the skilled reader of the patent.

The structure of the 420S was slightly different, but also fell outside the claims because the chassis was not "dish-like," and the structure was very similar to the 350S with a large rear frame for supporting the grass collector (Figure 13.10). Neither model could thus infringe the Rasenkatz patent, and the action could not succeed. The judge then went on to consider validity, starting with the argument from the defendants that "the claims were not fairly based on the matter disclosed in the specification" (an argument based on the U.K. 1949 Patent Act). The specification and claims must be looked at in a purposive way (using the Catnic approach), but having done that, it was clear that the patent was referring only to wheeled mowers. Claim 1, however, appeared to have a wider remit and wheels were not mentioned at all. The judge thus concluded that claim 1 (and all the other claims) was not fairly based on the complete specification, because it included hovermowers. Although he agreed with the narrow technical meaning of the word "spiral," it was not relevant, because the Zundapp lawnmower included a rising air duct of helical form, so the term was already known in the art.

The judge then turned to the question of obviousness, and he used the approach advocated in the Windsurfer case to evaluate the issue. First he looked at the way Flymo's designer had made the 350 and 420S models from the Husqvarna as his starting point (the judge was searching for the inventive step of the Rasenkatz mower). He identified the inventive step of the patent as being

> making a chassis with upstanding walls which ob-
> tained, in part, its strength [sic] from its co-extensive
> cover

This was the clam-like shell, or monocoque principle. When the designer seated a cover on his chassis to the Flymo mowers, he was not being inventive but simply producing a design variant. The judge could not identify any part of the design process that could be described as inventive. The Rasenkatz had played no part in the Flymo design sequence (Figure 13.15). If claim 1 was construed widely to include the Flymo mowers, then it was invalid for obviousness. He went on to consider the claim, if "properly construed," was also obvious in the light of the prior art. The only features that could be described as inventive were

1. Making a dish-like chassis with upturned walls defining the outer periphery
2. Mounting the motor in the body
3. Making the edges of the cover mate with the edges of the chassis

The defendants submitted that such a lawnmower would be an obvious design variant not requiring invention (Figure 13.14). The judge agreed, bearing in mind that it was based on hindsight reasoning. So even when correctly construed, the patent was obvious. The Zundapp lawnmower clearly disclosed the idea of a chassis with upstanding walls and an enveloping cover, and this was supported by the model made for the court. The judge then returned to the Windsurfer tasks. Having already defined the inventive step, he considered the differences with the Flymo models, which exhibited rear grass collectors and could not be envisaged by claim 1 of the patent-in-suit. The exact position of the joint between the chassis and cover was a matter of design choice (from the evidence of the expert shown in Figure 13.14 and the Flymo designer), not invention, so Rasenkatz was obvious in the light of Zundapp.

The court thus found that the patent was obvious on three different grounds: it included the Zundapp on proper construction, it included the Flymo mowers (on the plaintiff's construction of claim 1) and, quite separately, it also included the Flymo hovermower, a problem for a patent known as "lack of fair basis." It was clear that wheels are not an essential integer of claim 1 of the Rasenkatz mower, so it could be read as including a much older patent: the hovermower. It is interesting to note that such a decision ("invalid and not infringed") was so clear-cut that it was not appealed.[8] However, it is not common for patent court decisions to go so far. More commonly, a patent may be found perfectly valid, but not infringed. Another possibility is that some of the subsidiary claims are found to be invalid and require amendment for validity. Subsidiary claims are usually much less powerful than claim 1, and are normally inserted to catch those intent on copying but not willing to proceed so far as to infringe the main claim of a patent.

13.3.16   Afterword

Major patent trials are dramatic events because so much is at stake. Since the patent was rather old by the time the dispute came to trial, there would have been large royalties to be paid on all sales of the two Flymo models concerned if the case had gone against Flymo. Since Flymo would have been taking Black & Decker's ideas for many years, a royalty of 5 to 15% would have been payable to Black & Decker for the period of manufacture and sale of the two mowers concerned (15 and 12 years, respectively). Interest would also have been payable for the period over which the payment was due. However, this did not happen. The Rasenkatz patent was demonstrably weak, and too close to the prior art. The way claim 1 was interpreted by the plaintiffs to include the Flymo mowers meant that it also included the prior art, such as the Zundapp mower.

Both companies continue to design and produce new and innovative products for the market, a market that appears insatiable. DIY activities, in which Black & Decker specializes, continue to grow tremendously, although competition from cheap Far Eastern imports, such as the Workmate, is great. New products for gardening, such as devices for collecting leaves and other debris, continue to be developed. Flymo has developed a collecting mower, for example, where the grass is collected above the hood. Black & Decker made a similar product in the early 1990s, and the two companies clashed again over the Flymo patent. The case came to the Patents Court in 1996. To show how similar the two designs were (in Flymo's opinion), various experiments with grass collection were arranged for presentation before the court. They did not convince the court, however, and the court found that the Black & Decker model had not infringed the patent-in-suit. An attack on the validity of the latter also failed, producing a verdict of "valid but not infringed."

There are still many independents on the market that make mowers in a range of different materials. Decisions of the type made in the Flymo case are watched very closely by other manufacturers, who are aware that if the decision had gone against Flymo, they could be next in the frame for infringement proceedings. In the event, the decision freed the market for a wide range of competition, clearly good news for the consumer. Although thermoplastics have penetrated a substantial slice of the market, other materials continue to be used.

13.4   Electromechanical Devices

While the products studied in previous sections have been mechanical in function and operation, one of the most actively inventive areas of technology involves electrical, electronic or electromechanical machines and devices. One only has to look around at the growth in consumer products powered by electricity, for example, to appreciate the progress that has been made in the last few decades. While many such devices are entirely electrical in function, there is a large number where mechanical performance is also important if not critical to their function. The case study in this section examines just such a device: the RCD, or residual current device.

13.4.1   Residual Current Devices

Residual current devices protect human life by cutting the main current if a fault to earth occurs in a circuit; RCDs react so quickly that the escaping current cannot harm anyone who might be endangered by the escape.

It has been an objective of inventors to make such devices for many years. It is well known that simple fusible wire fuses placed in circuits react far too slowly to escape of current to prevent shock, injury or even death. The action depends on an overload creating heat that ultimately melts the fuse wire so that the circuit is broken, a notion originally conceived by Edison in the 1870s. The first devices to offer a better level of protection were circuit breakers, but they were designed primarily to protect equipment from the harmful effects of current surges, and they still did not react fast enough to protect life. They have been widely used for many years in mines and factories, and premises that use commercial electrical equipment, such as farms.

The turning point was when researchers collaborated with physiologists to determine the time delay that was critical to survival. Having determined the key threshold (about 50 msec), workers could then examine different design strategies to achieve a reaction time that was well below the threshold. It is an example of how engineers can work with physiologists to make new and useful life-saving devices. The demand for such protective devices has existed ever since electricity was generated and supplied toward the end of the 19th century, and it is rather surprising that the problem was solved only relatively recently. The invention of safety devices has, of course, a long and distinguished history, such as the 1841 invention of the Davy lamp, which enabled miners to work safely in gassy mines.

13.4.2   *Power Breaker v. Volex et al.*

The case study deals with a trial that was brought by the main patent holder of a key patent (Powerbreaker) (U.K. PAT 2141587) with a priority date of

June 13, 1983, against a new design of RCD actually designed in New Zealand, but imported to the U.K. by a large electrical manufacturer (Volex). The interest in the dispute arises from the way the technical effect was interpreted by the plaintiff, with expert evidence from leading electrical engineers, while the technical effect was in fact entirely mechanical in nature. The defense strategy focused on the mechanics of operation of the design, showing the court that it was this feature alone that distinguished the design of its product from the main claim of the patent-in-suit (which worked in a rather different way). It was also an example of a provisional patent battling it out against the recent prior art in the form of an existing and enforceable patent. Clearly, if the prior art was valid and infringed, then the provisional patent for the new device could not be valid. Much was at stake in the battle between the two parties to the action.

13.4.3 Patent-in-Suit

The patent, originally developed by Technology Research Corporation (Clearwater, FL), presents a series of figures that show how a preferred embodiment of the device works (Figure 13.17). As in all patent cases, the way the device works and the technical effect claimed has to be worked out by close reading of the specification taken together with the drawings provided. Claim 1 of the patent-in-suit reads as follows:

What We Claim Is

A resettable circuit closing device that is opened in the event of an undervoltage condition comprising; contact means biased to a normally open position; mechanical actuating means for closing said contact means; adjusting means to condition said actuating means to enable closing of said contact means; and electrically energised holding means separate from said adjusting means but which co-operates with said actuating means once conditioned to maintain the conditioning of said actuating means and close said contact means only when the voltage across said holding means exceeds a predetermined level.

In order to make sense of the claim, it is useful to subdivide the claim into its component clauses and focus on words that may be critical to its scope:

What We Claim Is

1. *A resettable circuit closing device that is opened in the event of an undervoltage condition comprising*
2. *Contact means biased to a normally open position;*
3. *Mechanical actuating means for closing said contact means;*

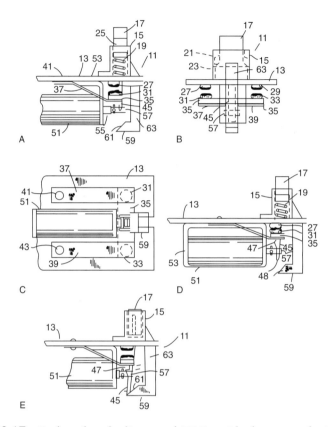

Figure 13.17 Preferred embodiment of TRC residual current device: (A), (B) (C) unprimed state with electrical contacts open; (D) fully primed state with elecrical contacts closed; (E) actuation with latch arm bent to one side by cam 61.

4. *Adjusting means to condition said actuating means to enable closing of said contact means;*

5. *And electrically energised holding means separate from said adjusting means but which co-operates with said actuating means once conditioned to maintain the conditioning of said actuating means and close said contact means only when the voltage across said holding means exceeds a pre-determined level.*

The key parts described in the claim (with their part numbers) include

        Contact means (contacts 27 and 31)
        Mechanical actuating means (leaf spring 37)
        Adjusting means (button 17) and
        Electrically energized holding means (armature 57)

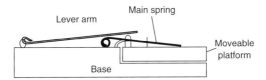

Figure 13.18   An unprimed mousetrap showing the main components.

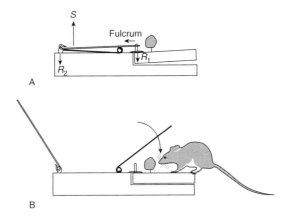

Figure 13.19   (A) Activated mousetrap showing balance of forces at (unstable) equilibrium and (B) rapid reaction of mainspring when platform is triggered.

As usual, the claim is stated in very general terms with numerous technical terms, and other words of common meaning that could have a technical connotation. The meaning of the claim is not immediately obvious, although the specification describes in general terms how a preferred embodiment of the device works in practice.

The sequence of figures shown in Figure 13.17 confirms that the device operates mechanically, in a way similar to the action of a very familiar small household machine: a mousetrap (Figure 13.18). Unlike an RCD mechanism, the mousetrap is not a precision device, but it can perform its function reasonably well. It is a device based on the interaction of several components, which must be primed and baited to achieve its final effect. In its primed state, several forces interact and are balanced in a state of static equilibrium. The state is unstable, however, and only needs a small trigger for the device to react to an intruder (Figure 13.19).

A mousetrap fulfills its function when the victim steps onto a spring-loaded platform to operate the main spring, which then swings over to hit the mouse. The main spring is held in place by a rigid lever that, in turn, is held in place by a hook attached to the platform onto which the mouse steps. In the case of an RCD, however, the device catches the electrical imp whenever a loss in voltage is detected. Any leakage of current will cause a drop in voltage, tripping the set of springs that are finely balanced in a metastable state of mechanical equilibrium. This state is maintained by a friction force between a bent arm and a bent leaf spring, so that any small movement of another rigid arm held in a solenoid will trip the device and cause the bent leaf spring to open the circuit.

13.4.4 Modeling the Technical Effect

It is helpful to redraw the action sequence shown in Figure 13.17 in a simplified diagrammatic way, so that the technical effect is clear and transparent. In addition, the balance of forces in the primed device should show exactly how the device is held in a metastable equilibrium. This would be the starting point, in any case, for quantitative analysis during the detailed design work which should precede prototyping, followed by tooling up for production models. The device is shown in schematic form in Figure 13.20, with the balance of forces in the primed device shown in Figure 13.21. The lower diagram identifies the principal forces acting against one another when the contacts are touching and the external circuit is complete. The schematic may then be compared with the situation as represented by the actual embodiment presented in the TRC patent-in-suit (Figure 13.17). Because various parts of the framework within which the device sits have been added, there are several extra forces shown, which are primarily reaction forces at fixing points. (Their addition, however, does not change the basic balance exhibited by Figure 13.21.)

A more comprehensive diagram of the TRC patent is shown in Figure 13.22. The solenoid, which holds an armature within it when current is flowing and the voltage is normal, is linked mechanically to the two leaf springs which lock together at a fulcrum. One of the leaf springs also makes an electrical contact, which is broken when the armature is released, following

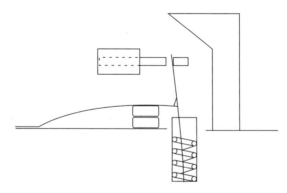

Figure 13.20 Schematic of TRC device primed and showing the coil spring and two leaf springs that power the action (inverted).

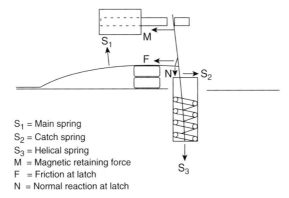

Figure 13.21 Simplified schematic balance of forces at equilibrium of the TRC device (inverted).

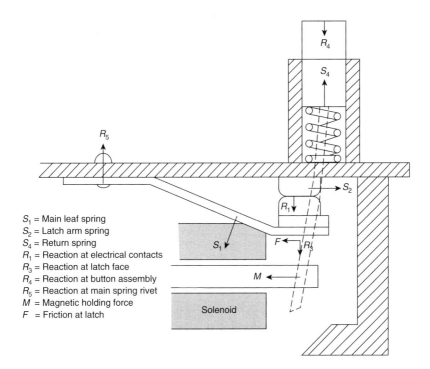

Figure 13.22 The TRC device shown with its frame and the full balance of forces acting at equilibrium in the primed state.

detection of an electrical current imbalance. This is the technical effect of the device, and it is a precision machine with very tight tolerances in order to be able to react almost instantly to current leakage in a circuit. Of course, it must perform that task repeatedly and reproducibly, so the device must also be totally reliable and robust, and thus constructed of wear and corrosion-resistant materials. Two metal leaf springs and a metal coil spring are the basis of the stored mechanical energy when primed, all working within the elastic limit of the metal. In the Hookean region of behavior, applied strain and the stress produced in the metal are completely reversible for thousands of cycles, so the reliability of the device is assured.

13.4.5 The Protector

The device accused of infringing the Powerbreaker patent in the action appeared, at first sight, to be very different from the Powerbreaker. It is known as the Protector. A notional equilibrium diagram of the set-up of the primed device is shown in Figure 13.23. The balance of forces in the primed state is shown in Figure 13.24. The sequence of actions exhibited in Figure 13.25 show how the Protector works. The Protector was developed by PDL, a plastics molding company based in New Zealand, and was the subject of a European Patent application (EPO PAT Appl. No. 526 071). The device consists of a set of rigid levers and coil springs, which looks quite different as a reaction

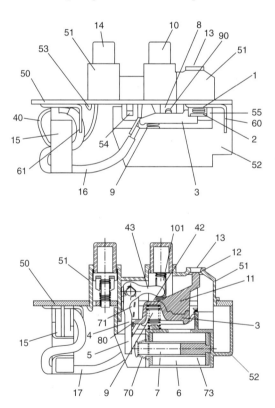

Figure 13.23 Sections of the Protector (from EP 526 071) showing various working elements of the device.

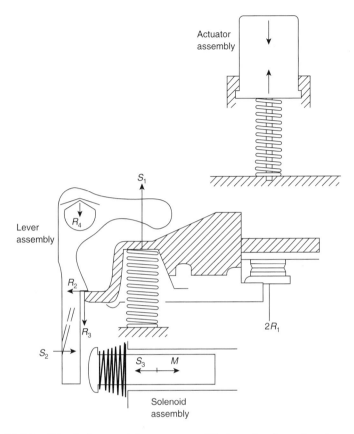

Figure 13.24 The balance of forces at equilibrium in the primed state of the Protector.

mechanism compared to the TRC device, but in fact it has a similar end result in cutting the electrical external circuit when a voltage drop is detected (Figure 13.25B to D).

Clearly there is a difference in the way each device reacts to an under-voltage condition, a difference that is reflected by the different component parts in each mechanism. The Protector is based on a set of rigid levers primed by operating a push button that is independent of the main mechanism. The potential energy of the system is raised by coil springs only, while the Powerbreaker uses two leaf springs and a coil spring to achieve its effect. The trigger action is quite different: in the case of the Powerbreaker, the armature is an integral part of the mechanism, being physically connected into the mechanism at all times, while the armature in the Protector acts independently. In the primed state, the solenoid is entirely separate in space and physically unconnected with the primed levers, making physical contact only when released by the solenoid (Figure 13.24). It achieves its effect by an

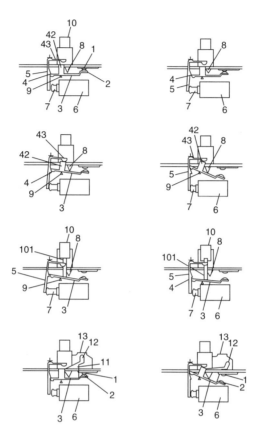

Figure 13.25 The sequence of events during the action of the Protector in guarding against leakage of electricity: (A) primed, (B–D) triggered, (E–G) reset, (H) unprimed.

impact blow, rather than by release of a continuous load. The Powerbreaker has a continuous load path between the trigger and the contacts, while that of the Protector is discontinuous.

A full and quantitative analysis of the mechanics of the Protector using both static and dynamic analysis was presented by the designer, as an appendix to his witness statement. The importance of presenting this evidence was to emphasize to the court the mechanical basis of both devices, and how the Protector mechanism differed substantially from the Powerbreaker in the way it operated. This claim was supported by the independent evidence of PDL's expert, who verified several key assumptions used in the rigorous mechanical analysis. Thus he measured the force constants of most of the springs, values that were in close agreement with those measured by PDL, and used in their analysis.

13.4.6   The Trial (Patents County Court)

The trial occurred over a 4-day period in August 1994 at the Patents County Court in London. Most of the oral evidence was given by experts. Two independent experts (both electrical engineers) reported for the plaintiff, and one independent expert (a materials engineer) reported for the defendant. In addition to the patent-in-suit, a considerable number of patents from the prior art were also examined by all the experts for evidence of obviousness. The evidence was rather weak, however, and arguments concentrated on the issue of infringement. Thus an important role for all the experts was the way in which they interpreted the integer 5 in claim 1 and, in particular, the term

electrically energized holding means

The defendant's expert interpreted the term as meaning that the Powerbreaker mechanism was referring to the solenoid and armature assembly of the Powerbreaker (Figure 13.22). The qualifier word "holding" was the key to understanding the way the armature worked with the leaf spring it connected to in the mechanism. It could mean several things. First, it could mean that the solenoid retained the armature when current flowed or second, it could be used in the sense of a grasping action between the armature and the leaf spring. He then turned to the description in the TRC patent of the preferred embodiment. The first time it is used is on page 5, lines 14–16:

> *The armature has a securing frame mounted on its free end to engage with and **hold** the elongate actuating member...*

The quotation indicates the patentee is using the term to show the physical grasping action between the two components. It is also used for a second time, where the patentee is explaining the action of the coil:

> *...so the power consumed by the electrically energized coil is only that required for a **holding** action.*

The term here is ambiguous, and could mean either alternative mentioned already. The final specific use of the term is:

> *Since the solenoid need only **hold** the actuating member in the flexed position...*

This quotation refers specifically to the grasping action of the armature in its physical interaction with the flexible latch spring. The expert concluded that the patentee clearly means the continuous grasping action between the armature and leaf spring. This action could not be reconciled with the way the Protector worked, by an impact blow from the retained armature (Figure 13.24 and Figure 13.25). In no way could the Protector armature be said to *hold* the rigid lever against which it worked when triggered. Loads cannot normally be transmitted through space, and when an object is *held*, it is in physical contact with the holder.

For this and other reasons, the expert believed that the Protector lacked this essential property required for the Powerbreaker, and that the Protector therefore fell outside claim 1 of the patent-in-suit. The expert maintained this view despite vigorous cross-examination, and the contrary views of the two electrical engineers acting on behalf of the plaintiff.

Cross-examination of the witness-of-fact for the defendants was remarkable only for one admission by the chief designer at PDL. The very vigorous cross-examination (rather in the manner of Marshall Hall, a famous British barrister of the Victorian period, who specialized in dramatic outbursts in court) ended with a final admission that the witness had the Powerbreaker patent in front of him when designing the Protector. The cross-examining barrister accused the designer of theft of his client's intellectual property, to which the response was "Yes"!

It might seem that this was a damning reply and that the defendant's case was lost irretrievably. Not at all. Patent cases are decided by the meaning of words, and whether or not the Protector fell within the normal and reasonable interpretation of the claims of the Powerbreaker patent. The judge felt that it did not, and that the mechanics of the interaction were quite different in the two devices. In other words, the technical effect in the Protector was based on impact rather than continuous stress. This could produce different properties in the final Protector device when compared with the Powerbreaker.

In the final analysis, none of the mechanical analysis performed by both PDL and the expert acting on their behalf was raised by either counsel or brought into cross-examination. The reason for this perhaps lay in the fact that neither of the electrical engineers called by TRC/Powerbreaker brought their expertise to bear on the problem. The critical issue lay in the mechanics of the two devices, rather than in the electrical analysis of circuitry. On the other hand, this part of the written evidence would have been seen by the judge when reviewing the case documents just before the trial started. A video animation of the dynamics of the mechanical action of both the Protector and Powerbreaker was shown before the court, and helped to emphasize the critical differences between the two devices in the way in which they related to an undervoltage in the protected circuit. Thus all such specialist evidence helped bring about a fair result to the dispute, which was not appealed.

13.4.7   Afterword

The final result of the action being a judgment of "valid but not infringed" (the case was not appealed) has allowed free competition in the marketplace. Before the decision, Powerbreaker had an effective monopoly for small RCDs in the U.K., such as those used when cutting the lawn with an electrical mower. They are a standard 13-amp plug fitting, with a cover for the mechanism and a reset button to activate the device and allow current to flow in the external circuit. The Protector is sold widely in supermarkets and electrical stores, and the price has decreased steadily since the trial. This is good news for all consumers because safety must be a key consideration for all users of electricity. In fact, similar RCDs must now (through changes to Building Regulations in the U.K.) be fitted to the main circuit boards of all new properties in place of fuse wire. For older properties, the option is open to the consumer to replace fuses with RCDs, but this is a relatively low-cost option and provides much greater security against the chances of accidental electrocution or electrical fires.

13.5   Endword

Despite the publicity given to biotechnology, computing and electronics, mechanics is still one of the most prolific areas of invention worldwide. The refuse bin is a good example of how simple ideas can be patented, and those ideas copied, provided they fall outside a reasonable interpretation of the valid patent claims. The market for such bins had expanded in Europe at such a rate as to create a demand that could be satisfied by several manufacturers. By changing the material of construction, the design changed and so avoided infringement of the original patent. The steel bin was in turn patented, with the new patent avoiding reference to the critical nature of the lifting lip and instead focusing on the bin lid. The same relatively small manufacturer has more recently patented a range of related inventions, including a compost bin and a device for weighing filled containers.

Lawnmower disputes will no doubt continue between leading and very large global manufacturers fighting for market share. Much greater care is needed in drafting patents, however, where the smallest advances in design are registered. The patentee's dilemma is at its critical edge due to the close proximity of prior art. The same is true of many other consumer products made by large companies and traded globally. A further danger lurks ever closer: the problem of imports from the tiger economies of the East, especially mainland China. By copying outdated patents, these companies can often improve designs and lower manufacturing costs by reducing a design to its bare bones. That process may encroach into enforceable patent technology by reverse engineering and designing around poorly drafted patents. But that competition already exists in advanced world economies, as the final case study demonstrated. By rethinking the mechanics of action of the TRC residual current device, PDL of New Zealand was able not just to avoid infringement, but also to improve the way the device works, and offer the consumer greater choice in the market (thus lowering prices through competition).

The role of the forensic engineer both in court actions and at earlier stages in the design process can improve both the efficiency of resolving disputes and product design. The expert role in court is essentially one of explaining the precise working of specific embodiments and real devices, the scope of patent claims, and the meaning of terms used in those claims in the context of the patent description, common general knowledge and the prior art. If these skills are exploited earlier, expensive litigation can be avoided altogether. Most forensic engineers who advise courts are also usually active in product liability cases, where their explanatory role is very similar. To understand how a product fails demands a knowledge of how it works without failing. Such subjects are unfortunately rarely taught in engineering textbooks, and are normally learned by experience harnessed to an appreciation of the background theory. By publicizing poor practice, or by direct advice to designers, forensic engineers can help improve product safety and reduce consequential injury, both in terms of injury to users or damage to property. As in IP litigation, product liability is now more international than formerly, due to the globalization of product design and trade between nations.

Many of the cases discussed in this chapter have a very clear international base. The wheeled refuse bin was originally developed in Germany, and was patented in Britain, where the dispute between plastic and steel occurred. The lawnmower also was designed in Germany and patented in both the U.K. and the U.S., being owned by a major U.S. manufacturer. Finally, the RCD was invented in the U.S., but it was challenged in the U.K. courts by a New Zealand company. It is a trend that will undoubtedly continue.

References

1. Battle, C., *The Patent Guide*, Allworth Books, New York, 1997.
2. Cornish, W.R., *Intellectual Property: Patents, Copyright, Trade Marks and Allied Rights*, 4th ed., Sweet & Maxwell, London, 1999; Cornish, W.R., Ed., *Cases and Materials on Intellectual Property*, 3rd ed., Sweet & Maxwell, London, 1999.

3. *Polaroid Corp. v. Eastman Kodak Co., Fleet Street Reports*, 25, 1977; *Reports of Patent Cases*, 379, 1977.

4. *Lucas v. Gaedor, Reports of Patent Cases*, 279, 1978.

5. *Catnic Components v. Hill & Smith, Reports of Patent Cases*, 183, 1982.

6. *Black & Decker Inc. v. Flymo Ltd., All England Law Reports,* 3, 158, 1991; *Weekly Law Reports,* 753, 1991; *Fleet Street Reports,* 93, 1991.

7. *Gillette Safety Razor Co. v. Anglo American Trading Co. Ltd., The Illustrated Official Journal (Patents) Reports of Patent Cases*, Vol. 30, 465, 1913.

8. *Black & Decker v. Flymo, Intellectual Property Decisions*, 14(5), 2, 1991.

Index